*THOMA*

# RELIQUES

OF

# ANCIENT ENGLISH POETRY:

CONSISTING OF

## Old Heroic Ballads, Songs,

AND OTHER PIECES OF OUR EARLIER POETS;

TOGETHER

WITH SOME FEW OF LATER DATE

*Volume 1*

Elibron Classics
www.elibron.com

Elibron Classics series.

© 2005 Adamant Media Corporation.

ISBN 1-4021-7381-4 (paperback)
ISBN 1-4021-2761-8 (hardcover)

This Elibron Classics Replica Edition is an unabridged facsimile of the edition published in 1866 by Bernhard Tauchnitz, Leipzig.

Elibron and Elibron Classics are trademarks of Adamant Media Corporation. All rights reserved.

This book is an accurate reproduction of the original. Any marks, names, colophons, imprints, logos or other symbols or identifiers that appear on or in this book, except for those of Adamant Media Corporation and BookSurge, LLC, are used only for historical reference and accuracy and are not meant to designate origin or imply any sponsorship by or license from any third party.

COLLECTION

OF

BRITISH AUTHORS.

VOL. 847.

# RELIQUES OF ANCIENT ENGLISH POETRY

BY

THOMAS PERCY.

IN THREE VOLUMES.

VOL. I.

# RELIQUES

OF

# ANCIENT ENGLISH POETRY:

CONSISTING OF

Old Heroic Ballads, Songs,

AND OTHER PIECES OF OUR EARLIER POETS;

TOGETHER

WITH SOME FEW OF LATER DATE.

BY

THOMAS PERCY,

LORD BISHOP OF DROMORE.

IN THREE VOLUMES.

VOL. I.

LEIPZIG

BERNHARD TAUCHNITZ

1866.

TO

THE RIGHT HONOURABLE

ELIZABETH

# COUNTESS OF NORTHUMBERLAND:

IN HER OWN RIGHT

BARONESS PERCY, LUCY, POYNINGS, FITZ-PAYNE, BRYAN, AND LATIMER.

---

Madam,

Those writers, who solicit the protection of the noble and the great, are often exposed to censure by the impropriety of their addresses: a remark that will perhaps be too readily applied to him who, having nothing better to offer than the rude Songs of ancient Minstrels, aspires to the patronage of the Countess of Northumberland, and hopes that the barbarous productions of unpolished ages can obtain the approbation or the notice of her, who adorns courts by her presence, and diffuses elegance by her example.

But this impropriety, it is presumed, will disappear, when it is declared that these poems are presented to your Ladyship, not as labours of art, but as effusions of nature, showing the first efforts of ancient genius, and exhibiting the customs and opinions of remote ages, — of ages that had been almost lost to memory, had not the gallant deeds of your illustrious Ancestors preserved them from oblivion.

No active or comprehensive mind can forbear some attention to the reliques of antiquity: it is prompted by natural curiosity to survey the progress of life and manners, and to inquire by what gradations barbarity was civilized, grossness refined, and ignorance instructed: but this curiosity, Madam, must be stronger in those who, like your Ladyship, can remark in every period the influence of some great Progenitor, and who still feel in their effects the transactions and events of distant centuries.

By such Bards, Madam, as I am now introducing to your presence, was the infancy of genius nurtured and advanced; by such were the minds of unlettered warriors softened and enlarged; by such was the memory of illustrious actions preserved and propagated; by such were the heroic deeds of the Earls of NORTHUMBERLAND sung at festivals in the hall of ALNWICK: and those Songs which the bounty of your ancestors rewarded, now return to your Ladyship by a kind of hereditary right; and, I flatter myself, will find such reception as is usually shown to poets and historians by those, whose consciousness of merit makes it their interest to be long remembered.

I am, Madam,

Your Ladyship's most humble,

and most devoted servant,

THOMAS PERCY.

MDCCLXV.

# CONTENTS

## OF VOLUME THE FIRST.

BOOK THE THIRD.

# ADVERTISEMENT

TO THE

FOURTH EDITION.

---

Twenty years have near elapsed since the last edition of this work appeared. But, although it was sufficiently a favourite with the public, and had long been out of print, the original Editor had no desire to revive it. More important pursuits had, as might be expected, engaged his attention; and the present edition would have remained unpublished, had he not yielded to the importunity of his friends, and accepted the humble offer of an Editor in a Nephew, to whom, it is feared, he will be found too partial.

These volumes are now restored to the public with such corrections and improvements as have occurred since the former impression; and the text in particular hath been amended in many passages by recurring to the old copies. The instances, being frequently trivial, are not always noted in the margin, but the alteration hath never been made without good reason; and especially in such pieces as were extracted from the folio Manuscript so often mentioned in the following pages, where any variation occurs from the former impression, it will be understood to have been given on the authority of that MS.

The appeal publicly made to Dr. Johnson in the first page of the following Preface, so long since as in the year 1765, and never once contradicted by him during so large a portion of his life, ought to have precluded every doubt concerning the existence of the MS. in question. But such, it seems, having been suggested, it may now be mentioned, that while this edition passed through his press, the MS. itself was left for near a year with Mr. Nichols, in whose house, or in that of its possessor, it was examined with more or less attention by many gentlemen of eminence in literature. At the first publication of these volumes, it had been in the hands of all, or most of his friends; but, as it could hardly be expected that he should continue to think of nothing else but these amusements of his youth, it was afterwards laid aside at his residence in the country. Of the many gentlemen above mentioned, who offered to give their testimony to the public, it will be sufficient to name the Honourable Daines Barrington, the Reverend Clayton Mordaunt Cracherode, and those eminent critics on Shakspeare, the Reverend Dr. Farmer, George Steevens, Esq., Edmund Malone, Esq., and Isaac Reed, Esq., to whom I beg leave to appeal for the truth of the following representation.

The MS. is a long narrow folio volume, containing one hundred and ninety-five Sonnets, Ballads, Historical Songs, and Metrical Romances, either in the whole or in part, for many of them are extremely mutilated and imperfect. The first and last leaves are wanting; and of fifty-four pages, near the beginning, half of every leaf hath been torn away, and several others are injured towards the end; besides that through a great part of the volume the top or bottom line, and sometimes both, have been cut off in the binding.

In this state is the MS. itself: and even where the leaves have suffered no injury, the transcripts, which seem to have been all made by one person, (they are at least all in the same kind of hand,) are sometimes extremely incorrect and faulty, being in such instances probably made from defective copies, or the imperfect recitation of illiterate singers; so that a considerable portion of the song or narrative is sometimes omitted, and miserable trash or nonsense not unfrequently introduced into pieces of considerable merit. And often the copyist grew so weary of his labour, as to write on without the least attention to the sense or meaning; so that the word which should form the rhyme is found misplaced in the middle of the line; and we have such blunders as these, *want and will*, for *wanton will*[1]; even *pan and wale*, for *wan and pale*[2], &c. &c.

Hence the public may judge how much they are indebted to the composer of this collection; who, at an early

1 This must have been copied from a reciter.

2 Thus we find in the fol. MS.

"His visage waxed pan and wale."

period of life, with such materials and such subjects, formed a work which hath been admitted into the most elegant libraries, and with which the judicious antiquary hath just reason to be satisfied, while refined entertainment hath been provided for every reader of taste and genius.

THOMAS PERCY,
FELLOW OF ST. JOHN'S COLLEGE, OXFORD.

MDCCXCIV.

# PREFACE.

The reader is here presented with select remains of our ancient English Bards and Minstrels, an order of men who were once greatly respected by our ancestors, and contributed to soften the roughness of a martial and unlettered people by their songs and by their music.

The greater part of them are extracted from an ancient folio MS. in the Editor's possession, which contains near two hundred Poems, Songs, and Metrical Romances. This manuscript was written about the middle of the last century; but contains compositions of all times and dates, from the ages prior to Chaucer, to the conclusion of the reign of Charles I.[1]

This manuscript was shown to several learned and ingenious friends, who thought the contents too curious to be consigned to oblivion, and importuned the possessor to select some of them, and give them to the press. As most of them are of great simplicity, and seem to have been merely written for the people, he was long in doubt, whether, in the present state of improved literature, they could be deemed worthy the attention of the public. At length the importunity of his friends prevailed, and he could refuse nothing to such judges as the author of *The Rambler*, and the late Mr. Shenstone.

Accordingly such specimens of ancient poetry have been selected, as either show the gradation of our language, exhibit the progress of popular opinions, display the peculiar

[1] Chaucer quotes the old romance of "Libius Disconius," and some others, which are found in this MS. (See the Essay prefixed to vol. iii. p. 13, et seq.) It also contains several Songs relating to the Civil War in the last century, but not one that alludes to the Restoration.

manners and customs of former ages, or throw light on our earlier classical poets.

They are here distributed into VOLUMES, each of which contains an independent SERIES of poems, arranged chiefly according to the order of time, and showing the gradual improvements of the English language and poetry, from the earliest ages down to the present. Each VOLUME, or SERIES, is divided into three BOOKS, to afford so many pauses, or resting-places to the reader, and to assist him in distinguishing between the productions of the earlier, the middle, and the latter times.

In a polished age, like the present, I am sensible that many of these reliques of antiquity will require great allowances to be made for them. Yet have they, for the most part, a pleasing simplicity, and many artless graces, which, in the opinion of no mean critics[2], have been thought to compensate for the want of higher beauties, and, if they do not dazzle the imagination, are frequently found to interest the heart.

To atone for the rudeness of the more obsolete poems, each volume concludes with a few modern attempts in the same kind of writing; and, to take off from the tediousness of the longer narratives, they are every where intermingled with little elegant pieces of the lyric kind. Select ballads in the old Scottish dialect, most of them of the first-rate merit, are also interspersed among those of our ancient English minstrels; and the artless productions of these old rhapsodists are occasionally confronted with specimens of the composition of contemporary poets of a higher class, — of those who had all the advantages of learning in the times in which they lived, and who wrote for fame and for posterity. Yet, perhaps, the palm will be frequently due to the old strolling Minstrels, who composed their rhymes to be

[2] Mr. Addison, Mr. Dryden, and the witty Lord Dorset, &c. See the *Spectator*, No. 70. To these might be added many eminent judges now alive. The learned Selden appears also to have been fond of collecting these old things. See below.

sung to their harps, and who looked no further than for present applause, and present subsistence.

The reader will find this class of men occasionally described in the following volumes, and some particulars relating to their history in an Essay subjoined to this Preface.

It will be proper here to give a short account of the other Collections that were consulted, and to make my acknowledgments to those gentlemen who were so kind as to impart extracts from them; for, while this Selection was making, a great number of ingenious friends took a share in the work, and explored many large repositories in its favour.

The first of these that deserved notice was the Pepysian library at Magdalen College, Cambridge. Its founder, Samuel Pepys[3], Esq., Secretary of the Admiralty in the reigns of Charles II. and James II., had made a large collection of ancient English ballads, near 2000 in number, which he has left pasted in five volumes in folio; besides garlands and other smaller miscellanies. This Collection, he tells us, was "begun by Mr. Selden; improved by the addition of many pieces elder thereto in time; and the whole continued down to the year 1700; when the form peculiar till then thereto, viz. of the black-letter with pictures, seems (for cheapness' sake) wholly laid aside for that of the white letter without pictures."

In the Ashmole library at Oxford is a small collection of ballads made by Anthony Wood in the year 1676, containing somewhat more than 200. Many ancient popular poems are also preserved in the Bodleian library.

The archives of the Antiquarian Society at London contain a multitude of curious political poems in large folio volumes, digested under the several reigns of Henry VIII., Edward VI., Mary, Elizabeth, James I., &c.

In the British Museum is preserved a large treasure of

3 A life of our curious collector, Mr. Pepys, may be seen in "The Continuation of Mr. Collier's Supplement to his great Dictionary, 1715, at the end of vol. iii. folio. Art. PEP."

ancient English poems in MS., besides one folio volume of printed ballads.

From all these some of the best pieces were selected; and from many private Collections, as well printed as manuscript, particularly from one large folio volume which was lent by a lady.

Amid such a fund of materials, the Editor is afraid he has been sometimes led to make too great a parade of his authorities. The desire of being accurate has perhaps seduced him into too minute and trifling an exactness; and in pursuit of information he may have been drawn into many a petty and frivolous research. It was however necessary to give some account of the old copies; though often, for the sake of brevity, one or two of these only are mentioned, where yet assistance was received from several. Where any thing was altered that deserved particular notice, the passage is generally distinguished by two inverted 'commas:' and the Editor has endeavoured to be as faithful as the imperfect state of his materials would admit. For these old popular rhymes being many of them copied only from illiterate transcripts, or the imperfect recitation of itinerant ballad-singers, have, as might be expected, been handed down to us with less care than any other writings in the world. And the old copies, whether MS. or printed, were often so defective or corrupted, that a scrupulous adherence to their wretched readings would only have exhibited unintelligible nonsense, or such poor meagre stuff as neither came from the bard nor was worthy the press; when, by a few slight corrections or additions, a most beautiful or interesting sense hath started forth, and this so naturally and easily, that the Editor could seldom prevail on himself to indulge the vanity of making a formal claim to the improvement; but must plead guilty to the charge of concealing his own share in the amendments under some such general title as a "Modern Copy," or the like. Yet it has been his design to give sufficient intimation where any considerable liberties[4] were taken with the old copies, and to have retained, either in the text or margin, any word or phrase which was antique, obsolete, unusual, or peculiar; so that these might be safely quoted as of genuine and undoubted antiquity. His object was to please both the judicious antiquary and the reader of taste; and he hath endeavoured to gratify both without offending either.

The plan of the work was settled in concert with the late elegant Mr. Shenstone, who was to have borne a joint share in it, had not death unhappily prevented him[5]. Most of the modern pieces were of his selection and arrangement, and the Editor hopes to be pardoned, if he has retained some things out of partiality to the judgment of his friend. The old folio MS. above mentioned was a present from Humphrey Pitt, Esq., of Prior's-Lee, in Shropshire[6], to whom this public acknowledgment is due for that and many other obliging favours. To Sir David Dalrymple, Bart., of Hales, near Edinburgh, the Editor is indebted for most of the beautiful Scottish poems with which this little miscellany is enriched, and for many curious and elegant remarks with which they are illustrated. Some obliging communications of the same kind were received from John Mac Gowan, Esq., of Edinburgh; and many curious explanations of Scottish

4 Such liberties have been taken with all those pieces which have three asterisks subjoined, thus ***.

5 That the Editor hath not here underrated the assistance he received from his friend, will appear from Mr. Shenstone's own letter to the Rev. Mr. Graves, dated March 1st, 1761. See his Works, vol. iii. letter ciii. It is doubtless a great loss to this work, that Mr. Shenstone never saw more than about a third of one of these volumes, as prepared for the press.

6 Who informed the Editor that this MS. had been purchased in a library of old books, which was thought to have belonged to Thomas Blount, author of the *Jocular Tenures*, 1679, 4to., and of many other publications enumerated in Wood's Athenæ, ii. 73; the earliest of which is *The Art of making Devises*, 1646, 4to., wherein he is described to be "of the Inner Temple." If the collection was made by this lawyer, (who also published the *Law Dictionary*, 1671, folio,) it should seem, from the errors and defects with which the MS. abounds, that he had employed his clerk in writing the transcripts, who was often weary of his task.

words in the glossaries from John Davidson, Esq., of Edinburgh, and from the Rev. Mr. Hutchinson, of Kimbolton. Mr. Warton, who has twice done so much honour to the Poetry Professor's chair at Oxford, and Mr. Hest, of Worcester College, contributed some curious pieces from the Oxford libraries. Two ingenious and learned friends at Cambridge deserve the Editor's warmest acknowledgments: to Mr. Blakeway, late fellow of Magdalen College, he owes all the assistance received from the Pepysian library: and Mr. Farmer, Fellow of Emanuel, often exerted, in favour of this little work, that extensive knowledge of ancient English literature, for which he is so distinguished[7]. Many extracts from ancient MSS. in the British Museum, and other repositories, were owing to the kind services of Thomas Astle, Esq., to whom the public is indebted for the curious Preface

[7] To the same learned and ingenious friend, since Master of Emanuel College, the Editor is obliged for many corrections and improvements in his second and subsequent editions; as also to the Rev. Mr. Bowle, of Idmistone, near Salisbury, editor of the curious edition of *Don Quixote,* with Annotations, in Spanish, in 6 vols. 4to.; to the Rev. Mr. Cole, formerly of Blecheley, near Fenny-Stratford, Bucks; to the Rev. Mr. Lambe, of Noreham, in Northumberland, (author of a learned *History of Chess*, 1764, 8vo., and editor of a curious Poem on the *Battle of Flodden Field*, with learned notes, 1774, 8vo.); and to G. Paton, Esq., of Edinburgh. He is particularly indebted to two friends, to whom the public, as well as himself, are under the greatest obligations; to the Honourable Daines Barrington, for his very learned and curious *Observations on the Statutes,* 4to.: and to Thomas Tyrwhitt, Esq., whose most correct and elegant edition of Chaucer's *Canterbury Tales,* 5 vols. 8vo., is a standard book, and shows how an ancient English classic should be published. The Editor was also favoured with many valuable remarks and corrections from the Rev. Geo. Ashby, late Fellow of St. John's College, in Cambridge, which are not particularly pointed out, because they occur so often. He was no less obliged to Thomas Butler, Esq. F. A. S., agent to the Duke of Northumberland, and Clerk of the Peace for the county of Middlesex; whose extensive knowledge of ancient writings, records, and history has been of great use to the Editor in his attempts to illustrate the literature or manners of our ancestors. Some valuable remarks were procured by Samuel Pegge, Esq., author of that curious work the *Curialia,* 4to.; but this impression was too far advanced to profit by them all; which hath also been the case with a series of learned and ingenious annotations inserted in the *Gentleman's Magazine* for August, 1793; April, June, July, and October, 1794; and which, it is hoped, will be continued.

and Index annexed to the Harleian Catalogue[8]. The worthy librarian of the Society of Antiquaries, Mr. Norris, deserved acknowledgment for the obliging manner in which he gave the Editor access to the volumes under his care. In Mr. Garrick's curious collection of old Plays are many scarce pieces of ancient poetry, with the free use of which he indulged the Editor in the politest manner. To the Rev. Dr. Birch he is indebted for the use of several ancient and valuable tracts. To the friendship of Dr. Samuel Johnson he owes many valuable hints for the conduct of the work. And, if the glossaries are more exact and curious than might be expected in so slight a publication, it is to be ascribed to the supervisal of a friend, who stands at this time the first in the world for northern literature, and whose learning is better known and respected in foreign nations than in his own country. It is perhaps needless to name the Rev. Mr. Lye, editor of Junius's *Etymologicum*, and of the *Gothic Gospels*.

The names of so many men of learning and character the Editor hopes will serve as an amulet, to guard him from every unfavourable censure for having bestowed any attention on a parcel of Old Ballads. It was at the request of many of these gentlemen, and of others eminent for their genius and taste, that this little work was undertaken. To prepare it for the press has been the amusement of now and then a vacant hour amid the leisure and retirement of rural life, and hath only served as a relaxation from graver studies. It has been taken up at different times, and often thrown aside for many months, during an interval of four or five years. This has occasioned some inconsistencies and repetitions, which the candid reader will pardon. As great care has been taken to admit nothing immoral and indecent, the Editor hopes he need not be ashamed of having bestowed some of his idle hours on the ancient literature of our own country, or in rescuing from oblivion some pieces (though

8 Since Keeper of the Records in the Tower.

but the amusements of our ancestors) which tend to place in a striking light their taste, genius, sentiments, or manners.

*** Except in one paragraph, and in the notes subjoined, this preface is given with little variation from the first edition in MDCCLXV.

---

# AN ESSAY

ON

## THE ANCIENT MINSTRELS IN ENGLAND.

---

I. The MINSTRELS (A) were an order of men in the middle ages, who subsisted by the arts of poetry and music, and sang to the harp verses composed by themselves, or others [1]. They also appear to have accompanied their songs with mimickry and action; and to have practised such various means of diverting as were much admired in those rude times, and supplied the want of more refined entertainment (B). These arts rendered them extremely popular and acceptable in this and all the neighbouring countries; where no high scene of festivity was esteemed complete that was not set off with the exercise of their talents; and where, so long as the spirit of chivalry subsisted, they were protected and caressed, because their songs tended to do honour to the ruling passion of the times, and to encourage and foment a martial spirit.

The Minstrels seem to have been the genuine successors of the ancient Bards (C), who, under different names, were admired and revered, from the earliest ages, among the people of Gaul, Britain, Ireland, and the North; and indeed by almost all the first inhabitants of Europe, whether of

(A) The larger notes and illustrations referred to by the letters (A) (B) &c. are thrown together to the end of this Essay.

1 Wedded to no hypothesis, the Author hath readily corrected any mistakes which have been *proved* to be in this Essay; and considering the novelty of the subject, and the time, and place, when and where he first took it up, many such had been excusable.—That the term *minstrel* was not confined, as some contend, to a mere *musician,* in this country, any more than on the Continent, will be considered more fully in the last note (GG) at the end of this Essay.

Celtic or Gothic race[2]; but by none more than by our own Teutonic ancestors[3], particularly by all the Danish tribes[4]. Among these they were distinguished by the name of Scalds, a word which denotes "smoothers and polishers of language[5]." The origin of their art was attributed to Odin or Woden, the father of their gods, and the professors of it were held in the highest estimation. Their skill was considered as something divine; their persons were deemed sacred; their attendance was solicited by kings; and they were every where loaded with honours and rewards. In short, Poets and their art were held among them in that rude admiration, which is ever shown by an ignorant people to such as excel them in intellectual accomplishments.

As these honours were paid to Poetry and Song, from the earliest times, in those countries which our Anglo-Saxon ancestors inhabited before their removal into Britain, we may reasonably conclude, that they would not lay aside all their regard for men of this sort immediately on quitting their German forests. At least, so long as they retained their ancient manners and opinions, they would still hold them in high estimation. But as the Saxons, soon after their establishment in this island, were converted to Christianity, in proportion as literature prevailed among them, this rude admiration would begin to abate, and poetry would be no longer a peculiar profession. Thus the Poet and the Minstrel early with us became two persons (D). Poetry was cultivated by men of letters indiscriminately; and many of the most popular rhymes were composed amidst the leisure and retirement of monasteries. But the minstrels continued a distinct order of men for many ages after the Norman

[2] Vide Pelloutier Hist. des Celtes, tom. 1, l. 2, c. 6, 10.

[3] Tacit. de Mor. Germ. cap. 2.

[4] Vide Bartholin. De Causis contemptæ a Danis Mortis, lib. i. cap. 10.—Wormij Literatura Runic. ad finem.—See also "Northern Antiquities, or a Description of the Manners, Customs, &c., of the ancient Danes and other Northern Nations: from the French of M. Mallet." London, printed for T. Carnan, 1770. 2 vols. 8vo.

[5] Torfæi Præf. ad Orcad. Hist.—Pref. to "Five Pieces of Runic Poetry," &c.

conquest, and got their livelihood by singing verses to the harp at the houses of the great (E). There they were still hospitably and respectfully received, and retained many of the honours shown to their predecessors, the Bards and Scalds (F). And though, as their art declined, many of them only recited the compositions of others, some of them still composed songs themselves, and all of them could probably invent a few stanzas on occasion. I have no doubt but most of the old heroic ballads in this collection were composed by this order of men; for, although some of the larger metrical romances might come from the pen of the monks or others, yet the smaller narratives were probably composed by the minstrels who sang them. From the amazing variations which occur in different copies of the old pieces, it is evident they made no scruple to alter each other's productions; and the reciter added or omitted whole stanzas according to his own fancy or convenience.

In the early ages, as was hinted above, the profession of oral itinerant Poet was held in the utmost reverence among all the Danish tribes; and therefore we might have concluded, that it was not unknown or unrespected among their Saxon brethren in Britain, even if history had been altogether silent on this subject. The original country of our Anglo-Saxon ancestors is well known to have lain chiefly in the Cimbric Chersonese, in the tracts of land since distinguished by the name of Jutland, Angelen, and Holstein[6] The Jutes and Angles in particular, who composed two-thirds of the conquerors of Britain, were a Danish people, and their country at this day belongs to the crown of Denmark[7]; so that when the Danes again infested England, three or four hundred years after, they made war on the

[6] Vide Chronic. Saxon. à Gibson, pp. 12, 13, 4to.—Bed. Hist. Eccles. à Smith, lib. i. c. xv.—"Ealdsexe [Regio antiq. Saxonum] in cervice Cimbricae Chersonesi, Holsatiam proprie dictam, Dithmarsiam, Stormariam, et Wagriam, complectens." Annot. in Bed. à Smith, p. 52. Et vide Camdeni Britan.

[7] "Anglia Vetus, hodie etiam Anglen, sita est inter Saxones et Giotes [Jutos], habens oppidum capitale .... Sleswick." Ethelwerd. lib. i.

descendants of their own ancestors[8]. From this near affinity we might expect to discover a strong resemblance between both nations in their customs, manners, and even language; and, in fact, we find them to differ no more than would naturally happen between a parent country and its own colonies, that had been severed in a rude uncivilized state, and had dropt all intercourse for three or four centuries; especially if we reflect that the colony here settled had adopted a new religion, extremely opposite in all respects to the ancient Paganism of the mother-country; and that even at first, along with the original Angli, had been incorporated a large mixture of Saxons from the neighbouring parts of Germany; and afterwards, among the Danish invaders, had come vast multitudes of adventurers from the more northern parts of Scandinavia. But all these were only different tribes of the same common Teutonic stock, and spoke only different dialects of the same Gothic language[9].

From this sameness of original and similarity of manners we might justly have wondered, if a character, so dignified and distinguished among the ancient Danes as the Scald or Bard, had been totally unknown or unregarded in this sister nation. And indeed this argument is so strong, and, at the same time, the early annals of the Anglo-Saxons are so scanty and defective (G), that no objections from their silence could be sufficient to overthrow it. For if these popular bards were confessedly revered and admired in those very countries which the Anglo-Saxons inhabited before their removal into Britain, and if they were afterwards common and numerous among the other descendants of the same Teutonic ancestors, can we do otherwise than conclude, that men of this order accompanied such tribes as migrated hither; that they afterwards subsisted here, though perhaps with less splendour than in the North; and that there never was wanting a succession of them to hand down

8 See Northern Antiquities, &c. vol. i. pp. 7, 8, 185, 259, 260, 261.

9 Ibid. Preface, p. xxvi.

the art, though some particular conjunctures may have rendered it more respectable at one time than another? And this was evidently the case. For though much greater honours seem to have been heaped upon the northern Scalds, in whom the characters of historian, genealogist, poet, and musician, were all united, than appear to have been paid to the Minstrels and Harpers (H) of the Anglo-Saxons, whose talents were chiefly calculated to entertain and divert; while the Scalds professed to inform and instruct, and were at once the moralists and theologues of their Pagan countrymen; yet the Anglo-Saxon Minstrels continued to possess no small portion of public favour; and the arts they professed were so extremely acceptable to our ancestors, that the word *Glee*, which peculiarly denoted their art, continues still in our own language to be of all others the most expressive of that popular mirth and jollity, that strong sensation of delight, which is felt by unpolished and simple minds (I).

II. Having premised these general considerations, I shall now proceed to collect from history such particular incidents as occur on this subject; and, whether the facts themselves are true or not, they are related by authors who lived too near the Saxon times, and had before them too many recent monuments of the Anglo-Saxon nation, not to know what was conformable to the genius and manners of that people; and therefore we may presume, that their relations prove at least the existence of the customs and habits they attribute to our forefathers before the Conquest, whatever becomes of the particular incidents and events themselves. If this be admitted, we shall not want sufficient proofs to show that Minstrelsy and Song were not extinct among the Anglo-Saxons; and that the professor of them here, if not quite so respectable a personage as the Danish Scald, was yet highly favoured and protected, and continued still to enjoy considerable privileges.

Even so early as the first invasion of Britain by the

Saxons, an incident is recorded to have happened, which, if true, shows that the Minstrel or Bard was not unknown among this people; and that their princes themselves could, upon occasion, assume that character. Colgrin, son of that Ella who was elected king or leader of the Saxons in the room of Hengist[10], was shut up in York, and closely besieged by Arthur and his Britons. Baldulph, brother of Colgrin, wanted to gain access to him, and to apprize him of a reinforcement which was coming from Germany. He had no other way to accomplish his design, but to assume the character of a Minstrel. He therefore shaved his head and beard, and, dressing himself in the habit of that profession, took his harp in his hand. In this disguise he walked up and down the trenches without suspicion, playing all the while upon his instrument as a Harper. By little and little he advanced near to the walls of the city, and making himself known to the sentinels, was in the night drawn up by a rope.

Although the above fact comes only from the suspicious pen of Geoffry of Monmouth (K), the judicious reader will not too hastily reject it; because, if such a fact really happened, it could only be known to us through the medium of the British writers: for the first Saxons, a martial but unlettered people, had no historians of their own; and Geoffry, with all his fables, is allowed to have recorded many true events, that have escaped other annalists.

We do not however want instances of a less fabulous era, and more indubitable authority: for later history affords us two remarkable facts (L), which I think clearly show that the same arts of poetry and song, which were so much admired among the Danes, were by no means unknown or neglected in this sister nation; and that the privileges and honours which were so lavishly bestowed upon the northern Scalds, were not wholly withheld from the Anglo-Saxon Minstrels.

[10] See Rapin's Hist. (by Tindal, fol. 1732, vol. i. p. 36,) who places the incident here related under the year 495.

Our great King Alfred, who is expressly said to have excelled in music[1], being desirous to learn the true situation of the Danish army, which had invaded his realm, assumed the dress and character of a minstrel (M); when, taking his harp, and one of the most trusty of his friends disguised as a servant[2], (for in the early times it was not unusual for a minstrel to have a servant to carry his harp,) he went with the utmost security into the Danish camp: and, though he could not but be known to be a Saxon by his dialect, the character he had assumed procured him a hospitable reception. He was admitted to entertain the king at table, and stayed among them long enough to contrive that assault which afterwards destroyed them. This was in the year 878.

About sixty years after[3], a Danish king made use of the same disguise to explore the camp of our king Athelstan. With his harp in his hand, and dressed like a minstrel (N), Aulaff[4], king of the Danes, went among the Saxon tents; and, taking his stand near the king's pavilion, began to play, and was immediately admitted. There he entertained Athelstan and his lords with his singing and his music, and was at length dismissed with an honourable reward, though his songs must have discovered him to have been a Dane (O). Athelstan was saved from the consequences of this stratagem by a soldier, who had observed Aulaff bury the money which had been given him, either from some scruple of honour, or motive of superstition. This occasioned a discovery.

Now if the Saxons had not been accustomed to have minstrels of their own, Alfred's assuming so new and unusual a character would have excited suspicions among the

[1] By Bale and Spelman. See note (M). [2] Ibid.

[3] Anno 938. Vide Rapin, &c.

[4] So I think the name should be printed, rather than Anlaff, the more usual form, (the same traces of the letters express both names in MS.) Aulaff being evidently the genuine northern name Olaff, or Olave, Lat. Olaus. In the old Romance of *Horn-Childe*, (see vol. iii. page 22,) the name of the king his father is Allof, which is evidently Ollaf, with the vowels only transposed.

Danes. On the other hand, if it had not been customary with the Saxons to show favour and respect to the Danish Scalds, Aulaff would not have ventured himself among them, especially on the eve of a battle (P). From the uniform procedure, then, of both these kings we may fairly conclude that the same mode of entertainment prevailed among both people, and that the Minstrel was a privileged character with each.

But, if these facts had never existed, it can be proved from undoubted records, that the Minstrel was a regular and stated officer in the court of our Anglo-Saxon kings: for in Domesday-book, *Joculator Regis*, the King's Minstrel, is expressly mentioned in Gloucestershire; in which county it should seem that he had lands assigned him for his maintenance (Q).

III. We have now brought the inquiry down to the Norman conquest; and as the Normans had been a late colony from Norway and Denmark, where the Scalds had arrived to the highest pitch of credit before Rollo's expedition into France, we cannot doubt but this adventurer, like the other northern princes, had many of these men in his train, who settled with him in his new duchy of Normandy, and left behind them successors in their art: so that, when his descendant, William the Bastard, invaded this kingdom in the following century[5], that mode of entertainment could not but be still familiar with the Normans. And that this is not mere conjecture will appear from a remarkable fact, which shows that the arts of Poetry and Song were still as reputable among the Normans in France, as they had been among their ancestors in the north; and that the profession of Minstrel, like that of Scald, was still aspired to by the most gallant soldiers. In William's army was a valiant warrior, named Taillefer, who was distinguished no less for the minstrel-arts (R), than for his courage and intrepidity. This

[5] Rollo was invested in his new duchy of Normandy A.D. 912. William invaded England A.D. 1066.

man asked leave of his commander to begin the onset, and obtained it. He accordingly advanced before the army, and with a loud voice animated his countrymen with songs in praise of Charlemagne and Roland, and other heroes of France; then rushing among the thickest of the English, and valiantly fighting, lost his life.

Indeed, the Normans were so early distinguished for their minstrel-talents, that an eminent French writer (s) makes no scruple to refer to them the origin of all modern poetry, and shows that they were celebrated for their songs near a century before the Troubadours of Provence, who are supposed to have led the way to the poets of Italy, France, and Spain[6].

We see, then, that the Norman conquest was rather likely to favour the establishment of the minstrel profession in this kingdom, than to suppress it: and although the favour of the Norman conquerors would be probably confined to such of their own countrymen as excelled in the minstrel arts; and in the first ages after the Conquest no other songs would be listened to by the great nobility, but such as were composed in their own Norman French; yet as the great mass of the original inhabitants were not extirpated, these could only understand their own native Gleemen or Minstrels, who must still be allowed to exist, unless it can be proved that they were all proscribed and massacred, as, it is said, the Welsh Bards were afterwards by the severe policy of King Edward I. But this we know was not the case; and even the cruel attempts of that monarch, as we shall see below, proved ineffectual (s2).

The honours shown to the Norman or French Minstrels by our princes and great barons, would naturally have been imitated by their English vassals and tenants, even if no favour or distinction had ever been shown here to the same order of men in the Anglo-Saxon and Danish reigns. So that we cannot doubt but the English Harper and Songster would,

[6] Vide Hist. des Troubadours, 3 tom. passim; and vide Fableaux ou Contes du XII. et du XIII. Siècle, traduits, &c. avec des Notes historiques et critiques, &c. par M. Le Grand. Paris, 1781. 5 tom. 12mo.

at least in a subordinate degree, enjoy the same kind of honours, and be received with similar respect, among the inferior English gentry and populace. I must be allowed, therefore, to consider them as belonging to the same community, as subordinate members at least of the same college; and therefore, in gleaning the scanty materials for this slight history, I shall collect whatever incidents I can find relating to minstrels and their art, and arrange them, as they occur in our own annals, without distinction; as it will not be always easy to ascertain, from the slight mention of them by our regular historians, whether the artists were Norman or English. For it need not be remarked, that subjects of this trivial nature are but incidentally mentioned by our ancient annalists, and were fastidiously rejected by other grave and serious writers; so that, unless they were accidentally connected with such events as became recorded in history, they would pass unnoticed through the lapse of ages, and be as unknown to posterity as other topics relating to the private life and amusements of the greatest nations.

On this account it can hardly be expected that we should be able to produce regular and unbroken annals of the minstrel art and its professors, or have sufficient information whether every minstrel or harper composed himself, or only repeated, the songs he chanted. Some probably did the one, and some the other: and it would have been wonderful indeed, if men whose peculiar profession it was, and who devoted their time and talents to entertain their hearers with poetical compositions, were peculiarly deprived of all poetical genius themselves, and had been under a physical incapacity of composing those common popular rhymes which were the usual subjects of their recitation. Whoever examines any considerable quantity of these, finds them in style and colouring as different from the elaborate production of the sedentary composer at his desk or in his cell, as the rambling harper or minstrel was remote in his modes of life and habits of thinking from the retired scholar or the solitary monk (T).

It is well known that on the Continent, whence our Norman nobles came, the bard who composed, the harper who played and sang, and even the dancer and the mimic, were all considered as of one community, and were even all included under the common name of Minstrels[7]. I must therefore be allowed the same application of the term here, without being expected to prove that every singer composed, or every composer chanted, his own song; much less that every one excelled in all the arts which were occasionally exercised by some or other of this fraternity

IV. After the Norman conquest, the first occurrence which I have met with relating to this order of men is the founding of a priory and hospital by one of them: scil. the Priory and Hospital of St. Bartholomew, in Smithfield, London, by Royer or Raherus, the King's Minstrel, in the third year of King Henry I., A. D. 1102. He was the first Prior of his own establishment, and presided over it to the time of his death (T 2).

In the reign of King Henry II. we have upon record the name of Galfrid, or Jeffrey, a harper, who in 1180 received a corrody, or annuity, from the abbey of Hide, near Winchester; and, as in the early times every harper was expected to sing, we cannot doubt but this reward was given to him for his music and his songs; which, if they were for the solace of the monks there, we may conclude would be in the English language (U).

Under his romantic son, King Richard I., the minstrel profession seems to have acquired additional splendour. Richard, who was the great hero of chivalry, was also the distinguished patron of poets and minstrels. He was himself of their number, and some of his poems are still extant[8].

7 See notes (B) and (AA).

8 See a pathetic Song of his in Mr. Walpole's Catalogue of Royal Authors, vol. i. p. 5. The reader will find a translation of it into modern French, in Hist. Littéraire des Troubadours, 1774, 3 tom. 12mo. See vol. i. (p. 58), where some more of Richard's poetry is translated. In Dr. Burney's Hist. of Music, vol. ii. p. 238, is a poetical version of it in English.

They were no less patronized by his favourites and chief officers. His Chancellor, William Bishop of Ely, is expressly mentioned to have invited singers and minstrels from France, whom he loaded with rewards; and they in return celebrated him as the most accomplished person in the world (u 2). This high distinction and regard, although confined perhaps in the first instance to poets and songsters of the French nation, must have had a tendency to do honour to poetry and song among all his subjects, and to encourage the cultivation of these arts among the natives; as the indulgent favour shown by the monarch or his great courtiers to the Provencal *Troubadour*, or Norman *Rymour*, would naturally be imitated by their inferior vassals to the English Gleeman or Minstrel. At more than a century after the Conquest, the national distinctions must have begun to decline, and both the Norman and English languages would be heard in the houses of the great (u 3); so that probably about this era, or soon after, we are to date that remarkable intercommunity and exchange of each other's compositions, which we discover to have taken place at some early period between the French and English minstrels; the same set of phrases, the same species of characters, incidents, and adventures, and often the same identical stories, being found in the old metrical romances of both nations (v).

The distinguished service which Richard received from one of his own minstrels, in rescuing him from his cruel and tedious captivity, is a remarkable fact, which ought to be recorded for the honour of poets and their art. This fact I shall relate in the following words of an ancient writer[9].

"The Englishmen were more than a whole yeare without hearing any tydings of their King, or in what place he was

[9] Mons. Favine's Theatre of Honour and Knighthood, translated from the French. Lond. 1623, fol. tom. ii. p. 49. An elegant relation of the same event (from the French of Presid. Fauchet's "Recueil," &c.) may be seen in "Miscellanies in Prose and Verse, by Anna Williams, Lond. 1766." 4to. p. 46. It will excite the reader's admiration to be informed, that most of the pieces of that collection were composed under the disadvantage of a total deprivation of sight.

kept prisoner. He had trained up in his court a Rimer or Minstrill[10], called Blondell de Nesle, who (so saith the manuscript of Old Poesies[1], and an auncient manuscript French Chronicle,) being so long without the sight of his Lord, his life seemed wearisome to him, and he became confounded with melancholly. Knowne it was that he came backe from the Holy Land; but none could tell in what countrey he arrived. Whereupon this Blondel, resolving to make search for him in many countries, but he would heare some newes of him: after expence of divers dayes in travaile, he came to a towne[2] (by good hap) neere to the castell where his maister King Richard was kept. Of his host he demanded to whom the castell appertained, and the host told him that it belonged to the Duke of Austria. Then he enquired whether there were any prisoners therein detained or no; for alwayes he made such secret questionings wheresoever he came. And the hoste gave answer, there was one onely prisoner, but he knew not what he was, and yet he had bin detained there more than the space of a yeare. When Blondel heard this, he wrought such meanes, that he became acquainted with them of the castell, *as Minstrels doe easily win acquaintance any where*[3]*;* but see the King he could not, neither understand that it was he. One day he sat directly before a window of the castell, where King Richard was kept

10 Favine's words are, "Jongleur appellé Blondiaux de Nesle." (Paris, 1620, 4to. p. 1106.) But Fauchet, who has given the same story, thus expresses it, "Or ce roy ayant nourri un Menestrel appellé Blondel," &c. liv. ii. p. 92. "Des anciens Poëtes François." He is however said to have been another *Blondel*, not *Blondel* (or *Blondiaux*) *de Nesle;* but this no way affects the circumstances of the story.

1 This the author calls in another place "An ancient MS. of old Poesies, written about those very times."—From this MS. Favine gives a good account of the taking of Richard by the Duke of Austria, who sold him to the emperor. As for the MS. chronicle, it is evidently the same that supplied Fauchet with this story. See his "Recueil de l'Origine de la Langue et Poesie Françoise, Ryme, et Romans," &c. Par. 1581.

2 Tribales.—"Retrudi eum præcepit in Triballis: a quo carcere nullus ante dies istos exivit." Lat. Chron. of Otho of Austria: apud Favin.

3 "Comme Menestrels s'accointent legerement." Favine. (Fauchet expresses it in the same manner.)

prisoner, and began to sing a song in French, which King Richard and Blondel had sometime composed together. When King Richard heard the song, he knew it was Blondel that sung it; and when Blondel paused at halfe of the song, the King *began the other half, and completed it*[4]. Thus Blondel won knowledge of the King his maister, and returning home into England, made the Barons of the countrie acquainted where the King was." This happened about the year 1193.

The following old Provençal lines are given as the very original song[5]; which I shall accompany with an imitation offered by Dr. Burney, ii. 237.

BLONDEL.

| | |
|---|---|
| Domna vostra beutas | *Your beauty, lady fair,* |
| Elas bellas faissos | *None views without delight;* |
| Els bels oils amoros | *But still so cold an air* |
| Els gens cors ben taillats | *No passion can excite:* |
| Don sieu empresenats | *Yet this I patient see* |
| De vostra amor que mi lia. | *While all are shunn'd like me.* |

RICHARD.

| | |
|---|---|
| Si bel trop affansia | *No nymph my heart can wound* |
| Ja de vos non portrai | *If favour she divide,* |
| Que major honorai | *And smiles on all around* |
| Sol en votre deman | *Unwilling to decide:* |
| Que sautra des beisan | *I'd rather hatred bear* |
| Tot can de vos volria. | *Than love with others share.* |

The access which Blondel so readily obtained in the privileged character of a Minstrel, is not the only instance upon

[4] I give this passage corrected; as the English translator of Favine's book appeared here to have mistaken the original:—Scil. "Et quant Blondel eut dit la moitie de la Chanson, le Roy Richart se prist a dire l'autre moitie et l'acheva." Favine, p. 1106. Fauchet has also expressed it in nearly the same words. Recueil, p. 93.

[5] In a little romance or novel, entitled, "La Tour Tenebreuse, et les Jours Lumineux, Contes Angloises, accompagnez d'Historiettes, & tirez d'une ancienne Chronique composee par Richard, surnomme Cœur de Lion, Roy d'Angleterre," &c. Paris, 1705. 12mo.—In the preface to this romance the editor has given another song of Blondel de Nesle, as also a copy of the song written by King Richard, and published by Mr. Walpole, mentioned above (in note 8, page xxxi.); yet the two last are not in Provençal like the sonnet printed here; but in the old French, called *Langage Roman.*

record of the same nature (v 2). In this very reign of King Richard I., the young heiress of D'Evreux, Earl of Salisbury, had been carried abroad and secreted by her French relations in Normandy. To discover the place of her concealment, a knight of the Talbot family spent two years in exploring that province, at first under the disguise of a Pilgrim; till having found where she was confined, in order to gain admittance he assumed the dress and character of a Harper, and being a jocose person, exceedingly skilled in "the *Gests* of the antients[6]," (so they called the romances and stories which were the delight of that age,) he was gladly received into the family. Whence he took an opportunity to carry off the young lady, whom he presented to the king; and he bestowed her on his natural brother, William Longespee, (son of fair Rosamond,) who became in her right Earl of Salisbury (v 3).

The next memorable event which I find in history reflects credit on the English minstrels; and this was their contributing to the Rescue of one of the great Earls of Chester, when besieged by the Welsh. This happened in the reign of King John, and is related to this effect[7].

Hugh, the first Earl of Chester, in his charter of foundation of St. Werburg's Abbey in that city, had granted such a privilege to those who should come to Chester fair, that they should not be then apprehended for theft or any other misdemeanour, except the crime were committed during the fair. This special protection occasioning a multitude of loose people to resort to that fair, was afterwards of signal benefit to one of his successors. For Ranulph, the last Earl of Chester, marching into Wales with a slender attendance, was constrained to retire to his castle of Rothelan, (or Rhuydland,) to which the Welsh forthwith laid siege. In

[6] The words of the original, viz. "Citharisator homo jocosus in GESTIS antiquorum valde peritus," I conceive to give the precise idea of the ancient Minstrel. See note (v 2). That *Gesta* was appropriated to romantic stories, see note (I) part iv. (1.)

[7] See Dugdale (Bar. i. 42, 101), who places it after 13 John, A.D. 1212. See also Plot's Staffordsh. Camden's Britann. (Chesnire.)

this distress he sent for help to the Lord De Lacy, Constable of Chester: "Who, making use of the Minstrells of all sorts, then met at Chester fair; by the allurement of their musick, got together a vast number of such loose people, as, by reason of the before specified priviledge, were then in that city; whom he forthwith sent under the conduct of Dutton, (his steward,)" a gallant youth, who was also his son-in-law. The Welsh, alarmed at the approach of this rabble, supposing them to be a regular body of armed and disciplined veterans, instantly raised the siege and retired.

For this good service, Ranulph is said to have granted to De Lacy, by charter, the patronage and authority over the minstrels and the loose and inferior people: who, retaining to himself that of the lower artificers, conferred on Dutton the jurisdiction of the minstrels and harlots[8]: and under the descendants of this family the minstrels enjoyed certain privileges and protection for many ages. For even so late as the reign of Elizabeth, when this profession had fallen into such discredit that it was considered in law as a nuisance, the minstrels under the jurisdiction of the family of Dutton are expressly excepted out of all acts of parliament made for their suppression; and have continued to be so excepted ever since (w).

The ceremonies attending the exercise of this jurisdiction are thus described by Dugdale[9], as handed down to his time, viz. "That at midsummer fair there, all the Minstrels of that countrey resorting to Chester do attend the heir of Dutton, from his lodging to St. John's church, (he being then accompanied by many gentlemen of the countrey,) one of 'the Minstrels' walking before him in a surcoat of his arms depicted on taffata; the rest of his fellows proceeding (two and two) and playing on their several sorts of musical instruments. And after divine service ended, give the like attendance on him back to his lodging; where a COURT being kept by his [Mr. Dutton's] steward, and all the Minstrels

8 See the ancient record in Blount's Law Dictionary. (Art. Minstrel.)

9 Bar. i. p. 101.

formally called, certain orders and laws are usually made for the better government of that Society, with penalties on those who transgress."

In the same reign of King John we have a remarkable instance of a minstrel, who to his other talents superadded the character of Soothsayer, and by his skill in drugs and medicated potions was able to rescue a knight from imprisonment. This occurs in Leland's Narrative of the GESTES of Guarine (or Warren) and his sons, which he "excerptid owte of an old Englisch boke yn ryme[10]," and is as follows:—

Whitington Castle in Shropshire, which together with the coheiress of the original proprietor had been won in a solemn turnament by the ancestor of the Guarines[1], had, in the reign of King John, been seized by the Prince of Wales, and was afterwards possessed by Morice, a retainer of that prince, to whom the king, out of hatred to the true heir Fulco Guarine, (with whom he had formerly had a quarrel at chess[2],) not only confirmed the possession, but also made him governor of the Marches, of which Fulco himself had the custody in the time of King Richard. The Guarines demanded justice of the king, but obtaining no gracious answer, renounced their allegiance and fled into Britagne. Returning into England, after various conflicts, "Fulco resortid to one John of Raumpayne, a Sothsayer and Jocular and Minstrelle, and made hym his spy to Morice at Whitington." The privileges of this character we have already seen, and John so well availed himself of them, that in consequence of the intelligence which he doubtless procured, "Fulco and

10 Leland's Collectanea, vol. i. pages 261, 266, 267.

1 This old feudal custom of marrying an heiress to the knight who should vanquish all his opponents in solemn contest, &c., appears to be burlesqued in the Turnament of Totenham (see vol. ii. p. 11), as is well observed by the learned author of Remarks, &c. in Gent. Mag. for July, 1794, p. 613.

2 "John, sun to King Henry, and Fulco felle at variance at Chestes, [r. Chesse]; and John brake Fulco'[s] hed with the Chest borde: and then Fulco gave him such a blow, that he had almost killed hym." (Lel. Coll. i. p. 264.) A curious picture of courtly manners in that age! Notwithstanding this fray, we read in the next paragraph, that "King Henry dubbid Fulco & 3 of his bretherne Knightes at Winchestor."—Ibid.

his brethrene laide waite for Morice, as he went toward Salesbyri, and Fulco ther woundid hym: and Bracy," a knight, who was their friend and assistant, "cut off Morice ['s] hedde." This Sir Bracy being in a subsequent rencounter sore wounded, was taken and brought to King John; from whose vengeance he was, however, rescued by this notable minstrel; for "John Rampayne founde the meanes to cast them, that kepte Bracy, into a deadely slepe; and so he and Bracy cam to Fulco to Whitington," which on the death of Morice had been restored to him by the Prince of Wales. As no further mention occurs of the minstrel, I might here conclude this narrative; but I shall just add, that Fulco was obliged to flee into France, where, assuming the name of Sir Amice, he distinguished himself in justs and turnaments; and, after various romantic adventures by sea and land, having in the true style of chivalry rescued "certayne ladies owt of prison," he finally obtained the king's pardon, and the quiet possession of Whitington Castle.

In the reign of King Henry III. we have mention of Master Ricard, the king's harper, to whom in his thirty-sixth year (1252) that monarch gave not only forty shillings and a pipe of wine, but also a pipe of wine to Beatrice his wife[3]. The title of *Magister*, or Master, given to this minstrel, deserves notice, and shows his respectable situation.

V. The Harper, or Minstrel, was so necessary an attendant on a royal personage, that Prince Edward (afterwards King Edward I.), in his crusade to the Holy Land, in 1271, was not without his harper, who must have been officially very near his person; as we are told by a contemporary historian[4], that, in the attempt to assassinate that heroic prince, when he had wrested the poisoned knife out of the

[3] Burney's Hist. ii. p. 355.—Rot. Pip. An. 36 H. III. "Et in uno dolio vini empto & dato MAGISTRO RICARDO Citharistæ Regis, xl. sol. per br. Reg. Et in uno dolio empto & dato Beatrici uxori ejusdem Ricardi."

[4] Walter Hemmingford (vixit temp. Edw. I.), in Chronic. cap. 35, inter V. Hist. Ang. Scriptores, vol. ii. Oxon. 1687. fol. pag. 591.

Sarazen's hand, and killed him with his own weapon; the attendants, who had stood apart while he was whispering to their master, hearing the struggle, ran to his assistance, and one of them, to wit his harper, seizing a tripod, or trestle, struck the assassin on the head and beat out his brains[5]. And though the prince blamed him for striking the man after he was dead, yet his near access shows the respectable situation of this officer; and his affectionate zeal should have induced Edward to entreat his brethren, the Welsh bards, afterwards with more lenity.

Whatever was the extent of this great monarch's severity towards the professors of music and of song in Wales; whether the executing by martial law such of them as fell into his hands was only during the heat of conflict, or was continued afterwards with more systematic rigour[6]; yet in his own court the minstrels appear to have been highly favoured; for when, in 1306, he conferred the order of knighthood on his son and many others of the young nobility, a multitude of minstrels were introduced to invite and induce the new knights to make some military vow (x). And

Under the succeeding reign of King Edward II. such extensive privileges were claimed by these men, and by dissolute persons assuming their character, that it became a matter of public grievance, and was obliged to be reformed by an express regulation in A. D. 1315 (Y). Notwithstanding which, an incident is recorded in the ensuing year, which shows that minstrels still retained the liberty of entering at

5 "Accurrentes ad hæc Ministri ejus, qui a longe steterunt, invenerunt eum [scil. Nuntium] in terra mortuum, et apprehendit unus eorum tripodem, scilicet CITHAREDA SUUS, & percussit eum in capite, et effundit cerebrum ejus. Increpavitque eum Edwardus quod hominem mortuum percussisset." Ibid. These *Ministri* must have been upon a very confidential footing, as it appears above in the same chapter, that they had been made acquainted with the contents of the letters which the assassin had delivered to the prince from his master.

6 See Gray's Ode; and the Hist. of the Gwedir Family in "Miscellanies by the Hon. Daines Barrington," 1781, 4to. page 386; who, in the Laws, &c. of this monarch, could find no instances of severity against the Welsh. See his Observations on the Statutes, 4to., 4th edit. p. 358.

will into the royal presence, and had something peculiarly splendid in their dress. It is thus related by Stowe (z):

"In the year 1316, Edward the Second did solemnize his feast of Pentecost at Westminster, in the great hall; where sitting royally at the table with his peers about him, there entered a woman *adorned like a Minstrel*, sitting on a great horse trapped, *as Minstrels then used;* who rode round about the tables, shewing pastime; and at length came up to the King's table, and laid before him a letter, and forthwith turning her horse, saluted every one and departed." The subject of this letter was a remonstrance to the king on the favours heaped by him on his minions, to the neglect of his knights and faithful servants.

The privileged character of a minstrel was employed on this occasion, as sure of gaining an easy admittance; and a female the rather deputed to assume it, that, in case of detection, her sex might disarm the king's resentment. This is offered on a supposition that she was not a real minstrel; for there should seem to have been women of this profession (AA), as well as of the other sex; and no accomplishment is so constantly attributed to females, by our ancient bards, as their singing to, and playing on, the harp (AA 2).

In the fourth year of King Richard II. John of Gaunt erected at Tutbury, in Staffordshire, a Court of Minstrels, similar to that annually kept at Chester (page xxxvi.), and which, like a Court-Leet or Court-Baron, had a legal jurisdiction, with full power to receive suit and service from the men of this profession within five neighbouring counties, to enact laws and determine their controversies; and to apprehend and arrest such of them as should refuse to appear at the said court, annually held on the 16th of August. For this they had a charter, by which they were empowered to appoint a King of the Minstrels, with four officers to preside over them (BB). These were every year elected with great ceremony; the whole form of which, as observed in 1680, is described by Dr. Plot[7]: in whose time, however, they appear

[7] Hist. of Staffordshire, ch. 10. § 69—76, p. 433, et seqq., of which see ex-

to have lost their singing talents, and to have confined all their skill to wind and string music[8].

The minstrels seem to have been in many respects upon the same footing as the heralds: and the King of the Minstrels, like the King at Arms, was both here and on the Continent an usual officer in the courts of princes. Thus we have in the reign of King Edward I. mention of a King Robert, and others. And in 16 Edward II. is a grant to William de Morlee, "the King's Minstrel, styled *Roy de North*[9]," of houses which had belonged to another king, John le Boteler (BB 2). Rymer hath also printed a licence granted by King Richard II. in 1387, to John Caumz, the King of *his* Minstrels, to pass the seas, recommending him to the protection and kind treatment of all his subjects and allies[10].

In the subsequent reign of King Henry IV. we meet with no particulars relating to the Minstrels in England, but we find in the Statute Book a severe law passed against their brethren, the Welsh Bards; whom our ancestors could not distinguish from their own *Rimours*, *Minstralx;* for by these names they describe them (BB 3). This act plainly shows, that far from being extirpated by the rigorous policy of King Edward I., this order of men were still able to alarm the English government, which attributed to them "many diseases and mischiefs in Wales," and prohibited their meetings and contributions.

When his heroic son, King Henry V., was preparing his great voyage for France, in 1415, an express order was given for his minstrels, fifteen in number, to attend

tracts in Sir J. Hawkins's Hist. of Music, vol. ii. p. 64; and Dr. Burney's Hist. vol. ii. p. 360, et seqq.

N.B. The barbarous diversion of bull-running was no part of the original institution, &c., as is fully proved by the Rev. Dr. Pegge, in Archæologia, vol. ii. no. xiii. p. 86.

8 See the charge given by the steward. at the time of the election, in Plot's Hist. ubi supra; and in Hawkins, p. 67. Burney, p. 363-4.

9 So among the heralds *Norrey* was anciently styled *Roy d'Armes de North.* (Anstis, ii. 300.) And the Kings at Armes in general were originally called *Reges Heraldorum* (ibid. p. 302), as these were *Reges Minstrallorum.*

10 Rymer's Fœdera, tom. vii. p. 555.

him[1]: and eighteen are afterwards mentioned, to each of whom he allowed xii*d*. a-day, when that sum must have been of more than ten times the value it is at present[2]. Yet when he entered London in triumph after the battle of Agincourt, he, from a principle of humility, slighted the pageants and verses which were prepared to hail his return; and, as we are told by Holingshed[3], would not suffer "any Dities to be made and song by Minstrels, of his glorious victorie; for that he would whollie have the praise and thankes altogether given to God" (BB 4). But this did not proceed from any disregard for the professors of music or of song; for at the feast of Pentecost, which he celebrated in 1416, having the Emperor and the Duke of Holland for his guests, he ordered rich gowns for sixteen of his minstrels, of which the particulars are preserved by Rymer[4]. And having before his death orally granted an annuity of 100 shillings to each of his minstrels, the grant was confirmed in the first year of his son King Henry VI., A.D. 1423, and payment ordered out of the Exchequer[5].

The unfortunate reign of King Henry VI. affords no occurrences respecting our subject; but in his thirty-fourth year, A. D. 1456, we have in Rymer[6] a commission for impressing boys or youths, to supply vacancies by death among

1 Rymer's Fœdera, tom. ix. 255. 2 Ibid. p. 260.

3 See his Chronicle, sub anno 1415 (p. 1170). He also gives this other instance of the king's great modesty, "that he would not suffer his helmet to be carried with him, and shewed to the people, that they might behold the dintes and cuttes whiche appeared in the same, of such blowes and stripes as hee received the daye of the battell."—Ibid. Vid. T. de Elmham, c. 29. p. 72.

The prohibition against vain and secular songs would probably not include that inserted in our second vol. no. v. (p. 22,) which would be considered as a hymn. The original notes engraven on a plate at p. 21, may be seen reduced and set to score in Mr. Stafford Smith's "Collection of English Songs for three and four voices," and in Dr. Burney's Hist. of Music, ii. p. 384.

4 Tom. ix. 336.

5 Rymer, tom. x. 287. They are mentioned by name, being *ten* in number: one of them was named *Thomas Chatterton*.

6 Tom. xi. 375.

the king's minstrels: in which it is expressly directed that they shall be elegant in their limbs, as well as instructed in the minstrel art, wherever they can be found, for the solace of his majesty.

In the following reign, King Edward IV. (in his ninth year, 1469), upon a complaint that certain rude husbandmen and artificers of various trades had assumed the title and livery of the king's minstrels, and under that colour and pretence had collected money in divers parts of the kingdom, and committed other disorders, the king grants to Walter Haliday, *Marshal*, and to seven others his own minstrels, whom he names, a Charter[7], by which he creates, or rather restores, a Fraternity or perpetual Gild, (such as, he understands, the brothers and sisters of the fraternity of Minstrels had in times past,) to be governed by a Marshal, appointed for life, and by two Wardens, to be chosen annually; who are impowered to admit brothers and sisters into the said Gild, and are authorized to examine the pretensions of all such as affected to exercise the minstrel profession; and to regulate, govern, and punish them throughout the realm (those of Chester excepted). This seems to have some resemblance to the Earl Marshal's court among the Heralds, and is another proof of the great affinity and resemblance which the Minstrels bore to the members of the College of Arms.

It is remarkable that Walter Haliday, whose name occurs as Marshal in the foregoing Charter, had been retained in the service of the two preceding monarchs, King Henry V.[8] and VI.[9] Nor is this the first time he is mentioned as Marshal of the king's minstrels, for in the third year of this reign, 1464, he had a grant from King Edward of ten marks per annum during life, directed to him with that title[10].

[7] See it in Rymer, tom. xi. 642, and in Sir J. Hawkins, vol. iv. p. 366, note. The above Charter is recited in letters patent of King Charles I., 15th July (11 Anno Regni), for a Corporation of Musicians, &c. in Westminster, which may be seen, ibid.

[8] Rymer, ix. 255. [9] Ibid. xi. 375. [10] Ibid. xi. 512.

But besides their Marshal, we have also in this reign mention of a Serjeant of the Minstrels, who upon a particular occasion was able to do his royal master a singular service, wherein his confidential situation and ready access to the king at all hours is very apparent: for "as he [King Edward IV.] was in the north contray in the monneth of Septembre, as he lay in his bedde, one namid Alexander Carlile, that was *Sariaunt of the Mynstrellis*, cam to him in grete hast, and badde hym aryse for he hadde enemyes cummyng for to take him, the which were within vi. or vii. mylis, of the which tydinges the king gretely marveylid[1]," &c. This happened in the same year, 1469, wherein the king granted or confirmed the Charter for the Fraternity or Gild above-mentioned: yet this Alexander Carlile is not one of the eight minstrels to whom that Charter is directed[2].

The same Charter was renewed by King Henry VIII. in 1520, to John Gilman, his then Marshal, and to seven others his minstrels[3]: and on the death of Gilman, he granted in 1529 this office of Marshal of his Minstrels to Hugh Wodehouse[4], whom I take to have borne the office of his Serjeant over them[5].

VI. In all the establishments of royal and noble households, we find an ample provision made for the Minstrels, and their situation to have been both honourable and lucrative. In proof of this it is sufficient to refer to the Houshold-

[1] Here unfortunately ends a curious fragment (an. 9 E. IV.), ad calcem Sprotti Chron. ed. Hearne, Oxon. 1719, 8vo. Vide T. Warton's Hist. ii. p. 134. Note (c).

[2] Rymer, xi. 642. [3] Ibid. xiii. 705. [4] Ibid. tom. xiv. 2, 93.

[5] So I am inclined to understand the term SERVIENS *noster Hugo Wodehous*, in the original grant. (See Rymer, ubi supra.) It is needless to observe that *Serviens* expressed a Serjeant as well as a Servant. If this interpretation of Serviens be allowed, it will account for his placing Wodehouse at the head of his Gild, although he had not been one of the eight minstrels who had had the general direction. The Serjeant of his Minstrels, we may presume, was next in dignity to the Marshal, although he had no share in the government of the Gild.

Book of the Earl of Northumberland, A. D. 1512 (CC). And the rewards they received so frequently recur in ancient writers, that it is unnecessary to crowd the page with them here (CC2).

The name of Minstrel seems, however, to have been gradually appropriated to the Musician only, especially in the fifteenth and sixteenth centuries; yet we occasionally meet with applications of the term in its more enlarged meaning, as including the Singer, if not the Composer, of heroic or popular rhymes[6].

In the time of King Henry VIII. we find it to have been a common entertainment to hear verses recited, or moral speeches learned for that purpose, by a set of men who got their livelihood by repeating them, and who intruded without ceremony into all companies; not only in taverns, but in the houses of the nobility themselves. This we learn from Erasmus, whose argument led him only to describe a species of these men who *did not sing* their compositions; but the others that *did*, enjoyed, without doubt, the same privileges (DD).

For even long after, in the reign of Queen Elizabeth, it was usual "in places of assembly" for the company to be "desirous to heare of old adventures and valiaunces of noble knights in times past, as those of King Arthur and his knights of the round-table, Sir Bevys of Southampton, Guy of Warwicke, and others like," in "short and long meetres, and by breaches or divisions [sc. FITS[7]], to be more commodiously sung to the harpe," as the reader may be informed, by a courtly writer, in 1589[8]. Who himself had "written for pleasure, a little brief Romance or historicall Ditty . . . of the Isle of Great Britaine," in order to contribute to such entertainment. And he subjoins this caution: "Such as have not premonition hereof," (viz. that his poem

[6] See below, and Note (GG).

[7] See vol. ii. page 144.

[8] Puttenham in his *Arte of English Poesie,* 1589, 4to. p. 33. See the quotation in its proper order in vol. ii. page 144.

was written in short metre, &c., to be sung to the harp in such places of assembly,) "and consideration of the causes alledged, would peradventure reprove and disgrace every Romance, or short historicall ditty, for that they be not written in long meeters or verses Alexandrins," which constituted the prevailing versification among the poets of that age, and which no one now can endure to read.

And that the recital of such romances, sung to the harp, was at that time the delight of the common people, we are told by the same writer[9], who mentions that "common Rimers" were fond of using rhymes at short distances, "in small and popular Musickes song by these Cantabanqui," [the said common rhymers,] "upon benches and barrels heads," &c., "or else by blind Harpers, or such like Taverne Minstrels, that give a FIT of mirth for a groat; and their matter being for the most part stories of old time, as the tale of Sir Topas, the reportes of Bevis of Southampton, Guy of Warwicke, Adam Bell and Clymme of the Clough, and such other old romances, or historicall rimes," &c.; "also they be used in Carols and Rounds, and such like or lascivious Poemes, which are commonly more commodiously uttered by these Buffons, or Vices, in Playes, then by any other person. Such were the rimes of Skelton (usurping the name of a Poet Laureat), being in deede but a rude railing rimer, and all his doings ridiculous[10]."

But although we find here that the Minstrels had lost much of their dignity, and were sinking into contempt and neglect: yet that they still sustained a character far superior to any thing we can conceive at present of the singers of old ballads, I think may be inferred from the following representation.

When Queen Elizabeth was entertained at Killingworth Castle by the Earl of Leicester in 1575, among the many devices and pageants which were contrived for her entertainment, one of the personages introduced was to have

[9] Puttenham, &c. p. 69. (See vol. ii. ibid.)
[10] Puttenham, &c. p. 69.

been that of an ancient Minstrel; whose appearance and dress are so minutely described by a writer there present[1], and give us so distinct an idea of the character, that I shall quote the passage at large (EE).

"A Person very meet seemed he for the purpose, of a xlv years old, apparelled partly as he would himself. His cap off; his head seemly rounded Tonsterwise[2]; fair kembed, that with a sponge daintily dipt in a little capon's greace, was finely smoothed, to make it shine like a mallard's wing. His beard smugly shaven; and yet his shirt after the new trink, with ruffs fair starched, sleeked and glistering like a pair of new shoes, marshalled in good order with a setting stick, and strut, that every ruff stood up like a wafer. A side [*i. e.* long] gown of Kendal green, after the freshness of the year now, gathered at the neck with a narrow gorget, fastened afore with a white clasp and a keeper close up to the chin; but easily, for heat to undo when he list. Seemly begirt in a red caddis girdle; from that a pair of capped Sheffield knives hanging a' two sides. Out of his bosom drawn forth a lappet of his napkin[3], edged with a blue lace, and marked with a true love, a heart, and a D for Damian, for he was but a batchelor yet.

"His gown had side [*i. e.* long] sleeves down to midleg, slit from the shoulder to the hand, and lined with white cotton. His doublet-sleeves of black worsted: upon them a pair of poynets[4], of tawny chamlet laced along the wrist with blue threaden points, a wealt towards the hand of fustian-a-napes. A pair of red neather stocks. A pair of pumps on his feet, with a cross cut at the toes for corns; not

[1] See a very curious "Letter: whearin, part of the entertainment untoo the Queenz Maiesty, at Killingwoorth Castl, in Warwick Sheer, in this soomerz Progress 1575, iz signified," &c. bl. l. 4to. vid. p. 46, & seqq. (Printed in Nichols's *Collection of Queen Elizabeth's Progresses*, &c. in 2 vols. 4to.) We have not followed above the peculiar and affected orthography of this writer, who was named Ro. Laneham, or rather Langham.

[2] I suppose "tonsure-wise," after the manner of the monks.

[3] *i. e.* handkerchief. So in Shakspeare's *Othello*, passim.

[4] Perhaps, points.

new indeed, yet cleanly blackt with soot, and shining as a shoing horn.

"About his neck a red ribband suitable to his girdle. His *harp* in good grace dependent before him. His *wrest*[5] tyed to a green lace and hanging by. Under the gorget of his gown a fair flaggon chain (pewter[6] for) silver, as a *Squire Minstrel of Middlesex*, that travelled the country this summer season, unto fairs and worshipful mens houses. From his chain hung a scutcheon, with metal and colour, resplendant upon his breast, of the ancient arms of Islington."

This minstrel is described as belonging to that village. I suppose such as were retained by noble families wore the arms of their patrons hanging down by a silver chain[7], as a kind of badge. From the expression of Squire Minstrel above, we may conclude there were other inferior orders, as Yeomen Minstrels, or the like.

This minstrel, the author tells us a little below, "after three lowly courtsies, cleared his voice with a hem . . . and . . . wiped his lips with the hollow of his hand for 'filing his napkin, tempered a string or two with his *wrest*, and after a little warbling on his Harp for a prelude, came forth with a solemn song, warranted for story out of King Arthur's acts," &c. — This song the reader will find printed in this work, vol. iii. book i. no. 3.

[5] The key, or screw, with which he tuned his harp.

[6] The reader will remember that this was not a *real* minstrel, but only one personating that character; his ornaments therefore were only such as *outwardly* represented those of a real minstrel.

[7] As the house of Northumberland had anciently three minstrels attending on them in their castles in Yorkshire, so they still retain three in their service in Northumberland, who wear the badge of the family (a silver crescent on the right arm), and are thus distributed, viz.—One for the barony of Prudhoe, and two for the barony of Rothbury. These attend the court-leets and fairs held for the lord, and pay their annual suit and service at Alnwick Castle: their instrument being the ancient Northumberland bagpipe (very different in form and execution from that of the Scots; being smaller, and blown, not with the breath, but with a small pair of bellows).

This, with many other venerable customs of the ancient Lord Percys, was revived by their illustrious representatives the late Duke and Duchess of Northumberland.

Towards the end of the sixteenth century this class of men had lost all credit, and were sunk so low in the public opinion, that in the 39th year of Elizabeth[8], a statute was passed, by which "Minstrels, wandering abroad," were included among "rogues, vagabonds, and sturdy beggars," and were adjudged to be punished as such. This act seems to have put an end to the profession (EE 2).

VII. I cannot conclude this account of the ancient English Minstrels, without remarking that they are most of them represented to have been of the North of England. There is scarce an old historical song or ballad (FF) wherein a minstrel or harper appears, but he is characterized, by way of eminence, to have been "of the North Countrye[9]:" and indeed the prevalence of the northern dialect in such compositions, shows that this representation is real[10]. On the other hand, the scene of the finest Scottish ballads is

8 Anno Dom. 1597. Vid. Pult. Stat. p. 1110, 39 Eliz.

9 See pp. 58, 59, ver. 156, 180, &c.

10 Giraldus Cambrensis, writing in the reign of King Henry II., mentions a very extraordinary habit or propensity, which then prevailed in the north of England, beyond the Humber, for "symphonious harmony" or singing "in two parts, the one murmuring in the base, and the other warbling in the acute or treble." (I use Dr. Burney's version, vol. ii. p. 108.) This he describes as practised by their very children from the cradle; and he derives it from the Danes [so *Daci* signifies in our old writers] and Norwegians, who long over-ran and in effect new-peopled the Northern parts of England, where alone this manner of singing prevailed. (Vide Cambriæ Descriptio, cap. 13, and in Burney, ubi supra.) — Giraldus is probably right as to the origin or derivation of this practice, for the Danish and Icelandic Scalds had carried the arts of Poetry and Singing to great perfection at the time the Danish settlements were made in the North. And it will also help to account for the superior skill and fame of our northern minstrels and harpers afterwards, who had preserved and transmitted the arts of their Scaldic ancestors. See *Northern Antiquities*, vol. i. c. 13, p. 386, and *Five Pieces of Runic Poetry*, 1763, 8vo. — Compare the original passage in Giraldus, as given by Sir John Hawkins, i. 408, and by Dr. Burney, ii. 108, who are both at a loss to account for this peculiarity, and therefore doubt the fact. The credit of Giraldus, which hath been attacked by some partial and bigoted antiquaries, the reader will find defended in that learned and curious work, "Antiquities of Ireland, by Edward Ledwich, LL.D. &c., of Dublin, 1790," 4to. p. 207, & seqq.

laid in the south of Scotland, which should seem to have been peculiarly the nursery of Scottish minstrels. In the old song of *Maggy Lawder*, a piper is asked, by way of distinction, Come ze frae the Border[1]? — The martial spirit constantly kept up and exercised near the frontier of the two kingdoms, as it furnished continual subjects for their songs, so it inspired the inhabitants of the adjacent counties on both sides with the powers of poetry. Besides, as our southern metropolis must have been ever the scene of novelty and refinement, the northern countries, as being most distant, would preserve their ancient manners longest, and of course the old poetry, in which those manners are peculiarly described.

The reader will observe in the more ancient ballads of this collection, a cast of style and measure very different from that of contemporary poets of a higher class; many phrases and idioms, which the minstrels seem to have appropriated to themselves, and a very remarkable licence of varying the accent of words at pleasure, in order to humour the flow of the verse, particularly in the rhymes; as

1 This line being quoted from memory, and given as old Scottish poetry is now usually printed (see Note at the end of the Glossary), would have been readily corrected by the copy published in "Scottish Songs, 1794," 2 vols. 12mo. i. p. 267, thus (though apparently corrupted from the Scottish idiom),

"Live you upo' the Border?"

had not all confidence been destroyed by its being altered in the "Historical Essay" prefixed to that publication (p. cx.) to

"Ye live upo' the Border,"

the better to favour a position, that many of the Pipers "might live upon the border, for the conveniency of attending fairs, &c. in both kingdoms." But whoever is acquainted with that part of England, knows that on the English frontier, rude mountains and barren wastes reach almost across the island, scarcely inhabited by any but solitary shepherds, many of whom durst not venture into the opposite border on account of the ancient feuds and subsequent disputes concerning the Debatable Lands, which separated the boundaries of the two kingdoms, as well as the estates of the two great families of Percy and Douglas, till these disputes were settled, not many years since, by arbitration between the *present* Lord Douglas and the *late* Duke and Duchess of Northumberland.

Countrìe harpèr battèl mornìng
Ladìe singèr damsèl lovìng

instead of *coùntry*, *làdy*, *hàrper*, *sìnger*, &c.— This liberty is but sparingly assumed by the classical poets of the same age, or even by the latter composers of heroical ballads; I mean, by such as professedly wrote for the press. For it is to be observed, that so long as the Minstrels subsisted, they seem never to have designed their rhymes for literary publication, and probably never committed them to writing themselves: what copies are preserved of them were doubtless taken down from their mouths. But as the old Minstrels gradually wore out, a new race of Ballad-writers succeeded, an inferior sort of minor poets, who wrote narrative songs merely for the press. Instances of both may be found in the reign of Elizabeth. The two latest pieces in the genuine strain of the old minstrelsy that I can discover, are Nos. iii. and iv. of book iii. in this volume. Lower than these I cannot trace the old mode of writing.

The old minstrel ballads are in the northern dialect, abound with antique words and phrases, are extremely incorrect, and run into the utmost licence of metre; they have also a romantic wildness, and are in the true spirit of chivalry. The other sort are written in exacter measure, have a low or subordinate correctness, sometimes bordering on the insipid, yet often well adapted to the pathetic; these are generally in the southern dialect, exhibit a more modern phraseology, and are commonly descriptive of more modern manners. To be sensible of the difference between them, let the reader compare in this volume No. iii. of book iii. with No. xi. of book ii.

Towards the end of Queen Elizabeth's reign, (as is mentioned above,) the genuine old minstrelsy seems to have been extinct, and thenceforth the ballads that were produced were wholly of the latter kind, and these came forth in such abundance, that in the reign of James I. they began to be collected into little miscellanies, under the name of

Garlands, and at length to be written purposely for such collections (FF 2).

P.S. By way of Postscript, should follow here the discussion of the question whether the term *Minstrels* was applied in English to Singers, and Composers of Songs, &c., or confined to Musicians only. But it is reserved for the concluding note (GG).

---

# NOTES AND ILLUSTRATIONS

REFERRED TO IN

THE FOREGOING ESSAY.

---

(A) *The Minstrels, &c.*] The word *Minstrel* does not appear to have been in use here before the Norman conquest; whereas it had long before that time been adopted in France[1]. MENESTREL, so early as the eighth century, was a title given to the *Maestro di Capella* of King Pepin, the father of Charlemagne; and afterwards to the Coryphæus, or leader of any band of musicians. [Vide Burney's *Hist. of Music*, ii. 268.] This term *Menestrel*, *Menestrier*, was thus expressed in Latin, *Ministellus*, *Ministrellus*, *Ministrallus*, *Menesterellus*, &c. [Vide Gloss. Du Cange, & Supplem.]

Menage derives the French words above mentioned from *Ministerialis* or *Ministeriarius*, barbarous Latin terms, used in the middle ages to express a workman or artificer, (still called in Languedoc *Ministral*,) as if these men were styled ARTIFICERS or PERFORMERS by way of excellence. [Vide *Diction. Etym.*] But the origin of the name is given perhaps more truly by Du Cange: "MINISTELLI . . . . quos vulgo *Menestreux* vel *Menestriers* appellamus, quod minoribus aulæ *Ministris* accenserentur." [Gloss. iv. p. 769.] Accordingly, we are told, the word *Minister* is sometimes used pro *Mi-*

1 The Anglo-Saxon and primary English name for this character was *Gleeman* [see below, Note (I) sect. 1], so that, wherever the term *Minstrel* is in these pages applied to it before the Conquest, it must be understood to be only by anticipation. Another early name for this profession in English was *Jogeler*, or *Jocular*, Lat. *Joculator*. [See p. xxx. as also note (v 2), and note (Q).] To prevent confusion, we have chiefly used the more general word *Minstrel:* which (as the author of the Observ. on the Statutes hath suggested to the Editor) might have been originally derived from a diminutive of the Lat. *Minister:* scil. *Ministerellus, Ministrellus.*

*nistellus*, [ibid.] and an instance is produced which I shall insert at large in the next paragraph.

Minstrels sometimes assisted at divine service, as appears from the record of the 9th of Edward IV., quoted above in page xliii, by which Haliday and others are erected into a perpetual Gild, &c. See the original in Rymer, xi. 642. By part of this record it is recited to be their duty "to pray (*exorare:* which it is presumed they did by assisting in the chant, and musical accompaniment, &c.) in the King's chapel, and particularly for the departed souls of the King and Queen, when they shall die," &c. The same also appears from the passage in the Supplem. to Du Cange, alluded to above. "MINISTER . . . . pro *Ministellus* Joculator[2]."—Vetus Ceremoniale MS. B.M. deauratæ Tolos. "Item, etiam congregabuntur Piscatores, qui debent interesse isto die in processione cum *Ministris* seu Joculatoribus· quia ipsi Piscatores tenentur habere isto die *Joculatores*, seu *Mimos*, ob *honorem Crucis* — et vadunt primi ante processionem cum *Ministris* seu Joculatoribus semper pulsantibus usque ad Ecclesiam S Stephani." [Gloss. 773.] This may perhaps account for the clerical appearance of the Minstrels, who seem to have been distinguished by the *Tonsure*, which was one of the inferior marks of the clerical character[3]. Thus Geoffrey of Monmouth, speaking of one who acted the part of a Minstrel,

[2] *Ministers* seems to be used for *Minstrels* in the Account of the Inthronization of Abp. Neville (An. 6 Edw. IV.). "Then all the Chaplyns must say grace, and the *Ministers* do sing."—Vide Lelandi Collectanea, by Hearne, vol. vi. p. 13.

[3] It has, however, been suggested to the Editor by the learned and ingenious author of "Irish Antiquities," 4to., that the ancient *Mimi* among the Romans had their heads and beards shaven, as is shown by Salmasius in Notis ad Hist. August. Scriptores VI. Paris, 1620, fol. p. 385. So that this peculiarity had a classical origin, though it afterwards might make the Minstrels sometimes pass for Ecclesiastics, as appears from the instance given below. Dr. Burney tells us that Histriones, and Mimi, abounded in France in the time of Charlemagne (ii. 221), so that their profession was handed down in regular succession from the time of the Romans, and therewith some leading distinctions of their habit or appearance; yet with a change in their arts of pleasing, which latterly were most confined to singing and music.

says, "Rasit capillos suos et barbam." (See note K.) Again, a writer in the reign of Elizabeth, describing the habit of an ancient Minstrel, speaks of his head as "rounded Tonster-wise," (which I venture to read Tonsure-wise,) "his beard smugly shaven." See above, p. xlvii.

It must, however, be observed, that notwithstanding such clerical appearance of the Minstrels, and though they might be sometimes countenanced by such of the clergy as were of more relaxed morals, their sportive talents rendered them generally obnoxious to the more rigid ecclesiastics, and to such of the religious orders as were of more severe discipline; whose writings commonly abound with heavy complaints of the great encouragement shown to those men by the princes and nobles, and who can seldom afford them a better name than that of *Scurræ*, *Famelici*, *Nebulones*, &c., of which innumerable instances may be seen in Du Cange. It was even an established order in some of the monasteries, that no Minstrel should ever be suffered to enter the gates[4].

We have, however, innumerable particulars of the good cheer and great rewards given to the Minstrels in many of the convents, which are collected by T. Warton (i. 91, &c.) and others. But one instance, quoted from Wood's *Hist. Antiq.* Univ. Ox. i. 67, (sub an. 1224,) deserves particular mention. Two itinerant priests, on a supposition of their being *Mimi* or *Minstrels*, gained admittance. But the cellarer, sacrist, and others of the brethren, who had hoped to have been entertained by their diverting arts, &c., when they found them to be only two indigent ecclesiastics, who could only administer spiritual consolation, and were consequently disappointed of their mirth, beat them, and turned them out of the monastery. (Ibid. p. 92.) This passage furnishes an additional proof that a minstrel might, by his dress or appearance, be mistaken for an ecclesiastic.

[4] Yet in St. Mary's church at Beverley, one of the columns hath this inscription:—"Thys Pillar made the Mynstrylls:" having its capital decorated with figures of five men in short coats; one of whom holds an instrument resembling a lute. See Sir J. Hawkins, Hist. ii. 298.

(B) *The Minstrels use mimickry and action, and other means of diverting, &c.*] It is observable, that our old monkish historians do not use the words *Cantator*, *Citharœdus*, *Musicus*, or the like, to express a Minstrel in Latin, so frequently as *Mimus*, *Histrio*, *Joculator*, or some other word that implies gesture. Hence it might be inferred, that the Minstrels set off their songs with all the arts of gesticulation, &c.; or, according to the ingenious hypothesis of Dr. Brown, united the powers of melody, poem, and dance. [See his *History of the Rise of Poetry, &c.*]

But indeed all the old writers describe them as exercising various arts of this kind. Joinville, in his *Life of St. Lewis*, speaks of some Armenian Minstrels, who were very dexterous tumblers and posture-masters. "Avec le Prince vinrent trois Menestriers de la Grande Hyermenie (Armenia) . . . . . et avoient trois cors. — Quand ils encommenceoient a corner, vous dissiez que ce sont les voix de cygnes, . . . . . et fesoient les plus douces melodies.—Ils fesoient trois merveilleus *saus*, car on leur metoit une touaille desous les piez, et tournoient tout debout . . . . Les deux tournoient les testes arieres," &c. [See the extract at large, in the Hon. D. Barrington's *Observations on the Anc. Statutes*, 4to. 2d edit. p. 273, omitted in the last impression.]

This may also account for that remarkable clause in the press-warrant of Henry VI., "De Ministrallis propter solatium Regis providendis," by which it is required, that the boys, to be provided "in arte Ministrallatûs instructos," should also be "membris naturalibus elegantes." See above page xlii. xliii. (Observ. on the Anc. Stat. 4th edit. p. 337.)

Although by Minstrel was properly understood, in English, one who sung to the harp, or some other instrument of music, verses composed by himself or others; yet the term was also applied by our old writers to such as professed either music or singing separately, and perhaps to such as practised any of the sportive arts connected with these[5]. Music, however,

[5] Vide infra, note (AA).

being the leading idea, was at length peculiarly called Minstrelsy, and the name of Minstrel at last confined to the musician only.

In the French language all these arts were included under the general name of *Menestraudie*, *Menestraudise*, *Jonglerie*, &c. [Med. Lat. *Menestellorum Ars*, *Ars Joculatoria*, &c.] — "On peut comprendre sous le nom de *Jonglerie* tout ce qui appartient aux anciens chansonniers Provencaux, Normands, Picards, &c. Le corps de la Jonglerie etoit formé des *Trouvères*, ou *Troubadours*, qui composoient les chansons, et parmi lesquels il y avoit des *Improvisateurs*, comme on en trouve en *Italie;* des *Chanteurs*, ou *Chanteres*, qui executoient ou chantoient ces compositions; des *Conteurs* qui faisoient en vers ou en prose les contes, les recits, les histoires; des *Jongleurs* ou *Menestrels* qui accompagnoient de leurs instruments. — L'art de ces Chantres ou Chansonniers, etoit nommé la Science Gaie, *Gay Saber*." (Pref. *Anthologie Franç.* 1765, 8vo, p. 17.) — See also the curious Fauchet, (*De l'Orig. de la Lang. Fr.* p. 72, *&c.*) "Bien tost apres la division de ce grand empire François en tant de petits royaumes, duchez, et comtez, au lieu des Poetes commencerent a se faire cognoistre les *Trouverres*, et *Chanterres*, *Contëours*, et *Juglëours:* qui sont Trouveurs, Chantres, Conteurs, *Jongleurs*, ou Jugleurs, c'est à dire, *Menestriers* chantans avec la viole."

We see, then, that *Jongleur*, *Jugleur*, (Lat. *Joculator*, *Juglator*,) was a peculiar name appropriated to the Minstrels. "Les *Jongleurs* ne faisoient que chanter les poesies sur leurs instrumens. On les appelloit aussi *Menestrels:*" says Fontenelle, in his *Hist. du Théat. Franç.*, prefixed to his Life of Corneille.

(c) *Successors of the ancient Bards.*] That the Minstrels in many respects bore a strong resemblance both to the British Bards and to the Danish Scalds, appears from this, that the old monkish writers express them all, without distinction, by the same names in Latin. Thus Geoffrey of Monmouth, himself a Welshman, speaking of an old pagan British king, who excelled in singing and music so far as to be esteemed by his countrymen the patron deity of the Bards, uses the phrase *Deus Joculatorum;* which is the peculiar name given to the English and French Minstrels[6]. In like manner, William Malmesbury, speaking of a Danish king's assuming the profession of a Scald, expresses it by *Professus Mimum;* which was another name given to the Minstrels in Middle Latinity[7]. Indeed Du Cange, in his Glossary, quotes a writer, who positively asserts that the Minstrels of the middle ages were the same with the ancient Bards. I shall give a large extract from this learned glossographer, as he relates many curious particulars concerning the profession and arts of the Minstrels; whom, after the monks, he stigmatizes by the name of *Scurræ;* though he acknowledges their songs often tended to inspire virtue.

"Ministelli, dicti præsertim *Scurræ*, Mimi, Joculatores." .... "Ejusmodi *Scurrarum* munus erat principes non suis duntaxat ludicris oblectare, sed et eorum aures variis avorum, adeoque ipsorum principum laudibus, non sine *assentatione*, cum cantilenis et musicis instrumentis demulcere ....

"Interdum etiam virorum insignium et heroum gesta, aut explicata et jocunda narratione commemorabant, aut suavi vocis inflexione, fidibusque decantabant, quo sic dominorum, cæterorumque qui his intererant ludicris, nobilium animos ad *virtutem* capessendam, et summorum virorum imitationem accenderent: quod fuit olim apud Gallos Bardorum ministerium, ut auctor est Tacitus. Neque enim alios à *Ministellis*, veterum Gallorum *Bardos* fuisse pluribus probat Henricus Valesius ad 15 Ammiani. ...... Chronicon Bertrandi Guesclini.

"Qui veut avoir renom des bons et des vaillans
Il doit aler souvent a la pluie et au champs
Et estre en la bataille, ainsy que fu Rollans,
Les Quatre Fils Haimon, et Charlon li plus grans,
Li dus Lions de Bourges, et Guions de Connans,
Perceval li Galois, Lancelot, et Tristans,
Alexandres, Artus, Godfroi li Sachans,
De quoy cils MENESTRIERS font les nobles ROMANS."

[6] Vide notes (B) (K) (Q). [7] Vide note (N).

"Nicolaus de Braia describens solenne convivium, quo post inaugurationem suam proceres excepit Lud. VIII. rex Francorum, ait inter ipsius convivii apparatum, in medium prodiisse Mimum, qui regis laudes ad cytharam decantavit."—

Our author then gives the lines at length, which begin thus,

"Dumque fovent genium geniali munere Bacchi,
Nectare commixto curas removente Lyæo
Principis a facie, citharae celeberrimus arte
Assurgit Mimus, ars musica quem decoravit.
Hic ergo chorda resonante subintulit ista:
Inclyte rex regum, probitatis stemmate vernans,
Quem vigor et virtus extollit in æthera famæ," &c.

The rest may be seen in Du Cange, who thus proceeds, "Mitto reliqua similia, ex quibus omnino patet ejusmodi Mimorum et Ministellorum cantilenas ad virtutem principes excitasse. . . . Id præsertim in pugnæ præcinctu, dominis suis occinebant, ut martium ardorem in eorum animis concitarent: cujusmodi cantum *Cantilenam Rollandi* appellat Will. Malmesb. lib. 3.—Aimoinus, lib. 4. de Mirac. S. Bened. c. 37. 'Tanta vero illis securitas . . . ut *Scurram* se precedere facerent, qui musico instrumento res fortiter gestas et priorum bella præcineret, quatenus his acrius incitarentur.'" &c. As the writer was a monk, we shall not wonder at his calling the minstrel, *scurram*.

This word *scurra*, or some one similar, is represented in the Glossaries as the proper meaning of *Leccator*, (Fr. *Leccour*,) the ancient term by which the Minstrel appears to be expressed in the grant to Dutton, quoted above in page xxxvi. On this head I shall produce a very curious passage, which is twice quoted in Du Cange's Glossary (sc. ad verb. Menestellus et ad verb. Lecator).—"Philippus Mouskes in Philip. Aug. fingit Carolum M. Provincie comitatum Scurris et Mimis suis olim donasse, indeque postea tantum in hac regione poetarum munerum excrevisse.

"Quar quant li buens Rois Karlemaigne
Ot toute mise a son demaine

Provence, qui mult iert plentive
De vins, de bois, d'aigue, de rive,
As LECCOURS as MENESTREUS
Qui sont auques luxurieus
Le donna toute et departi."

(D) *The Poet and the Minstrel early with us became two persons.*] The word Scald comprehended both characters among the Danes, nor do I know that they had any peculiar name for either of them separate. But it was not so with the Anglo-Saxons. They called a poet Sceop, and Leoðƿyꞃhꞇa: the last of these comes from Leoð, a song; and the former answers to our old word *Maker* (Gr. *Ποιητης*), being derived from Scıppan or Sceopan, *formare, facere, fingere, creare* (Ang. to shape). As for the Minstrel, they distinguished him by the peculiar appellation of Gliȝman, and perhaps by the more simple title of Heaꞃpeꞃe, Harper. [See below, Notes (H), (I)]. This last title, at least, is often given to a Minstrel by our most ancient English rhymists. See in this work, vol. i. p. 58, &c. vol. iii. book i. no. 7, &c.

(E) *Minstrels . . . at the houses of the great, &c.*] Du Cange affirms, that in the middle ages the courts of princes swarmed so much with this kind of men, and such large sums were expended in maintaining and rewarding them, that they often drained the royal treasuries: especially, he adds, of such as were delighted with their flatteries ("præsertim qui ejusmodi Ministellorum assentationibus delectabantur"). He then confirms his assertion by several passages out of monastic writers, who sharply inveigh against this extravagance. Of these I shall here select only one or two, which show what kind of rewards were bestowed on these old Songsters.

"Rigordus de Gestis Philippi Aug. ann. 1185. Cum in curiis regum seu aliorum principum, frequens turba Histrionum convenire soleat, ut ab eis *aurum*, *argentum*, *equos*, seu *vestes*[8], quos persæpe mutare consueverunt principes, ab eis

[8] The Minstrels in France were received with great magnificence in the 14th century. Froissart, describing a Christmas entertainment given by the

extorqueant, verba joculatoria variis adulationibus plena proferre nituntur. Et ut magis placeant, quicquid de ipsis principibus probabiliter fingi potest, videlicet omnes delitias et lepores, et visu dignas urbanitates et cæteras ineptias, trutinantibus buccis in medium eructare non erubescunt. Vidimus quondam quosdam principes, qui *vestes* diu excogitatas, et variis florum picturationibus artificiosè elaboratas, pro quibus forsan 20 vel 30 marcas argenti consumpserant, vix revolutis septem diebus, *Histrionibus*, ministris diaboli, ad primam vocem dedisse," &c.

The curious reader may find a similar, though at the same time a more candid account, in that most excellent writer, Presid. Fauchet (*Recueil de la Lang. Fr.* p. 73), who says that, like the ancient Greek *Αοιδοι*, "Nos Trouverres, ainsi que ceux la, prenans leur subject sur les faits de vaillans (qu'ils appelloyent Geste, venant de *Gesta* Latin) alloyent . . . par les cours rejouir les Princes . . . Remportans des grandes recompences des seigneurs, qui bien souvent leur donnoyent jusques aux *robes* qu'ils avoyent vestues: et lesquelles ces Jugleours ne failloyent de porter aux autres cours, à fin d'inviter les seigneurs a pareille liberalité. Ce qui a duré si longuement, qu'il me *souvient avoir veu* Martin Baraton (ja viel Menestrier d'Orleans), lequel aux festes et nopces batoit un tabourin d'argent, semé des plaques aussi d'argent, gravees des armoiries de ceux a qui il avoit appris a *danser*."—Here we see that a minstrel sometimes performed the function of a dancing-master.

Fontenelle even gives us to understand, that these men were often rewarded with favours of a still higher kind. "Les princesses et les plus grandes dames y joignoient souvent leurs faveurs. Elles etoient fort foibles contre les beaux esprits."—*Hist. du Théat.* We are not to wonder, then, that

Comte de Foix, tells us, that "there were many Mynstrels, as well of hys own as of straungers, and eache of them dyd their devoyre in their faculties. The same day the Erle of Foix gave to Haraulds and Minstrelles the som of *fyve hundred frankes:* and gave to the Duke of Tourayns Mynstreles Gownes of Clothe of Gold furred with Ermyne valued at two hundred Frankes."—B. iii. c. 31, Eng. Trans. Lond. 1525. (Mr. C.)

this profession should be followed by men of the first quality, particularly the younger sons and brothers of great houses. "Tel qui par les partages de sa famille n'avoit que la moitié ou le quart d'une vieux chateaux bien seigneurial, alloit quelque temps courir le monde en rimant, et revenoit acquerir le reste de Chateau." — Fontenelle, *Hist. du Théat.* We see, then, that there was no improbable fiction in those ancient songs and romances, which are founded on the story of minstrels being beloved by kings' daughters, &c., and discovering themselves to be the sons of some sovereign prince, &c.

(F) The honours and rewards lavished upon the Minstrels were not confined to the Continent. Our own countryman Johannes Sarisburiensis (in the time of Henry II.) declaims no less than the monks abroad, against the extravagant favour shown to these men. "Non enim more nugatorum ejus seculi in *Histriones* et *Mimos*, et hujusmodi monstra hominum, ob famæ redemptionem et dilatationem nominis effunditis opes vestras," &c. [Epist. 247[9].]

The monks seem to grudge every act of munificence that was not applied to the benefit of themselves and their convents. They therefore bestow great applauses upon the Emperor Henry, who, at his marriage with Agnes of Poictou, in 1044, disappointed the poor Minstrels, and sent them away empty. "Infinitam Histrionum et Joculatorum multitudinem sine cibo et muneribus vacuam et mœrentem abire permisit." (Chronic. Virtziburg.) For which I doubt not but he was sufficiently stigmatized in the songs and ballads of those times. Vid. Du Cange, Gloss. tom. iv. p. 771, &c.

(G) *The annals of the Anglo-Saxons are scanty and defective.*] Of the few histories now remaining that were written before the Norman conquest, almost all are such short and naked sketches and abridgments, giving only a concise and general relation of the more remarkable events, that scarce any of

[9] Et vide Policraticon, cap. viii. &c.

the minute circumstantial particulars are to be found in them; nor do they hardly ever descend to a description of the customs, manners, or domestic economy of their countrymen. The *Saxon Chronicle*, for instance, which is the best of them, and upon some accounts extremely valuable, is almost such an epitome as Lucius Florus and Eutropius have left us of the Roman history. As for Ethelward, his book is judged to be an imperfect translation of the Saxon Chronicle[10]; and the *Pseudo-Asser*, or Chronicle of St. Neot, is a poor defective performance. How absurd would it be, then, to argue against the existence of customs or facts, from the silence of such scanty records as these! Whoever would carry his researches deep into that period of history, might safely plead the excuse of a learned writer, who had particularly studied the Ante-Norman historians. "Conjecturis (licet nusquam verisimili fundamento) aliquoties indulgemus . . . utpote ab Historicis jejune nimis et indiligenter res nostras tractantibus coacti . . . Nostri . . . nudâ factorum commemoratione plerumque contenti, reliqua omnia, sive ob ipsarum rerum, sive meliorum literarum, sive Historicorum officii ignorantiam, fere intacta prætereunt." Vide plura in Præfat. ad Ælfr. Vitam à Spelman. Ox. 1678. fol.

(H) *Minstrels and Harpers.*] That the Harp (*Cithara*) was the common musical instrument of the Anglo-Saxons, might be inferred from the very word itself, which is not derived from the British, or any other Celtic language, but of genuine Gothic original, and current among every branch of that people, viz. Ang. Sax. Heappe, Heappa. Iceland, Harpa, Haurpa. Dan. and Belg. Harpe. Germ. Harpffe, Harpffa. Gal. *Harpe*. Span. *Harpa*. Ital. *Arpa*. [Vid. Jun. Etym.—Menage Etym. &c.] As also from this, that the word Heappe is constantly used in the Anglo-Saxon versions, to express the Latin words *Cithara*, *Lyra*, and even *Cymbalum*: the word *Psalmus* itself being sometimes translated Heapp ꞅanᵹ, *Harp Song*. [Gloss. Jun. R. apud Lye Anglo-Sax. Lexic.]

10 Vide Nicolson's Eng. Hist. Lib. &c.

But the fact itself is positively proved by the express testimony of Bede, who tells us that it was usual at festival meetings for this instrument to be handed round, and each of the company to sing to it in his turn. See his *Hist. Eccles. Anglor.* lib. iv. c. 24, where, speaking of their sacred poet Cædmon, who lived in the times of the Heptarchy (ob. circ. 680), he says:—

"Nihil unquam frivoli et supervacui poematis facere potuit; sed ea tantummodo, quæ ad religionem pertinent, religiosam ejus linguam decebant. Siquidem in habitu sæculari usque ad tempora provectioris ætatis constitutus nil Carminum aliquando didicerat. Unde nonnunquam in convivio, cùm esset lætitiæ causa decretum ut omnes per ordinem *cantare* deberent, ille ubi appropinquare sibi *citharam* cernebat, surgebat à mediâ cænâ, et egressus, ad suam domum repedabat."

I shall now subjoin King Alfred's own Anglo-Saxon translation of this passage, with a literal interlineary English version.

"He . . næꝼꞃe nohꞇ leaſunᵹa. ne iꝺeleſ leoðeſ ƿýꞃcean ne
He . . never no leasings, nor idle songs compose ne
mihꞇe. ac eꝼne ða an ða ðe ꞇo æꝼeſꞇneſſe
might; but lo! only those things which to religion [piety]
belumpon. ⁊ hiſ ða æꝼeſꞇan ꞇunᵹan ᵹeꝺaꝼenoꝺe ſinᵹan:
belong, and his then pious tongue became to sing:
Wæſ he ſe man in ƿeoꞃolꞇ-haꝺe ᵹeſeꞇeꝺ oð ða
He was the [a] man in worldly [secular] state set to the
ꞇiꝺe ðe he ƿæſ oꝼ ᵹelýꝼeꝺꞃe ýlꝺe. ⁊ he næꝼꞃe ænig
time in which he was of an advanced age; and he never any
leoþ ᵹeleoꞃnoꝺe. ⁊ he ꝼoþꞃon oꝼꞇ in ᵹebeoꞃſcipe
song learned. And he therefore OFT in an entertainment,
ðonne ðæꞃ ƿæſ bliſſe inꞇinᵹa ᵹeꝺemeꝺ
when there was for merriment-sake adjudged [or decreed]
ꝥ hi ealle ſceolꝺan ðuꞃh enꝺebýꞃꝺneſſe be
that they ALL should through their turns by [to the]
heaꞃpan ſinᵹan. ðonne he ᵹeſeah ða heaꞃpan him nealæcean.
HARP SING; when he saw the HARP him approach,

ꝺonne aꞃaꞅ he ꝼoꞃ ꞅceome ꞅꞃam ꝺam ꞅẏmle. ꝧ ham eoꝺe
then arose he FOR SHAME from the supper, and home yode
ꞇo hıꞅ huꞅe."
[went] to his house.

Bed. *Hist. Eccl.* à Smith, Cantab. 1722, fol. p. 597.

In this version of Alfred's it is observable, (1) that he has expressed the Latin word *cantare*, by the Anglo-Saxon words "be heaꞃpan ꞅınᵹan," *sing to the harp*, as if they were synonymous, or as if his countrymen had no idea of singing unaccompanied with the harp: (2) that when Bede simply says, *surgebat a mediâ cœnâ*, he assigns a motive, "aꞃaꞅ ꝼoꞃ ꞅceome," *arose for shame:* that is, either from an austerity of manners, or from his being deficient in an accomplishment which so generally prevailed among his countrymen.

(I) *The word* Glee, *which peculiarly denoted their art*, *&c.*] This word *Glee* is derived from the Anglo-Saxon Ꮆlıᵹᵹ [Gligg], *Musica*, Music, Minstrelsy (Somn.). This is the common radix, whence arises such a variety of terms and phrases relating to the minstrel art, as affords the strongest internal proof, that this profession was extremely common and popular here before the Norman conquest. Thus we have

I.

(1) Ꮆlıƿ [Gliw], *Mimus*, a Minstrel.

Ꮆlıᵹman, ᵹlıᵹmon, ᵹlıman [Glee-man[1]], *Histrio*, *Mimus*, *Pantomimus;* all common names in Middle Latinity for a

1 *Gleeman* continued to be the name given to a Minstrel both in England and Scotland almost as long as this order of men continued.

In De Brunne's metrical version of Bishop Grosthead's *Manuel de Peche*, A. D. 1303 (see Warton, i. 61), we have this,

"—— Gode men, ye shall lere
When ye any *Gleman* here."

Fabyan (in his Chronicle, 1533, f. 32) translating the passage from Geoffrey of Monmouth, quoted below in p. lxxi. note (K), renders Deus *Joculatorum*, by God of *Gleemen*. (Warton's *Hist. Eng. Poet.* Diss. 1.) Fabyan died in 1592.

Dunbar, who lived in the same century, describing, in one of his poems, entitled "The Daunce," what passed in the infernal regions "amangis the Feyndis," says,

Minstrel: and Somner accordingly renders the original by a Minstrel, a Player on a Timbrel or Taber. He adds, a Fidler, but although the *Fythel* or *Fiddle* was an ancient instrument, by which the *Jogelar* or Minstrel sometimes accompanied his song (see Warton, i. 17), it is probable that Somner annexes here only a modern sense to the word, not having at all investigated the subject.

Glumen, gliȝmen [Glee-men]. *Histriones*, Minstrels. Hence

Gliȝmanna-yppe. *Orchestra* vel *Pulpitus.* The place where the Minstrels exhibited their performances.

(2) But their most proper and expressive name was

Gliphleoþpienð. *Musicus*, a Minstrel; and

Gliphleoþpienðlica. *Musicus*, Musical.

These two words include the full idea of the minstrel character, expressing at once their music and singing, being compounded of Glip, *Musicus*, *Mimus*, a Musician, Minstrel, and Leoð, *Carmen*, a Song.

(3) From the above word Gliȝȝ, the profession itself was called

Gliȝcpæft [Glig- or Glee-craft]. *Musica*, *Histrionia*, *Mimica*, *Gesticulatio:* which Somner rightly gives in English, Minstrelsy, Mimical Gesticulation, Mummery. He also adds, Stage-playing; but here again I think he substitutes an idea too modern, induced by the word *Histrionia*, which in Middle Latinity only signifies the minstrel art.

However, it should seem that both mimical gesticulation and a kind of rude exhibition of characters were sometimes attempted by the old minstrels: but

(4) As musical performance was the leading idea, so

Glioɲian, *Cantus musicos edere;* and

Gliȝbeam, ȝlipbeam [Glig- or Glee-beam]. *Tympanum:* a Timbrel or Taber. (So Somn.) Hence

---

"Na Menstralls playit to thame, but dowt
For *Gle-men* thaire wer haldin out,
Be day and eke by nycht."

See Poems from Bannatyne's MS. Edinb. 1770, 12mo. p. 30. Maitland's MS. at Cambridge reads here, *Gleive men.*

Ȝlẏpian. *Tympanum pulsare;* and

Ȝlip-meðen: Ȝliẏpiende-maðen [Glee-maiden]. *Tympanistria:* which Somner renders a She-Minstrel; for it should seem that they had females of this profession: one name for which was also Ȝlẏpbẏðenestra.

(5) Of congenial derivation to the foregoing, is

Ȝlẏpc [Glywc]. *Tibia*, a Pipe or Flute.

Both this and the common radix Ȝliȝȝ, are with great appearance of truth derived by Junius from the Icelandic Gliggur, *Flatus:* as supposing the first attempts at music among our Gothic ancestors, were from wind-instruments. Vide Jun. Etym. Ang. V. Glee.

II.

But the Minstrels, as is hinted above, did not confine themselves to the mere exercise of their primary arts of music and song, but occasionally used many other modes of diverting. Hence, from the above root was derived, in a secondary sense,

(1) Ȝleo, and pinsum ȝlip. *Facetiæ.*

Ȝleopian, *jocari;* to jest, or be merry: (Somn.) and

Ȝleopienð, *jocans;* jesting, speaking merrily: (Somn.)

Ȝliȝman also signified *Jocista*, a Jester.

Ȝliȝ-ȝamen [Glee-games], *joci.* Which Somner renders Merriments, or merry Jests, or Tricks, or Sports; Gamboles.

(2) Hence, again, by a common metonymy of the cause for the effect,

Ȝlie, *gaudium, alacritas, lætitia, facetiæ;* Joy, Mirth, Gladness, Cheerfulness, Glee [Somner.] Which last application of the word still continues, though rather in a low debasing sense.

III.

But however agreeable and delightful the various arts of the Minstrels might be to the Anglo-Saxon laity, there is reason to believe that, before the Norman conquest at least, they were not much favoured by the clergy, particularly by those of monastic profession. For, not to mention that the sportive talents of these men would be considered by those austere ecclesiastics as tending to levity and licentiousness, the Pagan origin of their art would excite in the monks an insuperable prejudice against it. The Anglo-Saxon Harpers and Gleemen were the immediate successors and imitators of the Scandinavian Scalds, who were the great promoters of Pagan superstition, and fomented that spirit of cruelty and outrage in their countrymen, the Danes, which fell with such peculiar severity on the religious and their convents. Hence arose a third application of words derived from Gliʒʒ, Minstrelsy, in a very unfavourable sense, and this chiefly prevails in books of religion and ecclesiastic discipline. Thus

(1) Gliʒ, is Ludibrium, *laughing to scorn*[2]. So in S. Basil. Regul. 11. Hi hæfðon him to ʒliʒe halƿenðe mineʒunʒe. *Ludibrio habebant salutarem ejus admonitionem* (10). This sense of the word was perhaps not ill-founded; for as the sport of rude uncultivated minds often arises from ridicule, it is not improbable but the old Minstrels often indulged a vein of this sort, and that of no very delicate kind. So again,

Gliʒ-man was also used to signify *Scurra*, a saucy Jester. (Somn.)

Gliʒ-ʒeorn. *Dicax, Scurriles jocos supra quàm par est amans.* Officium Episcopale, 3.

Gliƿian. *Scurrilibus oblectamentis indulgere: Scurram agere.* Canon. Edgar, 58.

(2) Again, as the various attempts to please, practised by an order of men who owed their support to the public favour, might be considered by those grave censors as mean and debasing: Hence came from the same root,

Gliƿer. *Parasitus, Assentator;* a Fawner, a Cogger, a Parasite, a Flatterer[3]. (Somn.)

[2] To *gleek*, is used in Shakspeare for 'to make sport, to jest,' &c.

[3] The preceding list of Anglo-Saxon words, so full and copious beyond any thing that ever yet appeared in print on this subject, was extracted from Mr. Lye's curious Anglo-Saxon Lexicon, in MS., but the arrangement here is the Editor's own. It had, however, received the sanction of Mr. Lye's approbation, and would doubtless have been received into his printed copy, had he lived to publish it himself.

## IV.

To return to the Anglo-Saxon word Ligg; notwithstanding the various secondary senses in which this word (as we have seen above) was so early applied: yet

The derivative *Glee* (though now chiefly used to express merriment and joy) long retained its first simple meaning, and is even applied by Chaucer to signify *music* and *minstrelsy*. (Vide Jun. Etym.) e. g.

"For though that the best harper upon live
Would on the beste sounid jolly harpe
That evir was, with all his fingers five
Touch aie o string, or aie o warble harpe,
Were his nailes poincted nevir so sharpe
It shoulde makin every wight to dull
To heare is GLEE, and of his strokes ful.
*Troyl.* lib. ii. 1030.

Junius interprets Glees by *Musica Instrumenta*, in the following passages of Chaucer's Third Boke of FAME.

".. Stoden .. the castell all aboutin
Of all maner of *Mynstrales*
And *Jestours* that tellen tales
Both of wepyng and of game,
And of all that longeth unto fame;
There herde I play on a harpe
That sowned both well and sharpe
Hym Orpheus full craftily;
And on this syde fast by
Sate the harper Orion;
And Eacides Chirion;
And other harpers many one,
And the Briton Glaskyrion."

After mentioning these, the great masters of the art, he proceeds;

"And small Harpers with her *Glees*
Sat under them in divers sees."
* * * * *

Again, a little below, the poet having enumerated the performers on all the different sorts of instruments, adds,

---

It should also be observed, for the sake of future researches, that without the assistance of the old English interpretations given by Somner, in his Anglo-Saxon Dictionary, the Editor of this book never could have discovered that *Glee* signified Minstrelsy, or *Gligman* a Minstrel.

"There sawe I syt in other sees
Playing upon other sundry *Glees*,
Which that I cannot neven[4]
More than starres ben in heven," &c.

Upon the above lines I shall only make a few observations:

(1) That by *Jestours*, I suppose we are to understand *Gestours;* scil. the relaters of Gests (Lat. *Gesta*), or stories of adventures both comic and tragical, whether true or feigned; I am inclined to add, whether in prose or verse. [Compare the record below, in marginal note subjoined to (v2).] Of the stories in prose, I conceive we have specimens in that singular book, the *Gesta Romanorum*, and this will account for its seemingly improper title. These were evidently what the French called *Conteours*, or Story Tellers, and to them we are probably indebted for the first prose Romances of chivalry; which may be considered as specimens of their manner.

(2) That the "Briton Glaskyrion," whoever he was, is apparently the same person with our famous harper Glasgerion, of whom the reader will find a tragical ballad in vol. iii. no. vii. b. i. In that song may be seen an instance of what was advanced above in note (E), of the dignity of the minstrel profession, or at least of the artifice with which the minstrels endeavoured to set off its importance.

Thus "a king's son is represented as appearing in the character of a harper or minstrel in the court of another king. He wears a collar (or gold chain) as a person of illustrious rank; rides on horseback, and is admitted to the embraces of a king's daughter."

The Minstrels lost no opportunity of doing honour to their art.

(3) As for the word *Glees*, it is to this day used in a musical sense, and applied to a peculiar piece of composition. Who has not seen the advertisements proposing a reward to him who should produce the best Catch, Canon, or *Glee?*

[4] Neven, *i. e.* name.

(K) *Comes from the pen of Geoffrey of Monmouth.*] Geoffrey's own words are, "Cum ergo alterius modi aditum [Boldulphus] non haberet, rasit capillos suos et barbam[5], cultumque *Joculatoris* cum Cythara fecit. Deinde intra castra deambulans, modulis quos in Lyra componebat, sese *Cytharistam* exhibebat." Galf. Monum. Hist. 4to. 1508, lib. vii. c. 1. That *Joculator* signifies precisely a Minstrel, appears not only from this passage, where it is used as a word of like import to *Citharista*, or Harper (which was the old English word for Minstrel), but also from another passage of the same author, where it is applied as equivalent to *Cantor*. See lib. i. cap. 22, where, speaking of an ancient (perhaps fabulous) British king, he says, "Hic omnes Cantores quos præcedens ætas habuerat et in modulis et in omnibus musicis instrumentis excedebat; ita ut Deus Joculatorum videretur." Whatever credit is due to Geoffrey as a relater of *facts*, he is certainly as good authority as any for the signification of *words*.

(L) *Two remarkable facts.*] Both of these facts are recorded by William of Malmesbury; and the first of them, relating to Alfred, by Ingulphus also. Now Ingulphus (afterwards Abbot of Croyland) was near forty years of age at the time of the Conquest[6], and, consequently, was as

5 Geoffrey of Monmouth is probably here describing the appearance of the Joculatores or Minstrels, as it was in his own time. For they apparently derived this part of their dress, &c. from the *Mimi* of the ancient Romans, who had their heads and beards shaven (see above, p. liv. note 3): as they likewise did the mimickry, and other arts of diverting, which they superadded to the composing and singing to the harp heroic songs, &c. which they inherited from their own progenitors the Bards and Scalds of the ancient Celtic and Gothic nations. The Longobardi had, like other Northern people, brought these with them into Italy. For in the year 774, when Charlemagne entered Italy and found his passage impeded, he was met by a minstrel of Lombardy, whose song promised him success and victory. "Contigit Joculatorem ex Longobardorum gente ad Carolum venire, et *Cantiunculam a se compositam,* rotando in conspectu suorum cantare." Tom. ii. p. 2, Chron. Monast. Noval. lib. iii. cap. x. p. 717. (T. Warton's Hist. vol. ii. Emend. of vol. i. p. 113.)

6 Natus 1030, scripsit 1091, obiit 1109.—Tanner.

proper a judge of the Saxon manners, as if he had actually written his history before that event; he is therefore to be considered as an Ante-Norman writer; so that, whether the fact concerning Alfred be true or not, we are assured from his testimony, that the *Joculator* or Minstrel was a common character among the Anglo-Saxons. The same also may be inferred from the relation of William of Malmesbury, who outlived Ingulphus but thirty-three years[7]. Both these writers had doubtless recourse to innumerable records and authentic memorials of the Anglo-Saxon times which never descended down to us; their testimony therefore is too positive and full to be overturned by the mere silence of the two or three slight Anglo-Saxon epitomes that are now remaining. Vide note (G).

As for Asser Menevensis, who has given a somewhat more particular detail of Alfred's actions, and yet takes no notice of the following story, it will not be difficult to account for his silence, if we consider that he was a rigid monk, and that the Minstrels, however acceptable to the laity, were never much respected by men of the more strict monastic profession, especially before the Norman conquest, when they would be considered as brethren of the Pagan Scalds[8]. Asser therefore might not regard Alfred's skill in Minstrelsy in a very favourable light; and might be induced to drop the circumstance related below, as reflecting, in his opinion, no great honour on his patron.

The learned editor of Alfred's Life in Latin, after having examined the scene of action in person, and weighed all the circumstances of the event, determines, from the whole collective evidence, that Alfred could never have gained the victory he did, if he had not with his own eyes previously seen the disposition of the enemy by such a stratagem as is

7 Obiit anno 1142.—Tanner.

8 (See above, p. lxviii.) Both Ingulph. and Will. of Malmesb. had been very conversant among the Normans, who appear not to have had such prejudices against the Minstrels as the Anglo-Saxons had.

here described. Vide Annot. in Ælfr. Mag. Vitam, p. 33. Oxon. 1678, fol.

(M) *Alfred...assumed the dress and character of a Minstrel.*] "Fingens se Joculatorem, assumpta cithara," &c. Ingulphi Hist. p. 869.—"Sub specie *mimi* . . . ut *Joculatoriæ* professor artis." Gul. Malmesb. l. ii. c. iv. p. 43. That both *Joculator* and *Mimus* signify literally a *Minstrel*, see proved in notes (B) (K) (N) (Q) &c. See also note (GG).

Malmesbury adds, "Unius tantum fidelissimi fruebatur conscientiâ." As this confidant does not appear to have assumed the disguise of a Minstrel himself, I conclude that he only appeared as the Minstrel's attendant. Now that the Minstrel had sometimes his servant or attendant to carry his harp, and even to sing to his music, we have many instances in the old metrical Romances, and even some in this present collection. See vol. i. Song vi.; vol. iii. Song vii., &c. Among the French and Provençal bards, the *Trouverre*, or Inventor, was generally attended with his singer, who sometimes also played on the harp, or other musical instrument. "Quelque fois durant le repas d'un prince on voyoit arriver un Trouverre inconnu avec ses Menestrels ou Jongleours, et il leur faisoit chanter sur leurs harpes ou vielles les vers qu'il avoit composés. Ceux qui faisoient les SONS aussi bien que les MOTS etoient les plus estimés."—*Fontenelle*, *Hist. du Theat.*

That Alfred excelled in music is positively asserted by Bale, who doubtless had it from some ancient MS., many of which subsisted in his time that are now lost: as also by Sir J. Spelman, who, we may conclude, had good authority for this anecdote, as he is known to have compiled his life of Alfred from authentic materials collected by his learned father: this writer informs us that Alfred "provided himself of musitians, not common, or such as knew but the practick part, but men skilful in the art itself, whose skill and service he yet further improved with his own instruction," page 199. This proves Alfred at least to have understood the theory of music; and how could this have been acquired without practising on some instrument? which we have seen above, note (H), was so extremely common with the Anglo-Saxons, even in much ruder times, that Alfred himself plainly tells us, it was *shameful* to be ignorant of it. And this commonness might be one reason why Asser did not think it of consequence enough to be particularly mentioned in his short life of that great monarch. This rigid monk may also have esteemed it a slight and frivolous accomplishment, savouring only of worldly vanity. He has, however, particularly recorded Alfred's fondness for the oral Anglo-Saxon poems and songs ["Saxonica poemata die nocteque . . . audiens . . . memoriter retinebat," p. 16. "Carmina Saxonica memoriter discere," &c. p. 43, et ib.]. Now the poems learnt by rote, among all ancient unpolished nations, are ever songs chanted by the reciter, and accompanied with instrumental melody[9].

(N) *With his harp in his hand, and dressed like a Minstrel.*] "Assumptâ manu citharâ . . . professus Mimum, qui hujusmodi arte stipem quotidianam mercaretur . . . Jussus abire pretium Cantus accepit." Malmesb. l. ii. c. 6. We see here that which was rewarded was (*not* any mimickry or tricks, but) his singing (*Cantus*); this proves, beyond dispute, what was the nature of the entertainment Aulaff afforded them. Perhaps it is needless by this time to prove to the reader that *Mimus*, in Middle Latinity, signifies a Minstrel, and *Mimia*, Minstrelsy, or the Minstrel-art. Should he doubt it, let him cast his eye over the two following extracts from Du Cange.

"MIMUS: Musicus, qui instrumentis musicis canit. Leges Palatinæ Jacobi II. Reg. Majoric. In domibus principum, ut tradit antiquitas, Mimi seu Joculatores licitè possunt esse. Nam illorum officium tribuit lætitiam . . . Quapropter volumus et ordinamus, quod in nostra curia Mimi debeant esse quinque, quorum duo sint tubicinatores, et tertius sit tabelerius

9 Thus Leoð, the Saxon word for a Poem, is properly a Song, and its derivative *Lied* signifies a Ballad to this day in the German tongue: and *Cantare*, we have seen above, is by Alfred himself rendered Be hearpan singan.

[*i. e.* a player on the tabor[10]. Lit. remiss. ann. 1374. Ad Mimos cornicitantes, seu buçinantes accesserunt."

"MIMIA, Ludus Mimicus, Instrumentum [potius, Ars Joculatoria]. Ann. 1482 . . . . *mimia* et cantu victum acquiro." Du Cange, Gloss. tom. iv. 1762. Supp. c. 1225.

(o) *To have been a Dane.*] The northern historians produce such instances of the great respect shown to the Danish Scalds in the courts of our Anglo-Saxon kings, on account of their musical and poetic talents (notwithstanding they were of so hateful a nation), that if a similar order of men had not existed here before, we cannot doubt but the profession would have been taken up by such of the natives as had a genius for poetry and music.

"Extant Rhythmi hoc ipso [Islandico] idiomate Angliæ, Hyberniæque Regibus oblati et liberaliter compensati, &c. Itaque hinc colligi potest linguam Danicam in aulis vicinorum regum principumque familiarem fuisse, non secus ac hodie in aulis principum peregrina idiomata in deliciis haberi cernimus. Imprimis Vita Egilli Skallagrimii id invicto argumento adstruit. Quippe qui interrogatus ab Adalsteino, Angliæ rege, quomodo manus Eirici Blodoxii, Northumbriæ

10 The *Tabour* or *Tabourin* was a common instrument with the French Minstrels, as it had also been with the Anglo-Saxon (vide p. lxiv.): thus in an ancient Fr. MS. in the Harl. collection (2253, 75) a Minstrel is described as riding on horseback and bearing his tabour.

"Entour son col porta son *Tabour*,
Depeynt de Or, e riche Açour."

See also a passage in Menage's *Diction. Etym.* [v. MENESTRIERS], where *Tabours* is used as synonymous to *Menestriers*.

Another frequent instrument with them was the *Viele*. This, I am told, is the name of an instrument at this day, which differs from a guitar, in that the player turns round a handle at the top of the instrument, and with his other hand plays on some keys that touch the chords and produce the sound.

See Dr. Burney's account of the Vielle, vol. ii. p. 263, who thinks it the same with the *Rote*, or wheel. See p. 270 in the note.

"Il ot un Jougleor a Sens,
Qui navoit pas sovent robe entiere;
Sovent estoit sans sa *Viele*."

*Fabliaux et Cont.* ii. 184, 185.

regis, postquam in ejus potestatem venerat, evasisset, cujus filium propinquosque occiderat, . . rei statim ordinem metro, nunc satis obscuro, exposuit, nequaquam ita narraturus non intelligenti." (Vide plura apud Torfæii Prefat. ad Orcad. Hist. fol.)

This same Egill was no less distinguished for his valour and skill as a soldier, than for his poetic and singing talents as a Scald; and he was such a favourite with our king Athelstan, that he at one time presented him with "duobus annulis et scriniis duobus bene magnis argento repletis. . . . Quinetiam hoc addidit, ut Egillus quidvis præterea a se petens, obtineret; bona mobilia, sive immobilia, præbendam vel præfecturas. Egillus porro regiam munificentiam gratus excipiens, Carmen Encomiasticon, à se linguâ Norvegicâ (quæ tum his regnis communis) compositum, regi dicat; ac pro eo, duas marcas auri puri (pondus marcæ . . 8 uncias æquabat) honorarii loco retulit." [Arngr. Jon. Rer. Islandic. lib. ii. p. 129.]

See more of Egill, in the "Five Pieces of Runic Poetry," p. 45, whose poem (there translated) is the most ancient piece all in rhyme that is, I conceive, now to be found in any European language, except Latin. See Egill's Islandic original, printed at the end of the English version in the said Five Pieces, &c.

(P) *If the Saxons had not been accustomed to have Minstrels of their own . . . and to show favour and respect to the Danish Scalds,*] if this had not been the case, we may be assured, at least, that the stories given in the text could never have been recorded by writers who lived so near the Anglo-Saxon times as Malmesbury and Ingulphus, who, though they might be deceived as to particular facts, could not be so as to the general manners and customs which prevailed so near their own times among their ancestors.

(Q) *In Domesday Book,* &c.] Extract. ex Libro Domesday: et vide Anstis Ord. Gart. ii. 304.

## Glowecesterscire.

Fol. 162. Col. 1. Berdic Joculator Regis habet iii villas, et ibi v. car. nil redd.

That *Joculator* is properly a Minstrel, might be inferred from the two foregoing passages of Geoffrey of Monmouth, (v. note K,) where the word is used as equivalent to *Citharista* in one place, and to *Cantor* in the other: this union forms the precise idea of the character.

But more positive proofs have already been offered, vide supra, pp. lvi. lvii. lxxiii. & lxxxv. note. See also Du Cange's Gloss. vol. iii. c. 1543. "JOGULATOR pro *Joculator*. Consilium Masil. an. 1381. Nullus Ministreys, Jogulator, audeat pinsare vel sonare instrumentum cujuscumque generis," &c. &c.

As the Minstrel was termed in French *Jongleur* and *Jugleur;* so he was called in Spanish *Jutglar* and *Juglar*. "Tenemos canciones y versos para recitar mui antiguos y memorias ciertas de los *Juglares*, que assistian en los banquetes, como los que pinta Homero." Prolog. a las Comed. de Cervantes, 1749, 4to.

"El anno 1328, en las siestas de la Coronacion del Rey, Don Alonso el IV. de Aragon, . . . .[1] el *Juglar Ramaset* cantò una Villanesca de la Composicion del . . infante [Don Pedro]: y otro Juglar, llamado Novellet, recitò y representò en voz y sin cantar mas de 600 versos, que hizo el Infante en el metro que llamaban Rima Vulgar." Ibid.

"Los Trobadores inventaron la Gaya Ciencia . . . . estos Trobadores eran casi todos de la primera Nobleza. — Es verdad, quem ya entonces se havian entrometido entre las diversiones Cortesanos, los Contadores, los Cantores, los *Juglares*, los Truanes, y los Bufones." — Ibid.

In England, the King's Juglar continued to have an establishment in the royal household down to the reign of Henry VIII. [Vide note (cc).] But in what sense the title was there applied does not appear. In Barklay's *Egloges*,

1 "Romanset Jutglar canta alt veux . . . devant lo senyor Rey." *Chron. d'Aragon*, apud du Cange, iv. 771.

written circ. 1514, Juglers and Pipers are mentioned together. Egl. iv. (Vide T. Warton's Hist. ii. 254.)

(R) *A valiant warrior, named Taillefer, &c.*] See Du Cange, who produces this as an instance, — "Quod Ministellorum munus interdum præstabant milites probatissimi. Le Roman De Vacce, MS.

"Quant il virent Normanz venir
Mout veissiez Engleiz fremir ....
Taillefer qui mout bien chantoit,
Sur un cheval, qui tost alloit,
Devant euls aloit chantant
De Kallemaigne et de Roullant,
Et d'Olivier de Vassaux,
Qui moururent en Rainschevaux."

"Qui quidem Taillefer a Gulielmo obtinuit ut primus in hostes irrueret, inter quos fortiter dimicando occubuit."
Gloss. tom. iv. 769, 770, 771.

"Les anciennes chroniques nous apprennent, qu'en premier rang de l'Armée Normande, un écuyer nommé Taillefer, monté sur un cheval armé, chanta la *Chanson de Roland*, qui fut si long tems dans les bouches des François, sans qu'il soit resté le moindre fragment. Le Taillefer après avoir *entonné* la chanson que les soldats répétoient, se jetta le premier parmi les Anglois, et fut tué." [Voltaire, Add. Hist. Univ. p. 69.]

The reader will see an attempt to restore the Chanson de Roland, with musical notes, in Dr. Burney's Hist. ii. p. 276. — See more concerning the Song of Roland, vol. iii. p. 12, note.

(s) *An eminent French writer, &c.*] "M. l'Evêque de la Ravalière, qui avoit fait beaucoup de recherches sur nos anciennes Chansons, prétend que c'est à la Normandie que nous devons nos premiers Chansonniers, non à la Provence, et qu'il y avoit parmi nous des Chansons en langue vulgaire avant celles de Provençaus, mais postérieurement au Règne de Philippe I., ou à l'an 1100." [v. Révolutions de la Langue

Françoise, à la suite des *Poesies du Roi de Navarre.*] "Ce seroit une antériorité de plus d'une demi siècle à l'époque des premiers troubadours, que leur historien Jean de Nostredame fixe à l'an 1162," &c. Pref. à *l'Anthologie Franç.*, 8vo. 1765.

This subject hath since been taken up and prosecuted at length in the Prefaces, &c. to M. Le Grand's "Fabliaux ou Contes du xii e et du xiii e Siecle, Paris, 1788." 5 tom. 12mo., who seems pretty clearly to have established the priority and superior excellence of the old Rimeurs of the north of France over the Troubadours of Provence, &c.

(s 2) *Their own native Gleemen or Minstrels must be allowed to exist.*] Of this we have proof positive in the old metrical Romance of *Horn-Child* (vol. iii. no. 1, p. 22), which although from the mention of Sarazens, &c. it must have been written at least after the first Crusade in 1096, yet, from its Anglo-Saxon language or idiom, can scarce be dated later than within a century after the Conquest. This, as appears from its very exordium, was intended to be sung to a popular audience, whether it was composed by, or for, a Gleeman or Minstrel. But it carries all the internal marks of being the production of such a composer. It appears of genuine English growth; for, after a careful examination, I cannot discover any allusion to French or Norman customs, manners, composition, or phraseology: no quotation "as the Romance sayth:" not a name or local reference which was likely to occur to a French Rimeur. The proper names are all of Northern extraction. Child *Horn* is the son of *Allof* (*i. e.* Olaf or Olave) king of *Sudenne* (I suppose Sweden), by his queen *Godylde* or *Godylt*. *Athulf* and *Fykenyld* are the names of subjects. *Eylmer* or *Aylmere* is king of *Westnesse* (a part of Ireland), *Rymenyld* is his daughter; as *Erminyld* is of another king *Thurstan;* whose sons are *Athyld* and *Beryld. Athelbrus* is steward of King Aylmer, &c. &c. All these savour only of a Northern origin, and the whole piece is exactly such a performance as one would expect from a

Gleeman or Minstrel of the north of England, who had derived his art and his ideas from his Scaldic predecessors there. So that this probably is the original from which was translated the old French fragment of *Dan Horn*, in the Harleian MS. 527, mentioned by Tyrwhitt (Chaucer iv. p. 68), and by T. Warton (Hist. i. 38), whose extract from Horn-Child is extremely incorrect.

Compare the style of Child-Horn with the Anglo-Saxon specimens in short verses and rhyme, which are assigned to the century succeeding the Conquest, in Hicke's *Thesaurus*, tom. i. cap. 24, pp. 224 and 231.

(T) *The different production of the sedentary composer and the rambling minstrel.*] Among the old metrical romances, a very few are addressed to readers, or mention reading: these appear to have been composed by writers at their desk, and exhibit marks of more elaborate structure and invention. Such is *Eglamour of Artas* (vol. iii. no. 20, p. 28), of which I find in a MS. copy in the Cotton library, A. 2, folio 3, the Second Fitte thus concludes,

> . . . . thus ferr have I red.

Such is *Ipomydon* (vol. iii. no. 23, page 29), of which one of the divisions (Sign. E. ii. b. in pr. copy) ends thus,

> Let hym go, God him spede
> Tyll efte-soone we of him reed [i. e. *read*].

So in *Amys and Amylion*[2] (vol. iii. no. 31, p. 34), in stanza 3rd we have

> In Geste as we rede,

and similar phrases occur in stanzas 34, 125, 140, 196, &c.

These are all studied compositions, in which the story is

[2] It ought to have been observed in its proper place in vol. iii. no. 31, page 30, that *Amys* and *Amylion* were no otherwise "Brothers," than as being fast friends: as was suggested by the learned Dr. Samuel Pegge, who was so obliging as to favour the Essayist formerly with a curious transcript of this poem, accompanied with valuable illustrations, &c.; and that it was his opinion, that both the fragment of the *Lady Bellesent*, mentioned in the same no. 31, and also the mutilated Tale, no. 37 (page 31), were only imperfect copies of the above romance of *Amys and Amylion*, which contains the two lines quoted in no. 37.

invented with more skill and ingenuity, and the style and colouring are of superior cast to such as can with sufficient probability be attributed to the minstrels themselves.

Of this class I conceive the romance of *Horn-Child* (mentioned in the last note (s2) and in vol. iii. no. 1, p. 22), which, from the naked unadorned simplicity of the story, I would attribute to such an origin.

But more evidently is such the *Squire of Lowe Degree* (vol. iii. no. 24, p. 29), in which is no reference to any French original, nothing like the phrase, which so frequently occurs in others, "as the Romance sayth[3]," or the like. And it is just such a rambling performance as one would expect from an itinerant bard. And

Such also is *A lyttel Geste of Robyn Hode*, &c., in 8 Fyttes, of which are extant two editions, 4to., in black-letter, described more fully in page 69 of this volume. — This is not only of undoubted English growth, but, from the constant satire aimed at abbots and their convents, &c., could not possibly have been composed by any monk in his cell.

Other instances might be produced; but especially of the former kind is *Syr Launfal* (vol. iii. no. 11, p. 26), the 121st stanza of which has

In Romances as we rede.

This is one of the best invented stories of that kind, and I

[3] Wherever the word *Romance* occurs in these metrical narratives, it hath been thought to afford decisive proof of a translation from the *Romance* or French language. Accordingly it is so urged by T. Warton (i. 146, note), from two passages in the pr. copy of *Sir Eglamour*, viz. sign. E 1.

In Romaunce as we rede.

Again in fol. ult.

In Romaunce this cronycle is.

But in the Cotton MS. of the original, the first passage is

As I herd a Clerke rede.

And the other thus,

In Rome this Gest cronycled ys.

So that I believe references to "the Romaunce," or the like, were often mere expletive phrases inserted by the oral Reciters; one of whom I conceive had altered or corrupted the old "Syr Eglamour" in the manner that the copy was printed.

believe the only one in which is inserted the name of the author.

(T2) *Royer or Raherus the King's Minstrel.*] He is recorded by Leland under both these names, in his *Collectanea*, scil. vol. i. p. 61.

"Hospitale S. Bartholomæi in West Smithfelde in London. Royer Mimus Regis fundator."

"Hosp. Sti. Barthol. Londini.

"Raherus Mimus Regis H. 1. primus fundator, an. 1102, 3 H. 1, qui fundavit etiam Priorat. Sti. Barthol." Ibid. p. 99.

That *Mimus* is properly a Minstrel in the sense affixed to the word in this essay, one extract from the accounts [Lat. *Computis*] of the priory of Maxtock, near Coventry, in 1441, will sufficiently show. — Scil. "Dat. Sex. Mimis Dni. Clynton cantantibus, citharisantibus, ludentibus," &c. iiiis. (T. Warton, ii. 106, note q.) The same year, the Prior gave to a *doctor prædicans*, for a sermon preached to them, only 6d.

In the Monasticon, tom. ii. pp. 166, 167, is a curious history of the founder of this priory, and the cause of its erection, which seems exactly such a composition as one of those which were manufactured by Dr. Stone, the famous legend-maker, in 1380 (see T. Warton's curious account of him, in vol. ii. p. 190, note), who required no materials to assist him in composing his Narratives, &c.; for in this legend are no particulars given of the founder, but a recital of miraculous visions exciting him to this pious work, of its having been before revealed to King Edward the Confessor, and predicted by three Grecians, &c. Even his minstrel profession is not mentioned, whether from ignorance or design, as the profession was perhaps falling into discredit when this legend was written. There is only a general indistinct account that he frequented royal and noble houses, where he ingratiated himself *suavitate joculari.* (This last is the only word that seems to have any appropriated meaning.) This will account for the indistinct incoherent account given by Stow. "Rahere, a pleasant-witted gentleman, and therefore in his time called the King's Minstrel." *Survey of Lond.* Ed. 1598, p. 308.

(U) *In the early times, every Harper was expected to sing.*] See on this subject King Alfred's Version of Cædmon, above in note (H), page lxiii.

So in Horn-Child, King Allof orders his steward Athelbrus to

—teche him of harpe and of song.

In the Squire of Lowe Degree, the King offers to his daughter,

Ye shall have harpe, sautry[4], and song.

And Chaucer, in his description of the Limitour or Mendicant Friar, speaks of harping as inseparable from singing (i. p. 11, ver. 268),

—in his harping, whan that he hadde songe.

(U2) *As the most accomplished, &c.*] See Hoveden, p. 103, in the following passage, which had erroneously been applied to King Richard himself, till Mr. Tyrwhitt (Chaucer, iv. page 62) showed it to belong to his Chancelor. "Hic ad augmentum et famam sui nominis, emendicata carmina, et rhythmos adulatorios comparabat; et de regno Francorum Cantores et Joculatores muneribus allexerat, ut de illo canerent in plateis: et jam dicebatur ubique, quod non erat talis in orbe." For other particulars relating to this Chancelor, see T. Warton's Hist. vol. ii. Addit. to p. 113 of vol. i.

(U3) *Both the Norman and English languages would be heard at the houses of the great.*] A remarkable proof of this is, that the most diligent inquirers after ancient English rhymes, find the earliest they can discover in the mouths of the Norman nobles. Such as that of Robert Earl of Leicester and

[4] The Harp (Lat. *Cithara*) differed from the Sautry, or Psaltry (Lat. *Psalterium*), in that the former was a stringed instrument, and the latter was mounted with wire: there was also some difference in the construction of the bellies, &c. See "Bartholomæus de proprietatibus rerum," as Englished by Trevisa and Batman, ed. 1584, in Sir J. Hawkins's Hist. ii. p. 285.

his Flemings in 1173, temp. Hen. II. (little more than a century after the Conquest) recorded by Lambarde in his Dictionary of England, p. 36.

> "Hoppe Wyliken, hoppe Wyliken
> Ingland is thine and myne," &c.

And that noted boast of Hugh Bigot, Earl of Norfolk, in the same reign of King Henry II., vide Camdeni Britannia (art. Suffolk), 1607, folio.

> "Were I in my castle of Bungey
> Vpon the riuer of Waueney
> I would ne care for the king of Cockeney."

Indeed many of our old metrical romances, whether originally English, or translated from the French to be sung to an English audience, are addressed to persons of high rank, as appears from their beginning thus,—"Listen, Lordings," and the like. These were prior to the time of Chaucer, as appears from vol. iii. p. 25, et seqq. And yet to his time our Norman nobles are supposed to have adhered to their French language.

(v) *That intercommunity, &c. between the French and English Minstrels, &c.*] This might, perhaps, in a great measure, be referred even to the Norman conquest, when the victors brought with them all their original opinions and fables; which could not fail to be adopted by the English Minstrels and others, who solicited their favour. This interchange, &c. between the Minstrels of the two nations, would be afterwards promoted by the great intercourse produced among all the nations of Christendom in the general Crusades, and by that spirit of chivalry which led Knights and their attendants, the Heralds and Minstrels, &c., to ramble about continually, from one court to another, in order to be present at solemn turnaments and other feats of arms.

(v2) *Is not the only instance, &c.*] The constant admission granted to Minstrels was so established a privilege, that it became a ready expedient to writers of fiction. Thus, in the old romance of *Horn-Child*, the Princess Rymenyld being confined in an inaccessible castle, the prince, her lover, and some assistant knights, with concealed arms, assume the minstrel character; and approaching the castle with their "Gleyinge" or Minstrelsy, are heard by the lord of it, who being informed they were "harpeirs, jogelers, and fythelers[5]," has them admitted, when

> "Horn sette him abenche [*i. e.* on a bench]
> Is [*i. e.* his] harpe he gan clenche
> He made Rymenild a lay."

This sets the princess a-weeping, and leads to the catastrophe; for he immediately advances to "the Borde" or table, kills the ravisher, and releases the lady.

(v 3) . . *assumed the dress and character of a Harper*, *&c.*] We have this curious *Historiette* in the records of Lacock Nunnery, in Wiltshire, which had been founded by this Countess of Salisbury. See Vincent's Discovery of Errors in Brooke's Catalogue of Nobility, &c. folio, pp. 445, 446, &c. Take the following extract (and see Dugdale's *Baron.* i. p. 175):

"Ela uxor Gullielmi Longespee primi, nata fuit apud Ambresbiriam, patre et matre Normannis.

"Pater itaque ejus defectus senio migravit ad Christum, A.D. 1196. Mater ejus ante biennium obiit. . . . . Interea Domina charissima clam per cognatos adducta fuit in Normanniam, et ibidem sub tutâ et arctâ custodiâ nutrita. Eodem

5 JOGELER (Lat. *Joculator*) was a very ancient name for a Minstrel. Of what nature the performance of the *Joculator* was, we may learn from the Register of St. Swithin's Priory at Winchester (T. Warton, i. 69). "Et cantabat JOCULATOR quidam nomine Herebertus Canticum *Colbrondi*, necnon *Gestum Emme* regine a judicio ignis liberate, in aula Prioris." His instrument was sometimes the FYTHELE, or Fiddle, Lat. *Fidicula:* which occurs in the Anglo-Saxon Lexicon. On this subject we have a curious passage from a MS. of the Lives of the Saints in metre, supposed to be earlier than the year 1200 (T. Warton's Hist. i. p. 17), viz.

> "Christofre him served longe
> The kynge loved melodye much of fithele and of songe:
> So that his Jogeler on a day beforen him gon to pleye faste,
> And in a tyme he nemped in his song the devil at laste."

tempore in Angliâ fuit quidam miles nomine Gulielmus Talbot, qui induit se habitum Peregrini [Anglice, *a Pilgrim*] in Normanniam transfretavit et moratus per duos annos, huc atque illuc vagans, ad explorandam dominam Elam Sarum. Et illâ inventâ, exuit habitum Peregrini, et induit se quasi Cytharisator et Curiam ubi morabatur intravit. Et ut erat homo Jocosus, in Gestis Antiquorum valde peritus, ibidem gratanter fuit acceptus quasi familiaris. Et quando tempus aptum invenit, in Angliam repatriavit, habens secum istam venerabilem dominam Elam et hæredem comitatus Sarum; et eam Regi Richardo præsentavit. Ac ille lætissime eam suscepit, et Fratri suo Guillelmo Longespee maritavit ....

"A. D. 1226, Dominus Guill. Longespee primus nonas Martii obiit. Ela vero uxor ejus 7 annis supervixit..... Una die Duo monasteria fundavit primo mane xvi. Kal. Maii, A. D. 1232, apud Lacock, in quo sanctæ degunt Canonissæ... Et Henton post nonam, anno vero ætatis suæ xlv." &c.

(w) For the preceding account, Dugdale refers to Monast. Angl. i. [r. ii.] p. 185, but gives it as enlarged by D. Powel, in his Hist. of Cambria, p. 196, who is known to have followed ancient Welsh MSS. The words in the Monasticon are,— "Qui accersitis *Sutoribus* Cestriæ et *Histrionibus*, festinanter cum exercitu suo venit domino suo facere succursum. Walenses vero videntes multitudinem magnam venientem, relictâ obsidione fugerunt.... Et propter hoc dedit Comes antedictus .... Constabulario dominationem Sutorum et Histrionum. Constabularius vero retinuit sibi et hæredibus suis dominationem Sutorum: et Histrionum dedit vero Seneschallo." (So the passage should apparently be pointed; but either *et* or *vero* seems redundant.)

We shall see below, in note (z), the proper import of the word *Histriones:* but it is very remarkable that this is not the word used in the grant of the Constable De Lacy to Dutton, but "Magisterium omnium *Leccatorum* et *Meretricium* totius Cestreshire, sicut liberius illum [sic] Magisterium teneo de Comite" (vid. Blount's *Ancient Tenures*, p. 156). Now, as under this grant the heirs of Dutton confessedly held for many ages a *magisterial* jurisdiction over all the Minstrels and Musicians of that county, and as it could not be conveyed by the word *Meretrices*, the natural inference is that the Minstrels were expressed by the term *Leccatores*. It is true, Du Cange, compiling his Glossary, could only find in the writers he consulted this word used in the abusive sense, often applied to every synonyme of the sportive and dissolute Minstrel, viz. *Scurra*, *vaniloquus*, *parasitus*, *epulo*, &c. (This I conceive to be the proper arrangement of these explanations, which only express the character given to the minstrel elsewhere: see Du Cange *passim*, and notes (c), (E), (F), (I), vol. iii. 2, &c.) But he quotes an ancient MS. in French metre, wherein the Leccour (Lat. *Leccator*) and the Minstrel are joined together, as receiving from Charlemagne a grant of the territory of Provence, and from whom the Provençal Troubadours were derived, &c. See the passage above in note (c), p. lvii.

The exception in favour of the family of Dutton is thus expressed in the Statute, Anno 39 Eliz. chap. iv. entitled, "An Act for punishment of Rogues, Vagabonds, and Sturdy Beggars."

"§ II. . . . All Fencers, Bearwards, Common Players of Enterludes, and *Minstrels*, wandering abroad (other than Players of Enterludes belonging to any Baron of this Realm, or any other honourable Personage of greater degree, to be authorised to play under the hand and seal of arms of such Baron or Personage): all Juglers, Tinkers, Pedlers, &c. . . . shall be adjudged and deemed Rogues, Vagabonds, and Sturdy Beggars, &c.

"§ X. Provided always, that this Act, or any thing therein contained, or any authority thereby given, shall not in any wise extend to disinherit, prejudice, or hinder, John Dutton, of Dutton, in the county of Chester, Esquire, his heirs or assigns, for, touching or concerning any liberty, preheminence, authority, jurisdiction, or inheritance, which the said John Dutton now lawfully useth, or hath, or lawfully may or ought to use within the County-Palatine of Chester, and the County of the City of Chester, or either of them, by reason of any ancient Charters of any Kings of this Land, or by reason of any prescription, usage, or title whatsoever.'

The same clauses are renewed in the last Act on this subject, passed in the reign of Geo. III.

(x) *Edward I . . . . . at the knighting of his son, &c.*] See Nic. Triveti Annales, Oxon. 1719, 8vo. p. 342.

"In festo Pentecostes Rex filium suum armis militaribus cinxit, et cum eo Comites Warenniæ et Arundeliæ, aliosque, quorum numerus ducentos et quadraginta dicitur excessisse. Eodem die cum sedisset Rex in mensa, novis militibus circumdatus, ingressa *Ministrellorum Multitudo*, portantium multiplici ornatu amictum, ut milites præcipue novos invitarent, et inducerent, ad vovendum factum armorum aliquod coram signo."

(y) *By an express regulation, &c.*] See in Hearne's Append. ad Lelandi Collectan. vol. vi. p. 36, "A Dietarie, Writtes published after the Ordinance of Earles and Barons, Anno Dom. 1315."

"Edward, by the grace of God, &c. to Sheriffes, &c. greetyng. Forasmuch as . . . . many idle persons, under colour of Mynstrelsie, and going in messages, and other faigned busines, have ben and yet be receaved in other mens houses to meate and drynke, and be not therwith contented yf they be not largely consydered with gyftes of the Lordes of the houses, &c. . . . We wyllyng to restrayne such outrageous enterprises and idleness, &c. have ordeyned . . . . that to the houses of Prelates, Earles, and Barons, none resort to meate and drynke, unlesse he be a Mynstrel, and of these Minstrels that there come none, except it be three or four Minstrels of Honour at the most in one day, unlesse he be desired of the Lorde of the House. And to the houses of meaner men that none come unlesse he be desired, and that such as shall come so, holde themselves contented with meate and drynke, and with such curtesie as the Maister of the House wyl shewe unto them of his owne good wyll, without their askyng of any thyng. And yf any one do agaynst this Ordinaunce, at the first tyme he to lose his Minstrelsie, and at the second tyme to forsweare his craft, and never to be receaved for a Minstrel in any house. . . . Yeven at Langley the vi. day of August, in the ix. yere of our reigne.'

These abuses arose again to as great a height as ever in little more than a century after, in consequence, I suppose, of the licentiousness that crept in during the civil wars of York and Lancaster. This appears from the Charter 9 E. IV., referred to in page xliii. "Ex querulosâ insinuatione .... Ministrallorum nostrorum accepimus qualiter nonnulli rudes agricolæ et artifices diversarum misterarum regni nostri Angliæ, finxerunt se fore Ministrallos, quorum aliqui Liberatam nostram eis minime datam portarent, seipsos etiam fingentes esse *Minstrallos nostros proprios*, cujus quidem Liberatæ ac dictæ artis sive occupationis Ministrallorum colore, in diversis partibus regni nostri prædicti grandes pecuniarum exactiones de ligeis nostris deceptive colligunt," &c.

Abuses of this kind prevailed much later in Wales, as appears from the famous Commission issued out in 9 Eliz. (1567), for bestowing the SILVER HARP on the best Minstrel, Rythmer, or Bard, in the principality of North Wales; of which a fuller account will be given below in note (B B 3).

(z) *It is thus related by Stow.*] See his Survey of London, &c., fol. 1633. p. 521. [Acc. of Westm. Hall.] Stow had this passage from Walsingham's Hist. Ang. . . . "Intravit quædam mulier ornata Histrionali habitu, equum bonum insidens Histrionaliter phaleratum, quæ mensas more Histrionum circuivit; et tandem ad Regis mensam per gradus ascendit, et quandam literam coram rege posuit, et retracto fræno (salutatis ubique discumbentibus) prout venerat ita recessit," &c. Anglic. Norm. Script. &c. Franc. 1603, fol. p. 109.

It may be observed here, that Minstrels and others often rode on horseback up to the royal table, when the kings were feasting in their great halls. See in this vol. p. 59, &c.

The answer of the porters (when they were afterwards blamed for admitting her) also deserves attention. "Non esse moris domus regiæ *Histriones* ab ingressu quomodolibet prohibere," &c. Walsingh.

That Stow rightly translated the Latin word *Histrio* here by *Minstrel*, meaning a musician that sung, and whose subjects were stories of chivalry, admits of easy proof: for in the *Gesta Romanorum*, chap. cxi., Mercury is represented as coming to Argus in the character of a Minstrel; when he "*incepit*, *more Histrionico*, fabulas dicere, et plerumque cantare." (T. Warton, iii. p. li.) And Muratori cites a passage in an old Italian chronicle, wherein mention is made of a stage erected at Milan: — "Super quo *Histriones cantabant*, sicut modo cantatur de Rolando et Oliverio."—*Antich. Ital.* ii. p. 6. (Observ. on the Statutes, 4th edit. p. 362.)

See also notes (E), page lx. &c., and (F), p. lxii. &c.

(AA) *There should seem to have been women of this profession.*] This may be inferred from the variety of names appropriated to them in the middle ages, viz. Anglo-Sax. Ᵹlıpmeðen [Glee-maiden], &c., ᵹlẏpıenðemaðen, ᵹlẏpbẏðeneꞅꞇꞃa (vide supra, p. lxvii.), Fr. *Jengleresse*, Med. Lat. *Joculatrix*, *Ministralissa*, *Fœmina Ministerialis*, &c. (Vide Du Cange, Gloss. and Suppl.)

See what is said in page xliii. concerning the "Sisters of the fraternity of Minstrels;" see also a passage quoted by Dr. Burney (ii. 315) from Muratori, of the Chorus of women singing through the streets, accompanied with musical instruments, in 1268.

Had the female described by Walsingham been a *Tombestere*, or Dancing-woman (see Tyrwhitt's Chaucer, iv. 307, and v. Gloss.), that historian would probably have used the word *Saltatrix*. (See T. Warton, i. 240, note *m*.)

These *Saltatrices* were prohibited from exhibiting in

churches and church-yards along with *Joculatores*, *Histriones*, with whom they were sometimes classed, especially by the rigid ecclesiastics, who censured, in the severest terms, all these sportive characters. (Vide T. Warton, in loco citato. et vide supra notes (E), (F), &c.)

And here I would observe, that although Fauchet and other subsequent writers affect to arrange the several members of the minstrel profession under the different classes of *Troverres* (or *Troubadours*), *Chanterres*, *Conteours*, and *Jugleurs*, &c. (vide page lvii.), as if they were distinct and separate orders of men, clearly distinguished from each other by these appropriate terms, we find no sufficient grounds for this in the oldest writers; but the general names in Latin, *Histrio*, *Mimus*, *Joculator*, *Ministrallus*, &c.; in French, *Menestrier*, *Menestrel*, *Jongleur*, *Jugleur*, &c.; and in English, *Jogeleur*, *Jugler*, *Minstrel*, and the like, seem to be given them indiscriminately. And one or other of these names seems to have been sometimes applied to every species of men whose business it was to entertain or divert (*joculari*), whether with poesy, singing, music, or gesticulation, singly, or with a mixture of all these. Yet as all men of this sort were considered as belonging to one class, order, or community (many of the above arts being sometimes exercised by the same person), they had all of them doubtless the same privileges, and it equally throws light upon the general history of the profession, to show what favour or encouragement was given, at any particular period of time, to any one branch of it. I have not, therefore, thought it needful to inquire, whether, in the various passages quoted in these pages, the word *Minstrel*, &c. is always to be understood in its exact and proper meaning of a Singer to the Harp, &c.

That men of very different arts and talents were included under the common name of *Minstrels*, &c., appears from a variety of authorities. Thus we have *Menestrels de Trompes*, and *Menestrels de Bouche*, in the Suppl. to Du Cange, c. 1227, and it appears still more evident from an old French Rhymer, whom I shall quote at large.

"Les Quens[6] manda les *Menestrels*;
Et si a fet[7] crier entre els,
Qui la meillor truffe[8] sauroit
Dire, ne faire, qu'il auroit
Sa robe d'escarlate neuve.
L'uns Menestrels à l'autre reuve
Fere son mestier, tel qu'il sot,
Li uns fet l'yvre, l'autre sot;
Li uns chante, li autre note;
Et li autres dit la riote;
Et li autres la jenglerie[9]
Cil qui sevent de jonglerie
Vielent par devant le Conte;
Aucuns ja qui fabliaus conte
Il i ot did mainte risée," &c.

*Fabliaux et Contes*, 12mo. tom. ii. p. 161.

And what species of entertainment was afforded by the ancient Juggleurs, we learn from the following citation from an old Romance, written in 1230.

"Quand les tables ostees furent
C'il *juggleurs* in pies esturent
S'ont vielles, et harpes prisees
Chansons, sons, vers, et reprises
Et *gestes* chanté nos ont."

Sir J. Hawkins, ii. 44, from Andr. Du Chene. See also Tyrwhitt's Chaucer, iv. p. 299.

All the before-mentioned sports went by the general name of *Ministralcia*, *Ministellorum Ludicra*, &c.— "Charta an. 1377, apud Rymer, vii. p. 160. 'Peracto autem prandio, ascendebat D. Rex in cameram suam cum Prælatis, Magnatibus, et Proceribus prædictis: et deinceps Magnates, Milites, et Domini, aliique Generosi diem illum, usque ad tempus cœnæ, in *tripudiis*, *coreis*, *et solempnibus Ministralciis*, præ gaudio solempnitatis illius continuarunt.'" — (Du Cange, Gloss. 773.) [This was at the Coronation of King Richard II.]

It was common for the Minstrels to dance, as well as to harp and sing (see above, note (E), p. lx.). Thus in the old romance of *Tirante el Blanco;* Val. 1511, the 14th cap. lib. ii.

[6] Le Compte. [7] Fait. [8] Sornette [a gibe, a jest, or flouting.]
[9] Janglerie, babillage, raillerie.

begins thus, "Despues que las Mesas fueron alçadas vinieron los Ministriles; y delante del Rey, y de la Reyna dançaron un rato: y despues truxeron colacion."

They also, probably, among their other feats, played tricks of sleight of hand: hence the word *Jugler* came to signify a performer of Legerdemain; and it was sometimes used in this sense (to which it is now appropriated) even so early as the time of Chaucer, who, in his *Squire's Tale* (ii. 108), speaks of the horse of brass, as

"—— like
An apparence ymade by som magike,
As JOGELOURS plaien at thise festes grete."

See also the *Frere's Tale*, l. p. 279, v. 7049.

(AA 2) *Females playing on the Harp.*] Thus in the old romance of *Syr Degore* (or *Degree*, vol. iii. no. 22, p. 28), we have [Sign. D. i.],

"The lady, that was so faire and bright,
Upon her bed she sate down ryght;
She harped notes swete and fine.
[Her mayds filled a piece of wine.]
And Syr Degore sate him downe,
For to hear the harpes sowne."

The fourth line being omitted in the pr. copy, is supplied from the folio MS.

In the *Squyr of Lowe Degree* (vol. iii. no. 24, p. 29), the king says to his daughter [Sign. D. i.]

"Ye were wont to harpe and syng,
And be the meryest in chamber comyng."

In the *Carle of Carlisle* (vol. iii. no. 10, p. 25), we have the following passage. [Folio MS. p. 451, v. 217.]

"Downe came a lady faire and free,
And sett her on the Carles knee:
One whiles shee harped another whiles song,
Both of paramours and louinge amonge."

And in the romance of *Eger and Grime* (vol. iii. no. 12, p. 26), we have [ibid. p. 127, col. 2], in part i. ver. 263,

"The ladye fayre of hew and hyde
Shee sate downe by the bed side
Shee laid a souter [psaltry] vpon her knee
Thereon shee plaid full lovesomelye.
. . . And her 2 maydens sweetlye sange."

A similar passage occurs in part iv. ver. 129 (page 136). But these instances are sufficient.

(BB) *A Charter . . . . . . to appoint a King of the Minstrels.*] Entitled, *Carta Le Roy de Ministraulx* (in Latin, *Histriones*, vide Plott, p. 437). A copy of this charter is printed in Monast. Anglic. i. 355, and in Blount's Law Diction. 1717 (art. *King.*)

That this was a most respectable officer, both here and on the Continent, will appear from the passages quoted below, and therefore it could only have been in modern times, when the proper meaning of the original terms *Ministraulz*, and *Histriones*, was forgot, that he was called *King of the Fiddlers;* on which subject see below, note (EE 2).

Concerning the *King of the Minstrels* we have the following curious passages collected by Du Cange, Gloss. iv. 773.

"*Rex Ministellorum;* supremus inter *Ministellos:* de cujus munere, potestate in cæteros *Ministellos* agit Charta Henrici IV. Regis Angliæ in Monast. Anglicano, tom. i. pag. 355. —Charta originalis an. 1338. Je Robert Caveron Roy des Menestreuls du Royaume de France. Aliæ ann. 1357 et 1362. Copin de Brequin Roy des Menestres du Royaume de France. Computum de auxiliis pro redemptione Regis Johannis, ann. 1367. Pour une *Couronne d'Argent* qu'il donna le jour de la Tiphaine au Roy des Menestrels.

"Regestum Magnorum Dierum Trecensium an. 1296. Super quod Joannes dictus Charmillons Juglator, cui Dominus Rex per suas literas tanquam *Regem Juglatorum* in civitate Trecensi Magisterium Juglatorum, quemadmodum suæ placeret voluntati, concesserat." Gloss. c. 1587.

There is a very curious passage in Pasquier's *Recherches de la France*, Paris, 1633, folio, liv. 7, ch. v. p. 611, wherein he appears to be at a loss how to account for the title of *Le*

*Roy*, assumed by the old composers of metrical romances: in one of which the author expressly declares himself to have been a *Minstrel.* The solution of the difficulty, that he had been *Le Roy des Menestrels*, will be esteemed more probable than what Pasquier here advances; for I have never seen the title of *Prince* given to a Minstrel, &c. scil. "A nos vieux Poetes . . . . comme . . fust qu'ils eussent certain jeux de prix en leurs Poesies, ils . . . . honoroient du nome, tantot de *Roy*, tantot de *Prince*, celuy qui avoit le mieux faict comme nous voyons entre les Archers, Arbalestiers, et Harquebusiers estre fait le semblable. Ainsi l'Autheur du Roman d'Oger le Danois s'appelle Roy.

"Icy endroict est cil Livre finez
Qui des enfans Oger est appellez
Or vueille Diex qu'il soit parachevez
En tel maniere kestre n'en puist blamez
Le Roy Adams [r. Adenes] ki il'est remez.

"Et en celuy de Cleomades,

"Ce Livre de Cleomades
Rimé-je le Roy Adenes
Menestre au bon Duc Henry.

"Mot de *Roy*, qui seroit très-mal approprié à un *Menestrier*, si d'ailleurs on ne le rapportoit à un jeu du priz: Et de faict il semble que de nostre temps, il y en eust encores quelque remarques, en ce que le mot de *Jouingleur* s'estant par succession de temps tourné en batelage, nous avons veu en nostre jeunesse les Jouingleurs se trouver à certain jour tous les ans en la ville de Chauny en Picardie, pour faire monstre de leur mestrier devant le monde, à qui mieux. Et ce que j'en dis icy n'est pas pour vilipender ces anciens Rimeurs, ainsi pour monstrer qu'il n'y a chose si belle qui ne s'anéantisse avec le temps."

We see here that, in the time of Pasquier, the poor Minstrel was sunk into as low estimation in France, as he was then or afterwards in England; but by his apology for comparing the *Jouingleurs*, who assembled to exercise their faculty, in his youth, to the ancient *Rimeurs*, it is plain they exerted their skill in rhyme.

As for king Adenes, or Adenez (whose name in the first passage above is corruptly printed *Adams*), he is recorded in the *Bibliothèque des Romans*, Amst. 1734, 12mo. vol. i. page 232, to have composed the two romances in verse above mentioned, and a third, entitled, *Le Roman de Bertin;* all three being preserved in a MS. written about 1270. His *Bon Duc Henry*, I conceive to have been Henry Duke of Brabant.

(BB2) *King of the Minstrels*, &c.] See Anstis's Register of the Order of the Garter, ii. p. 303, who tells us, "The President or Governour of the *Minstrels* had the like denomination of *Roy* in France and Burgundy; and in England, John of Gaunt constituted such an officer by a patent; and long before his time payments were made by the Crown to [a] King of the Minstrels by Edw. I. Regi Roberto Ministrallo scutifero ad arma commoranti ad vadia Regis anno 5to. [Bibl. Cotton. Vespas. c.16. f.3], as likewise [Libro Garderob. 25 E. I.] Ministrallis in die nuptiarum Comitissæ Holland filiæ Regis, Regi Pago, Johanni Vidulatori, &c. Morello Regi, &c. Druetto Monthaut, et Jacketto de Scot. Regibus, cuilibet eorum, xl. s. Regi Pagio de Hollandia, &c. Under Ed. II. we likewise find other entries, Regi Roberto et aliis Ministrallis facientibus Menistrallias [Ministralcias, qu.] suas coram Rege. [Bibl. Cotton. Nero, c. 8. p. 84. b. Comp. Garderob.] That King granted Willielmo de Morlee dicto Roy de North, Ministrallo Regis, domos quæ fuerunt Johannis le Boteler dicti Roy Brunhaud [Pat. de terr. forisfact. 16 E. III.]." He adds below (p. 304), a similar instance of a *Rex Juglatorum*, and that the "King of the Minstrels" at length was styled in France *Roy des Violons* (Furetiere Diction. Univers.), as with us, "King of the Fiddlers;" on which subject see below, note (EE2).

(BB3) The Statute 4 Hen. IV. (1402), c. 27, runs in these terms, "Item, pur eschuir plusieurs diseases et mischiefs qont advenuz devaunt ces heures en la terre de Gales par plusieurs Westours, Rymours, Minstralx, et autres Vacabondes, ordeignez est et establiz qe nul Westour, Rymour, Ministral ne Vacabond soit aucunement sustenuz en la terre de Gales pur faire kymorthas ou coillage sur la commune poeple illoeques." This is among the severe laws against the Welsh, passed during the resentment occasioned by the outrages committed under Owen Glendour; and as the Welsh Bards had excited their countrymen to rebellion against the English government, it is not to be wondered that the Act is conceived in terms of the utmost indignation and contempt against this class of men, who are described as *Rymours*, *Ministralx*, which are apparently here used as only synonymous terms to express the Welsh Bards with the usual exuberance of our Acts of Parliament; for if their *Ministralx* had been mere musicians, they would not have required the vigilance of the English legislature to suppress them. It was their songs exciting their countrymen to insurrection which produced "les diseases et mischiefs en la terre de Gales."

It is also submitted to the reader, whether the same application of the terms does not still more clearly appear in the Commission issued in 1567, and printed in Evan Evans's Specimens of Welch Poetry, 1764, 4to. p. v. for bestowing the Silver Harp on "the chief of that faculty." For after setting forth "that vagrant and idle persons, naming themselves *Minstrels*, *Rythmers*, and *Bards*, had lately grown into such intolerable multitude within the Principality in North Wales, that not only gentlemen and others by their shameless disorders are oftentimes disquieted in their habitations, but also expert *Minstrels* and *Musicians in tonge and cunynge* thereby much discouraged," &c. and "hindred [of] livings and preferment," &c., it appoints a time and place, wherein all "persons that intend to maintain their living by name or colour of *Minstrels*, *Rythmers*, or *Bards*," within five shires of N. Wales, "shall appear to show their learnings accordingly," &c. And the Commissioners are required to admit such as shall be found worthy, into and under the degrees heretofore in use, so that they may "use, exercise, and follow the sciences and faculties of their professions in such decent order as shall appertain to each of their degrees." And the rest are to return to some honest labour, &c. upon pain to be taken as sturdy and idle vagabonds, &c.

(BB 4) Holingshed translated this passage from Tho. de Elmham's "Vita et Gesta Henrici V." scil. "Soli Omnipotenti Deo se velle victoriam imputari . . . . in tantum, quod cantus de suo triumpho fieri, seu per Citharistas vel alios quoscunque cantari penitus prohibebat." [Edit. Hearnii, 1727, p. 72.] As in his version, Holingshed attributes the *making* as well as *singing* ditties to Minstrels, it is plain he knew that men of this profession had been accustomed to do both.

(C C) *The Houshold Book, &c.*] See Section V.

"Of the Noumbre of all my Lords Servaunts."

"Item, Mynstralls in Houshold, iij. viz. A Taberett, a Luyte, and a Rebecc." [The rebeck was a kind of fiddle with three strings.]

Sect. XLIV. 3.

"Rewardis to his Lordshipis Servaunts," &c.

"Item, My Lorde usith ande accustomyth to gyf yerly, when his Lordschipp is at home, to his Mynstrallis that be daly in his houshold, as his Tabret, Lute, ande Rebek, upon New-Yeres-day in the mornynge when they doo play at my Lordis chambre doure for his Lordschipe and my Lady, xx. s. Viz. xiij. s. iiij. d. for my Lorde, and vj. s. viij. d. for my Lady, if sche be at my Lords fyndynge, and not at hir owen; and for playing at my Lordis sone and heir chaumbre doure, the Lord Percy, ij. s. And for playinge at the chaumbre doures of my Lords yonger Sonnes, my yonge Maisters, after viii. d. the pece for every of them.—xxiij. s. iiij. d."

Sect. XLIV. 2.

"Rewardis to be yeven to strangers, as Players, Mynstralls, or any other," &c.

"Furst, my Lorde usith and accustomyth to gyf to the Kings Jugler; . . . . when they custome to come unto hym yerly, vj. s. viij. d.

"Item, my Lord usith and accustomyth to gyf yerely the Kynge or the Queenes Barwarde, if they have one, when they custom to com unto hym yerly,—vj. s. viij. d.

"Item, my Lorde usith and accustomyth to gyfe yerly to every Erlis Mynstrellis, when they custome to come to hym yerely, iij. s. iiij. d. Ande if they come to my Lord seldome, ones in ij or iij yeres, than vj. s. viij. d.

"Item, my Lorde usith and accustomedeth to gife yerely to an Erls Mynstrall, if he be his speciall lorde, frende, or kynsman, if they come yerely to his Lordschipe .... Ande if they come 'to my lord' seldome, ones in ii or iii yeres ...."

* * * * *

"Item, my Lorde useth ande accustomyth to gyf yerely a Dookes or Erlis Trumpetts, if they com vj together to his Lordshipp, viz. if they come yerly, vj. s. viij. d. Ande if they come but in ij or iij yeres, than x. s.

"Item, my Lorde useth and accustometh to gife yerly, when his Lordship is at home, to gyf to iij of the Kyngs Shams, when they com to my Lorde yerely, x. s."

* * * * *

I cannot conclude this note without observing, that in this enumeration the family Minstrels seem to have been musicians only, and yet both the Earl's Trumpets and the King's Shawms are evidently distinguished from the Earl's Minstrels and the King's Jugler. Now we find *Jugglers* still coupled with *Pipers* in Barklay's *Egloges*, circ. 1514. (Warton, ii. 254.)

(c c 2) The honours and rewards conferred on Minstrels, &c., in the middle ages, were excessive, as will be seen by many instances in these volumes; vid. notes (E), (F), &c. But more particularly with regard to English Minstrels, &c., see T. Warton's *Hist. of Eng. Poetry*, i. p. 89—92, 116, &c.; ii. 105, 106, 254, &c. Dr. Burney's *Hist. of Music*, ii. p. 316—319, 397—399, 427, 428.

On this head, it may be sufficient to add the following passage from the Fleta, lib. ii. c. 23. "Officium Elemosinarij est, Equos relictos, Robas, Pecuniam, et alia ad Elemosinam largiter recipere et fideliter distribuere; debet etiam Regem super Elemosinæ largitione crebris summonitionibus stimulare et præcipue diebus Sanctorum, et rogare ne Robas suas quæ magni sunt precij *Histrionibus*, Blanditoribus, Adulatoribus, Accusatoribus, vel *Menestrallis*, sed ad Elemosinæ suæ incrementum jubeat largiri." Et in c. 72. "Ministralli, vel Adulatoris."

(D D) *A species of men who did not sing, &c.*] It appears from the passage of Erasmus here referred to, that there still existed in England of that species of Jongleurs or Minstrels, whom the French called by the peculiar name of *Conteours*, or reciters in prose: it is in his *Ecclesiastes*, where he is speaking of such preachers as imitated the tone of beggars or mountebanks:—"Apud Anglos est simile genus hominum, quales apud Italos sunt Circulatores [Mountebanks] de quibus modo dictum est; qui irrumpunt in convivia Magnatum, aut in Cauponas Vinarias; et argumentum aliquod, quod edidicerunt, recitant; puta mortem omnibus dominari, aut laudem matrimonii. Sed quoniam ea lingua monosyllabis fere constat, quemadmodum Germanica; atque illi [sc. this peculiar species of Reciters] studio vitant cantum, nobis (sc. Erasmus, who did not understand a word of English) latrare videntur verius quam loqui." Opera, tom. v. c. 958. (Jortin, vol. ii. p. 193.) As Erasmus was correcting the vice of preachers, it was more to his point to bring an instance from the moral reciters of prose than from chanters of rhyme; though the latter would probably be more popular, and therefore more common.

(E E) This character is supposed to have been suggested by descriptions of Minstrels in the romance of *Morte Arthur;* but none, it seems, have been found which come nearer to it than the following, which I shall produce, not only that the reader may judge of the resemblance, but to show how nearly the idea of the Minstrel character given in this Essay corresponds with that of our old writers.

Sir Lancelot having been affronted by a threatening abusive letter, which Mark King of Cornwall had sent to Queen Guenever, wherein he "spake shame by her, and Sir Lancelot," is comforted by a knight named Sir Dinadan, who tells him, "I will make a *Lay* for him, and when it is made, I shall make an Harper to sing it before him. So anon he went and made it, and taught it an Harper, that hyght Elyot; and when hee could it, hee taught it to many Harpers. And so . . . the Harpers went straight unto Wales and Cornwaile to sing the Lay . . . which was the worst Lay that ever Harper sung with Harpe, or with any other instrument. And [at a] great feast that King Marke made for joy of [a] victorie which hee had, . . . came Eliot the Harper; . . . and because he was a curious Harper, men heard him sing the same Lay that Sir Dinadan had made, the which spake the most vilanie by King Marke of his treason, that ever man heard. When the Harper had sung his song to the end, King Marke was wonderous wroth with him, and said, Thou Harper, how durst thou be so bold to sing this song before me? Sir, said Eliot, wit you well I am a Minstrell, and I must doe as I am commanded of these Lords that *I bear the armes of*. And, Sir King, wit you well that Sir Dinadan a knight of the Round Table made this song, and he made me to sing it before you. Thou saiest well, said King Marke, I charge thee that thou hie thee fast out of my sight. So the Harper departed," &c. [Part ii. c. 113, ed. 1634. See also part iii. c. 5.]

(E E 2) *This Act seems to have put an end to the profession, &c.*] Although I conceive that the character ceased to exist, yet the appellation might be continued, and applied to Fiddlers, or other common musicians: which will account for the mistakes of Sir Peter Leicester, or other modern writers. (See his *Historical Antiquities of Cheshire*, 1673, p. 141.)

In this sense it is used in an Ordinance in the times of Cromwell (1656), wherein it is enacted, that if any of the "persons commonly called Fidlers or Minstrels shall at any time be taken playing, fidling, and making music in any inn, ale-house, or tavern, or shall be taken proffering themselves, or desiring, or intreating any . . . to hear them play or make music in any of the places aforesaid;" they are to be "adjudged and declared to be rogues, vagabonds, and sturdy beggars."

This will also account why John of Gaunt's King of the Minstrels at length came to be called, like *le Roy des Violons* in France, vide note (B B 2), King of the Fiddlers. See the common ballad entitled, "The Pedigree, Education, and Marriage of Robinhood with Clorinda, Queen of Tutbury Feast:" which, though prefixed to the modern collection on that subject[10], seems of much later date than most of the others; for the writer appears to be totally ignorant of all the old traditions concerning this celebrated outlaw, and has given him a very elegant bride instead of his old noted lemman "Maid Marian;" who, together with his chaplain, "Frier Tuck," were his favourite companions, and probably on that account figured in the old Morice dance, as may be seen by the engraving in Mr. Steevens's and Mr. Malone's editions of Shakspeare: by whom she is mentioned, 1 Hen. IV. act. iii. sc. 3. (See also Warton, i. 245, ii. 237.) Whereas, from this ballad's concluding with an exhortation to "pray for the King," and "that he may get children," &c., it is evidently posterior to the reign of Queen Elizabeth, and can scarce be older than the reign of King Charles I.; for King James I. had no issue after his accession to the throne of England. It may even have been written since the Restoration, and only express the wishes of the nation for issue on

[10] Of the twenty-four songs in what is now called *Robin Hood's Garland*, many are so modern as not to be found in Pepys's collection, completed only in 1700. In the folio MS. (described in p. xv.) are ancient fragments of the following, viz.—Robin Hood and the Beggar.—Robin Hood and the Butcher.—Robin Hood and Fryer Tucke.—Robin Hood and the Pindar.—Robin Hood and Queen Catharine, in two parts.—Little John and the four Beggars, and "Robin Hoode his Death." This last, which is very curious, has no resemblance to any that have been published; and the others are extremely different from the printed copies; but they unfortunately are in the beginning of the MS., where half of every leaf hath been torn away.

the marriage of their favourite King Charles II., on his marriage with the Infanta of Portugal. I think it is not found in the Pepys collection.

(F F) *Historical song, or ballad.*] The English word *ballad* is evidently from the French *balade*, as the latter is from the Italian *ballata;* which the Crusca Dictionary defines, *canzone, che si canta ballando*, "A song which is sung during a dance." So Dr. Burney [ii. 342], who refers to a collection of *Ballette* published by Gastaldi, and printed at Antwerp in 1596 [iii. 226].

But the word appears to have had an earlier origin: for in the decline of the Roman empire these trivial songs were called *ballistea* and *saltatiunculæ*. *Ballisteum*, Salmasius says, is properly *ballistium*. Gr. *Βαλλιστεῖον*. "*ἀπὸ τοῦ βαλλίζω* .... *Βαλλιστία Saltatio* . . . Ballistium igitur est quod vulgo vocamus *ballet;* nam inde deducta vox nostra." Salmas. Not. in Hist. Ang. Scriptores, vi. p. 349.

In the Life of the Emperor Aurelian by Fl. Vopiscus may be seen two of these *ballistea*, as sung by the boys skipping and dancing, on account of a great slaughter made by the emperor with his own hand in the Sarmatic war. The first is,

"Mille, mille, mille decollavimus,
Unus homo mille decollavimus,
Mille vivat, qui mille occidit.
Tantum vini habet nemo
Quantum fudit sanguinis."

The other was,

"Mille Sarmatas, mille Francos
Semel et semel occidimus.
Mille Persas quærimus."

Salmasius (in loc.) shows that the trivial poets of that time were wont to form their metre of Trochaic Tetrametre Catalectics, divided into distichs. [Ibid. p. 350.] This becoming the metre of the hymns in the church service, to which the monks at length superadded rhyming terminations, was the origin of the common trochaic metre in the modern languages.

This observation I owe to the learned author of *Irish Antiquities*, 4to.

(FF 2) *Little Miscellanies named Garlands, &c.*] In the Pepysian and other libraries are preserved a great number of these in black-letter, 12mo., under the following quaint and affected titles, viz.

1. A Crowne Garland of Goulden Roses gathered out of England's Royal Garden, &c., by Richard Johnson, 1612. [In the Bodleian library.] — 2. The Golden Garland of Princely Delight. — 3. The Garland of Good-will, by T. D. 1631. — 4. The Royal Garland of Love and Delight, by T. D. — 5. The Garland of Delight, &c., by Tho. Delone. — 6. The Garland of Love and Mirth, by Thomas Lanfier. — 7. Cupid's Garland set round with Guilded Roses. — 8. The Garland of Withered Roses, by Martin Parker, 1656. — 9. The Shepherd's Garland of Love, Loyalty, &c. — 10. The Country Garland. — 11. The Golden Garland of Mirth and Merriment. — 12. The Lover's Garland. — 13. Neptune's fair Garland. — 14. England's fair Garland. — 15. Robin Hood's Garland. — 16. The Maiden's Garland. — 17. A Loyal Garland of Mirth and Pastime. — 18. A Royal Garland of New Songs. — 19. The Jovial Garland, 8th edit. 1691. — &c. &c. &c.

This sort of petty publications had anciently the name of Penny-Merriments: as little religious tracts of the same size were called Penny-Godlinesses. In the Pepysian library are multitudes of both kinds.

(GG) *The term Minstrel was not confined to a mere musician in this country any more than on the Continent.*] The discussion of the question, whether the term Minstrel was applied in England to singers and composers of songs, &c., or confined to the performers on musical instruments, was properly reserved for this place, because much light hath already been thrown upon the subject in the preceding notes, to which it will be sufficient to refer the reader.

That on the Continent the Minstrel was understood not to be a mere musician, but a singer of verses, hath been shown in notes (B), (C), (E), (AA), &c.[1] And that he was also a maker of them, is evident from the passage in (C), p. lvii., where the most noted romances are said to be of the composition of these men. And in (BB), p. xciv., we have the titles of some of which a Minstrel was the author, who has himself left his name upon record.

The old English names for one of this profession were Gleeman[2], Jogeler[3], and latterly Minstrel; not to mention Harper, &c. In French he was called *Jongleur* or *Jugleur*, *Menestrel* or *Menestrier*[4]. The writers of the middle ages expressed the character in Latin by the words *Joculator*, *Mimus*, *Histrio*, *Ministrellus*, &c. These terms, however modern critics may endeavour to distinguish and apply them to different classes, and although they may be sometimes mentioned as if they were distinct, I cannot find, after a very strict research, to have had any settled appropriate difference, but they appear to have been used indiscriminately by the oldest writers, especially in England; where the most general and comprehensive name was latterly Minstrel, Lat. *Ministrellus*, &c.

Thus *Joculator* (Eng. Jogeler, or Juglar) is used as synonymous to *Citharista*, note (K), p. lxxi., and to *Cantor* (ibid.), and to *Minstrel.* (Vide infra, p. cvi.) We have also positive proof that the subjects of his songs were gestes and romantic tales. (V2) note.

So *Mimus* is used as synonymous to *Joculator*, (M), p. lxxiii. He was rewarded for his singing, (N), p. lxxiv., and he both sang, harped, and dealt in that sport (T2) which is elsewhere called *Ars Joculatoria*, (M), ubi supra.

[1] That the French Minstrel was a singer and composer, &c., appears from many passages translated by M. Le Grand, in *Fabliaux ou Contes, &c.* See tom. i. p. 37, 47; ii. 306, 313, et seqq.; iii. 266, &c. Yet this writer, like other French critics, endeavours to reduce to distinct and separate classes the men of this profession, under the precise names of *Fablier, Conteur, Menetrier, Menestrel*, and *Jongleur* (tom. i. pref. p. xcviii.), whereas his own Tales confute all these nice distinctions, or prove at least that the title of *Menetrier*, or Minstrel, was applied to them all.

[2] See p. lxv. [3] See p. lxxxv. [4] See p. xxxiii. note.

Again, *Histrio* is also proved to have been a singer, (Z), p. lxxxix., and to have gained rewards by his *Verba Joculatoria*, (E), p. lx. And *Histriones* is the term by which the French word *Ministraulx* is most frequently rendered into Latin, (W), p. lxxxvi.; (BB), p. xciv., &c.

The fact therefore is sufficiently established, that this order of men were in England, as well as on the Continent, *singers:* so that it only becomes a dispute about words, whether here, under the more general name of Minstrels, they are described as having *sung.*

But in proof of this, we have only to turn to so common a book as T. Warton's *History of English Poetry;* where we shall find extracted from records the following instances.

Ex Registr. Priorat. S. Swithin Winton. (sub anno 1374.) "In festo Alwyni Epi.... Et durante pietancia in Aula Conventus sex Ministralli, cum quatuor Citharisatoribus, faciebant Ministralcias suas. Et post cenam, in magna camera arcuata Dom. Prioris cantabant idem *Gestum* in qua Camera suspendebatur, ut moris est, magnum dorsale Prioris habens picturas trium Regum Colein. Veniebant autem dicti Joculatores a Castello Domini Regis et ex familia Epi." (vol. ii. p. 174.) Here the Minstrels and Harpers are expressly called *Joculatores;* and as the Harpers had musical instruments, the singing must have been by the Minstrels, or by both conjointly.

For that Minstrels sang we have undeniable proof in the following entry in the Accompt roll of the Priory of Bicester, in Oxfordshire (under the year 1432). "Dat. Sex Ministrallis de Bokyngham *cantantibus* in refectorio Martyrium Septem Dormientium in Festo Epiphanie, iv. s." (Vol. ii. p. 175.)

In like manner our old English writers abound with passages wherein the Minstrel is represented as singing. To mention only a few:

In the old romance of *Emaré* (vol. iii. no. 15, p. 27), which, from the obsoleteness of the style, the nakedness of the story, the barrenness of incidents, and some other particulars, I should judge to be next in point of time to *Horn-Child*, we have

—"I have herd Menstrelles syng yn sawe."
Stanza 27.

In a poem of Adam Davie (who flourished about 1312), we have this distich,

"Merry it is in halle to here the harpe,
The Minstrelles synge, the Jogelours carpe."
T. Warton, i. p. 225.

So William of Nassyngton (circ. 1480) as quoted by Mr. Tyrwhitt (Chaucer, iv. 319),

—"I will make no vain carpinge
Of dedes of armys ne of amours
As dus Mynstrelles and Jestours [Gestours]
That makys carpinge in many a place
Of Octaviane and Isembrase,
And of many other Jestes [Gestes]
And namely whan they come to festes[5].

See also the description of the Minstrel in note (EE) from *Morte Arthur*, which appears to have been compiled about the time of this last writer. (See T. Warton, ii. 235.)

By proving that Minstrels were singers of the old romantic songs and gestes, &c. we have in effect proved them to have been the makers at least of some of them. For the names of their authors being not preserved, to whom can we so probably ascribe the composition of many of these old popular rhymes, as to the men who devoted all their time and talents to the recitation of them? especially as in the rhymes themselves Minstrels are often represented as the makers or composers.

Thus in the oldest of all, *Horn-Child*, having assumed the character of a Harper or Jogeler, is in consequence said (fo. 92) to have

"made Rymenild [his mistress] a lay."

In the old romance of *Emaré*, we have this exhortation to

[5] The fondness of the English (even the most illiterate) to hear Tales and Rhymes, is much dwelt on by Rob. de Brunne, in 1330. (Warton, i. pp. 59, 65, 75.) All Rhymes were then sung to the harp: even "Troilus and Cresseide," though almost as long as the Æneid, was to be "redde ..... or else songe." 1. ult. (Warton, i. 388.)

Minstrels, as composers, otherwise they could not have been at liberty to choose their subjects (st. 2).

"Menstrelles that walken fer and wyde
Her and ther in every a syde
In mony a dyverse londe
Sholde ut her bygynnyng
Speke of that rightwes kyng
That made both see and londe," &c.

And in the old song or geste of *Guy and Colbronde* (vol. iii. no. 4, p. 23), the Minstrel thus speaks of himself in the first person:

"When meate and drinke is great plentye
Then lords and ladyes still wil be
And sitt and solace lythe
Then itt is time for MEE to speake
Of keene knights and kempes great
Such carping for to kythe."

We have seen already that the Welsh *Bards*, who were undoubtedly composers of the songs they chanted to the harp, could not be distinguished by our legislators from our own *Rimers*, *Minstrels*. Vide (BB 3), and p. xli.

And that the Provençal *Troubadour* of our King Richard, who is called by M. Favine *Jongleur*, and by M. Fauchet *Menestrel*, is by the old English translator termed a Rhymer or Minstrel when he is mentioning the fact of his composing some verses (p. xxxiii.).

And lastly, that Holingshed, translating the prohibition of King Henry V., forbidding any songs to be composed on his victory, or to be sung by harpers or others, roundly gives it, he would not permit "any ditties to be made and sung by Minstrels on his glorious victory," &c. Vide p. xlii., and note (BB 4).

Now that this order of men, at first called Gleemen, then Jugglers, and afterwards more generally Minstrels, existed here from the Conquest, who entertained their hearers with chanting, to the harp or other instruments, songs and tales of chivalry, or, as they were called, *gests*[6] and romances in

[6] GESTS at length came to signify adventures or incidents in general. So in a narrative of the Journey into Scotland, of Queen Margaret and her

verse in the English language, is proved by the existence of the very compositions they so chanted, which are still preserved in great abundance; and exhibit a regular series from the time our language was almost Saxon, till after its improvements in the age of Chaucer, who enumerates many of them. And as the Norman French was in the time of this bard still the courtly language, it shows that the English was not thereby excluded from affording entertainment to our nobility, who are so often addressed therein by the title of *lordings:* and sometimes more positively, "lords and ladies." (p. cviii.)

And though many of these were translated from the French, others are evidently of English origin[7], which appear in their turns to have afforded versions into that language; a sufficient proof of that intercommunity between the French and English Minstrels which hath been mentioned in a preceding page. Even the abundance of such translations into English, being all adapted for popular recitation, sufficiently establishes the fact, that the English Minstrels had a great demand for such compositions, which they were glad to supply, whether from their own native stores or from other languages.

We have seen above, that the *Joculator*, *Mimus*, *Histrio*, whether these characters were the same, or had any real difference, were all called Minstrels; as was also the Harper[8], when the term implied a singer, if not a composer, of songs, &c. By degrees the name of Minstrel was extended to vocal and instrumental musicians of every kind: and as in the

attendants, on her marriage with King James IV. in 1503 [in Appendix to Leland. Collect. iv. p. 265], we are promised an account "of their Gestys and manners during the said Voyage."

[7] The romance of *Richard Cœur de Lion* (no. 25) I should judge to be of English origin, from the names Wardrewe and Eldrede, &c. vol. iii. pp. 29, 15 &c. As is also *Eger and Grime* (no. 12), vol. iii. p. 26, wherein a knight is named Sir Gray Steel, and a lady who excels in surgery is called *Loospaine*, or *Lose-pain:* these surely are not derived from France.

[8] See the Romance of *Sir Isenbras* (vol. iii. no. 14. p. 27), sign. a.

"Harpers loved him in Hall
With other Minstrels all."

establishment of royal and noble houses the latter would necessarily be most numerous, so we are not to wonder that the band of music (entered under the general name of Minstrels) should consist of instrumental performers chiefly, if not altogether: for, as the composer or singer of heroic tales to the harp would necessarily be a solitary performer, we must not expect to find him in the band along with the trumpeters, fluters, &c.

However, as we sometimes find mention of "Minstrels of music[9]:" so at other times we hear of "expert Minstrels and Musicians of tongue and cunning," (BB 3), p. xcvi.[10], meaning doubtless by the former Singers, and probably by the latter phrase Composers of songs. Even "Minstrels music" seems to be applied to the species of verse used by Minstrels in the passage quoted below[1].

But although, from the predominancy of instrumental music, Minstrelsy was at length chiefly to be understood in this sense, yet it was still applied to the poetry of Minstrels so late as the time of Queen Elizabeth, as appears in the following extract from Puttenham's *Arte of English Poesie*, p. 9. Who, speaking of the first composers of Latin verses in rhyme, says, "All that they wrote to the favor or prayse

[9] T. Warton, ii. 258, note (a), from Leland's Collect. (vol. iv. Append. edit. 1774, p. 267.)

[10] The curious author of the *Tour in Wales*, 1773, 4to. p. 435, I find to have read these words "in toune and contrey;" which I can scarce imagine to have been applicable to Wales at that time. Nor can I agree with him in the representation he has given (p. 367) concerning the *Cymmorth* or meeting, wherein the Bards exerted their powers to excite their countrymen to war; as if it were by a deduction of the particulars he enumerates, and as it should seem in the way of harangue, &c. After which, "the band of minstrels ...... struck up; the harp, the *crwth*, and the pipe filled the measures of enthusiasm, which the others had begun to inspire." Whereas it is well known, that the Bard chanted his enthusiastic effusions to the harp; and as for the term *Minstrel*, it was not, I conceive, at all used by the Welsh; and in English it comprehended both the bard and the musician.

[1] "Your ordinarie rimers use very much their measures in the odde, as nine and eleven, and the sharpe accent upon the last sillable, which therefore makes him go ill favouredly and like a MINSTRELS MUSICKE." (Puttenham's Arte of Eng. Poesie, 1589, p. 59.) This must mean his vocal music, otherwise it appears not applicable to the subject.

of princes, they did it in such manner of Minstralsie; and thought themselves no small fooles, when they could make their verses go all in *ryme*."

I shall conclude this subject with the following description of Minstrelsy given by John Lidgate at the beginning of the 15th century, as it shows what a variety of entertainments were then comprehended under this term, together with every kind of instrumental music then in use.

—"Al maner MYNSTRALCYE,
That any man kan specifye.
Ffor there were Rotys of Almayne,
And eke of Arragon, and Spayne:
SONGES, Stampes, and eke Daunces;
Divers plente of plesaunces:
And many unkouth NOTYS NEW
OF SWICHE FOLKE AS LOVID TREUE[2].

And instrumentys that did excelle,
Many moo than I kan telle.
Harpys, Fythales, and eke Rotys
Well according to her [*i. e.* their] notys,
Lutys, Ribibles, and Geternes,
More for estatys, than tavernes:
Orgay[n]s, Cytolis, Monacordys.—
There were Trumpes, and Trumpettes,
Lowde Shall[m]ys, and Doucettes."

T. Warton, ii. 225, note (*).

2 By this phrase I understand, new Tales or narrative Rhymes composed by the Minstrels on the subject of true and faithful Lovers, &c.

END OF THE ESSAY.

---

☞ *The foregoing Essay on the Ancient Minstrels has been very much enlarged and improved since the first edition, with respect to the Anglo-Saxon Minstrels, in consequence of some objections proposed by the reverend and learned Mr. Pegge, which the reader may find in the second volume of the* ARCHÆOLOGIA, *printed by the Antiquarian Society; but which that gentleman has since retracted in the most liberal and candid manner in the third volume of the* ARCHÆOLOGIA, No. xxxiv. p. 310.

*And in consequence of similar objections respecting the English Minstrels after the Conquest, the subsequent part hath been much enlarged, and additional light thrown upon the subject; which, to prevent cavil, hath been extended to* MINSTRELSY *in all its branches, as it was established in England, whether by natives or foreigners.*

I never heard the old song of Percie and Douglas, that I found not my heart moved more than with a trumpet: and yet 'it' is sung but by some blinde crowder, with no rougher voice, than rude style; which beeing so evill apparelled in the dust and cobweb of that uncivill age, what would it work, trimmed in the gorgeous eloquence of Pindare!

Sir Philip Sydney's Defence of Poetry.

# RELIQUES

OF

# ANCIENT POETRY.

*&c.*

---

## SERIES THE FIRST.

## BOOK I.

---

### I.

### The Ancient Ballad of Chevy-Chase.

The fine heroic song of Chevy-Chase has ever been admired by competent judges. Those genuine strokes of nature and artless passion, which have endeared it to the most simple readers, have recommended it to the most refined; and it has equally been the amusement of our childhood, and the favourite of our riper years.

Mr. Addison has given an excellent critique[1] on this very popular ballad, but is mistaken with regard to the antiquity of the common received copy; for this, if one may judge from the style, cannot be older than the time of Elizabeth, and was probably written after the eulogium of Sir Philip Sidney: perhaps in consequence of it. I flatter myself, I have here recovered the genuine antique poem, the true original song; which appeared rude even in the time of Sir Philip, and caused him to lament that it was so evil-appareled in the rugged garb of antiquity.

This curiosity is printed from an old manuscript, at the

[1] *Spectator*, No. 70, 74.

end of Hearne's Preface to Gul. Nubrigiensis Hist. 1719, 8vo, vol. i. To the MS. copy is subjoined the name of the author, RYCHARD SHEALE[2]: whom Hearne had so little judgment as to suppose to be the same with a R. Sheale, who was living in 1588. But whoever examines the gradation of language and idiom in the following volumes, will be convinced that this is the production of an earlier poet. It is indeed expressly mentioned among some very ancient songs in an old book intituled, The Complaint of Scotland[3], (fol. 42,) under the title of the HUNTIS OF CHEVET, where the two following lines are also quoted:

> The Perssee and the Mongumrye mette[4]
> That day, that day, that gentil day[5]:

Which, though not quite the same as they stand in the ballad, yet differ not more than might be owing to the author's quoting from memory. Indeed, whoever considers the style and orthography of this old poem, will not be inclined to place it lower than the time of Henry VI.; as, on the other hand, the mention of James the Scottish King[6], with one or two anachronisms, forbids us to assign it an earlier date. King James I., who was prisoner in this kingdom at the death of his father[7], did not wear the crown of Scotland till the second year of our Henry VI.[8], but before the end of that long reign, a third James had mounted the throne[9]. A succession of two or three Jameses, and the long detention of one of them in England, would render the name familiar to the English, and dispose a poet in those rude times to give it to any Scottish king he happened to mention.

[2] Subscribed, after the usual manner of our old poets, expliceth [explicit] quoth Rychard Sheale.

[3] One of the earliest productions of the Scottish press now to be found. The title-page was wanting in the copy here quoted; but it is supposed to have been printed in 1540. See Ames.

[4] See Pt. 2. v. 25.

[5] See Pt. 1. v. 99.

[6] Pt. 2. v. 36, 140.

[7] Who died Aug. 5, 1406, in the seventh year of our Hen. IV.

[8] James I. was crowned May 22, 1424; murdered, Feb. 21, 1436-7.

[9] In 1460. Hen. VI. was deposed 1461; restored and slain, 1471.

So much for the date of this old ballad: with regard to its subject, although it has no countenance from history, there is room to think it had originally some foundation in fact. It was one of the laws of the Marches, frequently renewed between the two nations, that neither party should hunt in the other's borders, without leave from the proprietors or their deputies[10]. There had long been a rivalship between the two martial families of Percy and Douglas, which, heightened by the national quarrel, must have produced frequent challenges and struggles for superiority, petty invasions of their respective domains, and sharp contests for the point of honour, which would not always be recorded in history. Something of this kind we may suppose gave rise to the ancient ballad of the HUNTING A' THE CHEVIAT[1]. Percy, Earl of Northumberland, had vowed to hunt for three days in the Scottish border without condescending to ask leave from Earl Douglas, who was either lord of the soil, or lord-warden of the Marches. Douglas would not fail to resent the insult, and endeavour to repel the intruders by force: this would naturally produce a sharp conflict between the two parties; something of which, it is probable, did really happen, though not attended with the tragical circumstances recorded in the ballad; for these are evidently borrowed from the BATTLE OF OTTERBOURN[2], a very different event, but which after-times would easily confound with it. That battle might be owing to some such previous affront as this of CHEVY-CHASE, though it has escaped the notice of historians. Our poet has evidently jumbled the two events together; if, indeed, the lines[3] in which this mistake is made are not

[10] Item ... Concordatum est, quod, ... NULLUS unius partis vel alterius ingrediatur terras, boschas, forrestas, warrenas, loca, dominia quæcunque alicujus partis alterius subditi, causa venandi, piscandi, aucupandi, disportum aut solatium in eisdem, aliave quacunque de causa, ABSQUE LICENTIA ejus .... ad quem ... loca ..... pertinent, aut de deputatis suis prius capt. et obtent. Vide Bp. Nicholson's *Leges Marchiarum*, 1705, 8vo. pp. 27, 51.

[1] This was the original title. See the ballad, Pt. 1. v. 101. Pt. 2. v. 165.

[2] See the next ballad.

[3] Vide Pt. 2. v. 167.

rather spurious, and the after-insertion of some person, who did not distinguish between the two stories.

Hearne has printed this ballad without any division of stanzas, in long lines, as he found it in the old written copy; but it is usual to find the distinction of stanzas neglected in ancient MSS., where, to save room, two or three verses are frequently given in one line undivided. See flagrant instances in the Harleian Catalogue, No. 2253, s. 29, 34, 61, 70, et passim.

---

### THE FIRST FIT.[4]

The Persè owt of Northombarlande,
  And a vowe to God mayd he,
That he wolde hunte in the mountayns
  Off Chyviat within dayes thre,
In the mauger of doughtè Dogles,
  And all that ever with him be.

The fattiste hartes in all Cheviat
  He sayd he wold kill, and cary them away:
Be my feth, sayd the dougheti Doglas agayn,
  I wyll let that hontyng yf that I may.

Then the Persè owt of Banborowe cam,
  With him a myghtye meany:
With fifteen hondrith archares bold;
  The wear chosen out of shyars thre[5].

Ver. 5, maggcr in Hearne's P. C. [Printed Copy.] V. 11, The the Persè. P. C. V. 13, archardes bolde off blood and bone. P. C.

[4] Fit, see v. 100.

[5] By these "shyars thre" is probably meant three districts in Northumberland, which still go by the name of *shires*, and are all in the neighbourhood of Cheviot. These are *Island-shire*, being the district so named from Holy-Island: *Norehamshire*, so called from the town and castle of Noreham (or Norham); and *Bamboroughshire*, the ward or hundred belonging to Bamborough-castle and town.

This begane on a monday at morn
In Cheviat the hillys so he;
The chyld may rue that ys un-born,
It was the mor pittè.

The dryvars thorowe the woodes went
For to reas the dear;
Bomen bickarte uppone the bent
With ther browd aras cleare.

Then the wyld thorowe the woodes went
On every syde shear;
Grea-hondes thorowe the greves glent
For to kyll thear dear.

The begane in Chyviat the hyls above
Yerly on a monnyn day;
Be that it drewe to the oware off none
A hondrith fat hartes ded there lay.

The blewe a mort uppone the bent,
The semblyd on sydis shear;
To the quyrry then the Persè went
To se the bryttlynge off the deare.

He sayd, It was the Duglas promys
This day to meet me hear;
But I wyste he wold faylle verament:
A gret oth the Persè swear.

At the laste a squyar of Northombelonde
Lokyde at his hand full ny,
He was war ath the doughetie Doglas comynge:
With him a myghtè meany,

Both with spear, 'byll,' and brande:
Yt was a myghti sight to se.

V. 19, throrowe. P.C. V. 31, blwe a mot. P.C. V. 42, myghtte, P.C. passim. V. 43, brylly. P.C.

Hardyar men both off hart nar hande
 Wear not in Christiantè.

The wear twenty hondrith spear-men good
 Withouten any fayle;
The wear borne a-long be the watter a Twyde,
 Yth bowndes of Tividale.

Leave off the brytlyng of the dear, he sayde,
 And to your bowys tayk good heed;
For never sithe ye wear on your mothars borne
 Had ye never so mickle need.

The dougheti Dogglas on a stede
 He rode att his men beforne;
His armor glytteryde as dyd a glede;
 A bolder barne was never born.

Tell me 'what' men ye ar, he says,
 Or whos men that ye be:
Who gave youe leave to hunte in this
 Chyviat chays in the spyt of me?

The first mane that ever him an answear mayd,
 Yt was the good lord Persè:
We wyll not tell the 'what' men we ar, he says,
 Nor whos men that we be;
But we wyll hount hear in this chays
 In the spyte of thyne, and of the.

The fattiste hartes in all Chyviat
 We have kyld, and cast to carry them a-way.
Be my troth, sayd the doughtè Dogglas agayn,
 Ther-for the ton of us shall de this day.

V. 48, withowte . . . feale. P. C. V. 52, boys look ye tayk. P. C. V. 54, ned. P. C. V. 59, whos. P. C. V. 65, whoys. P. C. V. 71, agay. P. C.

Then sayd the doughtè Doglas
  Unto the lord Persè:
To kyll all thes giltles men,
  A-las! it wear great pittè.

But, Persè, thowe art a lord of lande,
  I am a yerle callyd within my contre;
Let all our men uppone a parti stande;
  And do the battell off the and of me.

Nowe Cristes corse on his crowne, sayd the lord Persè,
  Who-soever ther-to says nay.
Be my troth, doughtè Doglas, he says,
  Thow shalt never se that day;

Nethar in Ynglonde, Skottlonde, nar France,
  Nor for no man of a woman born,
But and fortune be my chance,
  I dar met him on man for on.

Then bespayke a squyar off Northombarlonde,
  Ric. Wytharynton[6] was his nam;
It shall never be told in Sothe-Ynglonde, he says,
  To kyng Herry the fourth for sham.

I wat youe byn great lordes twa,
  I am a poor squyar of lande;
I wyll never se my captayne fyght on a fylde,
  And stande my-selffe, and looke on,
But whyll I may my weppone welde
  I wyll not 'fayl' both harte and hande.

V. 81, sayd the the. P.C. V. 88, on, *i. e.* one.
V. 93, twaw. P.C.

[6] This is probably corrupted in the MS. for Rog. Widdrington, who was at the head of the family in the reign of King Edw. III. There were several successively of the names of *Roger* and *Ralph*, but none of the name of *Richard*, as appears from the genealogies in the Herald's office.

That day, that day, that dredfull day:
  The first FIT[7] here I fynde.
And you wyll here any mor athe hountyng athe Chyviat,
  Yet ys ther mor behynde.

---

### THE SECOND FIT.

THE Ynglishe men hade ther bowys yebent,
  Ther hartes were good yenoughe;
The first of arros that the shote off,
  Seven skore spear-men the sloughe.

Yet bydys the yerle Doglas uppon the bent,
  A captayne good yenoughe,
And that was sene verament,
  For he wrought hom both woo and wouche.

The Dogglas pertyd his ost in thre,
  Lyk a cheffe cheften off pryde,
With suar speares off myghttè tre
  The cum in on every syde.

Thrughe our Ynglishe archery
  Gave many a wounde full wyde;
Many a doughete the garde to dy,
  Which ganyde them no pryde.

The Ynglyshe men let thear bowys be,
  And pulde owt brandes that wer bright;
It was a hevy syght to se
  Bryght swordes on basnites lyght.

Thorowe ryche male, and myne-ye-ple
  Many sterne the stroke downe streight:

V. 101, youe. . . . hountyng. P. C. V. 3, first, *i. e.* flight. V. 5, byddys. P. C. V. 17, boys. P. C. V. 18, briggt. P. C. V. 21, throrowe. P. C. V. 22, done. P. C.

[7] FIT, vide Gloss.

Many a freyke, that was full free,
Ther undar foot dyd lyght.

At last the Duglas and the Persè met,
Lyk to captayns of myght and mayne;
The swapte togethar tyll the both swat
With swordes, that wear of fyn myllàn.

Thes worthè freckys for to fyght
Ther-to the wear full fayne,
Tyll the bloode owte off thear basnetes sprente,
As ever dyd heal or rayne.

Holde the, Persè, sayd the Doglas,
And i' feth I shall the brynge
Wher thowe shalte have a yerls wagis
Of Jamy our Scottish kynge.

Thoue shalte have thy ransom fre,
I hight the hear this thinge,
For the manfullyste man yet art thowe,
That ever I conqueryd in filde fightyng.

Nay 'then' sayd the lord Persè,
I tolde it the beforne,
That I wolde never yeldyde be
To no man of a woman born.

With that ther cam an arrowe hastely
Forthe off a mightie wane[8],
Hit hathe strekene the yerle Duglas
In at the brest bane.

V. 26, to, *i. e.* two. Ibid. and of, P. C. V. 32, ran. P. C.
V. 33, helde. P. C.

[8] Wane, *i. e.* ane. *one*, sc. *man*: an arrow came from a mighty one: from a mighty man.

Thoroue lyvar and longs bathe
 The sharp arrowe ys gane,
That never after in all his lyffe days
 He spayke mo wordes but ane,
That was[9], Fyghte ye, my merry men, whyllys ye may,
 For my lyff days ben gan.

The Persè leanyde on his brande,
 And sawe the Duglas de;
He tooke the dede man be the hande,
 And sayd, Wo ys me for the!

To have savyde thy lyffe I wold have pertyd with
 My landes for years thre,
For a better man of hart, nare of hande
 Was not in all the north countrè.

Off all that se a Skottishe knyght,
 Was callyd Sir Hewe the Mongon-byrry,
He sawe the Duglas to the deth was dyght;
 He spendyd a spear a trusti tre:

He rod uppon a corsiare
 Throughe a hondrith archery;
He never styntyde, nar never blane
 Tyll he came to the good lord Persè.

He set uppone the lord Persè
 A dynte, that was full soare;
With a suar spear of a myghtè tre
 Clean thorow the body he the Persè bore,

Athe tothar syde, that a man myght se,
 A large cloth yard and mare:
Towe bettar captayns wear nat in Cristiantè,
 Then that day slain wear thare.

V. 49, throroue. P.C. V. 74, ber. P.C. V. 78, ther. P.C.

[9] This seems to have been a gloss added.

An archar of Northomberlonde
  Say slean was the lord Persè,
He bar a bende-bow in his hande,
  Was made off trusti tre:

An arow, that a cloth yarde was lang,
  To th' hard stele halyde he;
A dynt, that was both sad and soar,
  He sat on Sir Hewe the Mongon-byrry.

The dynt yt was both sad and 'soar,'
  That he of Mongon-byrry sete;
The swane-fethars, that his arrowe bar,
  With his hart blood the wear wete[10].

Ther was never a freake wone foot wolde fle,
  But still in stour dyd stand,
Heawyng on yche othar, whyll the myght dre,
  With many a bal ful brande.

This battell begane in Chyviat
  An owar befor the none,
And when even-song bell was rang
  The battell was nat half done.

The tooke 'on' on ethar hand
  Be the lyght off the mone;
Many hade no strength for to stande,
  In Chyviat the hyllys abone.

Of fifteen hondrith archers of Ynglonde
  Went away but fifti and thre;
Of twenty hondrith spear-men of Skotlonde,
  But even five and fifti:

V. 80, Say, *i.e.* sawe. V. 84, haylde. P. C. V. 87, sar. P. C. V. 102, abou. P. C.

[10] This incident is taken from the battle of Otterbourn; in which Sir Hugh Montgomery, Knt. (son of John Lord Montgomery) was slain with an arrow. Vide Crawfurd's Peerage.

But all wear slayne Cheviat within:
The hade no strengthe to stand on he:
The chylde may rue that is un-borne,
It was the mor pittè.

Thear was slayne with the lord Persè
Sir John of Agerstone,
Sir Roger the hinde Hartly,
Sir Wyllyam the bolde Hearone.

Sir Jorg the worthè Lovele
A knyght of great renowen,
Sir Raff the ryche Rugbè
With dyntes wear beaten dowene.

For Wetharryngton my harte was wo,
That ever he slayne shulde be;
For when both his leggis wear hewyne in to,
He knyled and fought on hys kne.

Ther was slayne with the dougheti Douglas
Sir Hewe the Mongon-byrry,
Sir Davye Lwdale, that worthè was,
His sistars son was he:

Sir Charles a Murrè, in that place,
That never a foot wolde fle;
Sir Hewe Maxwell, a lorde he was,
With the Duglas dyd he dey.

So on the morrowe the mayde them byears
Off byrch, and hasell so 'gray';
Many wedous with wepyng tears[1],
Cam to fach ther makys a-way.

V. 108, strenge . . . . hy. P. C. V. 115, lóule. P. C. V. 121, in to, *i. e.* in two. V. 122, Yet he . . . . kny. P. C. V. 132, gay. P. C.

[1] A common pleonasm, see the next poem, Fit 2nd, v. 155. So Harding in his *Chronicle*, chap. 140, fol. 148, describing the death of Richard I., says,

Tivydale may carpe off care,
  Northombarlond may mayk grat mone,
For towe such captayns, as slayne wear thear,
  On the march perti shall never be none.

Word ys commen to Edden-burrowe
  To Jamy the Skottishe kyng,
That dougheti Duglas, lyff-tenant of the Merches,
  He lay slean Chyviot with-in.

His handdes dyd he weal and wryng,
  He sayd, Alas, and woe ys me!
Such another captayn Scotland within,
  He said, y-feth shuld never be.

Worde ys commyn to lovly Londone
  Till the fourth Harry our kyng,
That lord Persè, leyff-tennante of the Merchis,
  He lay slayne Chyviat within.

God have merci on his soll, sayd kyng Harry,
  Good lord, yf thy will it be!
I have a hondrith captayns in Yynglonde, he sayd,
  As good as ever was hee:
But Persè, and I brook my lyffe,
  Thy deth well quyte shall be.

As our noble kyng made his a-vowe,
  Lyke a noble prince of renowen,
For the deth of the lord Persè,
  He dyd the battel of Hombyll-down:

V. 136, mon. P.C. V. 138, non. P.C.

For the names in this and the foregoing page, see the remarks at the end of the next ballad.

V. 146, ye seth. P.C. V. 149, cheyff tennante. P.C.

---

He shrove him then unto Abbots thre
With great sobbyng . . . . and wepyng teares.

So likewise Cavendish, in his *Life of Cardinal Wolsey*, chap. 12, p. 31, 4to. "When the Duke heard this, he replied with weeping teares," &c.

Wher syx and thritte Skottish knyghtes
  On a day wear beaten down:
Glendale glytteryde on ther armor bryght,
  Over castill, towar, and town.

This was the hontynge off the Cheviat;
  That tear begane this spurn:
Old men that knowen the grownde well yenoughe,
  Call it the Battell of Otterburn.

At Otterburn began this spurne:
  Uppon a monnyn day:
Ther was the dougghtè Doglas slean,
  The Persè never went away.

Ther was never a tym on the march partes
  Sen the Doglas, and the Persè met,
But yt was marvele, and the rede blude ronne not,
  As the reane doys in the stret.

Jhesue Crist our balys bete,
  And to the blys us brynge!
Thus was the hountynge of the Chevyat:
  God send us all good ending!

---

*** The style of this and the following ballad is uncommonly rugged and uncouth, owing to their being writ in the very coarsest and broadest northern dialect.

The battle of Hombyll-down, or Humbledon, was fought Sept. 14, 1402 (anno 3 Hen. IV.), wherein the English, under the command of the E. of Northumberland and his son Hotspur, gained a complete victory over the Scots. The village of Humbledon is one mile north-west from Wooller in Northumberland. The battle was fought in the field below the village, near the present turnpike-road, in a spot called ever since *Red-Riggs*. Humbledon is in Glendale Ward, a district so named in this county, and mentioned above in ver. 163.

---

## II.

## The Battle of Otterbourne.

The only battle, wherein an Earl of Douglas was slain fighting with a Percy, was that of Otterbourn, which is the subject of this ballad. It is here related with the allowable partiality of an English poet, and much in the same manner as it is recorded in the English Chronicles. The Scottish writers have, with a partiality at least as excusable, related it no less in their own favour. Luckily we have a very circumstantial narrative of the whole affair from Froissart, a French historian, who appears to be unbiassed. Froissart's relation is prolix; I shall therefore give it as abridged by Carte, who has however had recourse to other authorities, and differs from Froissart in some things, which I shall note in the margin.

In the twelfth year of Richard II., 1388, "The Scots taking advantage of the confusions of this nation, and falling with a party into the west Marches, ravaged the country about Carlisle, and carried off 300 prisoners. It was with a much greater force, headed by some of the principal nobility, that, in the beginning of August[1], they invaded Northumberland: and having wasted part of the county of Durham[2], advanced to the gates of Newcastle; where, in a skirmish, they took a 'penon' or colours[3] belonging to Henry Lord Percy, surnamed Hotspur, son to the Earl of Northumberland. In their retreat home, they attacked the castle of Otterbourn; and in the evening of August 9 (as the English writers say, or rather, according to Froissart, August 15),

[1] Froissart speaks of both parties (consisting in all of more than 40,000 men) as entering England at the same time; but the greater part by way of Carlisle.

[2] And, according to the ballad, that part of Northumberland called Bamboroughshire, a large tract of land so named from the town and castle of Bamborough, formerly the residence of the Northumbrian kings.

[3] This circumstance is omitted in the ballad. Hotspur and Douglas were two young warriors much of the same age.

after an unsuccessful assault were surprised in their camp, which was very strong, by Henry, who at the first onset put them into a good deal of confusion. But James Earl of Douglas rallying his men, there ensued one of the best-fought actions that happened in that age; both armies showing the utmost bravery[4]: the Earl Douglas himself being slain on the spot[5]; the Earl of Murrey mortally wounded; and Hotspur[6], with his brother Ralph Percy, taken prisoners. These disasters on both sides have given occasion to the event of the engagement's being disputed: Froissart (who derives his relation from a Scotch knight, two gentlemen of the same country, and as many of Foix[7]) affirming that the Scots remained masters of the field; and the English writers insinuating the contrary. These last maintain that the English had the better of the day; but night coming on, some of the northern lords, coming with the Bishop of Durham to their assistance, killed many of them by mistake, supposing them to be Scots; and the Earl of Dunbar at the same time falling on another side upon Hotspur, took him and his brother prisoners, and carried them off while both parties were fighting. It is at least certain, that immediately after this battle the Scots engaged in it made the best of their way home: and the same party was taken by the other corps about Carlisle."

Such is the account collected by Carte, in which he

[4] Froissart says the English exceeded the Scots in number three to one, but that these had the advantage of the ground, and were also fresh from sleep, while the English were greatly fatigued with their previous march.

[5] By Henry L. Percy, according to this ballad, and our old English historians, as Stow, Speed, &c.; but borne down by numbers, if we may believe Froissart.

[6] Hotspur (after a very sharp conflict) was taken prisoner by John Lord Montgomery, whose eldest son Sir Hugh was slain in the same action with an arrow, according to Crawfurd's Peerage (and seems also to be alluded to in the foregoing ballad, p. 11), but taken prisoner and exchanged for Hotspur, according to this ballad.

[7] Froissart (according to the Eng. Translation) says he had his account from two squires of England, and from a knight and squire of Scotland, soon after the battle.

seems not to be free from partiality: for prejudice must own that Froissart's circumstantial account carries a great appearance of truth, and he gives the victory to the Scots. He however does justice to the courage of both parties; and represents their mutual generosity in such a light, that the present age might edify by the example. "The Englyshmen on the one partye, and Scottes on the other party, are good men of warre, for whan they mete, there is a hard fighte without sparynge. There is no hoo[8] betwene them as long as speares, swordes, axes, or dagers wyll endure: but lay on eche upon other: and whan they be well beaten, and that the one party hath obtayned the victory, they than glorifye so in their dedes of armes, and are so joyfull, that suche as be taken, they shall be ransomed or they go out of the felde[9]; so that shortely ECHE OF THEM IS SO CONTENTE WITH OTHER, THAT AT THEIR DEPARTYNGE, CURTOYSLY THEY WILL SAYE, GOD THANKE YOU. But in fyghtynge one with another there is no playe, nor sparynge."—Froissart's Cronycle (as translated by Sir Johan Bourchier Lord Berners,) cap. cxlij.

The following ballad is (in this present edition) printed from an old MS. in the Cotton Library[10] (Cleopatra, c. iv.), and contains many stanzas more than were in the former copy, which was transcribed from a MS. in the Harleian Collection [No. 293, fol. 52]. In the Cotton MS. this poem has no title, but in the Harleian copy it is thus inscribed, "A songe made in R. 2. his tyme of the battele of Otterburne, betweene Lord Henry Percye earle of Northomberlande and the earle Douglas of Scotlande. Anno 1388." But this title is erroneous, and added by some ignorant transcriber of after-times: for, 1. The battle was not fought by the Earl of Northumberland, who was absent, nor is once

[8] So in Langham's letter concerning Queen Elizabeth's entertainment at Killingworth Castle, 1575, 12mo. p. 61, "Heer was no ho in devout drinkyng."

[9] *i. e.* They scorn to take the advantage, or to keep them lingering in long captivity.

[10] The notice of this MS. I must acknowledge, with many other obligations, owing to the friendship of Thomas Tyrwhitt, Esq. late Clerk of the House of Commons.

mentioned in the ballad; but by his son SIR HENRY PERCY, Knt. surnamed HOTSPUR (in those times they did not usually give the title of LORD to an earl's eldest son). 2. Although the battle was fought in Richard II.'s time, the song is evidently of later date, as appears from the poet's quoting the Chronicles in Pt. II. ver. 26; and speaking of Percy in the last stanza as dead. It was however written, in all likelihood, as early as the foregoing song, if not earlier; which perhaps may be inferred from the minute circumstances with which the story is related, many of which are recorded in no chronicle, and were probably preserved in the memory of old people. It will be observed, that the authors of these two poems have some lines in common; but which of them was the original proprietor must depend upon their priority; and this the sagacity of the reader must determine.

---

YT felle abowght the Lamasse tyde,
  When husbonds wynn ther haye,
The dowghtye Dowglasse bowynd hym to ryde,
  In Ynglond to take a praye:

The yerlle of Fyffe[1], withowghten stryffe,
  He bowynd hym over Sulway[2]:
The grete wolde ever together ryde;
  That race they may rue for aye.

Over 'Ottercap' hyll they[3] came in,
  And so dowyn by Rodelyffe cragge,

Ver. 2. wynn their heaye. Harl. MS. This is the Northumberland phrase to this day: by which they always express "getting in their hay." The orig. MS. reads here *winn their waye.*

[1] Robert Stuart, second son of King Robert II.

[2] *i. e.* "Over Solway frith." This evidently refers to the other division of the Scottish army, which came in by way of Carlisle. Bowynd, or bounde him; *i. e.* hied him. Vide Gloss.

[3] They: sc. the Earl of Douglas and his party.—The several stations here mentioned, are well-known places in Northumberland. Ottercap hill

Upon Grene 'Leyton' they lyghted dowyn,
  Styrande many a stagge[4]:

And boldely brente Northomberlonde,
  And haryed many a towyn;
They dyd owr Ynglyssh men grete wrange,
  To battell that were not bowyn.

Then spake a berne upon the bent,
  Of comforte that was not colde,
And sayd, We have brent Northomberlond,
  We have all welth in holde.

Now we have haryed all Bamboroweshyre,
  All the welth in the worlde have wee;
I rede we ryde to Newe Castell,
  So styll and stalwurthlye.

Uppon the morowe, when it was daye,
  The standards schone fulle bryght;
To the Newe Castelle the toke the waye,
  And thether they cam fulle ryght.

Sir Henry Percy laye at the Newe Castelle,
  I telle yow withowtten drede;
He had byn a marche-man[5] all hys dayes,
  And kepte Barwyke upon Twede.

To the Newe Castell when they cam,
  The Skottes they cryde on hyght,

is in the parish of Kirk-Whelpington, in Tynedaleward. Rodeliff- (or as it is more usually pronounced Rodeley-) Cragge is a noted cliff near Rodeley, a small village in the parish of Hartburn, in Morpethward: it lies south-east of Ottercap. Green Leyton is another small village in the same parish of Hartburn, and is south-east of Rodeley. — Both the orig. MSS. read here corruptly, Hoppertop and Lynton.

[4] This line is corrupt in both the MSS. viz. 'Many a styrande stage.'— Stags have been killed within the present century on some of the large wastes in Northumberland.

[5] Marche-man, *i. e.* a scourer of the Marches.

9*

Syr Harye Percy, and thou byste within,
  Com to the fylde, and fyght:

For we have brente Northomberlonde,
  Thy eritage good and ryght;
And syne my logeyng I have take,
  With my brande dubbyd many a knyght.

Sir Harry Percy cam to the walles
  The Skottyssh oste for to se;
"And thow hast brente Northomberlond,
  Full sore it rewyth me.

Yf thou hast haryed all Bambarowe shyre,
  Thow hast done me grete envye;
For the trespasse thow hast me done,
  The tone of us schall dye."

Where schall I byde the? sayd the Dowglas,
  Or where wylte thow come to me?
"At Otterborne in the hygh way[6],
  Ther maist thow well logeed be

The roo full rekeles ther sche rinnes,
  To make the game and glee:
The fawkon and the fesaunt both,
  Amonge the holtes on 'hee.'

Ther maist thow have thy welth at wyll,
  Well looged ther maist be.
Yt schall not be long, or I com the tyll,"
  Sayd Syr Harry Percye.

V. 39, *syne* seems here to mean *since*. V. 53, Roe-bucks were to be found upon the wastes not far from Hexham in the reign of George I.:— Whitfield, Esq., of Whitfield, is said to have destroyed the last of them. V. 56, hye. MSS.

[6] Otterbourn stands near the old Watling-street road, in the parish of Elsdon. The Scots were encamped in a grassy plain near the river Read. The place where the Scots and English fought is still called Battle Riggs.

Ther schall I byde the, sayd the Dowglas,
By the fayth of my bodye.
Thether schall I com, sayd Syr Harry Percy;
My trowth I plyght to the.

A pype of wyne he gave them over the walles,
For soth, as I yow saye:
Ther he mayd the Douglas drynke,
And all hys oste that daye.

The Dowglas turnyd hym homewarde agayne,
For soth withowghten naye,
He tooke his logeyng at Oterborne
Uppon a Wedyns-day:

And ther he pyght hys standerd dowyn,
Hys gettyng more and lesse,
And syne he warned hys men to goo
To chose ther geldyngs gresse.

A Skottysshe knyght hoved upon the bent,
A wache I dare well saye:
So was he ware on the noble Percy
In the dawnynge of the daye.

He prycked to his pavyleon dore,
As faste as he myght ronne,
Awaken, Dowglas, cryed the knyght,
For hys love, that syttes yn trone.

Awaken, Dowglas, cryed the knyght,
For thow maiste waken wyth wynne.
Yender have I spyed the prowde Percy,
And seven standardes wyth hym.

Nay by my trowth, the Douglas sayed,
It ys but a fayned taylle:

V. 77, upon the best bent. MS.

He durste not loke on my bred banner,
  For all Ynglonde so haylle.

Was I not yesterdaye at the Newe Castell,
  That stonds so fayre on Tyne?
For all the men that Percy hade,
  He cowde not garre me ones to dyne.

He stepped owt at hys pavelyon dore,
  To loke and it were lesse;
Araye yow, lordyngs, one and all,
  For here bygynnes no peysse.

The yerle of Mentaye[7], thow arte my eme,
  The fowarde I gyve to the:
The yerlle of Huntlay cawte and kene,
  He schall wyth the be.

The lorde of Bowghan[8] in armure bryght
  On the other hand he schall be:
Lorde Jhonstone, and lorde Maxwell,
  They to schall be with me.

Swynton fayre fylde upon your pryde
  To batell make yow bowen:
Syr Davy Scotte, Syr Walter Stewarde,
  Syr Jhon of Agurstone.

A FYTTE.

---

The Perssy came byfore hys oste,
  Wych was ever a gentyll knyght,
Upon the Dowglas lowde can he crye,
  I wyll holde that I have hyght:

For thow haste brente Northumberlonde,
  And done me grete envye;

V. 1, 13, Pearcy, al. MS.   V. 4, I will hold to what I have promised.

[7] The Earl of Menteith.   [8] The Lord Buchan.

For thys trespasse thou hast me done,
  The tone of us schall dye.

The Dowglas answerde hym agayne
  With grete wurds up on 'hee,'
And sayd, I have twenty agaynst 'thy' one[9],
  Byholde and thow maiste see.

Wyth that the Percye was grevyd sore,
  For sothe as I yow saye:
[10][He lyghted dowyn upon his fote,
  And schoote his horsse clene away.

Every man sawe that he dyd soo,
  That ryall was ever in rowght;
Every man schoote hys horsse him froo,
  And lyght him rowynde abowght.

Thus Syr Hary Percye toke the fylde,
  For soth, as I yow saye:
Jesu Cryste in hevyn on hyght
  Dyd helpe hym well that daye.

But nyne thowzand, ther was no moo;
  The cronykle wyll not layne:
Forty thowsande Skottes and fowre
  That day fowght them agayne.

But when the batell byganne to joyne,
  In hast ther came a knyght,
'Then' letters fayre furth hath he tayne
  And thus he sayd full ryght:

My lorde, your father he gretes yow well,
  Wyth many a noble knyght;

Ver. 10, hye. MSS.     Ver. 11, the one. MS.

[9] He probably magnifies his strength, to induce him to surrender.
[10] All that follows, included in brackets, was not in the first edition.

He desyres yow to byde
  That he may see thys fyght.

The Baron of Grastoke ys com owt of the west,
  Wyth hym a noble companye;
All they loge at your fathers thys nyght,
  And the Battel fayne wold they see.

For Jesu's love, sayd Syr Harye Percy,
  That dyed for yow and me,
Wende to my lorde my Father agayne,
  And saye thow saw me not with yee:

My trowth ys plyght to yonne Skottysh knyght,
  It nedes me not to layne,
That I schulde byde hym upon thys bent,
  And I have hys trowth agayne:

And if that I wende off thys grownde
  For soth unfoughten awaye,
He wolde me call but a kowarde knyght
  In hys londe another daye.

Yet had I lever to be rynde and rente,
  By Mary that mykel maye;
Then ever my manhod schulde be reprovyd
  Wyth a Skotte another daye.

Wherfore schote, archars, for my sake,
  And let scharpe arowes flee:
Mynstrells, playe up for your waryson,
  And well quyt it schall be.

Every man thynke on hys trewe love,
  And marke hym to the Trenite:
For to God I make myne avowe
  This day wyll I not fle.

The blodye Harte in the Dowglas armes,
  Hys standerde stode on hye;

That every man myght full well knowe:
  By syde stode Starres thre.

The whyte Lyon on the Ynglysh parte,
  Forsoth as I yow sayne;
The Lucetts and the Cressawnts both:
  The Skotts faught them agayne[1].]

Uppon sent Andrewe lowde cane they crye,
  And thrysse they schowte on hyght,
And syne marked them one owr Ynglysshe men,
  As I have tolde yow ryght.

Sent George the bryght owr ladyes knyght,
  To name they[2] were full fayne,
Owr Ynglysshe men they cryde on hyght,
  And thrysse the schowtte agayne.

Wyth that scharpe arowes bygan to flee,
  I tell yow in sertayne;
Men of armes byganne to joyne;
  Many a dowghty man was ther slayne.

The Percy and the Dowglas mette,
  That ether of other was fayne;
They schapped together, whyll that the swette,
  With swords of fyne Collayne;

Tyll the blood from ther bassonetts ranne,
  As the roke doth in the rayne.
Yelde the to me, sayd the Dowglàs,
  Or ells thow schalt be slayne:

[1] The arms of Douglas are pretty accurately emblazoned in the former stanza, especially if the readings were, *The crowned harte,* and *Above stode starres thre,* it would be minutely exact at this day. As for the Percy family, one of their ancient badges or cognizances was *a white lyon,* statant; and the *silver crescent* continues to be used by them to this day: they also give *three luces argent* for one of their quarters.

[2] *i. e.* The English.

For I see, by thy bryght bassonet,
  Thow arte sum man of myght;
And so I do by thy burnysshed brande,
  Thow art an yerle, or ells a knyght[3].

By my good faythe, sayd the noble Percy,
  Now haste thou rede full ryght,
Yet wyll I never yelde me to the,
  Whyll I may stonde and fyght.

They swapped together, whyll that they swette,
  Wyth swordes scharpe and long;
Ych on other so faste they beette,
  Tyll ther helmes cam in peyses dowyn.

The Percy was a man of strenghth,
  I tell yow in thys stounde,
He smote the Dowglas at the swordes length,
  That he felle to the growynde.

The sworde was scharpe and sore can byte,
  I tell yow in sertayne;
To the harte he cowde hym smyte,
  Thus was the Dowglas slayne.

The stonderds stode styll on eke syde,
  With many a grevous grone;
Ther the fowght the day, and all the nyght,
  And many a dowghty man was 'slone.'

Ther was no freke, that ther wolde flye,
  But styffly in stowre can stond,
Ychone hewyng on other whyll they myght drye,
  Wyth many a baylllefull bronde.

V. 116, slayne. MSS.

[3] Being all in armour, he could not know him.

Ther was slayne upon the Skottes syde,
  For soth and sertenly,
Syr James a Dowglas ther was slayne,
  That daye that he cowde dye.

The yerlle of Mentaye he was slayne,
  Grysely groned uppon the growynd;
Syr Davy Scotte, Syr Walter Steward,
  Syr 'John' of Agurstonne[4].

Syr Charlles Morrey in that place
  That never a fote wold flye;
Sir Hughe Maxwell, a lord he was,
  With the Dowglas dyd he dye.

Ther was slayne upon the Skottes syde,
  For soth as I yow saye,
Of fowre and forty thowsande Scotts
  Went but eyghtene awaye.

Ther was slayne upon the Ynglysshe syde,
  For soth and sertenlye,
A gentell knyght, Sir John Fitz-hughe,
  Yt was the more petye.

Syr James Harebotell ther was slayne,
  For hym ther hartes were sore,
The gentyll 'Lovelle' ther was slayne,
  That the Percyes standerd bore.

Ther was slayne uppon the Ynglyssh perte,
  For soth as I yow saye;

V. 124, *i. e.* he died that day. V. 143, Covelle. MS. For the names in this page, see the remarks at the end of this ballad.

[4] Our old minstrel repeats these names, as Homer and Virgil do those of their heroes:

—— fortemque Gyam, fortemque Cloanthum, &c. &c.

Both the MSS. read here, "Sir James:" but see above, Pt. 1. ver. 112.

Of nyne thowsand Ynglyssh men
  Fyve hondert cam awaye:

The other were slayne in the fylde,
  Cryste kepe ther sowles from wo,
Seyng ther was so fewe fryndes
  Agaynst so many a foo.

Then one the morne they mayd them beeres
  Of byrch, and haysell graye;
Many a wydowe with wepyng teyres
  Ther makes they fette awaye.

Thys fraye bygan at Otterborne
  Bytwene the nyghte and the day:
Ther the Dowglas lost hys lyfe,
  And the Percy was lede awaye[5].

Then was ther a Scottyshe prisoner tayne,
  Syr Hughe Mongomery was hys name,
For soth as I yow saye
  He borowed the Percy home agayne[6].

Now let us all for the Percy praye
  To Jesu most of myght,
To bryng hys sowle to the blysse of heven,
  For he was a gentyll knyght.

---

*** Most of the names in the two preceding ballads are found to have belonged to families of distinction in the North, as may be made appear from authentic records. Thus, in

THE ANCIENT BALLAD OF CHEVY-CHASE.

Pag. 12. ver. 112. *Agerstone.*] The family of Haggerston

V. 153, one, *i. e.* on.  V. 165, Percyes. Harl. MS.

[5] Sc. captive.

[6] In the Cotton MS. is the following note on ver. 164, in an ancient hand: —"Syr Hewe Mongomery takyn prizonar, was delyvered for the restorynge of Perssy."

of Haggerston, near Berwick, has been seated there for many centuries, and still remains. Thomas Haggerston was among the commissioners returned for Northumberland in 12 Hen. VI. 1433 (Fuller's *Worthies*, p. 310.) The head of this family at present is Sir Thomas Haggerston, Bart., of Haggerston above mentioned.

N. B. The name is spelt Agerstone, as in the text, in Leland's *Itinerary*, vol. vii. p. 54.

Ver. 113. *Hartly.*] Hartley is a village near the sea, in the barony of Tinemouth, about seven miles from North-Shields. It probably gave name to a family of note at that time.

Ver. 114. *Hearone.*] This family, one of the most ancient, was long of great consideration in Northumberland. Haddeston, the *Caput Baroniæ* of Heron, was their ancient residence. It descended, 25 Edw. I., to the heir general, Emeline Heron, afterwards Baroness Darcy.—Ford, &c. and Bockenfield (*in com. eodem*), went at the same time to Roger Heron, the heir male, whose descendants were summoned to Parliament: Sir William Heron of Ford Castle being summoned 44 Edw. III.—Ford Castle hath descended by heirs general to the family of Delaval (mentioned in the next article). Robert Heron, Esq., who died at Newark in 1753, (father of the Right Hon. Sir Richard Heron, Bart.) was heir male of the Herons of Bockenfield, a younger branch of this family. Sir Thomas Heron Middleton, Bart., is heir male of the Herons of Chip-Chase, another branch of the Herons of Ford Castle.

Ver. 115. *Lovele.*] Joh. de Lavale, miles, was sheriff of Northumberland 34 Hen. VII. Joh. de Lavele, mil. in the 1 Ed. VI. and afterwards (Fuller, 313). In Nicholson this name is spelt Da Lovel, p. 304. This seems to be the ancient family of Delaval, of Seaton Delaval, in Northumberland, whose ancestor was one of the twenty-five barons appointed to be guardians of Magna Charta.

Ver. 117. *Rugbè.*] The ancient family of Rokeby in Yorkshire seems to be here intended. In Thoresby's *Ducat.*

*I eod.* p. 253, fol. is a genealogy of this house, by which it appears that the head of the family about the time when this ballad was written, was Sir Ralph Rokeby, Knt., Ralph being a common name of the Rokebys.

Ver. 119. *Wetharryngton.*] Rog. de Widrington was sheriff of Northumberland in 36 of Edw. III. (Fuller, p. 311.) Joh. de Widrington in 11 of Hen. IV., and many others of the same name afterwards. See also Nicholson, p. 331. Of this family was the late Lord Witherington.

Ver. 124. *Mongon-byrry.*] Sir Hugh Montgomery was son of John Lord Montgomery, the lineal ancestor of the present Earl of Eglington.

Ver. 125. *Lwdale.*] The ancient family of the Liddels were originally from Scotland, where they were lords of Liddel Castle, and of the barony of Buff (vide Collins's Peerage). The head of this family is the present Lord Ravensworth, of Ravensworth Castle, in the county of Durham.

### IN THE BATTLE OF OTTERBOURNE.

Pag. 22. ver. 101. *Mentaye.*] At the time of this battle, the earldom of Menteith was possessed by Robert Stewart, Earl of Fife, third son of K. Robert II., who, according to Buchanan, commanded the Scots that entered by Carlisle. But our minstrel had probably an eye to the family of Graham, who had this earldom when the ballad was written. See Douglas's *Peerage of Scotland*, 1764, fol.

Ver. 103. *Huntlay.*] This shows this ballad was not composed before 1449; for in that year Alexander, Lord of Gordon and Huntley, was created Earl of Huntley by K. James II.

Ver. 105. *Bowghan.*] The Earl of Buchan at that time was Alexander Stewart, fourth son of K. Robert II.

Ver. 107. *Jhonstone—Maxwell.*] These two families of Johnston Lord of Johnston, and Maxwell Lord of Maxwell, were always very powerful on the borders. Of the former family is Johnston Marquis of Annandale: of the latter is

Maxwell Earl of Nithsdale. I cannot find that any chief of this family was named Sir Hugh; but Sir Herbert Maxwell was about this time much distinguished (see Doug.). This might have been originally written Sir H. Maxwell, and by transcribers converted into Sir Hugh. See above, in No. I. v. 90, *Richard* is contracted into *Ric.*

Ver. 109. *Swynton.*] *i. e.* The Laird of Swintone, a small village within the Scottish border, three miles from Norham. This family still subsists, and is very ancient.

Ver. 111. *Scotte.*] The illustrious family of Scot, ancestors of the Duke of Buccleugh, always made a great figure on the borders. Sir Walter Scot was at the head of this family when the battle was fought; but his great-grandson, Sir David Scot, was the hero of that house when the ballad was written.

Ibid. *Stewarde.*] The person here designed was probably Sir Walter Stewart, Lord of Dalswinton and Gairlies, who was eminent at that time. (See Doug.) From him is descended the present Earl of Galloway.

Ver. 112. *Agurstone.*] The seat of this family was sometimes subject to the kings of Scotland. Thus Richardus Hagerstoun, miles, is one of the Scottish knights who signed a treaty with the English in 1249, temp. Hen. III. (Nicholson, p. 2, note.) It was the fate of many parts of Northumberland often to change their masters, according as the Scottish or English arms prevailed.

Ver. 129. *Morrey.*] The person here meant was probably Sir Charles Murray of Cockpoole, who flourished at that time, and was ancestor of the Murrays sometime Earls of Annandale. See Doug. Peerage.

Ver. 139. *Fitz-hughe.*] Dugdale (in his Baron. vol. i. p. 403) informs us, that John, son of Henry Lord Fitz-hugh, was killed at the battle of Otterbourne. This was a Northumberland family. Vide Dugd. p. 403, col. 1, and Nicholson, pp. 33, 60.

Ver. 141. *Harebotell.*] Harbottle is a village upon the river Coquet, about ten miles west of Rothbury. The family of Harbottle was once considerable in Northumberland. (See Fuller, pp. 312, 313.) A daughter of Sir Guischard Harbottle, Knt., married Sir Thomas Percy, Knt., son of Henry, the fifth, and father of Thomas, the seventh, Earls of Northumberland.

---

## III.

## The Jew's Daughter,

A SCOTTISH BALLAD,

Is founded upon the supposed practice of the Jews in crucifying or otherwise murthering Christian children, out of hatred to the religion of their parents: a practice which hath been always alleged in excuse for the cruelties exercised upon that wretched people, but which probably never happened in a single instance. For if we consider, on the one hand, the ignorance and superstition of the times when such stories took their rise, the virulent prejudices of the monks who record them, and the eagerness with which they would be catched up by the barbarous populace as a pretence for plunder; on the other hand, the great danger incurred by the perpetrators, and the inadequate motives they could have to excite them to a crime of so much horror, we may reasonably conclude the whole charge to be groundless and malicious.

The following ballad is probably built upon some Italian legend, and bears a great resemblance to the *Prioresse's Tale* in Chaucer: the poet seems also to have had an eye to the known story of *Hugh of Lincoln*, a child said to have been there murthered by the Jews in the reign of Henry III. The conclusion of this ballad appears to be wanting: what it probably contained may be seen in Chaucer. As for Mirry-land Toun, it is probably a corruption of Milan (called by the Dutch Meylandt) Town: the Pa is evidently the river Po; although the Adige, not the Po, runs through Milan.

Printed from a MS. copy sent from Scotland.

---

THE rain rins doun through Mirry-land toune,
  Sae dois it doune the Pa:
Sae dois the lads of Mirry-land toune,
  Quhan they play at the ba'.

Than out and cam the Jewis dochtèr,
  Said, Will ye cum in and dine?
I winnae cum in, I cannae cum in,
  Without my play-feres nine.

Scho powd an apple reid and white
  To intice the zong thing in:
Scho powd an apple white and reid,
  And that the sweit bairne did win.

And scho has taine out a little pen-knife,
  And low down by her gair,
Scho has twin'd the zong thing and his life;
  A word he nevir spak mair.

And out and cam the thick thick bluid,
  And out and cam the thin;
And out and cam the bonny herts bluid:
  Thair was nae life left in.

Scho laid him on a dressing borde,
  And drest him like a swine,
And laughing said, Gae nou and pley
  With zour sweit play-feres nine.

Scho rowd him in a cake of lead,
  Bade him lie stil and sleip.
Scho cast him in a deip draw-well,
  Was fifty fadom deip.

Quhan bells wer rung, and mass was sung,
  And every lady went hame:
Than ilka lady had her zong sonne,
  Bot lady Helen had nane.

Scho rowd hir mantil hir about,
  And sair sair gan she weip:
And she ran into the Jewis castèl,
  Quhan they were all asleip.

My bonny sir Hew, my pretty sir Hew,
  I pray thee to me speik:
'O lady, rinn to the deip draw-well
  'Gin ze zour sonne wad seik.'

Lady Helen ran to the deip draw-well,
  And knelt upon her kne:
My bonny sir Hew, an ze be here,
  I pray thee speik to me.

The lead is wondrous heavy, mither,
  The well is wondrous deip,
A keen pen knife sticks in my hert,
  A word I dounae speik.

Gae hame, gae hame, my mither deir,
  Fetch me my windling sheet,
And at the back o' Mirry-land toun,
  Its thair we twa sall meet.

* * * * *

---

## IV.

## Sir Cauline.

This old romantic tale was preserved in the Editor's folio MS., but in so very defective and mutilated a condition (not from any chasm in the MS., but from great omission in the transcript, probably copied from the faulty recitation of some illiterate minstrel), that it was necessary to supply several stanzas in the first part, and still more in the second, to connect and complete the story.

There is something peculiar in the metre of this old ballad: it is not unusual to meet with redundant stanzas of six lines; but the occasional insertion of a double third or fourth line, as ver. 31, 44, &c. is an irregularity I do not remember to have seen elsewhere.

It may be proper to inform the reader before he comes to Pt. 2. v. 110, 111, that the ROUND TABLE was not peculiar to the reign of K. Arthur, but was common in all the ages of chivalry. The proclaiming a great tournament (probably with some peculiar solemnities) was called "holding a Round Table." Dugdale tells us, that the great baron Roger de Mortimer "having procured the honour of knighthood to be conferred 'on his three sons' by K. Edw. I. he, at his own costs, caused a tourneament to be held at Kenilworth; where he sumptuously entertained an hundred knights, and as many ladies, for three days; the like whereof was never before in England; and there began the ROUND TABLE (so called by reason that the place wherein they practised those feats was environed with a strong wall made in a round form). And upon the fourth day, the golden lion, in sign of triumph, being yielded to him, he carried it (with all the company) to Warwick." — It may further be added, that Matthew Paris frequently calls jousts and tournaments *Hastiludia Mensæ Rotundæ*.

As to what will be observed in this ballad of the art of healing being practised by a young princess, it is no more than what is usual in all the old romances, and was conformable to real manners: it being a practice derived from the earliest times among all the Gothic and Celtic nations, for women, even of the highest rank, to exercise the art of surgery. In the *Northern Chronicles* we always find the young damsels stanching the wounds of their lovers, and the wives those of their husbands[1]. And even so late as the time of Q. Elizabeth, it is mentioned among the accomplishments of the ladies of her court, that the "eldest of them are *skilful in*

[1] See *Northern Antiquities*, &c., vol. i. p. 318; vol. ii. p. 100; *Mémoires de la Chevalerie*, tom. i. p. 44.

*surgery.*" See Harrison's *Description of England*, prefixed to Holingshed's Chronicle, &c.

---

THE FIRST PART.

In Ireland, ferr over the sea,
  There dwelleth a bonnye kinge;
And with him a yong and comlye knighte,
  Men call him syr Caulìne.

The kinge had a ladye to his daughter,
  In fashyon she hath no peere;
And princely wightes that ladye wooed
  To be theyr wedded feere.

Syr Cauline loveth her best of all,
  But nothing durst he saye;
Ne descreeve his counsayl to no man,
  But deerlye he lovde this may.

Till on a daye it so beffell,
  Great dill to him was dight;
The maydens love removde his mynd,
  To care-bed went the knighte.

One while he spred his armes him fro,
  One while he spred them nye:
And aye! but I winne that ladyes love,
  For dole now I mun dye.

And whan our parish-masse was done,
  Our kinge was bowne to dyne:
He says, Where is syr Cauline,
  That is wont to serve the wyne?

Then aunswerde him a courteous knighte,
  And fast his handes gan wringe:
Sir Cauline is sicke, and like to dye
  Without a good leechìnge.

Fetche me downe my daughter deere,
  She is a leeche fulle fine:
Goe take him doughe, and the baken bread,
And serve him with the wyne soe red;
  Lothe I were him to tine.

Fair Christabelle to his chaumber goes,
  Her maydens followyng nye:
O well, she sayth, how doth my lord?
  O sicke, thou fayr ladyè.

Nowe ryse up wightlye, man, for shame,
  Never lye soe cowardlee;
For it is told in my fathers halle,
  You dye for love of mee.

Fayre ladye, it is for your love
  That all this dill I drye:
For if you wold comfort me with a kisse,
Then were I brought from bale to blisse,
  No lenger wold I lye.

Sir knighte, my father is a kinge,
  I am his onlye heire;
Alas! and well you knowe, syr knighte,
  I never can be youre fere.

O ladye, thou art a kinges daughtèr,
  And I am not thy peere,
But let me doe some deedes of armes
  To be your bacheleere.

Some deedes of armes if thou wilt doe,
  My bacheleere to bee,
(But ever and aye my heart wold rue,
  Giff harm shold happe to thee,)

Upon Eldridge hill there groweth a thorne,
  Upon the mores brodinge;

And dare ye, syr knighte, wake there all nighte
 Untill the fayre morninge?

For the Eldridge knighte, so mickle of mighte,
 Will examine you beforne;
And never man bare life awaye,
 But he did him scath and scorne.

That knighte he is a foul paynim,
 And large of limb and bone;
And but if heaven may be thy speede,
 Thy life it is but gone.

Nowe on the Eldridge hilles Ile walke[2],
 For thy sake, fair ladie;
And Ile either bring you a ready tokèn,
 Or Ile never more you see.

The lady is gone to her own chaumbère,
 Her maydens following bright:
Syr Cauline lope from care-bed soone,
And to the Eldridge hills is gone,
 For to wake there all night.

Unto midnight, that the moone did rise,
 He walked up and downe;
Then a lightsome bugle heard he blowe
 Over the bents soe browne:
Quoth hee, If cryance come till my heart,
 I am ffar from any good towne[3].

And soone he spyde on the mores so broad,
 A furyous wight and fell;
A ladye bright his brydle led,
 Clad in a fayre kyrtèll:

[2] Perhaps wake, as in ver. 61.
[3] This line is restored from the folio MS.

And soe fast he called on syr Cauline,
O man, I rede thee flye,
For, 'but' if cryance come till thy heart,
I weene but thou mun dye.

He sayth, 'No cryance comes till my heart,
Nor, in faith, I wyll not flee;
For, cause thou minged not Christ before,
The less me dreadeth thee.

The Eldridge knighte, he pricked his steed;
Syr Cauline bold abode:
Then either shooke his trustye speare,
And the timber these two children[4] bare
Soe soone in sunder slode.

Then tooke they out theyr two good swordes,
And layden on full faste,
Till helme and hawberke, mail and sheelde,
They all were well-nye brast.

The Eldridge knight was mickle of might,
And stiffe in stower did stande,
But syr Cauline with a 'backward' stroke,
He smote off his right-hand;
That soone he with paine and lacke of bloud
Fell downe on that lay-land.

Then up syr Cauline lift his brande
All over his head so hye:
And here I sweare by the holy roode,
Nowe, caytiffe, thou shalt dye.

Then up and came that ladye brighte,
Faste wringing of her hande:
For the maydens love, that most you love,
Withold that deadlye brande:

V. 109, aukeward. MS.

[4] i. e. Knights. See the Preface to *Child Waters*, vol. iii.

For the maydens love, that most you love,
  Now smyte no more I praye;
And aye whatever thou wilt, my lord,
  He shall thy hests obaye.

Now sweare to mee, thou Eldridge knighte,
  And here on this lay-land,
That thou wilt believe on Christ his laye,
  And therto plight thy hand:

And that thou never on Eldridge come
  To sporte, gamon, or playe:
And that thou here give up thy armes
  Until thy dying daye.

The Eldridge knighte gave up his armes
  With many a sorrowfulle sighe;
And sware to obey syr Caulines hest,
  Till the tyme that he shold dye.

And he then up and the Eldridge knighte
  Sett him in his saddle anone,
And the Eldridge knighte and his ladye
  To theyr castle are they gone.

Then he tooke up the bloudy hand,
  That was so large of bone,
And on it he founde five ringes of gold
  Of knightes that had be slone.

Then he tooke up the Eldridge sworde,
  As hard as any flint:
And he tooke off those ringès five,
  As bright as fyre and brent.

Home then pricked syr Caulìne
  As light as leafe on tree:
I-wys he neither stint ne blanne,
  Till he his ladye see.

Then downe he knelt upon his knee
  Before that lady gay:
O ladye, I have bin on the Eldridge hills:
  These tokens I bring away.

Now welcome, welcome, syr Cauline,
  Thrice welcome unto mee,
For now I perceive thou art a true knighte,
  Of valour bolde and free.

O ladye, I am thy own true knighte,
  Thy hests for to obaye:
And mought I hope to winne thy love! ——
  No more his tonge colde say.

The ladye blushed scarlette redde,
  And fette a gentill sighe:
Alas! syr knight, how may this bee,
  For my degree's soe highe?

But sith thou hast hight, thou comely youth,
  To be my batchilere,
Ile promise if thee I may not wedde,
  I will have none other fere.

Then shee held forthe her lilly-white hand
  Towards that knighte so free:
He gave to it one gentill kisse,
His heart was brought from bale to blisse,
  The teares sterte from his ee.

But keep my counsayl, syr Cauline,
  Ne let no man it knowe;
For and ever my father sholde it ken,
  I wot he wolde us sloe.

From that daye forthe that ladye fayre
  Lovde syr Cauline the knighte:

From that daye forthe he only joyde
Whan shee was in his sight.

Yea, and oftentimes they mette
Within a fayre arboùre,
Where they in love and sweet daliaunce
Past manye a pleasaunt houre.

---

*** In this conclusion of the First Part, and at the beginning of the Second, the reader will observe a resemblance to the story of *Sigismunda and Guiscard*, as told by Boccace and Dryden: see the latter's description of the lovers meeting in the cave, and those beautiful lines which contain a reflection so like this of our poet, "everye white," &c viz.—

"But as extremes are short of ill and good,
And tides at highest mark regorge their flood;
So Fate, that could no more improve their joy,
Took a malicious pleasure to destroy.
Tancred, who fondly loved," &c.

---

## PART THE SECOND.

Everye white will have its blacke,
And everye sweete its sowre:
This founde the ladye Christabelle
In an untimely howre.

For so it befelle as syr Cauline
Was with that ladye faire,
The kinge her father walked forthe
To take the evenyng aire:

And into the arboure as he went
To rest his wearye feet,
He found his daughter and syr Cauline
There sette in daliaunce sweet.

The kinge hee sterted forthe, i-wys,
  And an angrye man was hee:
Nowe, traytoure, thou shalt hange or drawe,
  And rewe shall thy ladiè.

Then forthe syr Cauline he was ledde,
  And throwne in dungeon deepe:
And the ladye into a towre so hye,
  There left to wayle and weepe.

The queene she was syr Caulines friend,
  And to the kinge sayd shee:
I praye you save syr Caulines life,
  And let him banisht bee.

Now, dame, that traitor shall be sent
  Across the salt sea fome:
But here I will make thee a band,
If ever he come within this land,
  A foule deathe is his doome.

All woe-begone was that gentil knight
  To parte from his ladyè;
And many a time he sighed sore,
  And cast a wistfulle eye:
Faire Christabelle, from thee to parte,
  Farre lever had I dye.

Faire Christabelle, that ladye bright,
  Was had forthe of the towre;
But ever shee droopeth in her minde,
As nipt by an ungentle winde
  Doth some faire lillye flowre.

And ever shee doth lament and weepe
  To tint her lover soe:
Syr Cauline, thou little think'st on mee,
  But I will still be true.

Manye a kinge, and manye a duke,
And lords of high degree,
Did sue to that fayre ladye of love;
But never shee wolde them nee.

When manye a daye was past and gone,
Ne comforte she colde finde,
The kynge proclaimed a tourneament,
To cheere his daughters mind:

And there came lords, and there came knights,
Fro manye a farre countryè,
To break a spere for theyr ladyes love
Before that faire ladyè.

And many a ladye there was sette
In purple and in palle:
But faire Christabelle soe woe-begone
Was the fayrest of them all.

Then manye a knighte was mickle of might
Before his ladye gaye;
But a stranger wight, whom no man knewe,
He wan the prize eche daye.

His acton it was all of blacke,
His hewberke, and his sheelde,
Ne noe man wist whence he did come,
Ne noe man knewe where he did gone,
When they came out the feelde.

And now three days were prestlye past
In feates of chivalrye,
When lo upon the fourth morninge
A sorrowfulle sight they see.

A hugye giaunt stiffe and starke,
All foule of limbe and lere;

Two goggling eyen like fire farden,
  A mouthe from eare to eare.

Before him came a dwarffe full lowe,
  That waited on his knee,
And at his backe five heads he bare,
  All wan and pale of blee.

Sir, quoth the dwarffe, and louted lowe,
  Behold that hend Soldàin!
Behold these heads I beare with me!
  They are kings which he hath slain.

The Eldridge knight is his own cousìne,
  Whom a knight of thine hath shent:
And hee is come to avenge his wrong,
And to thee, all thy knightes among,
  Defiance here hath sent.

But yette he will appease his wrath
  Thy daughters love to winne:
And but thou yeelde him that fayre mayd,
  Thy halls and towers must brenne.

Thy head, syr king, must goe with mee;
  Or else thy daughter deere;
Or else within these lists soe broad
  Thou must finde him a peere.

The king he turned him round aboute,
  And in his heart was woe:
Is there never a knighte of my round tablè,
  This matter will undergoe?

Is there never a knighte amongst yee all
  Will fight for my daughter and mee?
Whoever will fight yon grimme soldàn,
  Right fair his meede shall bee.

For hee shall have my broad lay-lands,
And of my crowne be heyre;
And he shall winne fayre Christabelle
To be his wedded fere.

But every knighte of his round tablè
Did stand both still and pale;
For whenever they lookt on the grim soldàn,
It made their hearts to quail.

All woe-begone was that fayre ladyè,
When she sawe no helpe was nye:
She cast her thought on her owne true-love,
And the teares gusht from her eye.

Up then sterte the stranger knighte,
Sayd, Ladye, be not affrayd:
Ile fight for thee with this grimme soldàn,
Thoughe he be unmacklye made.

And if thou wilt lend me the Eldridge sworde,
That lyeth within thy bowre,
I truste in Christe for to slay this fiende
Thoughe he be stiff in stowre.

Goe fetch him downe the Eldridge sworde,
The kinge he cryde, with speede:
Nowe heaven assist thee, courteous knighte;
My daughter is thy meede.

The gyaunt he stepped into the lists,
And sayd, Awaye, awaye:
I sweare, as I am the hend soldàn,
Thou lettest me here all daye.

Then forthe the stranger knight he came
In his blacke armoure dight:
The ladye sighed a gentle sighe,
"That this were my true knighte!"

And nowe the gyaunt and knighte be mett
  Within the lists soe broad;
And now with swordes soe sharpe of steele,
  They gan to lay on load.

The soldan strucke the knighte a stroke,
  That made him reele asyde;
Then woe-begone was that fayre ladyè,
  And thrice she deeply sighde.

The soldan strucke a second stroke,
  And made the bloude to flowe:
All pale and wan was that ladye fayre,
  And thrice she wept for woe.

The soldan strucke a third fell stroke,
  Which brought the knighte on his knee:
Sad sorrow pierced that ladyes heart,
  And she shriekt loud shriekings three.

The knighte he leapt upon his feete,
  All recklesse of the pain:
Quoth hee, But heaven be now my speede,
  Or else I shall be slaine.

He grasped his sworde with mayne and mighte,
  And spying a secrette part,
He drave it into the soldan's syde,
  And pierced him to the heart.

Then all the people gave a shoute,
  Whan they sawe the soldan falle:
The ladye wept, and thanked Christ,
  That had reskewed her from thrall.

And nowe the kinge with all his barons
  Rose uppe from offe his seate,
And downe he stepped intò the listes,
  That curteous knighte to greete

But he for payne and lacke of bloude
Was fallen intò a swounde,
And there all walteringe in his gore,
Lay lifelesse on the grounde.

Come downe, come downe, my daughter deare,
Thou art a leeche of skille;
Farre lever had I lose halfe my landes,
Than this good knighte sholde spille.

Downe then steppeth that fayre ladyè,
To helpe him if she maye;
But when she did his beavere raise,
It is my life, my lord, she sayes,
And shriekte and swound awaye.

Sir Cauline juste lifte up his eyes
When he hearde his ladye crye,
O ladye, I am thine owne true love;
For thee I wisht to dye.

Then giving her one partinge looke,
He closed his eyes in death,
Ere Christabelle, that ladye milde,
Begane to drawe her breathe.

But when she found her comelye knighte
Indeed was dead and gone,
She layde her pale cold cheeke to his,
And thus she made her moane:

O staye, my deare and onlye lord,
For mee thy faithfulle feere;
'Tis meet that I shold followe thee,
Who hast bought my love so deare.

Then fayntinge in a deadlye swoune,
And with a deep-fette sighe,
That burst her gentle heart in twayne,
Fayre Christabelle did dye.

---

## V.

# Edward, Edward.

### A SCOTTISH BALLAD.

FROM A MS. COPY TRANSMITTED FROM SCOTLAND.

Quhy dois zour brand sae drop wi' bluid,
Edward, Edward?
Quhy dois zour brand sae drop wi' bluid?
And quhy sae sad gang zee, O?
O, I hae killed my hauke sae guid,
Mither, mither:
O, I hae killed my hauke sae guid:
And I had nae mair bot hee, O.

Zour haukis bluid was nevir sae reid,
Edward, Edward:
Zour haukis bluid was nevir sae reid;
My deir son I tell thee, O.
O, I hae killed my reid-roan steid,
Mither, mither:
O, I hae killed my reid-roan steid,
That erst was sae fair and free, O.

Zour steid was auld, and ze hae gat mair,
Edward, Edward:
Zour steid was auld, and ze hae gat mair,
Sum other dule ze drie, O.
O, I hae killed my fadir deir,
Mither, mither:
O, I hae killed my fadir deir,
Alas! and wae is mee, O!

And quhatten penance wul ze drie for that,
Edward, Edward?
And quhatten penance will ze drie for that?
My deir son, now tell me, O.

Ile set my feit in zonder boat,
Mither, mither:
Ile set my feit in zonder boat,
And Ile fare ovir the sea, O.

And quhat wul ze doe wi' zour towirs and zour ha',
Edward, Edward?
And quhat wul ze doe wi' zour towirs and zour ha',
That were sae fair to see, O?
Ile let thame stand til they doun fa',
Mither, mither:
Ile let thame stand til they doun fa',
For here nevir mair maun I bee, O.

And quhat wul ze leive to zour bairns and zour wife,
Edward, Edward?
And quhat wul ze leive to zour bairns and zour wife,
Quhan ze gang ovir the sea, O?
The warldis room, let thame beg throw life,
Mither, mither:
The warldis room, let thame beg throw life,
For thame nevir mair wul I see, O.

And quhat wul ze leive to zour ain mither deir,
Edward, Edward?
And quhat wul ze leive to zour ain mither deir?
My deir son, now tell me, O.
The curse of hell frae me sall ze beir,
Mither, mither:
The curse of hell frae me sall ze beir,
Sic counseils ze gave to me, O.

This curious song was transmitted to the Editor by Sir David Dalrymple, Bart., late Lord Hailes.

---

## VI.

## King Estmere.

This old romantic Legend (which is given from two copies, one of them in the Editor's folio MS. but which contained very great variations,) bears marks of great antiquity, and perhaps ought to have taken place of any in this volume. It should seem to have been written while a great part of Spain was in the hands of the Saracens or Moors, whose empire there was not fully extinguished before the year 1491. The Mahometans are spoken of in v. 49, &c., just in the same terms as in all other old romances. The author of the ancient legend of *Sir Bevis* represents his hero, upon all occasions, breathing out defiance against

"Mahound and Termagaunte[1];"

and so full of zeal for his religion, as to return the following polite message to a Paynim king's fair daughter, who had fallen in love with him, and sent two Saracen knights to invite him to her bower:

"I wyll not ones stirre off this grounde,
To speake with an heathen hounde,
Unchristian houndes, I rede you fle,
Or I your harte bloud shall se[2]."

Indeed they return the compliment, by calling him elsewhere "a Christen hounde[3]."

This was conformable to the real manners of the barbarous ages: perhaps the same excuse will hardly serve our bard for the situations in which he has placed some of his royal personages. That a youthful monarch should take a journey into another kingdom to visit his mistress *incog.* was a piece of gallantry paralleled in our own Charles I.; but that King Adland should be found lolling or leaning at his gate, (v. 35) may be thought, perchance, a little out of character. And yet the great painter of manners, Homer,

[1] See a short Memoir at the end of this ballad. [2] Sign. C. ij. b.
[3] Sign. C. i. b.

did not think it inconsistent with decorum to represent a king of the Taphians rearing himself at the gate of Ulysses to inquire for that monarch, when he touched at Ithaca, as he was taking a voyage with a ship's cargo of iron to dispose of in traffic[4]. So little ought we to judge of ancient manners by our own.

Before I conclude this article, I cannot help observing that the reader will see in this ballad the character of the old minstrels (those successors of the bards) placed in a very respectable light[5]: here he will see one of them represented mounted on a fine horse, accompanied with an attendant to bear his harp after him, and to sing the poems of his composing. Here he will see him mixing in the company of kings without ceremony; no mean proof of the great antiquity of this poem. The farther we carry our inquiries back, the greater respect we find paid to the professors of poetry and music among all the Celtic and Gothic nations. Their character was deemed so sacred, that under its sanction our famous King Alfred (as we have already seen[6]) made no scruple to enter the Danish camp, and was at once admitted to the king's head-quarters[7]. Our poet has suggested the same expedient to the heroes of this ballad. All the histories of the North are full of the great reverence paid to this order of men. Harold Harfagre, a celebrated king of Norway, was wont to seat them at his table above all the officers of his court: and we find another Norwegian king placing five of them by his side in a day of battle, that they might be eye-witnesses of the great exploits they were to celebrate[8]. As to Estmere's riding into the hall while the kings were at table, this was usual in the ages of chivalry; and even to

[4] Odyss. A. 105.

[5] See vol. ii. note subjoined to 1st pt. of *Beggar of Bednal*, &c.

[6] See the Essay on the ancient Minstrels prefixed to this vol.

[7] Even so late as the time of Froissart, we find Minstrels and Heralds mentioned together, as those who might securely go into an enemy's country. Cap. cxl.

[8] Bartholini Antiq. Dan. p. 173. Northern Antiquities, &c., vol. i. pp. 386, 389, &c.

this day we see a relic of this custom still kept up, in the Champion's riding into Westminster-hall during the coronation dinner[9].

---

Hearken to me, gentlemen,
  Come and you shall heare;
Ile tell you of two of the boldest brethren,
  That ever born y-were.

The tone of them was Adler yonge,
  The tother was kyng Estmere;
The were as bolde men in their deedes,
  As any were farr and neare.

As they were drinking ale and wine
  Within kyng Estmeres halle:
When will ye marry a wyfe, brothèr,
  A wyfe to gladd us all?

Then bespake him kyng Estmere,
  And answered him hastilee:
I knowe not that ladye in any lande,
  That is able[10] to marry with mee.

Kyng Adland hath a daughter, brother,
  Men call her bright and sheene;
If I were kynge here in your stead,
  That ladye shold be queene.

Sayes, Reade me, reade me, deare brother,
  Throughout merry Englànd,
Where we might find a messenger
  Betweene us two to sende.

Ver. 14, hartilye. fol. MS.

[9] See also the account of Edw. II. in the Essay on the Minstrels.
[10] He means fit, suitable.

Sayes, You shall ryde yourselfe, brothèr,
Ile beare you companèe;
Many throughe fals messengers are deceived,
And I feare lest soe shold wee.

Thus the renisht them to ryde
Of twoe good renisht steedes,
And when they came to kyng Adlands halle,
Of red golde shone their weedes.

And when the came to kyng Adlands halle
Before the goodlye yate,
Ther they found good kyng Adlànd
Rearing himselfe theratt.

Nowe Christ thee save, good kyng Adlànd;
Nowe Christ thee save and see,
Sayd, You be welcome, kyng Estmere,
Right hartilye to mee.

You have a daughter, sayd Adler yonge,
Men call her bright and sheene,
My brother wold marrye her to his wiffe,
Of Englande to be queene.

Yesterdaye was att my dere daughtèr
Syr Bremor the kyng of Spayne;
And then she nicked him of naye,
I feare sheele do youe the same.

The kyng of Spayne is a foule paynim,
And 'leeveth on Mahound;
And pitye it were that fayre ladyè
Shold marrye a heathen hound.

But grant to me, sayes kyng Estmere,
For my love I you praye;

V. 27, many a man . . . is. fol. MS. V. 46, the king his sonne of Spayn. fol. MS.

That I may see your daughter dere
  Before I goe hence awaye.

Althoughe itt is seven yeare and more
  Syth my daughter was in halle,
She shall come downe once for your sake
  To glad my guestès alle.

Downe then came that mayden fayre,
  With ladyes lacede in pall,
And halfe a hondred of bolde knightes,
  To bring her from bowre to hall;
And eke as manye gentle squieres,
  To waite upon them all.

The talents of golde, were on her head sette,
  Hunge lowe downe to her knee;
And everye rynge on her small fingèr,
  Shone of the chrystall free.

Sayes, Christ you save, my deare madàme;
  Sayes, Christ you save and see.
Sayes, You be welcome, kyng Estmere,
  Right welcome unto mee.

And iff you lovè me, as you saye,
  So well and hartilèe,
All that ever you are comen about
  Soone sped now itt may bee.

Then bespake her father deare:
  My daughter, I saye naye;
Remember well the kyng of Spayne,
  What he sayd yesterdaye.

He wold pull downe my halles and castles,
  And reave me of my lyfe:
And ever I feare that paynim kyng,
  Iff I reave him of his wyfe

Your castles and your towres, father,
  Are stronglye built aboute;
And therefore of that foule paynìm
  Wee neede not stande in doubte.

Plyght me your troth, nowe, kyng Estmère,
  By heaven and your righte hande,
That you will marrye me to your wyfe,
  And make me queene of your land.

Then kyng Estmere he plight his troth
  By heaven and his righte hand,
That he wolde marrye her to his wyfe,
  And make her queene of his land.

And he tooke leave of that ladye fayre,
  To goe to his owne countree,
To fetche him dukes and lordes and knightes,
  That marryed the might bee.

They had not ridden scant a myle,
  A myle forthe of the towne,
But in did come the kynge of Spayne,
  With kempès many a one.

But in did come the kyng of Spayne,
  With manye a grimme baròne,
Tone day to marrye kyng Adlands daughter,
  Tother daye to carrye her home.

Then shee sent after kyng Estmère
  In all the spede might bee,
That he must either returne and fighte,
  Or goe home and lose his ladyè.

One whyle then the page he went,
  Another whyle he ranne;
Till he had oretaken king Estmere,
  I wis, he never blanne.

Tydinges, tydinges, kyng Estmere!
  What tydinges nowe, my boye?
O tydinges I can tell to you,
  That will you sore annoye.

You had not ridden scant a myle,
  A myle out of the towne,
But in did come the kyng of Spayne
  With kempès many a one:

But in did come the kyng of Spayne
  With manye a grimme baròne,
Tone day to marrye king Adlands daughter,
  Tother daye to carrye her home.

That ladye fayre she greetes you well,
  And ever-more well by mee:
You must either turne againe and fighte,
  Or goe home and lose your ladyè.

Sayes, Reade me, reade me, deare brothèr,
  My reade shall ryde[1] at thee,
Whiche way we best may turne and fighte,
  To save this fayre ladyè.

Now hearken to me, sayes Adler yonge,
  And your reade must rise[2] at me,
I quicklye will devise a waye
  To sette thy ladye free.

My mother was a westerne woman,
  And learned in gramaryè[3],
And when I learned at the schole,
  Something shee taught itt me.

[1] Sic MS. It should probably be *ryse, i. e.,* my counsel shall arise from thee. See ver. 140.

[2] Sic MS.

[3] See note at the end of this ballad.

There groweth an hearbe within this fielde,
And iff it were but knowne,
His color, which is whyte and redd,
It will make blacke and browne:

His color, which is browne and blacke,
Itt will make redd and whyte;
That sword is not in all Englande,
Upon his coate will byte.

And you shal be a harper, brother,
Out of the north countrèe;
And Ile be your boye, so faine of fighte,
To beare your harpe by your knee.

And you shall be the best harpèr,
That ever tooke harpe in hand;
And I will be the best singèr,
That ever sung in this land.

Itt shal be written in our forheads
All and in grammaryè,
That we towe are the boldest men,
That are in all Christentyè.

And thus they renisht them to ryde,
On towe good renish steedes;
And whan the came to kyng Adlands hall,
Of redd gold shone their weedes.

And whan the came to kyng Adlands hall
Untill the fayre hall yate,
There they found a proud portèr;
Rearing himselfe theratt.

Sayes, Christ thee save, thou proud portèr;
Sayes, Christ thee save and see.
Nowe you be welcome, sayd the portèr,
Of what land soever ye bee.

We been harpers, sayd Adler yonge,
  Come out of the northe countrèe;
We beene come hither untill this place,
  This proud weddinge for to see.

Sayd, And your color were white and redd,
  As it is blacke and browne,
Ild saye king Estmere and his brother
  Were comen untill this towne.

Then they pulled out a ryng of gold,
  Layd itt on the porters arme:
And ever we will thee, proud portèr,
  Thow wilt saye us no harme.

Sore he looked on kyng Estmère,
  And sore he handled the ryng,
Then opened to them the fayre hall yates,
  He lett for no kind of thyng.

Kyng Estmere he light off his steede
  Up att the fayre hall board;
The frothe, that came from his brydle bitte,
  Light on kyng Bremors beard.

Sayes, Stable thy steede, thou proud harpèr,
  Go stable him in the stalle;
Itt doth not beseeme a proud harpèr
  To stable 'him' in a kyngs halle.

My ladd he is so lither, he sayd,
  He will do nought that's meete;
And aye that I cold but find the man,
  Were able him to beate.

Thou speakst proud words, sayd the Paynim king,
  Thou harper here to mee:
There is a man within this halle,
  That will beate thy lad and thee.

V. 202, to stable his steede, fol. MS.

O lett that man come downe, he sayd,
  A sight of him wold I see;
And whan hee hath beaten well my ladd,
  Then he shall beate of mee.

Downe then came the kemperye man,
  And looked him in the eare;
For all the gold, that was under heaven,
  He durst not neigh him neare.

And how nowe, kempe, sayd the kyng of Spayne,
  And how what aileth thee?
He sayes, Itt is written in his forhead
  All and in gramaryè,
That for all the gold that is under heaven,
  I dare not neigh him nye.

Kyng Estmere then pulled forth his harpe,
  And played thereon so sweete:
Upstarte the ladye from the kynge,
  As hee sate at the meate.

Now stay thy harpe, thou proud harpèr,
  Now stay thy harpe, I say;
For an thou playest as thou beginnest,
  Thou'lt till[4] my bride awaye.

He strucke upon his harpe agayne,
  And playd both fayre and free;
The ladye was so pleasde theratt,
  She laught loud laughters three.

Nowe sell me thy harpe, sayd the kyng of Spayne,
  Thy harpe and stryngs eche one,
And as many gold nobles thou shalt have,
  As there be stryngs thereon.

[4] *i. e.* entice. Vide Gloss. For *gramarye,* see the end of this ballad.

And what wold ye doe with my harpe, he sayd,
Iff I did sell it yee?
"To playe my wiffe and me a FITT[5],
When abed together we bee."

Now sell me, quoth hee, thy bryde soe gay,
As shee sitts laced in pall,
And as many gold nobles I will give,
As there be rings in the hall.

And what wold ye doe with my bryde soe gay,
Iff I did sell her yee?
More seemelye it is for her fayre bodye
To lye by mee than thee.

Hee played agayne both loud and shrille,
And Adler he did syng,
"O ladye, this is thy owne true love;
Noe harper, but a kyng.

O ladye, this is thy owne true love,
As playnlye thou mayest see;
And Ile rid thee of that foule paynim,
Who partes thy love and thee."

The ladye looked, the ladye blushte,
And blushte and lookt agayne,
While Adler he hath drawne his brande,
And hath the Sowdan slayne.

Up then rose the kemperye men,
And loud they gan to crye:
Ah! traytors, yee have slayne our kyng,
And therefore yee shall dye.

Kyng Estmere threwe the harpe asyde,
And swith he drew his brand;

[5] *i. e.* a tune or strain of music. See Gloss.

And Estmere he, and Adler yonge
  Right stiffe in stour can stand.

And aye their swordes soe sore can byte,
  Throughe help of Gramaryè,
That soone they have slayne the kempery men,
  Or forst them forth to flee.

Kyng Estmere tooke that fayre ladyè,
  And marryed her to his wyfe,
And brought her home to merrye Englànd
  With her to leade his lyfe.

---

⁂ The word *Gramarye*, which occurs several times in the foregoing poem, is probably a corruption of the French word *Grimoire*, which signifies a conjuring-book in the old French romances, if not the art of necromancy itself.

⁂ *Termagaunte* (mentioned above in p. 51) is the name given in the old romances to the god of the Saracens: in which he is constantly linked with *Mahound*, or Mahomet. Thus, in the legend of *Syr Guy* the Soudan (Sultan) swears,

> "So helpe me *Mahowne* of might,
> And *Termagaunt* my God so bright."
>
> Sign. p. iij. b.

This word is derived by the very learned editor of Junius from the Anglo-Saxon Tẏꞃ very, and Maᵹan mighty. As this word has so sublime a derivation, and was so applicable to the true God, how shall we account for its being so degraded? Perhaps Tẏꞃ-maᵹan or *Termagant* had been a name originally given to some Saxon idol, before our ancestors were converted to Christianity, or had been the peculiar attribute of one of their false deities; and therefore the first Christian missionaries rejected it as profane, and improper to be applied to the true God. Afterwards, when the irruptions of the Saracens into Europe, and the Crusades into the East, had brought them acquainted with a new species of unbelievers, our ignorant ancestors, who thought all that did not receive the Christian law were necessarily Pagans and Idolaters, supposed the Mahometan creed was in all respects the same with that of their Pagan forefathers, and therefore made no scruple to give the ancient name of *Termagant* to the god of the Saracens; just in the same manner as they afterwards used the name of Sarazen to express any kind of Pagan or Idolater. In the ancient romance of *Merline* (in the Editor's folio MS.) the Saxons themselves that came over with Hengist, because they were not Christians, are constantly called Sarazens.

However that be, it is certain that, after the times of the Crusades, both Mahound and Termagaunt made their frequent appearance in the Pageants and religious Enterludes of the barbarous ages; in which they were exhibited with gestures so furious and frantic, as to become proverbial. Thus Skelton speaks of Wolsey,

> "Like *Mahound* in a play,
> No man dare him withsay."
> Ed. 1736, p. 158.

And Bale, describing the threats used by some Papist magistrates to his wife, speaks of them as "grennyng upon her lyke *Termagauntes* in a playe." [Actes of Engl. Votaryes, pt. 2. fo. 83. ed. 1550. 12mo.] Hence we may conceive the force of Hamlet's expression in Shakspeare, where, condemning a ranting player, he says, "I could have such a fellow whipt for ore-doing *Termagant*: it out-herods Herod." A. iii. sc. 3. By degrees the word came to be applied to an outrageous turbulent person, and especially to a violent brawling woman, to whom alone it is now confined: and this the rather, as, I suppose, the character of Termagant was anciently represented on the stage after the eastern mode, with long robes or petticoats.

Another frequent character in the old Pageants or Enterludes of our ancestors, was the Sowdan or Soldan, representing a grim eastern tyrant. This appears from a curious passage in Stow's Annals, (p. 458.) In a stage-play "the people know right well that he that plaieth the Sowdain, is percase a sowter [shoe-maker], yet if one should cal him by his owne name, while he standeth in his majestie, one of his tormentors might hap to break his head." The Sowdain, or Soldan, was a name given to any Sarazen king (being only a more rude pronunciation of the word *Sultan*,) as the Soldan of Egypt, the Soudan of Persia, the Sowdan of Babylon, &c., who were generally represented as accompanied with grim Sarazens, whose business it was to punish and torment Christians.

I cannot conclude this short memoir without observing, that the French romancers, who had borrowed the word Termagant from us, and applied it as we in their old romances, corrupted it into *Tervagaunte:* and from them La Fontaine took it up, and has used it more than once in his tales. This may be added to the other proofs adduced in these volumes, of the great intercourse that formerly subsisted between the old minstrels and legendary writers of both nations, and that they mutually borrowed each other's romances.

---

## VII.

## Sir Patrick Spence,

### A SCOTTISH BALLAD,

Is given from two MS. copies, transmitted from Scotland. In what age the hero of this ballad lived, or when this fatal expedition happened that proved so destructive to the Scots nobles, I have not been able to discover; yet am of opinion that their catastrophe is not altogether without foundation in history, though it has escaped my own researches. In the infancy of navigation, such as used the northern seas were very liable to shipwreck in the wintry months: hence a law was enacted in the reign of James the Third, (a law which was frequently repeated afterwards,) "That there be na schip frauched out of the realm with any staple gudes, fra the feast of Simons day and Jude, unto the feast of the purification of our Lady, called Candelmess." Jam. III. Parlt. 2. ch. 15.

In some modern copies, instead of Patrick Spence hath been substituted the name of Sir Andrew Wood, a famous Scottish admiral, who flourished in the time of our Edward IV., but whose story hath nothing in common with this of the ballad. As Wood was the most noted warrior of Scotland, it is probable that, like the Theban Hercules, he hath engrossed the renown of other heroes.

---

The king sits in Dumferling toune,
  Drinking the blude-reid wine:
O quhar will I get guid sailòr,
  To sail this schip of mine?

Up and spak an eldern knicht,
  Sat at the kings richt kne:
Sir Patrick Spence is the best sailòr,
  That sails upon the se.

The king has written a braid letter[1],
  And signd it wi' his hand;
And sent it to Sir Patrick Spence,
  Was walking on the sand.

The first line that Sir Patrick red,
  A loud lauch lauched he:
The next line that Sir Patrick red
  The teir blinded his ee.

O quha is this has don this deid,
  This ill deid don to me;
To send me out this time o' the zeir,
  To sail upon the se?

[1] A braid letter, *i. e.* open, or patent; in opposition to *close* rolls.

Mak hast, mak haste, my mirry men all,
Our guid schip sails the morne.
O say na sae, my master deir,
For I feir a deadlie storme.

Late late yestreen I saw the new moone
Wi' the auld moone in hir arme;
And I feir, I feir, my deir mastèr,
That we will com to harme.

O our Scots nobles wer richt laith
To weet their cork-heild schoone;
Bot lang owre a' the play wer playd,
Their hats they swam aboone.

O lang, lang, may their ladies sit
Wi' thair fans into their hand,
Or eir they se Sir Patrick Spence
Cum sailing to the land.

O lang, lang, may the ladies stand
Wi' thair gold kems in their hair,
Waiting for thair ain deir lords,
For they'll se thame na mair.

Have owre, have owre to Aberdour[2],
It's fiftie fadom deip:
And thair lies guid Sir Patrick Spence,
Wi' the Scots lords at his feit[3],

[2] A village lying upon the river Forth, the entrance to which is sometimes denominated *De mortuo mari.*

[3] An ingenious friend thinks the author of *Hardyknute* has borrowed several expressions and sentiments from the foregoing and other old Scottish songs in this collection.

---

## VIII.

### Robin Hood and Guy of Gisborne.

We have here a ballad of Robin Hood (from the Editor's folio MS.) which was never before printed, and carries marks of much greater antiquity than any of the common popular songs on this subject.

The severity of those tyrannical forest-laws that were introduced by our Norman kings, and the great temptation of breaking them by such as lived near the royal forests, at a time when the yeomanry of this kingdom were every where trained up to the long-bow, and excelled all other nations in the art of shooting, must constantly have occasioned great number of outlaws, and especially of such as were the best marksmen. These naturally fled to the woods for shelter, and forming into troops, endeavoured by their numbers to protect themselves from the dreadful penalties of their delinquency. The ancient punishment for killing the king's deer, was loss of eyes and castration: a punishment far worse than death. This will easily account for the troops of banditti which formerly lurked in the royal forests, and from their superior skill in archery, and knowledge of all the recesses of those unfrequented solitudes, found it no difficult matter to resist or elude the civil power.

Among all these, none was ever more famous than the hero of this ballad, whose chief residence was in Shirewood Forest, in Nottinghamshire: the heads of whose story, as collected by Stow, are briefly these.

"In this time [about the year 1190, in the reign of Richard I.] were many robbers, and outlawes, among the which Robin Hood, and Little John, renowned theeves, continued in woods, despoyling and robbing the goods of the rich. They killed none but such as would invade them; or by resistance for their own defence.

"The saide Robert entertained an hundred tall men and good archers with such spoiles and thefts as he got, upon whom four hundred (were they ever so strong) durst not give the onset. He suffered no woman to be oppressed, violated, or otherwise molested: poore mens goods he spared, abundantlie relieving them with that which by theft he got from abbeys and the houses of rich carles: whom Maior (the historian) blameth for his rapine and theft, but of all theeves he affirmeth him to be the prince and the most gentle theefe." — *Annals*, p. 159.

The personal courage of this celebrated outlaw, his skill in archery, his humanity, and especially his levelling principle of taking from the rich and giving to the poor, have in all ages rendered him the favourite of the common people: who, not content to celebrate his memory by innumerable songs and stories, have erected him into the dignity of an earl. Indeed it is not impossible but our hero, to gain the more respect from his followers, or they to derive the more credit to their profession, may have given rise to such a report themselves: for we find it recorded in an epitaph, which, if genuine, must have been inscribed on his tombstone near the nunnery of Kirk-lees in Yorkshire; where (as the story goes) he was bled to death by a treacherous nun, to whom he applied for phlebotomy:

> Hear undernead dis laitl stean
> laiz robert earl of huntingtun
> nea arcir ver az hie sae geud
> an pipl kauld im Robin Heud
> sick utlawz as hi an is men
> vil England nivir si agen
> obiit 24 kal. dekembris, 1247[1].

This epitaph appears to me suspicious; however, a late Antiquary has given a pedigree of Robin Hood, which, if genuine, shows that he had real pretensions to the earldom of Huntington, and that his true name was ROBERT FITZOOTH[2]. Yet the most ancient poems on Robin Hood make no

[1] See Thoresby's *Ducat. Leod.* p. 576. *Biog. Brit.* vi. 3933.
[2] Stukeley, in his *Palæographia Britannica,* No. II. 1746.

mention of this earldom. He is expressly asserted to have been a yeoman[3] in a very old legend in verse, preserved in the archives of the public library at Cambridge[4] in eight FYTTES or Parts, printed in black letter, quarto, thus inscribed, "℄ Here begynneth a lytell geste of Robyn hode and his meyne, and of the proude sheryfe of Notyngham." The first lines are,

"Lythe and lysten, gentylmen,  
That be of fre-bore blode:  
I shall you tell of a good YEMAN,  
His name was Robyn hode.

Robyn was a proude out-lawe,  
Whiles he walked on grounde;  
So curteyse an outlawe as he was one,  
Was never none yfounde," &c.

The printer's colophon is, "℄ Explicit Kinge Edwarde and Robin hode and Lyttel Johan. Enprented at London in Fletestrete at the sygne of the sone by Wynkin de Worde." In Mr. Garrick's collection[5] is a different edition of the same poem, "℄ Imprinted at London upon the thre Crane wharfe by Wyllyam Copland," containing at the end a little dramatic piece on the subject of Robin Hood and the Friar, not found in the former copy, called, "A newe playe for to be played in Maye games very plesaunte and full of pastyme. ℄ (∴) D."

I shall conclude these preliminary remarks with observing, that the hero of this ballad was the famous subject of popular songs so early as the time of K. Edw. III. In the *Visions of Pierce Plowman*, written in that reign, a monk says,

I can rimes of Roben Hod, and Randal of Chester,  
But of our Lorde and our Lady, I lerne nothyng at all.  
Fol. 26, ed. 1550.

See also in Bp. Latimer's Sermons[6] a very curious and characteristical story, which shows what respect was shown to the memory of our archer in the time of that prelate.

3 See also the following ballad, v. 147.

4 Num. D. 5, 2.

5 Old Plays, 4to. K. vol. x.

6 Serm. 6th before K. Ed. Apr. 12, fol. 75. Gilpin's *Life of Lat.* p. 122.

The curious reader will find many other particulars relating to this celebrated outlaw, in Sir John Hawkins's *Hist. of Music*, vol. iii. p. 410. 4to.

For the catastrophe of Little John, who, it seems, was executed for a robbery on Arbor-hill, Dublin, (with some curious particulars relating to his skill in archery,) see Mr. J. C. Walker's ingenious "Memoir on the Armour and Weapons of the Irish," p. 129, annexed to his "Historical Essay on the Dress of the ancient and modern Irish." Dublin, 1788. 4to.

Some liberties were, by the Editor, taken with this ballad; which, in this edition, hath been brought nearer to the folio MS.

---

When shaws beene sheene, and shradds full fayre,
  And leaves both large and longe,
Itt is merrye walkyng in the fayre forrèst
  To heare the small birdes songe.

The woodweele sang, and wold not cease,
  Sitting upon the spraye,
Soe lowde, he wakened Robin Hood,
  In the greenwood where he lay.

Now by my faye, sayd jollye Robìn,
  A sweaven I had this night;
I dreamt me of tow wighty yemen,
  That fast with me can fight.

Methought they did mee beate and binde,
  And tooke my bow mee froe;
Iff I be Robin alive in this lande,
  Ile be wroken on them towe.

Ver. 1. It should perhaps be *swards: i. e.* the surface of the ground: viz. "when the fields are in their beauty."

Sweavens are swift, master, quoth John,
  As the wind blowes ore the hill;
For if itt be never so loude this night,
  To-morrow it may be still.

Buske yee, bowne yee, my merry men all,
  And John shall goe with mee,
For Ile goe seeke yond wight yeomen,
  In greenwood where the bee.

Then they cast on their gownes of grene,
  And tooke theyr bowes each one;
And they away to the greene forrèst
  A shooting forth are gone;

Untill they came to the merry greenwood,
  Where they had gladdest to bee,
There were the ware of a wight yeomàn,
  That body leaned to a tree.

A sword and a dagger he wore by his side,
  Of manye a man the bane;
And he was clad in his capull hyde
  Topp and tayll and mayne.

Stand you still, master, quoth Little John,
  Under this tree so grene,
And I will go to yond wight yeoman
  To know what he doth meane.

Ah! John, by me thou settest noe store,
  And that I farley finde:
How offt send I my men beffore,
  And tarry my selfe behinde?

It is no cunning a knave to ken,
  And a man but heare him speake;
And itt were not for bursting of my bowe,
  John, I thy head wold breake.

As often wordes they breeden bale,
So they parted Robin and John;
And John is gone to Barnesdale:
The gates[7] he knoweth eche one.

But when he came to Barnesdale,
Great heavinesse there hee hadd,
For he found tow of his owne fellòwes
Were slaine both in a slade.

And Scarlette he was flying a-foote
Faste over stocke and stone,
For the proud sheriffe with seven score men
Fast after him is gone.

One shoote now I will shoote, quoth John,
With Christ his might and mayne;
Ile make yond fellow that flyes soe fast,
To stopp he shall be fayne.

Then John bent up his long bende-bowe,
And fetteled him to shoote:
The bow was made of tender boughe,
And fell down at his foote.

Woe worth, woe worth thee, wicked wood,
That ere thou grew on a tree;
For now this day thou art my bale,
My boote when thou shold bee.

His shoote it was but loosely shott,
Yet flewe not the arrowe in vaine,
For itt mett one of the sherriffes men,
Good William a Trent was slaine.

It had bene better of William a Trent
To have bene abed with sorrowe,

[7] *i. e.* ways, passes, paths, ridings. *Gate* is a common word in the North for *way*.

Than to be that day in the green wood slade
  To meet with Little Johns arrowe.

But as it is said, when men be mett
  Fyve can doe more than three,
The sheriffe hath taken little John,
  And bound him fast to a tree.

Thou shalt be drawen by dale and downe,
  And hanged hye on a hill.
But thou mayst fayle of thy purpose, quoth John,
  If itt be Christ his will.

Let us leave talking of little John,
  And thinke of Robin Hood,
How he is gone to the wight yeomàn,
  Where under the leaves he stood.

Good morrowe, good fellowe, sayd Robin so fayre,
  "Good morrowe, good fellow, quoth he."
Methinkes by this bowe thou beares in thy hande
  A good archere thou sholdst bee.

I am wilfulle of my waye, quo' the yeman,
  And of my morning tyde.
Ile lead thee through the wood, sayd Robin;
  Good fellow, Ile be thy guide.

I seeke an outlàwe, the straunger sayd,
  Men call him Robin Hood;
Rather Ild meet with that proud outlàwe
  Than fortye pound soe good.

Now come with me, thou wighty yeman,
  And Robin thou soone shalt see:
But first let us some pastime find
  Under the greenwood tree.

First let us some masterye make
  Among the woods so even,
We may chance to meet with Robin Hood
  Here att some unsett steven.

They cutt them down two summer shroggs,
  That grew both under a breere,
And sett them threescore rood in twaine
  To shoote the prickes y-fere.

Leade on, good fellowe, quoth Robin Hood,
  Leade on, I doe bidd thee.
Nay by my faith, good fellowe, hee sayd,
  My leader thou shalt bee.

The first time Robin shot at the pricke,
  He mist but an inch it froe;
The yeoman he was an archer good,
  But he cold never shoote soe.

The second shoote had the wightye yeman,
  He shot within the garlànde;
But Robin he shott far better than hee,
  For he clave the good pricke wande.

A blessing upon thy heart, he sayd;
  Goode fellowe, thy shooting is goode;
For an thy hart be as good as thy hand,
  Thou wert better than Robin Hoode.

Now tell me thy name, good fellowe, sayd he,
  Under the leaves of lyne.
Nay by my faith, quoth bolde Robìn,
  Till thou have told me thine.

I dwell by dale and downe, quoth hee,
  And Robin to take Ime sworne;
And when I am called by my right name
  I am Guy of good Gisbòrne.

My dwelling is in this wood, sayes Robin,
By thee I set right nought:
I am Robin Hood of Barnèsdale,
Whom thou so long hast sought.

He that had neyther beene kithe nor kin,
Might have seen a full fayre sight,
To see how together these yeomen went
With blades both browne[8] and bright.

To see how these yeomen together they fought
Two howres of a summers day:
Yett neither Robin Hood nor sir Guy
Them fettled to flye away.

Robin was reachles on a roote,
And stumbled at that tyde;
And Guy was quicke and nimble with-all,
And hitt him ore the left side.

Ah deere Lady, sayd Robin Hood, thou,
Thou art but mother and may',
I think it was never mans destinye
To dye before his day.

Robin thought on our lady deere,
And soone leapt up againe,

[8] The common epithet for a sword or other offensive weapon, in the old metrical romances, is *brown:* as "brown brand," or "brown sword: brown bill," &c., and sometimes even "bright brown sword." Chaucer applies the word *rustie* in the same sense; thus he describes the *Reve:*

"And by his side he bare a rustic blade."
Prol. ver. 620.

And even thus the god Mars:

"And in his hand he had a rousty swoord."
Test. of Cressid. 188.

Spenser has sometimes used the same epithet: see Warton's Observ. vol. ii. p. 62. It should seem from this particularity, that our ancestors did not pique themselves upon keeping their weapons bright: perhaps they deemed it more honourable to carry them stained with the blood of their enemies.

And strait he came with a 'backward' stroke,
  And he sir Guy hath slayne.

He took sir Guys head by the hayre,
  And stuck itt upon his bowes end:
Thou hast beene a traytor all thy life,
  Which thing must have an ende.

Robin pulled forth an Irish knife,
  And nicked sir Guy in the face,
That he was never on woman born,
  Cold tell whose head it was.

Saies, Lye there, lye there, now sir Guye,
  And with me be not wrothe;
If thou have had the worst strokes at my hand,
  Thou shalt have the better clothe.

Robin did off his gowne of greene,
  And on sir Guy did throwe,
And hee put on that capull hyde,
  That cladd him topp to toe.

The bowe, the arrowes, and little horne,
  Now with me I will beare;
For I will away to Barnèsdale,
  To see how my men doe fare.

Robin Hood sett Guyes horne to his mouth,
  And a loud blast in it did blow,
That beheard the sheriffe of Nottingham,
  As he leaned under a lowe.

Hearken, hearken, sayd the sheriffe,
  I heare nowe tydings good,
For yonder I heare sir Guyes horne blowe,
  And he hath slaine Robin Hoode.

Ver. 163, awkwarde. MS.

Yonder I heare sir Guyes horne blowe,
  Itt blowes soe well in tyde,
And yonder comes that wightye yeoman,
  Cladd in his capull hyde.

Come hyther, come hyther, thou good sir Guy,
  Aske what thou wilt of mee.
O I will none of thy gold, sayd Robin,
  Nor I will none of thy fee:

But now I have slaine the master, he sayes,
  Let me goe strike the knave;
For this is all the rewarde I aske;
  Nor noe other will I have.

Thou art a madman, said the sheriffe,
  Thou sholdst have had a knightes fee:
But seeing thy asking hath beene soe bad,
  Well granted it shale be.

When Little John heard his master speake,
  Well knewe he it was his steven:
Now shall I be looset, quoth Little John,
  With Christ his might in heaven.

Fast Robin hee hyed him to Little John,
  He thought to loose him belive;
The sheriffe and all his companye
  Fast after him can drive.

Stand abacke, stand abacke, sayd Robin;
  Why draw you mee so neere?
Itt was never the use in our countryè,
  Ones shrift another shold heere.

But Robin pulled forth an Irysh knife,
  And losed John hand and foote,
And gave him sir Guyes bow into his hand,
  And bade it be his boote.

Then John he took Guyes bow in his hand,
His boltes and arrowes eche one:
When the sheriffe saw Little John bend his bow,
He fettled him to be gone.

Towards his house in Nottingham towne,
He fled full fast away;
And soe did all the companye:
Not one behind wold stay.

But he cold neither runne soe fast,
Nor away soe fast cold ryde,
But little John with an arrowe soe broad,
He shott him into the 'backe'-syde.

---

*** The title of *Sir* was not formerly peculiar to knights, it was given to priests, and sometimes to very inferior personages.

Dr. Johnson thinks this title was applied to such as had taken the degree of A. B. in the universities, who are still styled *Domini*, "Sirs," to distinguish them from Undergraduates, who have no prefix, and from Masters of Arts, who are styled *Magistri*, "Masters."

---

## IX.

## An Elegy on Henry, Fourth Earl of Northumberland.

The subject of this poem, which was written by Skelton, is the death of Henry Percy, fourth Earl of Northumberland, who fell a victim to the avarice of Henry VII. In 1489, the parliament had granted the king a subsidy, for carrying on the war in Bretagne. This tax was found so heavy in the North, that the whole country was in a flame. The Earl of Northumberland, then lord-lieutenant for Yorkshire, wrote to inform the king of the discontent, and praying an abatement. But nothing is so unrelenting as avarice: the king wrote back, that not a penny should be abated. This message being delivered by the earl with too little caution, the populace rose, and supposing him to be the promoter of their calamity, broke into his house, and murdered him, with several of his attendants; who yet are charged by Skelton with being backward in their duty on this occasion. This melancholy event happened at the earl's seat at Cocklodge, near Thirske, in Yorkshire, April 28, 1489. See Lord Bacon, &c.

If the reader does not find much poetical merit in this old poem, (which yet is one of Skelton's best,) he will see a striking picture of the state and magnificence kept up by our ancient nobility during the feudal times. This great earl is described here as having among his menial servants, *knights*, *squires*, and even *barons:* see v. 32, 183, &c.; which, however different from modern manners, was formerly not unusual with our greater barons, whose castles had all the splendour and offices of a royal court, before the laws against Retainers abridged and limited the number of their attendants.

John Skelton, who commonly styled himself Poet-Laureat, died June 21, 1529. The following poem, which appears to have been written soon after the event, is printed from an ancient MS. copy, preserved in the British Museum, being much more correct than that printed among Skelton's Poems, in bl. let. 12mo. 1568. It is addressed to Henry Percy, fifth Earl of Northumberland, and is prefaced, &c. in the following manner:

*Poeta Skelton Laureatus libellum suum metrice alloquitur.*

Ad dominum properato meum mea pagina Percy,
  Qui Northumbrorum jura paterna gerit.
Ad nutum celebris tu prona repone leonis,
  Quæque suo patri tristia justa cano.
Ast ubi perlegit, dubiam sub mente volutet
  Fortunam, cuncta quæ male fida rotat.
Qui leo sit felix, et Nestoris occupet annos;
  Ad libitum cujus ipse paratus ero.

———

### Skelton Laureat upon the dolorus dethe and much lamentable chaunce of the moost honorable Erle of Northumberlande.

I wayle, I wepe, I sobbe, I sigh ful sore
The dedely fate, the dolefulle destenny
Of him that is gone, alas! without restore,
Of the blode[1] royall descendinge nobelly;
Whos lordshepe doutles was slayne lamentably
Thorow treson ageyn hym compassyd and wrought;
Trew to his prince, in word, in dede, and thought.

Of hevenly poems, O Clyo calde by name
In the college of musis goddess hystoriall,
Adres the to me, whiche am both halt and lame
In elect uteraunce to make memoryall:
To the for soccour, to the for helpe I call
Myne homely rudnes and drighnes to expelle
With the freshe waters of Elyconys welle.

Of noble actes auncyently enrolde,
Of famous princis and lordes of astate,
By thy report ar wonte to be extold,
Regestringe trewly every formare date;
Of thy bountie after the usuall rate,
Kyndle in me suche plenty of thy noblès,
Thes sorrowfulle dities that I may shew expres.

In sesons past who hathe harde or sene
Of formar writinge by any presidente
That vilane hastarddis in ther furious tene,

[1] The mother of Henry, first Earl of Northumberland, was Mary daughter to Henry Earl of Lancaster, whose father Edmond was second son of King Henry III. The mother and wife of the second Earl of Northumberland were both lineal descendants of King Edward III. The Percys also were lineally descended from the Emperor Charlemagne and the ancient kings of France, by their ancestor Josceline de Lovaine (son of Godfrey Duke of Brabant), who took the name of Percy on marrying the heiress of that house in the reign of Hen. II. Vide Camden's *Britan.* Edmonson, &c.

Fulfyld with malice of froward entente,
Confeterd togeder of commoun concente
Falsly to slo ther moste singular goode lorde?
It may be registerde of shamefull recorde.

So noble a man, so valiaunt lorde and knight,
Fulfilled with honor, as all the worlde dothe ken;
At his commaundement, whiche had both day and night
Knightis and squyers, at every season when
He calde upon them, as menyall houshold men:
Were no thes commones uncurteis karlis of kynde
To slo their owne lorde? God was not in their minde.

And were not they to blame, I say also,
That were aboute hym, his owne servants of trust,
To suffre hym slayn of his mortall fo?
Fled awaye from hym, let hym ly in the dust:
They bode not till the rekening were discust.
What shuld I flatter? what shulde I glose or paynt?
Fy, fy for shame, their harts wer to faint.

In Englande and Fraunce, which gretly was redouted
Of whom both Flaunders and Scotland stode in drede;
To whome grete astates obeyde and lowttede;
A mayny of rude villayns made him for to blede:
Unkindly they slew hym, that holp them oft at nede:
He was their bulwark, their paves, and their wall,
Yet shamfully they slew him; that shame mot them befal.

I say, ye commoners, why wer ye so stark mad?
What frantyk frensy fyll in youre brayne?
Where was your wit and reson, ye shuld have had?
What willfull foly made yow to ryse agayne
Your naturall lord? alas! I cannot fayne.
Ye armed you with will, and left your wit behynd;
Well may you be called comones most unkynd.

He was your chyfteyne, your shelde, your chef defence,
Redy to assyst you in every tyme of nede:

Your worship depended of his excellence:
  Alas! ye mad men, to far ye did excede:
  Your hap was unhappy, to ill was your spede:
What movyd you agayn hym to war or to fight?
What aylde you to sle your lord agyn all right?

The grounde of his quarel was for his sovereyn lord,
  The welle concernyng of all the hole lande,
Demaundyng soche dutyes as nedis most acord
  To the right of his prince which shold not be withstand;
  For whos cause ye slew hym with your awne hande:
But had his nobill men done wel that day,
Ye had not been hable to have saide him nay.

But ther was fals packinge, or els I am begylde:
  How-be-it the matter was evident and playne,
For yf they had occupied ther spere and ther shelde,
  This noble man doutles had not be slayne.
  But men say they wer lynked with a double chayn,
And held with the commouns under a cloke,
Whiche kindeled the wyld fyre that made all this smoke.

The commouns renyed ther taxes to pay
  Of them demaunded and asked by the kinge;
With one voice importune, they playnly said nay:
  They buskt them on a bushment themself in baile to bringe:
  Agayne the kings plesure to wrastle or to wringe,
Bluntly as bestis withe boste and with cry
They saide, they forsede not, nor carede not to dy.

The noblenes of the northe this valiant lorde and knyght,
  As man that was innocent of trechery or trayne,
Presed forthe boldly to witstand the myght,
  And, lyke marciall Hector, he fauht them agayne,
  Vigorously upon them with myght and with mayne,
Trustinge in noble men that wer with hym there:
Bot all they fled from hym for falshode or fere.

Barons, knights, squyres, one and alle,
  Togeder with servaunts of his famuly,
Turnd their backis, and let ther master fall,
  Of whos [life] they counted not a flye;
  Take up whos wolde for them, they let hym ly.
Alas! his golde, his fee, his annuall rente
Upon suche a sort was ille bestowde and spent.

He was envyronde aboute on every syde
  Withe his enemys, that were stark mad and wode;
Yet whils he stode he gave them woundes wyde:
  Alas for routhe! what thouche his mynde were goode,
  His corage manly, yet ther he shed his bloode!
All left alone, alas! he fawte in vayne;
For cruelly amonge them ther he was slayne.

Alas for pite! that Percy thus was spylt,
  The famous erle of Northumberlande:
Of knightly prowès the sworde pomel and hylt,
  The myghty lyoun[2] doutted by se and lande!
  O dolorous chaunce of fortuns fruward hande!
What man remembring how shamfully he was slayne,
From bitter weepinge hymself kan restrayne?

O cruell Mars, thou dedly god of war!
  O dolorous teusday, dedicate to thy name,
When thou shoke thy sworde so noble a man to mar!
  O grounde ungracious, unhappy be thy fame,
  Whiche wert endyed with rede blode of the same!
Moste noble erle! O fowle mysuryd grounde
Whereon he gat his fynal dedely wounde!

O Atropos, of the fatall systers thre,
  Goddes mooste cruell unto the lyf of man,
All merciles, in the ys no pitè!

[2] Alluding to his crest and supporters. *Doutted* is contracted for *redoubted.*

O homycide, whiche sleest all that thou kan,
So forcibly upon this erle thow ran,
That with thy sworde enharpid of mortall drede,
Thou kit asonder his perfight vitall threde!

My wordis unpullysht be nakide and playne,
Of aureat poems they want ellumynynge;
Bot by them to knoulege ye may attayne
Of this lordis dethe and of his murdrynge.
Which whils he lyvyd had fuyson of every thing,
Of knights, of squyers, chef lord of toure and toune,
Tyll fykkill fortune began on hym to frowne.

Paregall to dukis, with kings he myght compare,
Sourmountinge in honor all erls he did excede,
To all cuntreis aboute hym reporte me I dare.
Lyke to Eneas benygne in worde and dede,
Valiaunt as Hector in every marciall nede,
Provydent, discrete, circumspect, and wyse,
Tyll the chaunce ran agyne him of fortunes duble dyse.

What nedethe me for to extoll his fame
With my rude pen enkankerd all with rust?
Whos noble actis shew worsheply his name,
Transcendyng far myne homely muse, that must
Yet sumwhat wright supprisid with hartly lust,
Truly reportinge his right noble astate,
Immortally whiche is immaculate.

His noble blode never disteynyd was,
Trew to his prince for to defende his right,
Doublenes hatinge, fals maters to compas,
Treytory and treson he bannesht out of syght,
With trowth to medle was all his hole delyght,
As all his kuntrey kan testefy the same:
To slo suche a lord, alas, it was grete shame

If the hole quere of the musis nyne
  In me all onely wer sett and comprisyde,
Enbrethed with the blast of influence dyvyne,
  As perfightly as could be thought or devysyd;
  To me also allthouche it were promysyde
Of laureat Phebus holy the eloquence,
All were to littill for his magnyficence.

O yonge lyon, bot tender yet of age,
  Grow and encrese, remembre thyn astate,
God the assyst unto thyn herytage,
  And geve the grace to be more fortunate,
  Agayne rebellyouns arme to make debate.
And, as the lyoune, whiche is of bestis kinge,
Unto thy subjectis be kurteis and benyngne.

I pray God sende the prosperous lyf and long,
  Stabille thy mynde constant to be and fast,
Right to mayntein, and to resist all wronge,
  All flattringe faytors abhor and from the cast,
  Of foule detraction God kepe the from the blast,
Let double delinge in the have no place,
And be not light of credence in no case.

Wythe hevy chere, with dolorous hart and mynd,
  Eche man may sorow in his inward thought,
Thys lords death, whose pere is hard to fynd
  Allgyf Englond and Fraunce were thorow saught.
  Al kings, all princes, all dukes, well they ought
Bothe temporall and spirituall for to complayne
This noble man, that crewelly was slayne.

More specially barons, and those knygtes bold,
  And all other gentilmen with hym enterteynd
In fee, as menyall men of his housold,
Whom he as lord worsheply manteynd:
  To sorowfull weping they ought to be constreynd,

As oft as thei call to ther remembraunce,
Of ther good lord the fate and dedely chaunce.

O perlese prince of hevyn emperyalle,
That with one worde formed al thing of noughte;
Hevyn, hell, and erth obey unto thi kall;
Which to thy resemblance wondersly hast wrought
All mankynd, whom thou full dere hast boght,
With thy blode precious our finaunce thou dyd pay,
And us redemed, from the fendys pray:

To the pray we, as prince imcomperable,
As thou art of mercy and pite the well,
Thou bringe unto thy joye etermynable
The sowle of this lorde from all daunger of hell,
In endles blis with the to byde and dwell
In thy palace above the orient,
Where thou art lorde, and God omnipotent.

O quene of mercy, O lady full of grace,
Maiden moste pure, and goddis moder dere,
To sorowfull harts chef comfort and solace,
Of all women O floure withouten pere,
Pray to thy son above the starris clere,
He to vouchesaf by thy mediatioun
To pardon thy servant, and bringe to salvacion.

In joy triumphaunt the hevenly yerarchy,
With all the hole sorte of that glorious place,
His soule mot receyve into ther company
Thorowe bounte of hym that formed all solace:
Well of pite, of mercy, and of grace,
The father, the son, and the holy goste
In Trinitate one God of myghts moste.

*** I have placed the foregoing poem of Skelton's before the following extract from Hawes, not only because it was written first, but because I think Skelton is in general to be considered as the earlier poet, many of his poems being written long before Hawes's *Graunde Amour.*

---

## X.

## The Tower of Doctrine.

The reader has here a specimen of the descriptive powers of Stephen Hawes, a celebrated poet in the reign of Henry VII., though now little known. It is extracted from an allegorical poem of his (written in 1505) intitled, "The History of Graunde Amoure and La Belle Pucel, called the Palace of Pleasure," &c. 4to. 1555. See more of Hawes in *Ath. Ox.* v. i. p. 6, and Warton's *Observ.* v. ii. p. 105. He was also author of a book intitled, "The Temple of Glass. Wrote by Stephen Hawes, gentleman of the bedchamber to K. Henry VII." Pr. for Caxton, 4to. no date.

The following stanzas are taken from chap. iii. and iv. of the History above mentioned. "How Fame departed from Graunde Amoure and left him with Governaunce and Grace, and howe he went to the Tower of Doctrine," &c. As we are able to give no small lyric piece of Hawes's, the reader will excuse the insertion of this extract.

---

I loked about and saw a craggy roche,
  Farre in the west neare to the element,
And as I dyd then unto it approche,
  Upon the toppe I sawe refulgent
  The royal tower of Morall Document,
Made of fine copper, with turrettes fayre and hye,
Which against Phebus shone soe marveylously,

That for the very perfect bryghtnes
  What of the tower and of the cleare sunne,
I could nothyng behold the goodlines
  Of that palaice, whereas Doctrine did wonne:
  Tyll at the last, with mysty wyndes donne,
The radiant brightnes of golden Phebus
Auster gan cover with clowde tenebrus.

Then to the tower I drewe nere and nere,
  And often mused of the great hyghnes
Of the craggy rocke, which quadrant did appeare:
  But the fayre tower, (so much of ryches
  Was all about,) sexangled doubtles;
Gargeyld with greyhoundes, and with many lyons,
Made of fyne golde; with divers sundry dragons[1].

The little 'turretts' with ymages of golde
  About was set, whiche with the wynde aye moved
With propre vices, that I did well beholde
  About the tower, in sundry wyse they hoved
  With goodly pypes, in their mouthes ituned,
That with the wynd they pyped a daunce
Iclipped *Amour de la hault plesaunce.*

The toure was great of marveylous wydnes,
  To whyche ther was no way to passe but one,
Into the toure for to have an intres:
  A grece there was ychesyld all of stone
  Out of the rocke, on whyche men dyd gone
Up to the toure, and in lykewyse dyd I
Wyth bothe the Grayhoundes in my company[2]:

Tyll that I came unto a ryall gate,
  Where I saw stondynge the goodly Portres,

Ver. 25, towers. P. C.

[1] Greyhounds, lions, dragons, were at that time the royal supporters.

[2] This alludes to a former part of the poem.

Whyche axed me, from whence I came a-late;
  To whome I gan in every thynge expresse
  All myne adventure, chaunce, and busynesse,
And eke my name; I tolde her every dell:
Whan she herde this she lyked me right well.

Her name, she sayd, was called Countenaunce;
  Into the 'base' courte she dyd me then lede,
Where was a fountayne depured of plesance,
  A noble sprynge, a ryall conduyte-hede,
  Made of fyne golde enameled with reed;
And on the toppe four dragons blewe and stoute
Thys dulcet water in four partes dyd spoute.

Of whyche there flowed foure ryvers ryght clere,
  Sweter than Nylus[3] or Ganges was ther odoure;
Tygrys or Eufrates unto them no pere:
  I dyd than taste the aromatyke lycoure,
  Fragraunt of fume, and swete as any floure;
And in my mouthe it had a marveylous scent
Of divers spyces, I knewe not what it ment.

And after thys further forth me brought
  Dame Countenaunce into a goodly Hall,
Of jasper stones it was wonderly wrought:
  The wyndowes cleare depured all of crystall,
  And in the roufe on hye over all
Of golde was made a ryght crafty vyne;
Instede of grapes the rubies there did shyne.

The flore was paved with berall clarified,
  With pillers made of stones precious,
Like a place of pleasure so gayely glorified,
  It myght be called a palaice glorious,
  So muche delectable and solaçious;

V. 44, besy courte. P. C.  V. 49, partyes. P. C.

[3] Nysus P. C.

The hall was hanged hye and circuler
With cloth of arras in the rychèst maner.

That treated well of a ful noble story,
  Of the doubty waye to the Tower Perillous[4];
Howe a noble knyght should wynne the victory
  Of many a serpente foule and odious.

* * * * *

[4] The story of the poem.

---

## XI.

## The Child of Elle.

Is given from a fragment in the Editor's folio MS.; which, though extremely defective and mutilated, appeared to have so much merit, that it excited a strong desire to attempt a completion of the story. The reader will easily discover the supplemental stanzas by their inferiority, and at the same time be inclined to pardon it, when he considers how difficult it must be to imitate the affecting simplicity and artless beauties of the original.

*Child* was a title sometimes given to a knight. See Gloss.

---

On yonder hill a castle standes,
  With walles and towres bedight,
And yonder lives the Child of Elle,
  A younge and comely knighte.

The Child of Elle to his garden wente,
  And stood at his garden pale,
Whan, lo! he beheld fair Emmelines page
  Come trippinge downe the dale.

The Child of Elle he hyed him thence,
  Y-wis he stoode not stille,
And soone he mette faire Emmelines page
  Come climbing up the hille.

Nowe Christe thee save, thou little foot-page,
  Now Christe thee save and see!
Oh telle me how does thy ladye gaye,
  And what may thy tydinges bee?

My lady shee is all woe-begone,
  And the teares they falle from her eyne;
And aye she laments the deadlye feude
  Betweene her house and thine.

And here shee sends thee a silken scarfe
  Bedewde with many a teare,
And biddes thee sometimes thinke on her,
  Who loved thee so deare.

And here shee sends thee a ring of golde
  The last boone thou mayst have,
And biddes thee weare it for her sake,
  Whan she is layde in grave.

For, ah! her gentle heart is broke,
  And in grave soone must shee bee,
Sith her father hath chose her a new new love,
  And forbidde her to think of thee.

Her father hath brought her a carlish knight,
  Sir John of the north countràye,
And within three dayes shee must him wedde,
  Or he vowes he will her slaye.

Nowe hye thee backe, thou little foot-page,
  And greet thy ladye from mee,
And telle her that I her owne true love
  Will dye, or sette her free.

Nowe hye thee backe, thou little foot-page,
  And let thy fair ladye know
This night will I bee at her bowre-windòwe,
  Betide me weale or woe.

The boye he tripped, the boye he ranne,
  He neither stint ne stayd
Untill he came to fair Emmelines bowre,
  Whan kneeling downe he sayd,

O ladye, Ive been with thy own true love,
  And he greets thee well by mee;
This night will he bee at thy bowre-windòwe,
  And dye or sette thee free.

Nowe daye was gone, and night was come,
  And all were fast asleepe,
All save the ladye Emmeline,
  Who sate in her bowre to weepe:

And soone shee heard her true loves voice
  Lowe whispering at the walle,
Awake, awake, my deare ladyè,
  Tis I thy true love call.

Awake, awake, my ladye deare,
  Come, mount this faire palfràye:
This ladder of ropes will lette thee downe,
  Ile carrye thee hence awaye.

Nowe nay, nowe nay, thou gentle knight,
  Nowe nay, this may not bee;
For aye sould I tint my maiden fame,
  If alone I should wend with thee.

O ladye, thou with a knighte so true,
  Mayst safelye wend alone,
To my ladye mother I will thee bringe,
  Where marriage shall make us one.

"My father he is a baron bolde,
  Of lynage proude and hye;
And what would he saye if his daughtèr
  Awaye with a knight should fly?

Ah! well I wot, he never would rest,
  Nor his meate should doe him no goode,
Till he had slayne thee, Child of Elle,
  And seene thy deare hearts bloode."

O ladye, wert thou in thy saddle sette,
  And a little space him fro,
I would not care for thy cruel fathèr,
  Nor the worst that he could doe.

O ladye, wert thou in thy saddle sette,
  And once without this walle,
I would not care for thy cruel fathèr,
  Nor the worst that might befalle.

Faire Emmeline sighed, fair Emmeline wept,
  And aye her heart was woe:
At length he seizde her lilly-white hand,
  And downe the ladder he drewe:

And thrice he claspde her to his breste,
  And kist her tenderlie:
The teares that fell from her fair eyes,
  Ranne like the fountayne free.

Hee mounted himselfe on his steede so talle,
  And her on a faire palfràye,
And slung his bugle about his necke,
  And roundlye they rode awaye.

All this beheard her owne damsèlle,
  In her bed whereas shee ley,
Quoth shee, My lord shall knowe of this,
  Soe I shall have golde and fee.

Awake, awake, thou baron bolde!
  Awake, my noble dame!
Your daughter is fledde with the Child of Elle,
  To doe the deede of shame.

The baron he woke, the baron he rose,
And called his merrye men all:
"And come thou forth, Sir John the knighte,
The ladye is carried to thrall."

Fair Emmeline scant had ridden a mile,
A mile forth of the towne,
When she was aware of her fathers men
Come galloping over the downe:

And foremost came the carlish knight,
Sir John of the north countràye:
"Nowe stop, nowe stop, thou false traitòure,
Nor carry that ladye awaye.

For she is come of hye lynàge,
And was of a ladye borne,
And ill it beseems thee a false churles sonne
To carrye her hence to scorne."

Nowe loud thou lyest, Sir John the knight,
Nowe thou doest lye of mee;
A knight mee gott, and a ladye me bore,
Soe never did none by thee.

But light nowe downe, my ladye faire,
Light downe, and hold my steed,
While I and this discourteous knighte
Doe trye this arduous deede.

But light now downe, my deare ladyè,
Light downe, and hold my horse;
While I and this discourteous knight
Doe trye our valours force.

Fair Emmeline sighde, fair Emmeline wept,
And aye her heart was woe,
While twixt her love and the carlish knight
Past many a baleful blowe.

The Child of Elle hee fought soe well,
  As his weapone he wavde amaine,
That soone he had slaine the carlish knight,
  And layde him upon the plaine.

And nowe the baron, and all his men
  Full fast approached nye:
Ah! what may ladye Emmeline doe?
  Twere now no boote to flye.

Her lover he put his horne to his mouth,
  And blew both loud and shrill,
And soone he saw his owne merry men
  Come ryding over the hill.

"Nowe hold thy hand, thou bold baròn,
  I pray thee, hold thy hand,
Nor ruthless rend two gentle hearts,
  Fast knit in true loves band.

Thy daughter I have dearly lovde
  Full long and many a day;
But with such love as holy kirke
  Hath freelye sayd wee may.

O give consent, shee may be mine,
  And blesse a faithfull paire:
My lands and livings are not small,
  My house and lynage faire:

My mother she was an earles daughter,
  And a noble knyght my sire—
The baron he frownde, and turnde away
  With mickle dole and ire.

Fair Emmeline sighde, faire Emmeline wept,
  And did all tremblinge stand:
At lengthe she sprange upon her knee,
  And held his lifted hand.

Pardon, my lorde and father deare,
  This faire yong knyght and mee:
Trust me, but for the carlish knyght,
  I never had fled from thee.

Oft have you callde your Emmeline
  Your darling and your joye;
O let not then your harsh resolves
  Your Emmeline destroye.

The baron he stroakt his dark-brown cheeke,
  And turnde his heade asyde
To whipe awaye the starting teare,
  He proudly strave to hyde.

In deepe revolving thought he stoode,
  And musde a little space:
Then raisde faire Emmeline from the grounde,
  With many a fond embrace.

Here take her, Child of Elle, he sayd,
  And gave her lillye hand;
Here take my deare and only child,
  And with her half my land:

Thy father once mine honour wrongde
  In dayes of youthful pride;
Do thou the injurye repayre
  In fondnesse for thy bride.

And as thou love her, and hold her deare,
  Heaven prosper thee and thine:
And nowe my blessing wend wi' thee,
  My lovelye Emmeline.

---

*** From the word *kirke* in ver. 159, this hath been thought to be a Scottish ballad; but it must be acknowledged that the line referred to is among the additions supplied by the Editor: besides, in the northern counties of England, *kirk* is used in the common dialect for *church*, as well as beyond the Tweed.

---

## XII.

## Edom o' Gordon,

A SCOTTISH BALLAD,

WAS printed at Glasgow, by Robert and Andrew Foulis, 1755, 8vo. (twelve pages.) We are indebted for its publication (with many other valuable things in these volumes) to Sir David Dalrymple, Bart., who gave it as it was preserved in the memory of a lady.

The reader will here find it improved, and enlarged with several fine stanzas, recovered from a fragment of the same ballad, in the Editor's folio MS. It is remarkable that the latter is entitled *Captain Adam Carre*, and is in the English idiom. But whether the author was English or Scotch, the difference originally was not great. The English ballads are generally of the north of England, the Scottish are of the south of Scotland; and of consequence the country of ballad-singers was sometimes subject to one crown, and sometimes to the other, and most frequently to neither. Most of the finest old Scotch songs have the scene laid within twenty miles of England; which is indeed all poetic ground, green hills, remains of woods, clear brooks. The pastoral scenes remain: of the rude chivalry of former ages, happily nothing remains but the ruins of the castles, where the more daring and successful robbers resided. The house or castle of the RODES, stood about a measured mile south from Duns, in Berwickshire: some of the ruins of it may be seen to this day. The Gordons were anciently seated in the same county. The two villages of East and West Gordon lie about ten miles from the castle of the Rodes[1]: the fact,

[1] This ballad is well known in that neighbourhood, where it is entitled

however, on which the ballad is founded, happened in the north of Scotland (see p. 103). It contains but too just a picture of the violences practised in the feudal times all over Europe.

From the different titles of this ballad, it should seem that the old strolling bards or minstrels (who gained a livelihood by reciting these poems) made no scruple of changing the names of the personages they introduced, to humour their hearers. For instance, if a Gordon's conduct was blameworthy in the opinion of that age, the obsequious minstrel would, when among Gordons, change the name to Car, whose clan or sept lay further west, and *vice versâ*. In the third volume the reader will find a similar instance. See the song of *Gil Morris*, the hero of which had different names given him, perhaps from the same cause.

It may be proper to mention, that in the folio MS., instead of the "Castle of the Rodes," it is the "Castle of Brittons-borrow," and also "Diactoars," or "Dratours-borrow," for it is very obscurely written, and "Capt. Adam Carre" is called the "Lord of Westerton-town." Uniformity required that the additional stanzas supplied from that copy should be clothed in the Scottish orthography and idiom: this has therefore been attempted, though perhaps imperfectly.

---

IT fell about the Martinmas,
Quhen the wind blew schril and cauld,
Said Edom o' Gordon to his men,
We maun draw to a hauld.

And quhat a hauld sall we draw till
My mirry men and me?
We wul gae to the house o' the Rodes,
To see that fair ladìe.

*Adam o' Gordon.* It may be observed, that the famous freebooter, whom Edward the First fought with, hand to hand, near Farnham, was named Adam Gordon.

The lady stude on hir castle wa',
  Beheld baith dale and down:
There she was ware of a host of men
  Cum ryding towards the toun.

O see ze nat, my mirry men a'?
  O see ze nat quhat I see?
Methinks I see a host of men:
  In marveil quha they be.

She weend it had been hir luvely lord,
  As he cam ryding hame;
It was the traitor Edom o' Gordon,
  Quha reckt nae sin nor shame.

She had nae sooner buskit hirsel,
  And putten on hir goun,
Till Edom o' Gordon and his men
  Were round about the toun.

They had nae sooner supper sett,
  Nae sooner said the grace,
Till Edom o' Gordon and his men,
  Were light about the place.

The lady ran up to hir towir head,
  Sa fast as she could hie,
To see if by her fair speechès
  She could wi' him agree.

But quhan he see this lady saif,
  And hir yates all locked fast,
He fell into a rage of wrath,
  And his look was all aghast.

Cum doun to me, ze lady gay,
  Cum doun, cum doun to me:
This night sall ye lig within mine armes,
  To-morrow my bride sall be.

I winnae cum doun, ze fals Gordòn,
  I winnae cum doun to thee;
I winnae forsake my ain dear lord,
  That is sae far frae me.

Give owre zour house, ze lady fair,
  Give owre zour house to me,
Or I sall brenn yoursel therein,
  Bot and zour babies three.

I winnae give owre, ze fals Gordòn,
  To nae sik traitor as zee;
And if ze brenn my ain dear babes,
  My lord sall make ze drie.

But reach me hether my guid bend-bowe,
  Mine arrows one by one;
For, but an I pierce that bluidy butcher,
  My babes we been undone.

She stude upon her castle wa',
  And let twa arrows flee:
She mist that bluidy butchers hart,
  And only raz'd his knee[2].

Set fire to the house, quo' fals Gordòn,
  All wood wi' dule and ire:
Fals lady, ze sall rue this deid,
  As ze brenn in the fire.

Wae worth, wae worth ze, Jock my man,
  I paid ze weil zour fee;
Quhy pow ze out the ground-wa stane,
  Lets in the reek to me?

[2] The two foregoing stanzas are improved in this edition by more ancient readings, communicated lately to the publisher. In the former edition they were evidently modernized, viz., "Reach my pistol, Glaud, my man, And charge ze weil my gun:" and below, "let twa bullets flee."

And ein wae worth ze, Jock my man,
I paid ze weil zour hire;
Quhy pow ze out the ground-wa stane,
To me lets in the fire?

Ze paid me weil my hire, lady;
Ze paid me weil my fee:
But now Ime Edom o' Gordons man,
Maun either doe or die.

O than bespaik hir little son,
Sate on the nourice' knee:
Sayes, Mither deare, gi owre this house,
For the reek it smithers me.

I wad gie a' my gowd, my childe,
Sae wad I a' my fee,
For ane blast o' the westlin wind,
To blaw the reek frae thee.

O then bespaik hir dochter dear,
She was baith jimp and sma:
O row me in a pair o' sheits,
And tow me owre the wa.

The rowd hir in a pair o' sheits,
And towd hir owre the wa:
But on the point of Gordons spear
She gat a deadly fa.

O bonnie bonnie was hir mouth,
And cherry were hir cheiks,
And clear clear was hir zellow hair,
Whareon the reid bluid dreips.

Then wi' his spear he turnd hir owre,
O gin her face was wan!

Ver. 98, 102. O gin, &c. a Scottish idiom to express great admiration.

He sayd, Ze are the first that eir
  I wisht alive again.

He turnd hir owre and owre again,
  O gin hir skin was whyte!
I might ha spared that bonnie face,
  To hae been sum mans delyte.

Busk and boun, my merry men a',
  For ill dooms I doe guess;
I cannae luik in that bonny face,
  As it lyes on the grass.

Thame, luiks to freits, my master deir,
  Then freits wil follow thame:
Let it neir be said brave Edom o' Gordon
  Was daunted by a dame.

But quhen the ladye see the fire
  Cum flaming owre hir head,
She wept and kist her children twain,
  Sayd, Bairns, we been but dead.

The Gordon then his bougill blew,
  And said, Awa', awa';
This house o' the Rodes is a' in flame,
  I hauld it time to ga'.

O then bespyd hir ain dear lord,
  As hee cam owr the lee;
He sied his castle all in blaze
  Sa far as he could see.

Then sair, O sair his mind misgave,
  And all his hart was wae;
Put on, put on, my wighty men,
  So fast as ze can gae.

V. 109, 110, thame, &c. *i. e.* them that look after omens of ill luck, ill luck will follow.

Put on, put on, my wighty men,
So fast as ze can drie;
For he that is hindmost of the thrang,
Sall neir get guid o' me.

Than sum they rade, and sum they rin,
Fou fast out-owr the bent;
But eir the foremost could get up,
Baith lady and babes were brent.

He wrang his hands, he rent his hair,
And wept in teenefu' muid:
O traitors, for this cruel deid
Ze sall weep teirs o' bluid.

And after the Gordon he is gane,
Sa fast as he might drie;
And soon i' the Gordon's foul hartis bluid,
He's wroken his dear ladie.

---

*** Since the foregoing ballad was first printed, the subject of it has been found recorded in Abp. Spotswood's *History of the Church of Scotland*, p. 259; who informs us, that

"Anno 1571. In the north parts of Scotland, Adam Gordon (who was deputy for his brother the Earl of Huntley) did keep a great stir; and under colour of the queen's authority, committed divers oppressions, especially upon the Forbes's .... having killed Arthur Forbes, brother to the Lord Forbes. .... Not long after he sent to summon the house of Tavoy, pertaining to Alexander Forbes. The Lady refusing to yield without direction from her husband, he put fire unto it, and burnt her therein with children and servants, being twenty-seven persons in all.

"This inhuman and barbarous cruelty made his name

odious, and stained all his former doings; otherwise he was held very active and fortunate in his enterprises."

This fact, which had escaped the Editor's notice, was in the most obliging manner pointed out to him by an ingenious writer, who signs his name H. H. (Newcastle, May 9,) in the *Gentleman's Magazine* for May, 1775, p. 219.

END OF THE FIRST BOOK.

# RELIQUES

OF

# ANCIENT POETRY.

*&c.*

---

## SERIES THE FIRST.

## BOOK II.

---

### I.

### Ballads that illustrate Shakspeare.

Our great dramatic poet having occasionally quoted many ancient ballads, and even taken the plot of one, if not more, of his plays from among them, it was judged proper to preserve as many of these as could be recovered, and, that they might be the more easily found, to exhibit them in one collective view.

This Second Book is therefore set apart for the reception of such ballads as are quoted by Shakspeare, or contribute in any degree to illustrate his writings: this being the principal point in view, the candid reader will pardon the admission of some pieces that have no other kind of merit.

The design of this book being of a dramatic tendency, it may not be improperly introduced with a few observations on the origin of the English stage, and on the conduct of our first dramatic poets, a subject which though not unsuccessfully handled by several good writers already[1], will yet perhaps admit of some further illustration.

[1] Bp. Warburton's *Shakesp.* vol. v. p. 338.—Pref. to Dodsley's *Old Plays.*

## ON THE ORIGIN OF THE ENGLISH STAGE, ETC.

It is well known that dramatic poetry in this and most other nations of Europe, owes its origin, or at least its revival, to those religious shows, which in the dark ages were usually exhibited on the more solemn festivals. At those times they were wont to represent in the churches the lives and miracles of the Saints, or some of the more important stories of Scripture. And as the most mysterious subjects were frequently chosen, such as the Incarnation, Passion, and Resurrection of Christ, &c., these exhibitions acquired the general name of MYSTERIES. At first they were probably a kind of dumb shows, intermingled, it may be, with a few short speeches; at length they grew into a regular series of connected dialogues, formally divided into acts and scenes. Specimens of these in their most improved state (being at best but poor artless compositions) may be seen among Dodsley's *Old Plays*, and in Osborne's *Harleyan Miscel.* How they were exhibited in their most simple form, we may learn from an ancient novel, often quoted by our old dramatic poets[2], entitled . . . a merye Jest of a man that was called Howleglas[3], &c., being a translation from the Dutch language, in which he is named *Ulenspiegle.* Howleglas, whose waggish-tricks are the subject of this book, after many adventures comes to live with a priest, who makes him his parish-clerk. This priest is described as keeping a *leman*, or concubine, who had but one eye, to whom Howleglas owed a grudge for revealing his rogueries to his master. The story thus proceeds, . . . . "And than in the meane season, while Howleglas was parysh clarke, at Easter they should play the Resurrection of our Lorde: and for because than

—Riccoboni's *Acct. of Theat. of Europe, &c. &c.* These were all the author had seen when he first drew up this Essay.

[2] See Ben Jonson's *Poetaster,* act iii. sc. 4, and his Masque of *The Fortunate Isles.* Whalley's edit. vol. ii. p. 49, vol. vi. p. 190.

[3] Howleglas is said in the Preface to have died in M.CCCC.L. At the end of the book, M.CCC.L.

the men wer not learned, nor could not read, the priest toke his leman, and put her in the grave for an Aungel: and this seing Howleglas, toke to him iij of the simplest persons that were in the towne, that played the iij Maries; and the person [i. e. parson or rector] played Christe, with a baner in his hand. Than saide Howleglas to the symple persons: Whan the Aungel asketh you, whom you seke, you may saye, The parsons leman with one iye. Than it fortuned that the tyme was come that they must playe, and the Aungel asked them whom they sought; and than sayd they, as Howleglas had shewed and lerned them afore, and than answered they, We seke the priests leman with one iye. And than the prieste might heare that he was mocked. And whan the priestes leman herd that, she arose out of the grave, and would have smyten with her fist Howleglas upon the cheke, but she missed him and smote one of the simple persons that played one of the thre Maries; and he gave her another; and than toke she him by the heare [hair]; and that seing his wyfe, came running hastely to smite the priestes leman; and than the priest seeing this, caste down hys baner and went to helpe his woman, so that the one gave the other sore strokes, and made great noyse in the churche. And than Howleglas seying them lyinge together by the eares in the bodi of the churche, went his way out of the village, and came no more there[4]."

As the old Mysteries frequently required the representation of some allegorical personage, such as Death, Sin, Charity, Faith, and the like, by degrees the rude poets of those unlettered ages began to form complete dramatic pieces, consisting entirely of such personifications. These they entitled *Moral Plays*, or *Moralities*. The Mysteries were very inartificial, representing the Scripture stories simply according to the letter. But the Moralities are not devoid of invention: they exhibit outlines of the dramatic art; they

[4] ¶. Imprynted ..... by Wyllyam Copland: without date, in 4to. bl. let. among Mr. Garrick's *Old Plays*, K. vol. x.

contain something of a fable or plot, and even attempt to delineate characters and manners. I have now before me two that were printed early in the reign of Henry VIII.; in which I think one may plainly discover the seeds of Tragedy and Comedy; for which reason I shall give a short analysis of them both.

One of them is entitled Every Man[5]. The subject of this piece is the summoning of Man out of the world by Death; and its moral, that nothing will then avail him but a well-spent life and the comforts of religion. This subject and moral are opened in a monologue spoken by the *Messenger* (for that was the name generally given by our ancestors to the prologue on their rude stage): then God[6] is represented; who, after some general complaints on the degeneracy of mankind, calls for *Deth*, and orders him to bring before his tribunal *Every-man*, for so is called the personage who represents the human race. *Every-man* appears, and receives the summons with all the marks of confusion and terror. When *Deth* is withdrawn, *Every-man* applies for relief in this distress to *Fellowship*, *Kindred*, *Goods*, or Riches, but they successively renounce and forsake him. In this disconsolate state he betakes himself to *Good-dedes*, who, after upbraiding him with his long neglect of her[7], introduces him to her sister *Knowledge*, and she leads him to the "holy man, *Confession*," who appoints him penance: this he inflicts upon himself on the stage, and then withdraws to receive the sacraments of the priest. On his return he begins to wax faint, and after *Strength*, *Beauty*, *Discretion*, and *Five Wits*[8] have all taken their final leave of him, gradually expires on the stage; *Good-dedes* still accompanying him to the last. Then an Aungell descends to sing his *requiem:* and the

[5] This play has been reprinted by Mr. Hawkins in his *Origin of the English Drama*, 3 vols. 12mo. Oxford, 1773. See vol. i. p. 27.

[6] The second person of the Trinity seems to be meant.

[7] Those above mentioned are male characters.

[8] *i. e.* The five Senses. These are frequently exhibited as five distinct personages upon the Spanish stage (see Riccoboni, p. 98); but our moralist has represented them all by one character.

epilogue is spoken by a person called *Doctour*, who recapitulates the whole, and delivers the moral:

> "¶. This memoriall men may have in mynde,
> Ye herers, take it of worth old and yonge,
> And forsake Pryde, for he disceyveth you in thende,
> And remembre Beautè, Five Witts, Strength, and Discrecion,
> They all at last do Every-man forsake;
> Save his Good Dedes there dothe he take:
> But beware, for and they be small,
> Before God he hath no helpe at all," &c.

From this short analysis it may be observed, that **Every Man** is a grave solemn piece, not without some rude attempts to excite terror and pity, and therefore may not improperly be referred to the class of Tragedy. It is remarkable, that in this old simple drama the fable is conducted upon the strictest model of the Greek tragedy. The action is simply one; the time of action is that of the performance; the scene is never changed, nor the stage ever empty. *Every-man*, the hero of the piece, after his first appearance, never withdraws, except when he goes out to receive the sacraments, which could not well be exhibited in public; and during his absence, *Knowledge* descants on the excellence and power of the priesthood, somewhat after the manner of the Greek chorus. And, indeed, except in the circumstance of *Every-man's* expiring on the stage, the "Samson Agonistes" of Milton is hardly formed on a severer plan[9].

The other play is entitled **Hick-Scorner**[10], and bears no distant resemblance to Comedy: its chief aim seems to be to exhibit characters and manners, its plot being much less regular than the foregoing. The prologue is spoken by *Pity*, represented under the character of an aged pilgrim; he is joined by *Contemplacyon* and *Perseverance*, two holy men, who, after lamenting the degeneracy of the age, declare their resolution of stemming the torrent. *Pity* then is left

9 See more of *Every Man*, in vol. ii. Pref. to b. ii. Note.

10 **Imprynted by me Wynkyn de Worde**, no date; in 4to. bl. let. This play has also been reprinted by Mr. Hawkins in his *Origin of the English Drama*, vol. i. p. 69.

upon the stage, and presently found by *Frewyll*, representing a lewd debauchee, who, with his dissolute companion *Imaginacion*, relate their manner of life, and not without humour describe the stews and other places of base résort. They are presently joined by *Hick-scorner*, who is drawn as a libertine returned from travel, and, agreeably to his name, scoffs at religion. These three are described as extremely vicious, who glory in every act of wickedness; at length two of them quarrel, and *Pity* endeavours to part the fray; on this they fall upon him, put him in the stocks, and there leave him. *Pity*, thus imprisoned, descants in a kind of lyric measure on the profligacy of the age, and in this situation he is found by *Perseverance* and *Contemplacyon*, who set him at liberty, and advise him to go in search of the delinquents. As soon as he is gone, *Frewyll* appears again; and, after relating in a very comic manner some of his rogueries and escapes from justice, is rebuked by the two holy men, who, after a long altercation, at length convert him and his libertine companion *Imaginacion* from their vicious course of life; and then the play ends with a few verses from *Perseverance*, by way of epilogue. This, and every Morality I have seen, conclude with a solemn prayer. They are all of them in rhyme; in a kind of loose stanza, intermixed with distichs.

It would be needless to point out the absurdities in the plan and conduct of the foregoing play; they are evidently great. It is sufficient to observe, that, bating the moral and religious reflection of *Pity*, &c. the piece is of a comic cast, and contains a humorous display of some of the vices of the age. Indeed the author has generally been so little attentive to the allegory, that we need only substitute other names to his personages, and we have real characters and living manners.

We see, then, that the writers of these moralities were upon the very threshold of real Tragedy and Comedy; and therefore we are not to wonder that tragedies and comedies in form soon after took place, especially as the revival of learning about this time brought them acquainted with the Roman and Grecian models.

II. At what period of time the Moralities had their rise here, it is difficult to discover; but plays of Miracles appear to have been exhibited in England soon after the Conquest. Matthew Paris tells us, that Geoffrey, afterwards Abbot of St. Alban's, a Norman, who had been sent for over by Abbot Richard to take upon him the direction of the school of that monastery, coming too late, went to Dunstable, and taught in the abbey there; where he caused to be acted (probably by his scholars) a MIRACLE-PLAY OF ST. CATHARINE, composed by himself[1]. This was long before the year 1119, and probably within the eleventh century. The above play of ST. CATHARINE was, for aught that appears, the first spectacle of this sort that was exhibited in these kingdoms; and an eminent French writer thinks it was even the first attempt towards the revival of dramatic entertainments in all Europe; being long before the representations of Mysteries in France, for these did not begin till the year 1398[2].

But whether they derived their origin from the above exhibition or not, it is certain that holy plays, representing the miracles and sufferings of the Saints, appear to have been no novelty in the reign of Henry II., and a lighter sort of interludes were not then unknown[3]. In Chaucer's time,

[1] *Apud Dunestapliam .... quendam ludum de sancta Katerina (quem* MIRACULA *vulgariter appellamus) fecit. Ad quæ decoranda, petiit a sacrista sancti Albani, ut sibi Capæ Chorales accommodarentur, et obtinuit. Et fuit ludus ille de sancta Katerina.* Vitæ Abbat. ad fin Hist. Mat. Paris, folio, 1639, p. 56. We see here that Plays of Miracles were become common enough in the time of Mat. Paris, who flourished about 1240; but that indeed appears from the more early writings of Fitz-Stephens, quoted below.

[2] Vide Abrégé *Chron. de l'Hist. de France*, par M. Henault, à l'ann. 1179.

[3] See Fitz-Stephens's Description of London, preserved by Stow, *Londonia pro spectaculis theatralibus, pro ludis scenicis, ludos habet sanctiores, representationes miraculorum, &c.* He is thought to have written in the reign of Henry II., and to have died in that of Richard I. It is true at the end of this book we find mentioned *Henricum regem tertium;* but this is doubtless Henry the Second's son, who was crowned during the life of his father, in 1170, and is generally distinguished as *Rex juvenis, Rex filius,* and sometimes they were jointly named *Reges Angliæ.* From a passage in his Chap. *De Religione,*

"Plays of Miracles" in Lent were the common resort of idle gossips[4]. They do not appear to have been so prevalent on the continent, for the learned historian of the Council of Constance[5] ascribes to the English the introduction of plays into Germany. He tells us that the emperor, having been absent from the council for some time, was, at his return, received with great rejoicings; and that the English Fathers in particular did, upon that occasion, cause a sacred comedy to be acted before him on Sunday, January 31st, 1417; the subjects of which were: — THE NATIVITY OF OUR SAVIOUR; THE ARRIVAL OF THE EASTERN MAGI; and THE MASSACRE BY HEROD. Thence it appears, says this writer, that the Germans are obliged to the English for the invention of this sort of spectacles, unknown to them before that period.

The fondness of our ancestors for dramatic exhibitions of this kind, and some curious particulars relating to this subject, will appear from the HOUSHOLD-BOOK of the fifth Earl of Northumberland, A. D. 1512[6], whence I shall select a few extracts, which show that the exhibiting Scripture Dramas on the great festivals entered into the regular establishment, and formed part of the domestic regulations of our ancient nobility: and, what is more remarkable, that it was as much the business of the Chaplain in those days to compose PLAYS for the family, as it is now for him to make sermons.

"My Lordes Chapleyns in Household vj. *viz.* The Almonar, and if he be a maker of INTERLUDYS, than he to have a servaunt to the intent for writynge of the PARTS; and ells to have non. The maister of Gramer," &c. — *Sect.* v. p. 44.

"Item. — My lorde usith and accustomyth to gyf yerely,

it should seem that the body of St. Thomas à Becket was just then a new acquisition to the church of Canterbury.

[4] See Prologue to *Wife of Bath's Tale,* v. 6137, Tyrwhitt's ed.

[5] M. L'Enfant. Vide *Hist. du Conc. de Constance,* vol. ii. p. 440.

[6] "The regulations and establishments of the household of Hen. Alg. Percy, 5th Earl of Northumb. Lond. 1770," 8vo. Whereof a small impression was printed by order of the late Duke and Duchess of Northumberland to bestow in presents to their friends. Although begun in 1512, some of the regulations were composed so late as 1525.

if is lordship kepe a chapell and be at home, them of his lordschipes chapell, if they doo play the Play of the NATIVITE uppon Cristynmes day in the mornyinge in my lords chappell before his lordship, — xxs." — *Sect.* xliv. p. 343.

"Item . . . to them of his lordship chappell and other his lordshipis servaunts that doeth play the Play before his lordship upon SHROF-TEWSDAY at night yerely in reward — xs." — *Ibid.* p. 345.

"Item . . . to them . . . that playth the Play of RESURRECTION upon Estur day in the mornnynge in my lordis 'chapell' before his lordshipe — xxs." — *Ibid.*

"Item. — My lorde useth and accustomyth yerly to gyf hym which is ordynede to be the MASTER OF THE REVELLS yerly in my lordis hous in Cristmas for the overseyinge and orderinge of his lordschips Playes, Interludes, and Dresinge that is plaid before his lordship in his hous in the xijth dayes of Cristenmas, and they to have in rewarde for that caus yerly — xxs." — *Ibid.* p. 346.

"Item. — My lorde useth and accustomyth to gyf every of the iiij Parsones that his lordschip admyted as his PLAYERS to com to his lordship yerly at Cristynmes ande at all other such tymes as his lordship shall commande them for playing of Playe and Interludes affor his lordship, in his lordshipis hous for every of their fees for an hole yere — . . ." — *Ibid.* p. 351.

"Item. — To be payd . . . for rewards to PLAYERS for Plays playd at Christynmas by Stranegeres in my house after xx*d.*[7] every play, by estimacion somme xxxiij*s.* iiij[8]." — *Sect.* i. p. 22.

"Item. — My lorde usith, and accustometh to gif yerely when his lordshipp is at home, to every erlis Players that comes to his lordshipe betwixt Cristynmas ande Candelmas, if he be his special lorde and frende and kynsman — xx*s* " — *Sect.* xliv. p. 340.

[7] This was not so small a sum then as it may now appear; for in another part of the MS. the price ordered to be given for a fat ox is but 13*s.* 4*d.*, and for a lean one 8*s*.

[8] At this rate, the number of Plays acted must have been twenty.

"Item. — My lorde usith and accustomyth to gyf yerely when his lordship is at home to every lordis Players, that comyth to his lordshipe betwixt Crystynmas ande Candelmas — xs." — *Ibid.*

The reader will observe the great difference in the rewards here given to such Players as were retainers of noble personages, and such as are styled Strangers, or, as we may suppose, only strollers. The profession of the common player was about this time held by some in low estimation. In an old satire entitled *Cock Lorreles Bote*[9], the author, enumerating the most common trades or callings, as carpenters, coopers, joiners, &c., mentions

> "*Players*, purse-cutters, money-batterers,
> Golde-washers, tomblers, jogelers,
> Pardoners," &c.—*Sign.* B. vj.

III. It hath been observed already that plays of Miracles, or Mysteries, as they were called, led to the introduction of Moral Plays, or Moralities, which prevailed so early, and became so common, that towards the latter end of King Henry the VIIth's reign John Rastel, brother-in-law to Sir Thomas More, conceived a design of making them the vehicle of science and natural philosophy. With this view he published '¶. A new interlude and a mery of the nature of the iiii elements declarynge many proper points of phylosophy naturall, and of dyvers straunge landes[10],' &c. It is

[9] Pr. at the Sun in Fleet-street, by W. de Worde: no date, b. l. 4to.

[10] Mr. Garrick has an imperfect copy, (*Old Plays*, I. vol. iii.) The Dramatis Personæ are, "¶. The Messengere [or Prologue] Nature naturate. Humanytè. Studyous Desire. Sensuall Appetyte. The Taverner. Experyence. Ygnoraunce. (Also yf ye lyste ye may brynge in a dysgysynge.)" Afterwards follows a table of the matters handled in the interlude. Among which are "¶. Of certeyn conclusions prouvynge the yerthe must nedes be rounde, and that it hengyth in the myddes of the fyrmament, and that yt is in circumference above xxi M. myle."—— "¶. Of certeyne points of cosmographye — and of dyvers straunge regyons, — and of the new found landys and the maner of the people." This part is extremely curious, as it shows what notions were entertained of the new American discoveries by our own countrymen.

observable that the poet speaks of the discovery of America as then recent:

> —— "Within this xx yere
> Westwarde be founde new landes,
> That we never harde tell of before this," &c.

The West Indies were discovered by Columbus in 1492, which fixes the writing of this play to about 1510, (two years before the date of the above Houshold-Book). The play of Hick-Scorner was probably somewhat more ancient, as he still more imperfectly alludes to the American discoveries, under the name of "the Newe founde Ilonde." Sign. A. vij.

It is observable that in the older Moralities, as in that last mentioned, Every-man, &c. there is printed no kind of stage direction for the exits and entrances of the personages, no division of acts and scenes. But in the moral interlude of Lusty Juventus[1], written under Edward VI., the exits and entrances begin to be noted in the margin[2]: at length in Queen Elizabeth's reign, Moralities appeared formally divided into acts and scenes, with a regular prologue, &c. One of these is reprinted by Dodsley.

Before we quit this subject of the very early printed Plays, it may just be observed that, although so few are now extant, it should seem many were printed before the reign of Queen Elizabeth; as at the beginning of her reign, her INJUNCTIONS, in 1559, are particularly directed to the suppressing of "many Pamphlets, PLAYES, and Ballads; that no manner of person shall enterprize to print any such," &c. but under certain restrictions. — *Vide* Sect. v.

In the time of Henry VIII. one or two dramatic pieces had been published under the classical names of Comedy and Tragedy[3], but they appear not to have been intended

[1] Described in vol. ii. Preface to book ii. The Dramatis Personæ of this piece are, "¶. Messenger. Lusty Juventus. Good Counsaill. Knowledge. Sathan the devyll. Hypocrisie. Fellowship. Abominable-lyving [an Harlot]. God's-merciful-promises."

[2] I have also discovered some few *Exeats* and *Intrats* in the very old Interlude of the Four Elements.

[3] Bp. Bale had applied the name of Tragedy to his Mystery of Gods

for popular use: it was not till the religious ferments had subsided that the public had leisure to attend to dramatic poetry. In the reign of Elizabeth, tragedies and comedies began to appear in form, and could the poets have persevered, the first models were good. Gorboduc, a regular tragedy, was acted in 1561[4]; and Gascoigne, in 1566, exhibited Jocasta, a translation from Euripides, as also The Supposes, a regular comedy, from Ariosto: near thirty years before any of Shakspeare's were printed.

The people, however, still retained a relish for their old Mysteries and Moralities[5], and the popular dramatic poets seem to have made them their models. The graver sort of Moralities appear to have given birth to our modern Tragedy; as our Comedy evidently took its rise from the lighter interludes of that kind. And as most of these pieces contain an absurd mixture of religion and buffoonery, an eminent critic[6] has well deduced from thence the origin of our unnatural Tragi-comedies. Even after the people had been accustomed to tragedies and comedies, Moralities still kept their ground: one of them entitled The New Custom[7], was printed so late as 1573: at length they assumed the name of Masques[8], and

Promises, in 1538. In 1540, John Palsgrave, B.D. had republished a Latin comedy called Acolastus, with an English version. Holingshed tells us (vol. iii. p. 850,) that so early as 1520, the king had "a goodlie comedie of Plautus plaied" before him at Greenwich; but this was in Latin, as Mr. Farmer informs us in his curious "Essay on the Learning of Shakspeare." 8vo. p. 31.

[4] See Ames, p. 316. This play appears to have been first printed under the name of Gorboduc; then under that of Ferrex and Porrex, in 1569; and again, under Gorboduc, 1590. Ames calls the first edit. 4to.; Langbane, 8vo.; and Tanner, 12mo.

[5] The general reception the old Moralities had upon the stage, will account for the fondness of all our first poets for allegory. Subjects of this kind were familiar to every body.

[6] Bp. Warburt. Shaksp. vol. v.

[7] Reprinted among Dodsley's *Old Plays*, vol. i.

[8] In some of these appeared characters full as extraordinary as in any of the old Moralities. In Ben Jonson's Masque of Christmas, 1616, one of the personages is *Minced Pye*.

with some classical improvements became, in the two following reigns, the favourite entertainments of the court.

IV. The old Mysteries, which ceased to be acted after the Reformation, appear to have given rise to a third species of stage exhibition, which, though now confounded with Tragedy and Comedy, were by our first dramatic writers considered as quite distinct from them both: these were Historical Plays, or HISTORIES, a species of dramatic writing, which resembled the old Mysteries in representing a series of historical events, simply in the order of time in which they happened, without any regard to the three great unities. These pieces seem to differ from Tragedies, just as much as historical poems do from epic: as the Pharsalia does from the Æneid.

What might contribute to make dramatic poetry take this form was, that soon after the Mysteries ceased to be exhibited, there was published a large collection of poetical narratives, called The Mirrour for Magistrates[9], wherein a great number of the most eminent characters in English history are drawn relating their own misfortunes. This book was popular, and of a dramatic cast, and therefore, as an elegant writer[10] has well observed, might have its influence in producing Historical Plays. These narratives probably furnished the subjects, and the ancient Mysteries suggested the plan.

There appears indeed to have been one instance of an attempt at an HISTORICAL PLAY itself, which was perhaps as early as any Mystery on a religious subject; for such, I think, we may pronounce the representation of a memorable event in English history, that was EXPRESSED IN ACTION AND RHYMES. This was the old Coventry play of Hock Tuesday[1],

[9] The first part of which was printed in 1559.

[10] Walpole, Catal. of Royal and Noble Authors, vol. i. p. 166, 7.

[1] This must not be confounded with the Mysteries acted on Corpus Christi day by the Franciscans at Coventry, which were also called COVENTRY PLAYS, and of which an account is given from T. Warton's *History of English Poetry*, &c., in Malone's *Shakspeare*, vol. ii. part ii. p. 13, 14.

founded on the story of the massacre of the Danes, as it happened on St. Brice's night, November 13th, 1002[2]. The play in question was performed by certain men of Coventry, among the other shows and entertainments at Kenilworth Castle in July, 1575, prepared for Queen Elizabeth; and this the rather, "because the matter mentioneth how valiantly our English women, for the love of their country, behaved themselves."

The writer, whose words are here quoted[3], hath given a short description of the performance; which seems on that occasion to have been without recitation or rhymes, and reduced to mere dumb-show; consisting of violent skirmishes and encounters, first between Danish and English, "lance-knights on horseback," armed with spear and shield; and afterwards between "hosts" of footmen: which at length ended in the Danes being "beaten down, overcome, and many led captive by our English women[4]."

This play, it seems, which was wont to be exhibited in their city yearly, and which had been of great antiquity and long continuance there[5], had of late been suppressed, at the instance of some well-meaning but precise preachers, of whose "sourness" herein the townsmen complain; urging that their play was "without example of ill manners, pa-

[2] Not 1012, as printed in Laneham's letter, mentioned below.

[3] Ro. Laneham, whose LETTER, containing a full description of the Shows, &c. is reprinted at large in Nichols's "Progresses of Queen Elizabeth," &c., vol. i. 4to. 1788. That writer's orthography being peculiar and affected, is not here followed.

Laneham describes this play of Hock Tuesday, which was "presented in an historical cue by certain good-hearted men of Coventry," (p. 32,) and which was "wont to be play'd in their citie yearly," (p. 33,) as if it were peculiar to them, terming it "THEIR old storial show," (p. 32.) And so it might be as represented and expressed by them "after their manner," (p. 33,) although we are also told by Bevil Higgons, that St. Brice's EVE was still celebrated by the northern English in commemoration of this massacre of the Danes, the women beating brass instruments, and singing old rhymes, in praise of their cruel ancestors. See his *Short View of Eng. History*, 8vo. p. 17. (The Preface is dated 1734.)

[4] Laneham, p. 37. [5] Ibid. p. 33.

pistry, or any superstition[6];" which shows it to have been entirely distinct from a religious Mystery. But having been discontinued, and, as appears from the narrative, taken up of a sudden after the sports were begun, the players apparently had not been able to recover the old rhymes, or to procure new ones, to accompany the action; which, if it originally represented "the outrage and importable insolency of the Danes, the grievous complaint of Huna, King Ethelred's chieftain in wars[7]:" his counselling and contriving the plot to dispatch them; concluding with the conflicts above mentioned, and their final suppression, "expressed in actions and rhymes" after their manner[8], one can hardly conceive a more regular model of a complete drama, and if taken up soon after the event, it must have been the earliest of the kind in Europe[9].

Whatever this old play, or "storial show[10]," was at the time it was exhibited to Queen Elizabeth, it had probably our young Shakspeare for a spectator, who was then in his twelfth year, and doubtless attended with all the inhabitants of the surrounding country at these "princely pleasures of Kenelworth[1]," whence Stratford is only a few miles distant. And as the queen was much diverted with the Coventry Play, "whereat Her Majesty laught well," and rewarded the performers with two bucks, and five marks in money: who, "what rejoicing upon their ample reward, and what triumphing upon the good acceptance, vaunted their Play was never so dignified, nor ever any Players before so beatified:" but especially if our young bard afterwards gained admittance into the castle to see a Play, which the same evening, after supper, was there "presented of a very good theme, but so set forth by the actors' well-handling, that pleasure and

[6] Laneham, p. 33. [7] Ibid. p. 32. [8] Ibid. p. 33.

[9] The rhymes, &c., prove this play to have been in English; whereas Mr. Thomas Warton thinks the Mysteries composed before 1328 were in Latin. Malone's *Shaksp.* vol. ii. pt. ii. p. 9.

[10] Laneham, p. 32.

[1] See Nichols's *Progresses*, vol. i. p. 57.

mirth made it seem very short, though it lasted two good hours and more[2]," we may imagine what an impression was made on his infant mind. Indeed, the dramatic cast of many parts of that superb entertainment, which continued nineteen days, and was the most splendid of the kind ever attempted in this kingdom; the addresses to the queen in the personated characters of a Sybille, a Savage Man, and Sylvanus, as she approached or departed from the castle; and, on the water, by Arion, a Triton, or the Lady of the Lake, must have had a very great effect on a young imagination, whose dramatic powers were hereafter to astonish the world.

But that the Historical Play was considered by our old writers, and by Shakspeare himself, as distinct from Tragedy and Comedy, appears from numberless passages of their works. "Of late days," says Stow, "instead of those Stage-Playes[3] hath been used Comedies, Tragedies, Enterludes, and HISTORIES, both true and fayned." — Survey of London[4]. Beaumont and Fletcher, in the prologue to The Captain, say,

> "This is nor Comedy, nor Tragedy,
> Nor HISTORY."

Polonius in Hamlet commends the actors, as the best in the world, "either for Tragedie, Comedie, Historie, Pastorall," &c. And Shakspeare's friends, Heminge and Condell, in the first folio edition of his Plays, in 1623[5], have not only entitled their book "Mr. William Shakespeare's Comedies, HISTORIES, and Tragedies," but in their table of contents have arranged them under those three several heads; placing in the class of Histories, "King John, Richard II., Henry IV. two parts, Henry V., Henry VI. three parts, Richard III., and Henry VIII.;" to which they might have added such of

[2] Laneham, p. 38, 39. This was on *Sunday* evening, July 9.

[3] The Creation of the World, acted at Skinners-well in 1409.

[4] See Stow's *Survey of London*, 1603, 4to. p. 94, (said in the title page to be "written in 1598.") See also Warton's *Observations on Spenser*, vol. ii. p. 109.

[5] The same distinction is continued in the 2d and 3d folios, &c.

his other Plays as have their subjects taken from the old Chronicles, or Plutarch's Lives.

Although Shakspeare is found not to have been the first who invented this species of drama[6], yet he cultivated it with such superior success, and threw upon this simple inartificial tissue of scenes such a blaze of genius, that his HISTORIES maintain their ground in defiance of Aristotle and all the critics of the classic school, and will ever continue to interest and instruct an English audience.

Before Shakspeare wrote, Historical Plays do not appear to have attained this distinction, being not mentioned in Queen Elizabeth's licence, in 1574[7], to James Burbage and others, who are only empowered "to use, exercyse, and occupie the arte and facultye of playenge Comedies, Tragedies, Enterludes, Stage-Playes, and such other like." But when Shakspeare's HISTORIES had become the ornaments of the stage, they were considered by the public, and by himself, as a formal and necessary species, and are thenceforth so distinguished in public instruments. They are particularly inserted in the licence granted by King James I. in 1603[8] to W. Shakspeare himself, and the Players his fellows, who are authorised "to use and exercise the arte and faculty of playing Comedies, Tragedies, HISTORIES, Interludes, Morals, Pastorals, Stage-Plaies, and such like." The same merited distinction they continued to maintain after his death, till the theatre itself was extinguished; for they are expressly mentioned in a warrant in 1622, for licensing certain "late Comedians of Queen Anne deceased, to bring up children in the qualitie and exercise of playing Comedies, *Histories*, Interludes, Morals, Pastorals, Stage-Plaies, and such like[9]." The same appears in an admoni-

[6] See Malone's *Shaksp.* vol. i. part ii. p. 31.

[7] See Malone's *Shaksp.* vol. i. part ii. p. 37.

[8] Ibid. vol. i. part ii. p. 40.

[9] Ibid. p. 49. Here *Histories*, or Historical Plays, are found totally to have excluded the mention of Tragedies; a proof of their superior popularity. In an order for the king's comedians to attend King Charles I. in his summer's progress, 1636 (ibid. p. 144), *Histories* are not particularly men-

tion issued in 1637[10], by Philip Earl of Pembroke and Montgomery, then Lord Chamberlain, to the Master and Wardens of the Company of Printers and Stationers; wherein is set forth the complaint of His Majesty's servants the Players, that "diverse of their books of Comedyes and Tragedies, Chronicle-Historyes, and the like," had been printed and published to their prejudice, &c.

This distinction, we see, prevailed for near half a century; but after the Restoration, when the Stage revived for the entertainment of a new race of auditors, many of whom had been exiled in France, and formed their taste from the French theatre, Shakspeare's Histories appear to have been no longer relished; at least the distinction respecting them is dropt in the patents that were immediately granted after the king's return.

This appears, not only from the allowance to Mr. William Beeston, in June 1660[1], to use the house in Salisbury Court "for a Play-house, wherein Comedies, Tragedies, Tragi-Comedies, Pastoralls, and Interludes, may be acted," but also from the fuller grant (dated August 21, 1670)[2], to Thomas Killigrew, Esq. and Sir William Davenant, Knight, by which they have authority to erect two companies of players, and to fit up two theatres "for the representation of Tragydies, Comedyes, Playes, Operas, and all other entertainments of that nature."

But while Shakspeare was the favourite dramatic poet, his Histories had such superior merit, that he might well claim to be the chief, if not the only historic dramatist that kept possession of the English stage; which gives a strong support to the tradition mentioned by Gildon[3], that, in a conversation with Ben Jonson, our bard vindicated his Historical Plays, by urging, that as he had found "the nation

tioned; but so neither are Tragedies: they being briefly directed to "act Playes, Comedyes, and Interludes, without any lett," &c.

[10] Ibid. p. 139.

[1] This is believed to be the date by Mr. Malone, vol. ii. part ii. p. 239.

[2] Malone, vol. ii. pt. ii. p. 244. [3] Ibid. vol. vi. p. 427.

in general very ignorant of history, he wrote them in order to instruct the people in this particular." This is assigning not only a good motive, but a very probable reason for his preference of this species of composition; since we cannot doubt but his illiterate countrymen would not only want such instruction when he first began to write, notwithstanding the obscure dramatic chroniclers who precede him, but also that they would highly profit by his admirable Lectures on English History, so long as he continued to deliver them to his audience; and as it implies no claim to his being the *first* who introduced our chronicles on the stage, I see not why the tradition should be rejected.

Upon the whole, we have had abundant proof that both Shakspeare and his contemporaries considered his HISTORIES, or Historical Plays, as of a legitimate distinct species, sufficiently separate from Tragedy and Comedy; a distinction which deserves the particular attention of his critics and commentators, who, by not adverting to it, deprive him of his proper defence and best vindication for his neglect of the unities, and departure from the classical dramatic forms: for, if it be the first canon of sound criticism to examine any work by whatever rule the author prescribed for his own observance, then we ought not to try Shakspeare's HISTORIES by the general laws of Tragedy or Comedy. Whether the rule itself be vicious or not, is another inquiry; but certainly we ought to examine a work only by those principles according to which it was composed. This would save a deal of impertinent criticism.

V. We have now brought the inquiry as low as was intended, but cannot quit it without entering into a short description of what may be called the Economy of the ancient English Stage.

Such was the fondness of our forefathers for dramatic entertainments, that not fewer than *nineteen* play-houses had been opened before the year 1633, when Prynne published his *Histriomastix*[4]. From this writer it should seem that

[4] He speaks, in p. 492, of the Play-houses in Bishopsgate-street and on

"tobacco, wine, and beer[5]," were in those days the usual accommodations in the theatre.

With regard to the players themselves, the several companies were (as hath been already shown[6]) retainers, or menial servants to particular noblemen[7], who protected them in the exercise of their profession: and many of them were occasionally strollers, that travelled from one gentleman's house to another. Yet so much were they encouraged, that notwithstanding their multitude, some of them acquired large fortunes. Edward Allen, master of the play-house

Ludgate-hill, which are not among the seventeen enumerated in the Preface to Dodsley's *Old Plays*. Nay, it appears from Rymer's MSS. that *twenty-three* Play-houses had been at different periods open in London; and even *six* of them at one time.—See Malone's *Shakspeare*, vol. i. pt. ii. p. 48.

5 So, I think we may infer from the following passage, viz. "How many are there, who, according to their several qualities, spend 2*d.* 3*d.* 4*d.* 6*d.* 12*d.* 18*d.* 2*s.* and sometimes 4*s.* or 5*s.* at a play-house, day by day, if coach-hire, boat-hire, tobacco, wine, beere, and such like vaine expenses, which playes doe usually occasion, be cast into the reckoning?"—Prynne's *Histriomastix*, p. 322.

But that tobacco was smoked in the play-houses, appears from Taylor the Water-poet, in his Proclamation for Tobacco's Propagation. "Let *Play-houses*, drinking-schools, taverns, &c. be continually haunted with the contaminous vapours of it; nay (if it be possible), bring it into the CHURCHES, and there choak up their preachers." (Works, p. 253.) And this was really the case at Cambridge: James I. sent a letter in 1607, against "taking tobacco" in St. Mary's. So I learn from my friend Mr. Farmer.

A gentleman has informed me, that once going into a church in Holland, he saw the male part of the audience sitting with their hats on, smoking tobacco, while the preacher was holding forth in his morning-gown.

6 See the extracts above in p. 112, from the E. of Northumb. Houshold-Book.

7 See the Preface to Dodsley's *Old Plays*. The author of an old invective against the Stage, called *A third Blast of Retrait from Plaies, &c.* 1580, 12mo. says, "Alas! that private affection should so raigne in the nobilitie, that to pleasure their servants, and to upholde them in their vanitye, they should restraine the magistrates from executing their office!... They [the nobility] are thought to be covetous by permitting their servants ..... to live at the devotion or almes of other men, passing from countrie to countrie, from one gentleman's house to another, offering their service, which is a kind of beggerie. Who indeede, to speake more trulie, are become beggers for their servants. For commonlie the good-wil men beare to their Lordes, makes them draw the stringes of their purses to extend their liberalitie." Vide p. 75, 76, &c.

called the Globe, who founded Dulwich college, is a known instance. And an old writer speaks of the very inferior actors, whom he calls the Hirelings, as living in a degree of splendour, which was thought enormous in that frugal age[8].

At the same time the ancient prices of admission were often very low. Some houses had penny-benches[9]. The "two-penny gallery" is mentioned in the prologue to Beaumont and Fletcher's *Woman-Hater*[10]. And seats of three-pence and a groat seem to be intended in the passage of Prynne above referred to. Yet different houses varied in their prices: that play-house called the Hope had seats of

8 Stephen Gosson in his *Schoole of Abuse*, 1579, 12mo. fol. 23, says thus of what he terms in his margin *Players-men:* "Over lashing in apparel is so common a fault, that the very hyerlings of some of our players, which stand at revirsion of vi s. by the week, jet under gentlemen's noses in sutis of silke, exercising themselves to prating on the stage, and common scoffing when they come abrode, where they look askance over the shoulder at every man of whom the Sunday before they begged an almes. I speake not this, as though everye one that professeth the qualitie so abused himselfe, for it is well knowen, that some of them are sober, discreete, properly learned, honest housholders and citizens, well-thought on among their neighbours at home," [he seems to mean Edward Allen above mentioned,] "though the pryde of their shadowes (I mean those hangbyes, whom they succour with stipend) cause them to be somewhat il-talked of abroad."

In a subsequent period we have the following satirical fling at the showy exterior and supposed profits of the actors of that time. Vide Greene's *Groatsworth of Wit*, 1625, 4to.

"What is your profession?"—"Truly, Sir, .... I am a *Player*." "A Player? ... I took you rather for a Gentleman of great living; for if by outward habit men should be censured, I tell you, you would be taken for a substantial man." "So I am where I dwell .... What, though the world once went hard with me, when I was fayne to carry my playing-fardle a foot-backe: *Tempora Mutantur* .... for my very share in playing apparell will not be sold for *two hundred Pounds* .... Nay more, I can serve to make a pretty speech, for I was a country author, passing at a *Moral*," &c. See Roberto's Tale, Sign. D. 3. b.

9 So a MS. of Oldys, from Tom Nash, an old pamphlet-writer. And this is confirmed by Taylor the Water-poet, in his *Praise of Beggerie*, (p. 99,)

"Yet have I seen a begger with his many, [sc. vermin]
Come at a Play-house, all in for one penny."

10 So in the *Belman's Night-walks* by Decker, 1616, 4to. "Pay thy *two-pence* to a Player, in this gallery thou mayest sit by a harlot."

five several rates, from six-pence to half-a-crown[1]. But the general price of what is now called the Pit, seems to have been a shilling[2].

The day originally set apart for theatrical exhibition appears to have been Sunday; probably because the first dramatic pieces were of a religious cast. During a great part of Queen Elizabeth's reign the play-houses were only licensed to be opened on that day[3]. But before the end of her reign, or soon after, this abuse was probably removed.

The usual time of acting was early in the afternoon[4], plays being generally performed by day-light[5]. All female

1 Induct. to Ben. Jonson's *Bartholomew-fair:* an ancient satirical piece, called *The Blacke Booke*, Lond. 1604, 4to., talks of "the *six-penny roomes* in Play-houses," and leaves a legacy to one whom he calls "Arch-tobacco-taker of England, in ordinaries, upon *stages* both common and private."

2 Shaksp. Prol. to *Hen. VIII.*—Beaum. and Fletch. Prol. to the *Captain*, and to the *Mad-lover*. The pit probably had its name from one of the play-houses having been a cock-pit.

3 So Ste. Gosson, in his *Schoole of Abuse*, 1579, 12mo, speaking of the Players, says, "These, because they are allowed to play every Sunday, make iiii or v Sundayes at least every week," fol. 24. So the Author of *A Second and Third Blast of Retrait from Plaies*, 1580, 12mo. "Let the magistrate but repel them from the libertie of plaieng on the Sabboth-daie .... To plaie on the Sabboth is but a priviledge of sufferance, and might with ease be repelled, were it thoroughly followed." p. 61, 62. So again, "Is not the Sabboth of al other daies the most abused? ... Wherefore abuse not so the Sabboth-daie, my brethren; leave not the temple of the Lord."…. "Those unsaverie morsels of unseemelie sentences passing out of the mouth of a ruffenlie plaier, doth more content the hungrie humors of the rude multitude, and carrieth better rellish in their mouthes, than the bread of the worde," &c. Vide pp. 63, 65, 69, &c. I do not recollect that exclamations of this kind occur in Prynne, whence I conclude that this enormity no longer subsisted in his time.

It should also seem, from the author of the Third Blast above quoted, that the churches still continued to be used occasionally for theatres. Thus, in p. 77, he says, that the Players, (who, as hath been observed, were servants of the nobility,) "under the title of their maisters, or as reteiners, are priviledged to roave abroad, and permitted to publish their mametree in everie temple of God, and that throughout England, unto the horrible contempt of praier."

4 "He entertaines us (says Overbury in his Character of an Actor) in the best leisure of our life, that is, betweene meales; the most unfit time either for study, or bodily exercise." Even so late as in the reign of Charles II., plays generally began at three in the afternoon.

5 See *Biogr. Brit.* i. 117. n. D.

parts were performed by men, no English actress being ever seen on the public stage[6] before the civil wars.

Lastly, with regard to the play-house furniture and ornaments, a writer of King Charles the Second's time[7], who well remembered the preceding age, assures us, that in general "they had no other scenes nor decorations of the stage, but only old tapestry, and the stage strewed with rushes, with habits accordingly[8]." Yet Coryate thought our theatrical exhibitions, &c. splendid, when compared with what he saw abroad. Speaking of the Theatre for Comedies at Venice, he says, "The house is very beggarly and base in comparison of our stately play-houses in England: neyther can their actors compare with ours for apparrell, shewes, and musicke. Here I observed certaine things that I never saw before; for, I saw WOMEN ACT, a thing that I never saw before, though I have heard that it hath been sometimes used in London: and they performed it with as good a grace, action, gesture, and whatsoever convenient for a player, as ever I saw any masculine actor[9]."

6 I say "no *English* actress .... on the public stage," because Prynne speaks of it as an unusual enormity, that "they had Frenchwomen actors in a play not long since personated in Blackfriars Play-house." This was in 1629, vid. p. 215. And though female parts were performed by men or boys on the public stage, yet in Masques at court, the queen and her ladies made no scruple to perform the principal parts, especially in the reigns of James I. and Charles I.

Sir William Davenant, after the Restoration, introduced women, scenery, and higher prices. See Cibber's *Apology for his own Life.*

7 See a short discourse on the English Stage subjoined to Flecknor's *Loves Kingdom,* 1674, 12mo.

8 It appears from an Epigram of Taylor the Water-poet, that one of the principal theatres in his time, *viz.* the Globe, on the Bankside, Southwark, (which Ben Jonson calls the "Glory of the Bank, and Fort of the whole Parish,") had been covered with thatch till it was burnt down in 1613. (See Taylor's *Sculler,* Epig. 22, p. 31. Jonson's *Execration on Vulcan.*)

Puttenham tells us they used vizards in his time, "partly to supply the want of players, when there were more parts than there were persons, or that it was not thought meet to trouble....princes chambers with too many folkes." [*Art of Eng. Poes.* 1589, p. 26.] From the last clause it should seem that they were chiefly used at the *Masques* at court.

9 Coryate's *Crudities,* 4to. 1611, p. 247.

It ought, however, to be observed, that amid such a multitude of play-houses as subsisted in the metropolis before the civil wars, there must have been a great difference between their several accommodations, ornaments, and prices: and that some would be much more showy than others, though probably all were much inferior in splendour to the two great theatres after the Restoration.

---

*** The preceding Essay, although some of the materials are new arranged, hath received no alteration deserving notice, from what it was in the second edition, 1767, except in Sect. IV., which, in the present impression, hath been much enlarged.

This is mentioned, because, since it was first published, the History of the English Stage hath been copiously handled by Mr. Thomas Warton in his "History of English Poetry, 1774," &c., 3 vols. 4to. (wherein is inserted whatever in these volumes fell in with his subject); and by Edmond Malone, Esq., who, in his "Historical Account of the English Stage," (Shaksp. vol. i. pt. ii. 1790.) hath added greatly to our knowledge of the economy and usages of our ancient theatres.

END OF THE ESSAY.

## I.

## Adam Bell, Clym of the Clough, and William of Cloudesly,

Were three noted outlaws, whose skill in archery rendered them formerly as famous in the North of England, as Robin Hood and his fellows were in the midland counties. Their place of residence was in the forest of Englewood, not far from Carlisle (called corruptly in the ballad English-wood, whereas Engle- or Ingle-wood, signifies wood for firing). At what time they lived does not appear. The author of the common ballad on *The Pedigree, Education, and Marriage of Robin Hood*, makes them contemporary with Robin Hood's father, in order to give him the honour of beating them: viz.

> The father of *Robin* a forrester was,
>   And he shot in a lusty long-bow
> Two north-country miles and an inch at a shot,
>   As the Pindar of Wakefield does know:
>
> For he brought Adam Bell, and Clim of the Clough,
>   And William a Clowdéslee
> To shoot with our Forester for forty mark;
>   And our Forester beat them all three.
>
> *Collect. of Old Ballads,* 1727, vol. i. p. 67.

This seems to prove that they were commonly thought to have lived before the popular hero of Sherwood.

Our northern archers were not unknown to their southern countrymen, their excellence at the long-bow is often alluded to by our ancient poets. Shakspeare, in his comedy of *Much Ado about Nothing*, act i., makes Benedicke confirm his resolves of not yielding to love by this protestation, "If I do, hang me in a bottle like a cat[1], and shoot at me; and he that hits me, let him be clapt on the shoulder and called *Adam:*"

[1] Bottles formerly were of leather; though perhaps a wooden bottle might be here meant. It is still a diversion in Scotland to hang up a cat in a small cask, or firkin, half filled with soot; and then a parcel of clowns on horseback try to beat out the ends of it, in order to show their dexterity in escaping before the contents fall upon them.

meaning *Adam Bell*, as Theobald rightly observes, who refers to one or two other passages in our old poets wherein he is mentioned. The Oxford editor has also well conjectured that "Abraham Cupid," in *Romeo and Juliet*, act ii. sc. 1, should be "*Adam* Cupid," in allusion to our archer. Ben Jonson has mentioned *Clym o' the Clough* in his *Alchemist*, act i. sc. 2. And Sir William Davenant, in a mock poem of his, called *The long Vacation in London*, describes the attorneys and proctors as making matches to meet in Finsbury-fields.

"With loynes in canvas bow-case tyde[2]:
Where arrowes stick with mickle pride; . . . .
Like ghosts of *Adam Bell* and *Clymme*.
Sol sets for fear they'l shoot at him."
*Works*, p. 291, fol. 1673.

I have only to add further, concerning the principal hero of this ballad, that the Bells were noted rogues in the North so late as the time of Queen Elizabeth. See in Rymer's *Fœdera*, a letter from Lord William Howard to some of the officers of state, wherein he mentions them.

As for the following stanzas, which will be judged from the style, orthography, and numbers, to be very ancient, they are given (corrected in some places by a MS. in the Editor's old folio) from a black-letter quarto, **Imprinted at London in Lothburye by Wyllyam Copland** (no date). That old quarto edition seems to be exactly followed in "Pieces of Ancient Popular Poetry, &c. Lond. 1791," 8vo., the variations from which that occur in the following copy, are selected from many others in the folio MS. above mentioned; and when distinguished by the usual inverted 'comma,' have been assisted by conjecture.

In the same MS. this ballad is followed by another, entitled *Young Cloudeslee*, being a continuation of the present story, and reciting the adventures of William of Cloudesly's son: but greatly inferior to this both in merit and antiquity.

[2] *i. e.* Each with a canvass bow-case tied round his loins.

PART THE FIRST.

Mery it was in the grene forèst
Amonge the levès grene,
Wheras men hunt east and west
Wyth bowes and arrowes kene;

To raise the dere out of theyr denne;
Suche sightes hath ofte bene sene;
As by thre yemen of the north countrèy,
By them it is I meane.

The one of them hight Adam Bel,
The other Clym of the Clough[3],
The thyrd was William of Cloudesly,
An archer good ynough.

They were outlawed for venyson,
These yemen everychone;
They swore them brethren upon a day,
To Englyshe wood for to gone.

Now lith and lysten, gentylmen,
That of myrthes loveth to here:
Two of them were single men,
The third had a wedded fere.

Wyllyam was the wedded man,
Muche more then was hys care:
He sayde to hys brethren upon a day,
To Carleile he would fare,

For to speke with fayre Alyce his wife,
And with hys chyldren thre.
By my trouth, sayde Adam Bel,
Not by the counsell of me:

Ver. 24, *Caerlel* in P. C. passim.

[3] *Clym of the Clough* means Clem. [Clement] of the Cliff: for so Clough signifies in the North.

For if ye go to Carlile, brother,
And from thys wylde wode wende,
If that the justice may you take,
Your lyfe were at an ende.

If that I come not to-morrowe, brother,
By pryme to you agayne,
Truste you then that I am 'taken'
Or else that I am slayne.

He toke hys leave of hys brethren two,
And to Carlile he is gon:
There he knocked at his owne windòwe
Shortlye and anone.

Wher be you, fayre Alyce, he sayd,
My wife and chyldren three?
Lyghtly let in thyne owne husbànde,
Wyllyam of Cloudeslee.

Alas! then sayde fayre Alyce,
And syghed wonderous sore,
Thys place hath ben besette for you
Thys halfe a yere and more.

Now am I here, sayde Cloudeslee,
I would that in I were:
Now fetche us meate and drynke ynoughe,
And let us make good chere.

She fetched hym meate and drynke plentye,
Lyke a true wedded wyfe;
And pleased hym with that she had,
Whome she loved as her lyfe.

There lay an old wyfe in that place,
A lytle besyde the fyre,

V. 35, take. P. C., tane. MS.

Whych Wyllyam had found of charytyè
More than seven yere.

Up she rose, and forth shee goes,
Evill mote shee speede therfore;
For shee had sett no foote on ground
In seven yere before.

She went unto the justice hall,
As fast as she could hye:
Thys night, shee sayd, is come to town
Wyllyam of Cloudeslyè.

Thereof the justice was full fayne,
And so was the shirife also:
Thou shalt not trauaile hither, dame, for nought,
Thy meed thou shalt have ere thou go.

They gave to her a ryght good goune
Of scarlate, 'and of graine:'
She toke the gyft, and home she wente,
And couched her doune agayne.

They raysed the towne of mery Carleile
In all the haste they can;
And came thronging to Wyllyames house,
As fast as they might gone.

There they besette that good yemàn
Round about on every syde:
Wyllyam hearde great noyse of folkes
That thither-ward fast hyed.

Alyce opened a backe wyndòwe
And loked all aboute,
She was ware of the justice and shirife bothe,
Wyth a full great route.

V. 85, sic MS., shop window. P. C.

Alas! treason, cryed Alyce,
  Ever wo may thou be!
Goe into my chamber, husband, she sayd,
  Swete Wyllyam of Cloudeslee.

He toke hys sweard and hys bucler,
  Hys bow and hys chyldren thre,
And wente into hys strongest chamber,
  Where he thought surest to be.

Fayre Alyce, like a lover true,
  Took a pollaxe in her hande:
Said, He shall dye that cometh in
  Thys dore, whyle I may stand.

Cloudeslee bente a right good bowe,
  That was of a trusty tre,
He smote the justise on the brest,
  That hys arowe brest in three.

'A' curse on his harte, saide William,
  Thys day thy cote dyd on!
If it had ben no better then myne,
  It had gone nere thy bone.

Yelde the Cloudeslè, sayd the justise,
  And thy bowe and thy arrowes the fro.
'A' curse on hys hart, sayd fair Alyce,
  That my husband councelleth so.

Set fyre on the house, saide the sherife,
  Syth it wyll no better be,
And brenne we therin William, he saide,
  Hys wyfe and chyldren thre.

They fyred the house in many a place,
  The fyre flew up on hye:
Alas! then cryed fayre Alìce,
  I se we here shall dye.

William openyd a backe wyndòw,
  That was in hys chamber hie,
And there with sheetes he did let downe
  His wyfe and chyldren thre.

Have you here my treasure, sayde William,
  My wyfe and my chyldren thre:
For Christès love do them no harme,
  But wreke you all on me.

Wyllyam shot so wondrous well,
  Tyll hys arrowes were all agoe,
And the fyre so fast upon hym fell,
  That hys bowstryng brent in two.

The sparkles brent and fell upon
  Good Wyllyam of Cloudeslè:
Than was he a wofull man, and sayde,
  This is a cowardes death to me.

Leever had I, sayde Wyllyam,
  With my sworde in the route to renne,
Then here among myne enemyes wode
  Thus cruelly to bren.

He toke hys sweard and hys buckler,
  And among them all he ran,
Where the people were most in prece,
  He smot downe many a man.

There myght no man abyde hys stroakes,
  So fersly on them he ran:
Then they threw wyndowes, and dores on him,
  And so toke that good yemàn.

There they hym bounde both hand and fote,
  And in deepe dungeon him cast:
Now Cloudesle, sayd the justice,
  Thou shalt be hanged in hast.

V. 151, sic MS., hye justice. P. C.

'A payre of new gallowes, sayd the sherife,
  Now shal I for the make;'
And the gates of Carleil shal be shutte:
  No man shal come in therat.

Then shall not helpe Clym of the Cloughe,
  Nor yet shall Adam Bell,
Though they came with a thousand mo,
  Nor all the devels in hell.

Early in the mornynge the justice uprose,
  To the gates first gan he gone,
And commaunded to be shut full close
  Lightilè everychone.

Then went he to the markett place,
  As fast as he coulde hye;
There a payre of new gallowes he set up
  Besyde the pyllorye.

A lytle boy 'amonge them asked,'
  What meaneth that gallow-tre?
They sayde to hang a good yemàn,
  Called Wyllyam of Cloudeslè.

That lytle boye was the towne swyne-heard,
  And kept fayre Alyces swyne;
Oft he had seene William in the wodde,
  And geuen hym there to dyne.

He went out att a crevis in the wall,
  And lightly to the woode dyd gone;
There met he with these wightye yemen
  Shortly and anone.

Alas! then sayde that lytle boye,
  Ye tàry here all to longe;

V. 153, 4, are contracted from the fol. MS. and P. C. V. 179, yonge men. P. C.

Cloudeslee is taken, and dampned to death,
  All readye for to honge.

Alas! then sayd good Adam Bell,
  That ever we see thys daye!
He had better with us have taryed,
  So often as we dyd hym praye.

He myght have dwelt in grene forèste,
  Under the shadowes greene,
And have kepte both hym and us att reste,
  Out of all trouble and teene.

Adam bent a ryght good bow,
  A great hart sone hee had slayne;
Take that, chylde, he sayde, to thy dynner,
  And bryng me mine arrowe agayne.

Now go we hence, sayed these wightye yeomen,
  Tary we no longer here;
We shall hym borowe by God his grace,
  Though we bye itt full dere.

To Caerleil wente these good yemen,
  All in a mornyng of maye.
Here is a FYT[4] of Cloudeslye,
  And another is for to saye.

---

## PART THE SECOND.

AND when they came to mery Carleile,
  All in 'the' mornyng tyde,
They founde the gates shut them untyll
  About on every syde.

V. 190, sic MS., shadowes sheene. P. C. V. 197, jolly yeomen. MS., wight yong men. P. C.

[4] See Gloss.

Alas! then sayd good Adam Bell,
  That ever we were made men!
These gates be shut so wonderous fast,
  We may not come therein.

Then bespake him Clym of the Clough,
  Wyth a wyle we wyl us in bryng;
Let us saye we be messengers,
  Streyght come nowe from our king.

Adam said, I have a letter written,
  Now let us wysely werke,
We wyl saye we have the kynges seale;
  I holde the porter no clerke.

Then Adam Bell bete on the gates
  With strokes great and stronge,
The porter marveiled who was therat,
  And to the gates he thronge.

Who is there nowe, sayde the porter,
  That maketh all thys knockinge?
We be tow messengers, quoth Clim of the Clough,
  Be come ryght from our kyng.

We have a letter, sayd Adam Bel,
  To the justice we must itt bryng;
Let us in our message to do,
  That we were agayne to the kyng.

Here commeth none in, sayd the porter,
  By hym that dyed on a tre,
Tyll a false thefe be hanged up,
  Called Wyllyam of Cloudeslè.

Then spake the good yeman Clym of the Clough,
  And swore by Mary fre,
And if that we stande long wythout,
  Lyk a thefe hanged thou shalt be.

Lo! here we have the kyngès seale:
  What, Lurden, art thou wode?
The porter went[5] it had ben so,
  And lyghtly dyd off hys hode.

Welcome is my lordes seale, he saide;
  For that ye shall come in.
He opened the gate full shortlye;
  An euyl openyng for him.

Now are we in, sayde Adam Bell,
  Whereof we are full faine;
But Christ he knowes, that harowed hell,
  How we shall com out agayne.

Had we the keys, said Clim of the Clough,
  Ryght wel then shoulde we spede,
Then might we come out wel ynough
  When we se tyme and nede.

They called the porter to counsell,
  And wrang his necke in two,
And caste hym in a depe dongeon,
  And toke hys keys hym fro.

Now am I porter, sayd Adam Bel,
  Se brother the keys are here,
The worst porter to merry Carleile
  That 'the' had thys hundred yere.

And now wyll we our bowes bend,
  Into the towne wyll we go,
For to delyuer our dere brothèr,
  That lyeth in care and wo.

V. 38, Lordeyne. P. C.

[5] *i. e.* weened, *thought,* (which last is the reading of the folio MS.) Calais or Rouen was taken from the English by showing the governor, who could not read, a letter with the king's seal, which was all he looked at.

Then they bent theyr good ewe bowes,
And loked theyr stringes were round[6],
The markett place in mery Carleile
They beset that stound.

And, as they loked them besyde,
A paire of new galowes 'they' see,
And the justice with a quest of squyers,
Had judged William hanged to be.

And Cloudeslè lay redy there in a cart,
Fast bound both fote and hande;
And a stronge rop about hys necke,
All readye for to hange.

The justice called to him a ladde,
Cloudeslees clothes hee shold have,
To take the measure of that yemàn,
Thereafter to make hys grave.

I have sene as great mervaile, said Cloudesle,
As betweyne thys and pryme,
He that maketh a grave for mee
Hymselfe may lye therin.

Thou speakest proudlye, said the justice,
I shall thee hange with my hande.
Full wel herd this his brethren two,
There styll as they did stande.

Then Cloudeslè cast his eyen asyde,
And saw hys 'brethren twaine'
At a corner of the market place,
Redy the justice for to slaine.

[6] So Ascham in his *Toxophilus*, gives a precept; "The stringe must be rounde," (p. 149, ed. 1761): otherwise, we may conclude from mechanical principles, the arrow will not fly true.

I se comfort, sayd Cloudeslè,
  Yet hope I well to fare,
If I might have my handes at wyll
  Ryght lytle wolde I care.

Then spake good Adam Bell
  To Clym of the Clough so free,
Brother, se you marke the justyce wel;
  Lo! yonder you may him se:

And at the shyrife shote I wyll
  Strongly wyth arrowe kene;
A better shote in mery Carleile
  Thys seven yere was not sene.

They loosed their arrowes both at once,
  Of no man had they dread;
The one hyt the justice, the other the sheryfe,
  That both theyr sides gan blede.

All men voyded, that them stode nye,
  When the justice fell to the grounde,
And the sherife nye hym by;
  Eyther had his deathes wounde.

All the citezens fast gan flye,
  They durst no longer abyde:
There lyghtly they loosed Cloudeslee,
  Where he with ropes lay tyde.

Wyllyam start to an officer of the towne,
  Hys axe 'from' hys hande he wronge,
On eche syde he smote them downe
  Hee thought he taryed to long.

Wyllyam sayde to hys brethren two,
  Thys daye let us lyve and de,

V. 105, lowsed thre. P. C. V. 108, can bled. MS.

If ever you have nede, as I have now,
The same shall you finde by me.

They shot so well in that tyde,
Theyr stringes were of silke ful sure,
That they kept the stretes on every side;
That batàyle did long endure.

The fought together as brethren true,
Lyke hardy men and bolde,
Many a man to the ground they threw,
And many a herte made colde.

But when their arrowes were all gon,
Men preced to them full fast,
They drew theyr swordès then anone,
And theyr bowes from them they cast.

They went lyghtlye on theyr way,
Wyth swordes and buclers round;
By that it was mydd of the day,
They made many a wound.

There was many an out-horne[7] in Carleil blowen,
And the belles bacwàrd dyd ryng,
Many a woman sayde, Alas!
And many theyr handes dyd wryng.

The mayre of Carleile forth was com,
Wyth hym a ful great route:
These yemen dred hym full sore,
Of theyr lyves they stode in doute.

The mayre came armed a full great pace,
With a pollaxe in hys hande;

V. 148, For of. MS.

[7] *Outhorne* is an old term, signifying the calling forth of subjects to arms by the sound of a horn. See Cole's Lat. Dict., Bailey, &c.

Many a strong man wyth him was,
There in that stowre to stande.

The mayre smot at Cloudeslè with his bil,
Hys bucler he brast in two,
Full many a yeman with great evyll,
Alas! Treason they cryed for wo.
Kepe we the gates fast, they bad,
That these traytours thereout not go.

But al for nought was that they wrought,
For so fast they downe were layde,
Tyll they all thre, that so manfulli fought,
Were gotten without, abraide.

Have here your keys, sayd Adam Bel,
Myne office I here forsake,
And yf you do by my counsell
A new porter do ye make.

He threw theyr keys at theyr heads,
And bad them well to thryve[8],
And all that letteth any good yeman
To come and comfort his wyfe.

Thus be these good yemen gon to the wod,
And lyghtly, as lefe on lynde;
The lough and be mery in theyr mode,
Theyr enemyes were ferr behynd

When they came to Englyshe wode,
Under the trusty tre,
There they found bowes full good,
And arrowes full great plentye.

V. 175, merry green wood. MS.

[8] This is spoken ironically.

So God me help, sayd Adam Bell,
And Clym of the Clough so fre,
I would we were in mery Carleile,
Before that fayre meynye.

They set them downe, and made good chere,
And eate and dranke full well.
A second FYT of the wightye yeomen,
Another I wyll you tell.

---

PART THE THIRD.

As they sat in Englyshe wood,
Under the green-wode tre,
They thought they herd a woman wepe,
But her they mought not se.

Sore then syghed the fayre Alyce:
'That ever I sawe thys day!'
For nowe is my dere husband slayne:
Alas! and wel-a-way!

Myght I have spoken with hys dere brethren,
Or with eyther of them twayne,
To shew to them what him befell,
My hart were out of payne.

Cloudeslè walked a lytle beside,
He looked under the grene wood lynde,
He was ware of his wife, and chyldren three,
Full wo in harte and mynde.

Welcome, wyfe, then sayde Wyllyam,
Under 'this' trusti tre:
I had wende yesterdaye, by swete saynt John,
Thou sholdest me never 'have' se.

V. 185, See part i. ver. 197. V. 20, never had se. P. C. and MS.

"Now well is me that ye be here,
  My harte is out of wo."
Dame, he sayde, be mery and glad,
  And thanke my brethren two.

Herof to speake, said Adam Bell,
  I-wis it is no bote:
The meate, that we must supp withall,
  It runneth yet fast on fote.

Then went they downe into a launde,
  These noble archares all thre;
Eche of them slew a hart of greece,
  The best that they cold se.

Have here the best, Alyce, my wyfe,
  Sayde Wyllyam of Cloudeslye:
By cause ye so bouldly stode by me
  When I was slayne full nye.

Then went they to suppère
  Wyth suche meate as they had;
And thanked God of ther fortune:
  They wer both mery and glad.

And when they had supped well,
  Certayne wythouten lease,
Cloudeslè sayd, We wyll to our kyng,
  To get us a charter of peace.

Alyce shal be at our sojournyng
  In a nunnery here besyde;
My tow sonnes shall wyth her go,
  And there they shall abyde.

Myne eldest son shall go wyth me;
  For hym have 'you' no care:

V. 50, have I no care. P. C.

And he shall breng you worde agayn,
How that we do fare.

Thus be these yemen to London gone,
As fast as they myght 'he[9],'
Tyll they came to the kynges pallàce,
Where they woulde nedes be.

And whan they came to the kyngès courte,
Unto the pallace gate,
Of no man wold they aske no leave,
But boldly went in therat.

They preced prestly into the hall,
Of no man had they dreade:
The porter came after, and dyd them call,
And with them gan to chyde.

The usher sayde, Yemen, what wold ye have?
I pray you tell to me:
You myght thus make offycers shent:
Good syrs, of whence be ye?

Syr, we be out-lawes of the forest
Certayne withouten lease;
And hether we be come to our kynge,
To get us a charter of peace.

And whan they came before the kyng,
As it was the lawe of the lande,
The kneled downe without lettyng,
And eche held up his hand.

The sayed, Lord, we beseche the here,
That ye wyll graunt us grace;
For we have slayne your fat falow dere
In many a sondry place.

[9] *i. e.* hie, hasten.

What be your nams, then said our king,
Anone that you tell me?
They sayd, Adam Bell, Clim of the Clough,
And Wyllyam of Cloudeslè.

Be ye those theves, then sayd our kyng,
That men have tolde of to me?
Here to God I make an avowe,
Ye shal be hanged al thre.

Ye shal be dead without mercy,
As I am kynge of this lande.
He commandeth his officers everichone,
Fast on them to lay hande.

There they toke these good yemen,
And arested them al thre:
So may I thryve, sayd Adam Bell,
Thys game lyketh not me.

But, good lorde, we beseche you now,
That yee graunt us grace,
Insomuche as 'frelè' to you we come,
'As frely' we may fro you passe,

With such weapons as we have here,
Tyll we be out of your place;
And yf we lyve this hundreth yere,
We wyll aske you no grace.

Ye speake proudly, sayd the kynge;
Ye shall be hanged all thre.
That were great pitye, then sayd the quene,
If any grace myght be.

My lorde, whan I came fyrst into this lande
To be your wedded wyfe,

V. 111, 119, sic MS., bowne. P. C.

The fyrst boone that I wold aske,
  Ye would graunt it me belyfe:

And I never asked none tyll now;
  Therefore, good lorde, graunt it me.
Now aske it, madam, sayd the kynge,
  And graunted it shal be.

Then, good my lord, I you beseche.
  These yemen graunt ye me.
Madame, ye might have asked a boone,
  That shuld have been worth them all thre.

Ye myght have asked towres, and townes,
  Parkes and forestes plentè.
None soe pleasant to my pay, shee sayd;
  Nor none so lefe to me.

Madame, sith it is your desyre,
  Your askyng graunted shal be;
But I had lever have given you
  Good market townes thre.

The quene was a glad woman,
  And sayde, Lord, gramarcy:
I dare undertake for them,
  That true men shal they be.

But good my lord, speke som mery word,
  That comfort they may se.
I graunt you grace, then sayd our king;
  Washe, felos, and to meate go ye.

They had not setten but a whyle
  Certayne without lesynge,
There came messengers out of the north
  With letters to our kyng.

V. 130, God a mercye. MS.

And whan the came before the kynge,
They knelt downe on theyr kne:
And sayd, Lord, your officers grete you well,
Of Carleile in the north cuntrè.

How fareth my justice, sayd the kyng,
And my sherife also?
Syr, they be slayne without leasynge,
And many an officer mo.

Who hath them slayne, sayd the kyng;
Anone thou tell to me?
"Adam Bell, and Clime of the Clough,
And Wyllyam of Cloudeslè."

Alas for rewth! then sayd our kynge:
My hart is wonderous sore;
I had lever than a thousande pounde,
I had knowne of thys before;

For I have graunted them grace,
And that forthynketh me:
But had I knowne all thys before,
They had been hanged all thre.

The kyng hee opened the letter anone,
Himselfe he red it thro,
And founde how these outlawes had slain
Thre hundred men and mo:

Fyrst the justice, and the sheryfe,
And the mayre of Carleile towne:
Of all the constables and catchipolles
Alyve were 'scant' left one:

The baylyes, and the bedyls both,
And the sergeauntes of the law,

V. 168, left but one. MS., not one. P. C.

And forty fosters of the fe,
  These outlawes had yslaw:

And broke his parks, and slayne his dere;
  Of all they chose the best;
So perelous out-lawes, as they were,
  Walked not by easte nor west.

When the kynge this letter had red,
  In hys harte he syghed sore:
Take up the tables anone he bad,
  For I may eat no more.

The kyng called hys best archars
  To the buttes wyth hym to go:
I wyll se these felowes shote, he sayd,
  In the north have wrought this wo.

The kynges bowmen buske them blyve,
  And the quenes archers also;
So dyd these thre wyghtye yemen;
  With them they thought to go.

There twyse, or thryse they shote about
  For to assay theyr hande;
There was no shote these yemen shot,
  That any prycke[1] myght stand.

Then spake Wyllyam of Cloudeslè;
  By him that for me dyed,
I hold hym never no good archar,
  That shoteth at buttes so wyde.

'At what a butte now wold ye shote,'
  I pray thee tell to me?
At suche a but, syr, he sayd,
  As men use in my countrè.

V. 185, blythe, MS.

[1] *i. e.* mark.

Wyllyam wente into a fyeld,
And 'with him' his two brethren:
There they set up two hasell roddes
Full twenty score betwene.

I hold him an archar, said Cloudeslè,
That yonder wande cleveth in two
Here is none suche, sayd the kyng,
Nor none that can so do.

I shall assaye, syr, sayd Cloudeslè,
Or that I farther go.
Cloudesly with a bearyng arowe
Clave the wand in two.

Thou art the best archer, then said the king,
For sothe that ever I se.
And yet for your love, sayd Wyllyam,
I wyll do more maystery.

I have a sonne is seven yere olde,
He is to me full deare;
I wyll hym tye to a stake;
All shall se, that be here;

And lay an apple upon hys head,
And go syxe score hym fro,
And I my selfe with a brode arȯw
Shall cleve the apple in two.

Now haste the, then sayd the kyng,
By hym that dyed on a tre,
But yf thou do not, as thou hest sayde,
Hanged shalt thou be.

V. 202, 203, 212, to, P.C. V. 204, twenty score paces. P.C. *i. e.* 400 yards. V. 208, sic MS., none that can. P.C. V. 222, six-score paces. P.C., *i. e.* 120 yards.

And thou touche his head or gowne,
  In syght that men may se,
By all the sayntes that be in heaven.
  I shall hange you all thre.

That I have promised, said William,
  That I wyll never forsake.
And there even before the kynge
  In the earth he drove a stake:

And bound therto his eldest sonne,
  And bad hym stand styll thereat;
And turned the childes face him fro,
  Because he should not start.

An apple upon his head he set,
  And then his bowe he bent:
Syxe score paces they were meaten,
  And thether Cloudeslè went.

There he drew out a fayr brode arrowe,
  Hys bowe was great and longe,
He set that arrowe in his bowe,
  That was both styffe and stronge.

He prayed the people, that wer there,
  That they 'all still wold' stand,
For he that shoteth for such a wager,
  Behoveth a stedfast hand.

Muche people prayed for Cloudeslè,
  That his lyfe saved myght be,
And whan he made hym redy to shote,
  There was many weeping ee.

'But' Cloudeslè cleft the apple in two,
  'His sonne he did not nee.'

V. 243, sic MS., out met. P. C.   V. 252, steedye. MS.

Over Gods forbode, sayde the kinge,
  That thou shold shote at me.

I geve thee eightene pence a day,
  And my bowe shalt thou bere,
And over all the north countrè
  I make the chyfe rydère.

And I thyrtene pence a day, said the quene,
  By God, and by my fay;
Come feche thy payment when thou wylt,
  No man shall say the nay.

Wyllyam, I make the a gentleman
  Of clothyng, and of fe:
And thy two brethren, yemen of my chambre,
  For they are so semely to se.

Your sonne, for he is tendre of age,
  Of my wyne-seller he shall be;
And when he commeth to mans estate,
  Better avaunced shall he be.

And, Wyllyam, bring to me your wife, said the quene,
  Me longeth her sore to se:
She shall be my chefe gentlewoman,
  To governe my nurserye.

The yemen thanketh them curteously.
  To some byshop wyl we wend,
Of all the synnes, that we have done,
  To be assoyld at his hand.

So forth be gone these good yemen,
  As fast as they might 'he[2];'

V. 265, and I geve the xvii pence. P.C. V. 282, And sayd to some Bishopp wee will wend. MS.

[2] he, *i. e.* hie, hasten. See the Glossary.

And after came and dwelled with the kynge,
  And dyed good men all thre.

Thus endeth the lives of these good yemen;
  God send them eternall blysse.
And all, that with a hand-bowe shoteth,
  That of heven they never mysse. Amen.

---

## II.

## The Aged Lover renounceth Love.

The Grave-digger's song in *Hamlet*, act v. is taken from three stanzas of the following poem, though greatly altered and disguised, as the same were corrupted by the ballad-singers of Shakspeare's time; or perhaps so designed by the poet himself, the better to paint the character of an illiterate clown. The original is preserved among Surrey's Poems, and is attributed to Lord Vaux, by George Gascoigne, who tells us, it "was thought by some to be made upon his death-bed;" a popular error which he laughs at. (See his *Epist. to Yong Gent.* prefixed to his *Posies*, 1575, 4to.) It is also ascribed to Lord Vaux in a manuscript copy preserved in the British Museum[1]. This lord was remarkable for his skill in drawing feigned manners, &c. for so I understand an ancient writer. "The Lord Vaux his commendation lyeth chiefly in the facilitie of his meetre, and the aptnesse of his descriptions such as he taketh upon him to make, namely in sundry of his Songs, wherein he showeth the *counterfait action* very lively and pleasantly." *Arte of Eng. Poesie*, 1589, p. 51. See another song by this poet in vol. ii. no. viii.

[1] Harl. MSS. num. 1703, § 25. The readings gathered from that copy are distinguished here by inverted commas. The text is printed from the "Songs, &c. of the Earl of Surrey and others, 1557, 4to."

---

I LOTHE that I did love,
 In youth that I thought swete,
As time requires: for my behove
 Me thinkes they are not mete.

My lustes they do me leave,
 My fansies all are fled;
And tract of time begins to weave
 Gray heares upon my hed.

For age with steling steps,
 Hath clawde me with his crowch,
And lusty 'Youthe' away he leapes,
 As there had bene none such.

My muse doth not delight
 Me, as she did before:
My hand and pen are not in plight,
 As they have bene of yore.

For Reason me denies,
 'All' youthly idle rime;
And day by day to me she cries,
 Leave off these toyes in tyme.

The wrinkles in my brow,
 The furrowes in my face
Say, Limping age will 'lodge' him now,
 Where youth must geve him place.

The harbenger of death,
 To me I se him ride,
The cough, the cold, the gasping breath,
 Doth bid me to provide

Ver. 6, be. P. C. [printed copy in 1557.] · V. 10, *crowch* perhaps should be *clouch*, clutch, grasp. V. 11, life away she. P. C. V. 18, this. P. C. V. 23, sic ed. 1583; 'tis *hedge* in ed. 1557. hath caught him. MS.

A pikeax and a spade,
And eke a shrowding shete,
A house of clay for to be made
For such a guest most mete.

Me thinkes I hear the clarke,
That knoles the carefull knell,
And bids me leave my 'wearye' warke,
Ere nature me compell.

My kepers[2] knit the knot,
That youth doth laugh to scorne,
Of me that 'shall bee cleane' forgot,
As I had 'ne'er' been borne.

Thus must I youth geve up,
Whose badge I long did weare:
To them I yelde the wanton cup,
That better may it beare.

Lo here the bared skull;
By whose bald signe I know,
That stouping age away shall pull
'What' youthful yeres did sow.

For Beautie with her band,
These croked cares had wrought,
And shipped me into the lande,
From whence I first was brought.

And ye that bide behinde,
Have ye none other trust:
As ye of claye were cast by kinde,
So shall ye 'turne' to dust.

V. 30, wyndynge-sheete. MS. V. 34, bell. MS. V. 35, wofull. P. C. V. 38, did. P. C. V. 39, clene shal be. P. C. V. 40, not. P. C. V. 45, bare-hedde. MS. and some P. CC. V. 48, Which. P. C., That. MS. What *is conject.* V. 56, wast. P. C.

[2] Alluding perhaps to Eccles. xii. 3.

## III.

## Jephthah Judge of Israel.

In Shakspeare's *Hamlet*, act ii. sc. 7, the hero of the Play takes occasion to banter Polonius with some scraps of an old ballad, which has never appeared yet in any collection: for which reason, as it is but short, it will not perhaps be unacceptable to the reader: who will also be diverted with the pleasant absurdities of the composition. It was retrieved from utter oblivion by a lady, who wrote it down from memory as she had formerly heard it sung by her father. I am indebted for it to the friendship of Mr. Steevens.

It has been said that the original ballad, in black-letter, is among Anthony à Wood's Collection, in the Ashmolean Museum. But, upon application lately made, the volume which contained the song was missing, so that it can only now be given as in the former edition.

The banter of Hamlet is as follows:—

"*Hamlet*. 'O Jephtha, Judge of Israel,' what a treasure hadst thou!
*Polonius*. What a treasure had he, my lord?
*Ham*. Why, 'One faire daughter, and no more, The which he loved passing well.'
*Pol*. Still on my daughter.
*Ham*. Am not I i' th' right, old Jephtha?
*Pol*. If you call me Jephtha, my lord; I have a daughter, that I love passing well.
*Ham*. Nay, that follows not.
*Pol*. What follows then, my lord?
*Ham*. Why, 'As by lot, God wot;' and then, you know, 'It came to passe, As most like it was.' The first row of the pious chanson will shew you more."

Edit. 1793, vol. xv. p. 133.

---

Have you not heard these many years ago,
 Jeptha was judge of Israel?
He had one only daughter and no mo,
 The which he loved passing well:
  And, as by lott,
  God wot,

It so came to pass,
As Gods will was,
That great wars there should be,
And none should be chosen chief but he.

And when he was appointed judge,
And chieftain of the company,
A solemn vow to God he made;
If he returned with victory,
At his return,
To burn
The first live thing,
* * * * *
That should meet with him then,
Off his house, when he shoud return agen.

It came to pass, the wars was o'er,
And he returnd with victory;
His dear and only daughter first of all
Came to meet her father foremostly:
And all the way
She did play
On tabret and pipe,
Full many a stripe,
With note so high,
For joy that her father is come so nigh.

But when he saw his daughter dear
Coming on most foremostly,
He wrung his hands, and tore his hair,
And cryed out most piteously;
Oh! it's thou, said he,
That have brought me
Low,
And troubled me so,
That I know not what to do.

For I have made a vow, he sed,
The which must be replenished:
* * * * *
"What thou hast spoke
Do not revoke:
What thou hast said,
Be not affraid:
Altho' it be I;
Keep promises to God on high.

But, dear father, grant me one request,
That I may go to the wilderness,
Three months there with my friends to stay;
There to bewail my virginity;
And let there be,
Said she,
Some two or three
Young maids with me."
So he sent her away,
For to mourn, for to mourn, till her dying day.

---

## IV.

## A Robyn, Jolly Robyn.

In his *Twelfth Night*, Shakspeare introduces the Clown, singing part of the two first stanzas of the following song, which has been recovered from an ancient MS. of Dr. Harrington's, at Bath, preserved among the many literary treasures transmitted to the ingenious and worthy possessor by a long line of most respectable ancestors. Of these, only a small part hath been printed in the *Nugæ Antiquæ*, 3 vols. 12mo.; a work which the public impatiently wishes to see continued.

The song is thus given by Shakspeare, act iv. sc. 2, (Malone's edit. iv. 93.)

"*Clown.* Hey Robin, jolly Robin, [*singing.*]
Tell me how thy lady does.
*Malvolio.* Fool—
*Clown.* My lady is unkind perdy.
*Mal.* Fool—
*Clown.* Alas, why is she so?
*Mal.* Fool, I say—
*Clown.* She loves another. Who calls, ha?"

Dr. Farmer has conjectured that the song should begin thus:

"Hey, jolly Robin tell to me
How does thy lady do?
My lady is unkind perdy,
Alas! why is she so?"

But this emendation is now superseded by the proper readings of the old song itself, which is here printed from what appears the most ancient of Dr. Harrington's poetical MSS., and which has, therefore, been marked No. I. (*scil.* p. 68.) That volume seems to have been written in the reign of King Henry VIII., and as it contains many of the poems of Sir Thomas Wyat, hath had almost all the contents attributed to him by marginal directions, written with an old but later hand, and not always rightly, as, I think, might be made appear by other good authorities. Among the rest, this song is there attributed to Sir Thomas Wyat also; but the discerning reader will probably judge it to belong to a more obsolete writer.

In the old MS. to the third and fifth stanzas is prefixed this title, *Responce*, and to the fourth and sixth, *Le Plaintif:* but in the last instance so evidently wrong, that it was thought better to omit these titles, and to mark the changes of the dialogue by inverted commas. In other respects the MS. is strictly followed, except where noted in the margin. Yet the first stanza appears to be defective, and it should seem that a line is wanting, unless the four first words were lengthened in the tune.

---

A Robyn,
Jolly Robyn,
Tell me how thy leman doeth,
And thou shalt knowe of myn.

"My lady is unkynde perde."
Alack! why is she so?
"She loveth an other better than me;
And yet she will say no."

I fynde no such doublenes;
I fynde women true:
My lady loveth me dowtles,
And will change for no newe.

"Thou art happy while that doeth last;
But I say, as I fynde,
That women's love is but a blast,
And torneth with the wynde."

Suche folkes can take no harme by love,
That can abide their torn;
"But I alas can no way prove
In love, but lake and morne."

But if thou wilt avoyde thy harme,
Lerne this lessen of me,
At others fieres thy selfe to warme,
And let them warme with the.

Ver. 4, shall. MS.

---

## V.

## A Song to the Lute in Musicke.

THIS sonnet (which is ascribed to Richard Edwards[1] in the "Paradise of Daintie Devises," fo. 31, b.) is by Shak-

[1] See Wood's *Athen*, Tanner's *Biblioth.*, and Hawkins' *Hist. of Music.*

speare made the subject of some pleasant ridicule in his *Romeo and Juliet*, act iv. sc. 5, where he introduces Peter putting this question to the Musicians:

*Peter.* "....Why 'Silver Sound?' why 'Musicke with her silver sound?' what say you, Simon Catling?

*1st Musician.* Marry, sir, because silver hath a sweet sound.

*Pet.* Pretty! what say you, Hugh Rebecke?

*2nd Mus.* I say, silver sound, because Musicians sound for silver.

*Pet.* Pretty too! what say you, James Sound-post.

*3rd Mus.* Faith, I know not what to say.

*Pet.* ...I will say for you: It is 'Musicke with her silver sound,' because Musicians have no gold for sounding."

Edit. 1793, vol. xiv. p. 529.

This ridicule is not so much levelled at the song itself, (which for the time it was written is not inelegant,) as at those forced and unnatural explanations often given by us painful editors and expositors of ancient authors.

This copy is printed from an old quarto MS. in the Cotton Library, [Vesp. A. 25,] entitled "Divers things of Hen. viij's time:" with some corrections from *The Paradise of Dainty Devises*, 1596.

---

Where gripinge grefes the hart would wounde,
And dolefulle dumps the mynde oppresse,
There musicke with her silver-sound
With spede is wont to send redresse:
Of trobled mynds, in every sore,
Swete musicke hath a salve in store.

In joye yt maks our mirthe abounde,
In woe yt cheres our hevy sprites;
Be-strawghted heads relyef hath founde,
By musickes pleasaunt swete delightes:
Our senses all, what shall I say more?
Are subjecte unto musicks lore.

The Gods by musicke have theire prayse;
The lyfe, the soul therein doth joye:

For, as the Romayne poet sayes,
  In seas, whom pyrats would destroy,
A dolphin saved from death most sharpe
Arion playing on his harpe.

O heavenly gyft, that rules the mynd,
  Even as the sterne dothe rule the shippe!
O musicke, whom the gods assinde
  To comforte manne, whom cares would nippe!
Since thow both man and beste doest move,
What beste ys he, wyll the disprove?

---

## VI.

## King Cophetua and the Beggar-Maid,

Is a story often alluded to by our old dramatic writers. Shakspeare in his *Romeo and Juliet*, act ii. sc. 1, makes Mercutio say,

> ——"Her [Venus's] purblind son and heir,
> Young Adam[1] Cupid, he that shot so true,
> When King Cophetua loved the beggar-maid."

As the 13th line of the following ballad seems here particularly alluded to, it is not improbable but Shakspeare wrote it *shot so trim*, which the players or printers, not perceiving the allusion, might alter to *true.* The former, as being the more humorous expression, seems most likely to have come from the mouth of Mercutio[2].

In the 2d Part of *Hen. IV.* act. v. sc. 3, Falstaff is introduced affectedly saying to Pistoll,

> "O base Assyrian knight, what is thy news?
> Let king Cophetua know the truth thereof."

These lines Dr. Warburton thinks were taken from an old bombast play of *King Cophetua.* No such play is, I believe,

[1] See above, preface to Song i. Book ii. of this vol. p. 158, 159.

[2] Since this conjecture was first made, it has been discovered that *shot so trim* was the genuine reading. See Shakspeare, edit. 1793, xiv. 393.

now to be found; but it does not therefore follow that it never existed. Many dramatic pieces are referred to by old writers, which are not now extant, or even mentioned in any list[3]. In the infancy of the stage, plays were often exhibited that were never printed.

It is probably in allusion to the same play, that Ben Jonson says in his Comedy of *Every Man in his Humour*, act iii. sc. 4.

"I have not the heart to devour thee, an' I might be made as *rich* as King Cophetua."

At least there is no mention of King Cophetua's *riches* in the present ballad, which is the oldest I have met with on the subject.

It is printed from Rich. Johnson's *Crown Garland of Goulden Roses*, 1612, 12mo (where it is entitled simply, *A Song of a Beggar and a King*): corrected by another copy.

---

I READ that once in Affrica
  A princely wight did raine,
Who had to name Cophetua,
  As poets they did faine:
From natures lawes he did decline,
For sure he was not of my mind,
He cared not for women-kinde,
  But did them all disdaine.
But, marke, what hapned on a day,
As he out of his window lay,
He saw a beggar all in gray,
  The which did cause his paine.

The blinded boy, that shootes so trim,
  From heaven downe did hie;
He drew a dart and shot at him,
  In place where he did lye:

3 See Mere's *Wits Treas.* fol. 283. *Arte of Eng. Poes.* 1589, pp. 51, 111, 143, 169.

Which soone did pierse him to the quicke,
And when he felt the arrow pricke,
Which in his tender heart did sticke,
He looketh as he would dye.
What sudden chance is this, quoth he,
That I to love must subject be,
Which never thereto would agree,
But still did it defie?

Then from the window he did come,
And laid him on his bed.
A thousand heapes of care did runne
Within his troubled head:
For now he meanes to crave her love,
And now he seekes which way to proove
How he his fancie might remoove,
And not this beggar wed.
But Cupid had him so in snare,
That this poor begger must prepare
A salve to cure him of his care,
Or els he would be dead.

And, as he musing thus did lye,
He thought for to devise
How he might have her companye,
That so did 'maze his eyes.
In thee, quoth he, doth rest my life;
For surely thou shalt be my wife,
Or else this hand with bloody knife
The Gods shall sure suffice.
Then from his bed he soon arose,
And to his pallace gate he goes;
Full little then this begger knowes
When she the king espies.

The gods preserve your majesty,
The beggers all gan cry:

Vouchsafe to give your charity
  Our childrens food to buy.
The king to them his pursse did cast,
And they to part it made great haste;
This silly woman was the last
  That after them did hye.
The king he cal'd her back againe,
And unto her he gave his chaine;
And said, With us you shal remaine
  Till such time as we dye:

For thou, quoth he, shalt be my wife,
  And honoured for my queene;
With thee I meane to lead my life,
  As shortly shall be seene:
Our wedding shall appointed be,
And every thing in its degree:
Come on, quoth he, and follow me,
  Thou shalt go shift thee cleane.
What is thy name, faire maid? quoth he.
Penelophon[4], O king, quoth she:
With that she made a lowe courtsèy;
  A trim one as I weene.

Thus hand in hand along they walke
  Unto the king's pallàce:
The king with courteous comly talke
  This begger doth imbrace:
The begger blusheth scarlet red,
And straight againe as pale as lead,
But not a word at all she said,
  She was in such amaze.

[4] Shakspeare (who alludes to this ballad in his *Love's Labour Lost*, act iv. sc. 1,) gives the Beggar's name *Zenelophon*, according to all the old editions: but this seems to be a corruption; for *Penelophon*, in the text, sounds more like the name of a woman. The story of the King and the Beggar is also alluded to in King Rich. II. act v. sc. 3.

At last she spake with trembling voyce,
And said, O king, I doe rejoyce
That you wil take me for your choyce,
And my degree's so base.

And when the wedding day was come,
The king commanded strait
The noblemen both all and some
Upon the queene to wait.
And she behaved herself that day,
As if she had never walkt the way;
She had forgot her gowne of gray,
Which she did weare of late.
The proverbe old is come to passe,
The priest, when he begins his masse,
Forgets that ever clerke he was,
He knowth not his estate.

Here you may read, Cophetua,
Though long time fancie-fed,
Compelled by the blinded boy
The begger for to wed:
He that did lovers lookes disdaine,
To do the same was glad and faine,
Or else he would himselfe have slaine,
In storie, as we read.
Disdaine no whit, O lady deere,
But pitty now thy servant heere,
Least that it hap to thee this yeare,
As to that king it did.

And thus they led a quiet life
During their princely raine;
And in a tombe were buried both,
As writers sheweth plaine.

Ver. 90, *i.e.* tramped the streets. V. 105, Here the poet addresses himself to his mistress. V. 112, *sheweth* was anciently the plur. numb.

The lords they tooke it grievously,
The ladies tooke it heavily,
The commons cryed piteously,
  Their death to them was paine,
Their fame did sound so passingly,
That it did pierce the starry sky,
And throughout all the world did flye
  To every princes realme[5].

[5] An ingenious friend thinks the two last stanzas should change place.

---

## VII.

## Take thy Old Cloak about Thee,

Is supposed to have been originally a Scottish ballad. The reader here has an ancient copy in the English idiom, with an additional stanza (the 2d) never before printed. This curiosity is preserved in the Editor's folio MS. but not without corruptions, which are here removed by the assistance of the Scottish edit. Shakspeare in his *Othello*, act ii. has quoted one stanza, with some variations, which are here adopted: the old MS. readings are however given in the margin.

---

This winters weather itt waxeth cold,
  And frost doth freese on every hill,
And Boreas blowes his blasts soe bold,
  That all our cattell are like to spill;
Bell my wife, who loves no strife,
  She sayd unto me quietlie,
Rise up, and save cow Crumbockes life,
  Man, put thine old cloake about thee.

He.

O Bell, why dost thou flyte 'and scorne?'
  Thou kenst my cloak is very thin:

It is so bare and overworne
  A cricke he thereon cannot renn:
Then Ile noe longer borrowe nor lend,
  'For once Ile new appareld bee,
To-morrow Ile to towne and spend,'
  For Ile have a new cloake about mee.

SHE.

Cow Crumbocke is a very good cowe,
  She has been alwayes true to the payle,
Shee has helpt us to butter and cheese, I trow,
  And other things she will not fayle;
I wold be loth to see her pine,
  Good husband, councell take of mee,
It is not for us to go soe fine,
  Then take thine old cloake about thee

HE.

My cloake it was a very good cloake,
  Itt hath been alwayes true to the weare,
But now it is not worth a groat;
  I have had it four and forty yeare:
Sometime itt was of cloth in graine,
  'Tis now but a sigh clout as you may see,
It will neither hold out winde nor raine;
  Ill have a new cloake about mee.

SHE.

It is four and fortye yeeres agoe
  Since the one of us the other did ken,
And we have had betwixt us towe
  Of children either nine or ten;
Wee have brought them up to women and men;
  In the feare of God I trow they bee;
And why wilt thou thyself misken?
  Man, take thine old cloake about thee.

HE.

O Bell my wyfe, why dost thou 'floute!'
  Now is nowe, and then was then:
Seeke now all the world throughout,
  Thou kenst not clownes from gentlemen.
They are clad in blacke, greene, yellowe, or 'gray,'
  Soe far above their owne degree:
Once in my life Ile 'doe as they,'
  For Ile have a new cloake about mee.

SHE.

King Stephen was a worthy peere,
  His breeches cost him but a crowne,
He held them sixpence all too deere;
  Therefore he calld the taylor Lowne.
He was a wight of high renowne,
  And thouse but of a low degree:
Itt's pride that putts the countrye downe,
  Then take thine old cloake about thee.

HE.

'Bell my wife she loves not strife,
  Yet she will lead me if she can;
And oft, to live a quiet life,
  I am forced to yield, though Ime good-man;'
Itt's not for a man with a woman to threape,
  Unlesse he first give oer the plea:
As wee began wee now mun leave,
  And Ile take mine old cloake about mee.

Ver. 49, King Harry ... a very good king. MS. V. 50, I trow his hose cost but. MS. V. 51, He thought them 12*d*. to deere. MS. V. 52, clowne. MS. V. 53, He was king and wore the crowne. MS.

---

## VIII.

## Willow, Willow, Willow.

It is from the following stanzas that Shakspeare has taken his song of the *Willow*, in his *Othello*, act iv. sc. 3, though somewhat varied and applied by him to a female character. He makes Desdemona introduce it in this pathetic and affecting manner,

> "My mother had a maid call'd Barbara:
> She was in love; and he she lov'd prov'd mad,
> And did forsake her. She had a song of—Willow.
> An old thing 'twas, but it express'd her fortune;
> And she dyed singing it."—Ed. 1793, vol. xv., p. 613.

This is given from a black-letter copy in the Pepys Collection, thus entitled, "*A Lovers Complaint, being forsaken of his Love.* To a pleasant tune."

---

A poore soule sat sighing under a sicamore tree;
O willow, willow, willow!
With his hand on his bosom, his head on his knee;
O willow, willow, willow!
O willow, willow, willow!
Sing, O the greene willow shall be my garlànd.

He sigh'd in his singing, and after each grone,
Come willow, &c.
I am dead to all pleasure, my true-love is gone;
O willow, &c.
Sing, O the greene willow, &c.

My love she is turned; untrue she doth prove:
O willow, &c.
She renders me nothing but hate for my love.
O willow, &c.
Sing, O the greene willow, &c.

O pitty me (cried he) ye lovers, each one;
O willow, &c.
Her heart's hard as marble; she rues not my mone.
O willow, &c.
Sing, O the greene willow shall be my garlànd.

The cold streams ran by him, his eyes wept apace;
O willow, &c.
The salt tears fell from him, which drowned his face:
O willow, &c.
Sing, O the greene willow, &c.

The mute birds sate by him, made tame by his mones:
O willow, &c.
The salt tears fell from him, which softened the stones.
O willow, &c.
Sing, O the greene willow, &c.

Let nobody blame me, her scornes I do prove;
O willow, &c.
She was borne to be faire; I, to die for her love.
O willow, &c.
Sing, O the greene willow, &c.

O that beauty should harbour a heart that's so hard!
Sing willow, &c.
My true love rejecting without all regard.
O willow, &c.
Sing, O the greene willow, &c.

Let love no more boast him in palace, or bower;
O willow, &c.
For women are trothles, and flote in an houre.
O willow, &c.
Sing, O the greene willow, &c.

But what helps complaining? In vaine I complaine:
O willow, &c.

I must patiently suffer her scorne and disdaine.
O willowe, &c.
Sing, O the greene willow shall be my garlànd.

Come, all you forsaken, and sit down by me,
O willow, &c.
He that 'plaines of his false love, mine's falser than she.
O willow, &c.
Sing, O the greene willow, &c.

The willow wreath weare I, since my love did fleet;
O willow, &c.
A Garland for lovers forsaken most meete.
O willow, &c.
Sing, O the greene willow shall be my garlànd!

---

PART THE SECOND.

Lowe lay'd by my sorrow, begot by disdaine;
O willow, willow, willow!
Against her too cruell, still still I complaine,
O willow, willow, willow!
O willow, willow, willow!
Sing, O the greene willow shall be my garlànd!

O love too injurious, to wound my poore heart!
O willow, &c.
To suffer the triumph, and joy in my smart:
O willow, &c.
Sing, O the greene willow, &c.

O willow, willow, willow! the willow garlànd,
O willow, &c.
A sign of her falsenesse before me doth stand:
O willow, &c.
Sing, O the greene willow, &c.

As here it doth bid to despair and to dye,
O willow, &c.
So hang it, friends, ore me in grave where I lye:
O willow, &c.
Sing, O the greene willow shall be my garlànd.

In grave where I rest mee, hang this to the view,
O willow, &c.
Of all that doe knowe her, to blaze her untrue.
O willow, &c.
Sing, O the greene willow, &c.

With these words engraven, as epitaph meet,
O willow, &c.
"Here lyes one, drank poyson for potion most sweet."
O willow, &c.
Sing, O the greene willow, &c.

Though she thus unkindly hath scorned my love,
O willow, &c.
And carelesly smiles at the sorrowes I prove;
O willow, &c.
Sing, O the greene willow, &c.

I cannot against her unkindly exclaim,
O willow, &c.
Cause once well I loved her, and honoured her name:
O willow, &c.
Sing, O the greene willow, &c.

The name of her sounded so sweete in mine eare,
O willow, &c.
It rays'd my heart lightly, the name of my deare;
O willow, &c.
Sing, O the greene willow, &c.

As then 'twas my comfort, it now is my griefe;
O willow, &c.

It now brings me anguish, then brought me reliefe.
    O willow, &c.
Sing, O the greene willow shall be my garlànd!

Farewell, faire false hearted: plaints end with my breath!
    O willow, willow, willow!
Thou dost loath me, I love thee, though cause of my death.
    O willow, willow, willow!
    O willow, willow, willow!
Sing, O the greene willow shall be my garlànd.

---

## IX.

## Sir Lancelot Du Lake.

This ballad is quoted in Shakspeare's Second Part of *Henry IV.* act ii. sc. 4. The subject of it is taken from the ancient romance of *King Arthur*, (commonly called *Morte Arthur*,) being a poetical translation of chap. cviii. cix. cx. in Part 1st, as they stand in ed. 1634, 4to. In the older editions the chapters are differently numbered. This song is given from a printed copy, corrected in part by a fragment in the editor's folio MS.

In the same Play of 2 *Henry IV.*, *Silence* hums a scrap of one of the old ballads of Robin Hood. It is taken from the following stanza of *Robin Hood and the Pindar of Wakefield.*

> All this beheard three wighty yeomen,
>   'Twas Robin Hood, Scarlet, and John:
> With that they espyd the Jolly Pindàr
>   As he sate under a thorne.

That ballad may be found on every stall, and therefore is not here reprinted.

---

When Arthur first in court began,
  And was approved king,
By force of armes great victoryes wanne,
  And conquest home did bring.

Then into England straight he came
  With fifty good and able
Knights, that resorted unto him,
  And were of his round table:

And he had justs and turnaments,
  Wherto were many prest,
Wherein some knights did then excell
  And far surmount the rest.

But one Sir Lancelot du Lake,
  Who was approved well,
He for his deeds and feates of armes,
  All others did excell.

When he had rested him a while
  In play, and game, and sportt,
He said he wold goe prove himselfe
  In some adventurous sort.

He armed rode in forrest wide,
  And met a damsell faire,
Who told him of adventures great,
  Whereto he gave good eare.

Such wold I find, quoth Lancelott:
  For that cause came I hither.
Thou seemst, quoth she, a knight full good,
  And I will bring thee thither.

Wheras a mighty knight doth dwell,
  That now is of great fame:
Therfore tell me what wight thou art,
  And what may be thy name.

"My name is Lancelot du Lake."
  Quoth she, it likes me than:

Ver. 18, to sportt. MS. V. 29, *where* is often used by our old writers for *whereas:* here it is just the contrary.

Here dwelles a knight who never was
  Yet matcht with any man:

Who has in prison threescore knights
  And four, that he did wound;
Knights of king Arthurs court they be,
  And of his table round.

She brought him to a river side,
  And also to a tree,
Whereon a copper bason hung,
  And many shields to see.

He struck soe hard, the bason broke;
  And Tarquin soon he spyed:
Who drove a horse before him fast,
  Whereon a knight lay tyed.

Sir knight, then sayd Sir Lancelòtt,
  Bring me that horse-load hither,
And lay him downe, and let him rest;
  Weel try our force together:

For, as I understand, thou hast,
  Soe far as thou art able,
Done great despite and shame unto
  The knights of the Round Table.

If thou be of the Table Round,
  Quoth Tarquin speedilye,
Both thee and all thy fellowship
  I utterly defye.

That's over much, quoth Lancelott tho,
  Defend thee by and by.
They sett their speares unto their steeds,
  And each att other flye.

They coucht their speares, (their horses ran,
As though there had been thunder)
And strucke them each immidst their shields,
Wherewith they broke in sunder.

Their horsses backes brake under them,
The knights were both astound:
To avoyd their horsses they made haste
And light upon the ground.

They tooke them to their shields full fast,
Their swords they drew out than,
With mighty strokes most eagerlye
Each at the other ran.

They wounded were, and bled full sore,
For both for breath did stand,
And leaning on their swordes awhile,
Quoth Tarquine, Hold thy hand,

And tell to me what I shall aske.
Say on, quoth Lancelot tho.
Thou art, quoth Tarquine, the best knight
That ever I did know;

And like a knight, that I did hate:
Soe that thou be not hee,
I will deliver all the rest,
And eke accord with thee.

That is well sayd, quoth Lancelott;
But sith it must be soe,
What knight is that thou hatest thus?
I pray thee to me show.

His name is Lancelot du Lake,
He slew my brother deere;
Him I suspect of all the rest:
I would I had him here.

Thy wish thou hast, but yet unknowne,
  I am Lancelot du Lake,
Now knight of Arthurs Table Round;
  King Hauds son of Schuwake;

And I desire thee do thy worst.
  Ho, ho, quoth Tarquin tho,
One of us two shall end our lives
  Before that we do go.

If thou be Lancelot du Lake,
  Then welcome shalt thou bee;
Wherfore see thou thyself defend,
  For now defye I thee.

They buckled then together so,
  Like unto wild boares rashing[1],
And with their swords and shields they ran
  At one another slashing:

The ground besprinkled was with blood:
  Tarquin began to yield;
For he gave backe for wearinesse,
  And lowe did beare his shield,

This soone Sir Lancelot espyde,
  He leapt upon him then,
He pull'd him downe upon his knee,
  And rushing off his helm,

[1] *Rashing* seems to be the old hunting term to express the stroke made by the wild-boar with his fangs. To *rase* has apparently a meaning something similar. See Mr. Steevens's Note to *King Lear*, act iii. sc. 7, (ed. 1793, vol. xiv., p. 193,) where the quartos read,

"Nor thy fierce sister
In his anointed flesh *rash* boarish fangs."

So in *King Richard III.*, act iii. sc. 2, (vol. x., pp. 567, 583.)

"He dreamt
To night the boar had *rased* off his helm."

Forthwith he strucke his necke in two,
 And, when he had soe done,
From prison threescore knights and four
 Delivered everye one.

---

## X.

## Corydon's Farewell to Phillis,

Is an attempt to paint a lover's irresolution, but so poorly executed, that it would not have been admitted into this collection, if it had not been quoted in Shakspeare's *Twelfth Night*, act ii. sc. 3.—It is found in a little ancient miscellany, entitled *The Golden Garland of Princely Delights*, 12mo. bl. let.

In the same scene of the *Twelfth Night*, Sir Toby sings a scrap of an old ballad, which is preserved in the Pepys Collection, (vol. i. pp. 33. 496,) but as it is not only a poor dull performance, but also very long, it will be sufficient here to give the first stanza:

THE BALLAD OF CONSTANT SUSANNA.

There dwelt a man in Babylon
 Of reputation great by fame;
He took to wife a faire womàn,
 Susanna she was callde by name:
A woman fair and vertuous:
 Lady, lady:
Why should we not of her learn thus
 To live godly?

If this song of *Corydon*, &c. has not more merit, it is at least an evil of less magnitude.

---

Farewell, dear love; since thou wilt needs be gone,
Mine eyes do shew, my life is almost done.
 Nay I will never die, so long as I can spie
 There be many mo, though that she doe goe,
 There be many mo, I fear not:
 Why then let her goe, I care not.

Farewell, farewell; since this I find is true,
I will not spend more time in wooing you:
  But I will seek elsewhere, if I may find love there:
  Shall I bid her goe? what and if I doe?
    Shall I bid her goe and spare not?
    O no, no, no, I dare not.

Ten thousand times farewell;—yet stay a while:—
Sweet, kiss me once; sweet kisses time beguile:
  I have no power to move. How now am I in love?
  Wilt thou needs be gone? Go then, all is one.
    Wilt thou needs be gone? Oh, hie thee!
    Nay stay, and do no more deny me.

Once more adieu, I see loath to depart
Bids oft adieu to her, that holds my heart.
  But seeing I must lose thy love, which I did choose,
  Goe thy way for me, since that may not be.
    Goe thy ways for me. But whither?
    Goe, oh, but where I may come thither.

What shall I doe? my love is now departed.
She is as fair, as she is cruel-hearted.
  She would not be intreated, with prayers oft repeated,
  If she come no more, shall I die therefore?
    If she come no more, what care I?
    Faith, let her goe, or come, or tarry.

---

## XI.

## Gernutus the Jew of Venice.

In the *Life of Pope Sixtus V.*, translated from the Italian of Greg. Leti, by the Rev. Mr. Farneworth, folio, is a remarkable passage to the following effect:

"It was reported in Rome, that Drake had taken and plundered St. Domingo in Hispaniola, and carried off an immense booty. This account came in a private letter to

Paul Secchi, a very considerable merchant in the city, who had large concerns in those parts, which he had insured. Upon receiving this news, he sent for the insurer, Sampson Ceneda, a Jew, and acquainted him with it. The Jew, whose interest it was to have such a report thought false, gave many reasons why it could not possibly be true, and at last worked himself into such a passion, that he said, I'll lay you a pound of my flesh it is a lye. Secchi, who was of a fiery hot temper, replied, I'll lay you a thousand crowns against a pound of your flesh that it is true. The Jew accepted the wager, and articles were immediately executed betwixt them, That if Secchi won, he should himself cut the flesh with a sharp knife from whatever part of the Jew's body he pleased. The truth of the account was soon confirmed; and the Jew was almost distracted, when he was informed that Secchi had solemnly sworn he would compel him to an exact performance of his contract. A report of this transaction was brought to the Pope, who sent for the parties, and being informed of the whole affair, said, When contracts are made, it is but just they should be fulfilled, as this shall: take a knife therefore, Secchi, and cut a pound of flesh from any part you please of the Jew's body. We advise you, however, to be very careful; for if you cut but a scruple more or less than your due, you shall certainly be hanged."

The editor of that book is of opinion, that the scene between Shylock and Antonio in the *Merchant of Venice*, is taken from this incident. But Mr. Warton, in his ingenious *Observations on the Faerie Queen*, vol. i. p. 128, has referred it to the following ballad. Mr. Warton thinks this ballad was written before Shakspeare's play, as being not so circumstantial, and having more of the nakedness of an original. Besides, it differs from the play in many circumstances, which a mere copyist, such as we may suppose the ballad-maker to be, would hardly have given himself the trouble to alter. Indeed he expressly informs us, that he had his story from the Italian writers. See the *Connoisseur*, vol. i. no. 16.

After all, one would be glad to know what authority Leti had for the foregoing fact, or at least for connecting it with the taking of St. Domingo by Drake; for this expedition did not happen till 1585, and it is very certain that a play of the *Jewe*, "representing the greedinesse of worldly chusers, and bloody minds of usurers," had been exhibited at the play-house, called *The Bull*, before the year 1579, being mentioned in Steph. Gosson's *Schoole of Abuse*[1], which was printed in that year.

As for Shakspeare's *Merchant of Venice*, the earliest edition known of it is in quarto, 1600; though it had been exhibited before the year 1598, being mentioned, together with eleven other of his plays, in Mere's *Wits Treasury*, &c. 1598. 12mo. fol. 282. See Malone's Shakspeare.

The following is printed from an ancient black-letter copy in the Pepys Collection[2], entitled, "a new Song, shewing the crueltie of Gernutus, a Jewe, who lending to a merchant an hundred crowns, would have a pound of his fleshe, because he could not pay him at the time appointed. To the tune of *Black and Yellow*."

---

THE FIRST PART.

In Venice towne not long agoe
  A cruel Jew did dwell,
Which lived all on usurie,
  As Italian writers tell.

Gernutus called was the Jew,
  Which never thought to dye,
Nor ever yet did any good
  To them in streets that lie.

His life was like a barrow hogge,
  That liveth many a day,
Yet never once doth any good,
  Until men will him slay.

[1] Warton, ubi supra. [2] Compared with the Ashmole copy.

Or like a filthy heap of dung,
  That lieth in a whoard;
Which never can do any good,
  Till it be spread abroad.

So fares it with the usurer,
  He cannot sleep in rest,
For feare the thiefe will him pursue
  To plucke him from his nest.

His heart doth thinke on many a wile,
  How to deceive the poore;
His mouth is almost ful of mucke,
  Yet still he gapes for more.

His wife must lend a shilling,
  For every weeke a penny,
Yet bring a pledge, that is double worth,
  If that you will have any.

And see, likewise, you keepe your day,
  Or else you loose it all:
This was the living of the wife,
  Her cow she did it call.

Within that citie dwelt that time
  A marchant of great fame,
Which being distressed in his need,
  Unto Gernutus came:

Desiring him to stand his friend
  For twelve month and a day,
To lend to him an hundred crownes:
  And he for it would pay

Ver. 32, her *cow*, &c. seems to have suggested to Shakspeare Shylock's argument for usury taken from Jacob's management of Laban's sheep, act i. to which Antonio replies,

"Was this inserted to make interest good?
Or are your gold and silver *ewes* and rams?
*Shylock*. I cannot tell, I make it *breed as fast*."

Whatsoever he would demand of him,
  And pledges he should have.
No, (quoth the Jew with flearing lookes)
  Sir, aske what you will have.

No penny for the loane of it
  For one year you shall pay;
You may doe me as good a turne,
  Before my dying day.

But we will have a merry jeast,
  For to be talked long:
You shall make me a bond, quoth he,
  That shall be large and strong:

And this shall be the forfeyture;
  Of your owne fleshe a pound,
If you agree, make you the bond,
  And here is a hundred crownes.

With right good will! the marchant says:
  And so the bond was made.
When twelve month and a day drew on
  That backe it should be payd,

The marchants ships were all at sea,
  And money came not in;
Which way to take, or what to doe
  To thinke he doth begin:

And to Gernutus strait he comes
  With cap and bended knee,
And sayde to him, Of curtesie
  I pray you beare with mee.

My day is come, and I have not
  The money for to pay:
And little good the forfeyture
  Will doe you, I dare say.

With all my heart, Gernutus sayd,
  Commaund it to your minde:
In thinges of bigger waight then this
  You shall me ready finde.

He goes his way; the day once past
  Gernutus doth not slacke
To get a sergiant presently;
  And clapt him on the backe:

And layd him into prison strong,
  And sued his bond withall;
And when the judgement day was come,
  For judgement he did call.

The marchants friends came thither fast,
  With many a weeping eye,
For other means they could not find,
  But he that day must dye.

---

### THE SECOND PART.

"Of the Jews crueltie: setting foorth the mercifulnesse of the Judge towards the Marchant. To the tune of *Blacke and Yellow*."

Some offered for his hundred crownes
  Five hundred for to pay:
And some a thousand, two or three,
  Yet still he did denay.

And at the last ten thousand crownes
  They offered, him to save.
Gernutus sayd, I will no gold,
  My forfeite I will have.

A pound of fleshe is my demand,
  And that shall be my hire.
Then sayd the judge, Yet, good my friend,
  Let me of you desire

To take the flesh from such a place,
  As yet you let him live:
Do so, and lo! an hundred crownes
  To thee here will I give.

No: no: quoth he, no: judgment here:
  For this it shall be tride,
For I will have my pound of fleshe
  From under his right side.

It grieved all the companie
  His crueltie to see,
For neither friend nor foe could helpe
  But he must spoyled bee.

The bloudie Jew now ready is
  With whetted blade in hand[1],
To spoyle the bloud of innocent,
  By forfeit of his bond.

And as he was about to strike
  In him the deadly blow:
Stay (quoth the judge) thy crueltie;
  I charge thee to do so.

Sith needs thou wilt thy forfeit have,
  Which is of flesh a pound:
See that thou shed no drop of bloud,
  Nor yet the man confound.

For if thou doe, like murderer,
  Thou here shalt hanged be:
Likewise of flesh see that thou cut
  No more than longes to thee:

[1] The passage in Shakspeare bears so strong a resemblance to this, as to render it probable that the one suggested the other. See act iv. sc. 2. *Bass.* "Why doest thou whet thy knife so earnestly?" &c.

For if thou take either more or lesse
  To the value of a mite,
Thou shalt be hanged presently,
  As is both law and right.

Gernutus now waxt franticke mad,
  And wotes not what to say;
Quoth he at last, Ten thousand crownes,
  I will that he shall pay;

And so I graunt to set him free.
  The judge doth answere make;
You shall not have a penny given;
  Your forfeyture now take.

At the last he doth demaund
  But for to have his owne.
No, quoth the judge, doe as you list,
  Thy judgement shall be showne.

Either take your pound of flesh, quoth he,
  Or cancell me your bond.
O cruell judge, then quoth the Jew,
  That doth against me stand!

And so with griping grieved mind
  He biddeth them fare-well.
'Then' all the people prays'd the Lord,
  That ever this heard tell.

Good people, that doe heare this song,
  For trueth I dare well say,
That many a wretch as ill as hee
  Doth live now at this day;

That seeketh nothing but the spoyle
  Of many a wealthey man,

V. 61, *griped*. Ashmol. copy.

And for to trap the innocent
  Deviseth what they can.

From whome the Lord deliver me,
  And every Christian too,
And send to them like sentence eke
  That meaneth so to do.

---

⁂ Since the first edition of this book was printed, the Editor hath had reason to believe, that both Shakspeare and the author of this ballad, are indebted for their story of the Jew (however they came by it) to an Italian Novel, which was first printed at Milan in the year 1554, in a book entitled, *Il Pecorone, nel quale si contengono Cinquanta Novelle antiche, &c.*, republished at Florence about the year 1748 or 9. — The author was Ser. Giovanni Fiorentino, who wrote in 1378; thirty years after the time in which the scene of Boccace's *Decameron* is laid. (Vide *Manni, Istoria del Decamerone di Giov. Boccac.* 4to. Fior. 1744.)

That Shakspeare had his plot from the Novel itself, is evident from his having some incidents from it which are not found in the ballad: and I think it will also be found that he borrowed from the ballad some hints that were not suggested by the Novel. (See above, pt. ii. ver. 25, &c., where instead of that spirited description of *the whetted blade*, &c., the prose narrative coldly says, "The Jew had prepared a razor," &c. See also some other passages in the same piece.) This however is spoken with diffidence, as I have at present before me only the abridgment of the Novel which Mr. Johnson has given us at the end of his Commentary on Shakspeare's play. The translation of the Italian story at large, is not easy to be met with, having I believe never been published, though it was printed some years ago with this title, — "The Novel, from which the *Merchant of Venice* written by Shakespeare is taken, translated from the Italian. To which is added, a Translation of a Novel from the *Decamerone* of Boccaccio. London, Printed for M. Cooper, 1755," 8vo.

---

## XII.

### The Passionate Shepherd to his Love.

THIS beautiful sonnet is quoted in the *Merry Wives of Windsor*, act iii. sc. 1, and is ascribed (together with *the Reply*) to Shakspeare himself by all the modern editors of his smaller poems. A copy of this Madrigal, containing only four stanzas (the 4th and 6th being wanting) accompanied with the first of the answer, being printed in *The Passionate Pilgrime, and Sonnets to sundry Notes of Musicke*, by Mr. WILLIAM SHAKESPEARE. Lond. printed for W. Jaggard, 1599. Thus was this sonnet, &c. published as Shakspeare's in his life-time.

And yet there is good reason to believe that (not Shakspeare, but) Christopher Marlow wrote the song, and Sir Walter Raleigh the *Nymph's Reply*. For so we are positively assured by Isaac Walton, a writer of some credit, who has inserted them both in his *Compleat Angler*[1], under the character of "that smooth song, which was made by Kit. Marlow, now at least fifty years ago; and . . . an Answer to it, which was made by Sir Walter Raleigh in his younger days. . . . Old-fashioned poetry, but choicely good." It also passed for Marlow's in the opinion of his contemporaries; for in the old Poetical Miscellany, entitled *England's Helicon*, it is printed, with the name of Chr. Marlow subjoined to it: and the Reply is subscribed *Ignoto*, which is known to have been a signature of Sir Walter Raleigh. With the same signature *Ignoto*, in that Collection, is an imitation of Marlow's, beginning thus,

> "Come live with me, and be my dear,
> And we will revel all the year,
> In plains and groves," &c.

Upon the whole, I am inclined to attribute them to Mar-

1 First printed in the year 1653, but probably written some time before.

low and Raleigh, notwithstanding the authority of Shakspeare's Book of Sonnets. For it is well known, that as he took no care of his own compositions, so was he utterly regardless of what spurious things were fathered upon him. *Sir John Oldcastle*, the *London Prodigal*, and the *Yorkshire Tragedy*, were printed with his name at full length in the title-pages while he was living, which yet were afterwards rejected by his first editors, Heminge and Condell, who were his intimate friends, (as he mentions both in his will,) and therefore no doubt had good authority for setting them aside[2].

The following sonnet appears to have been (as it deserved) a great favourite with our earlier poets: for besides the imitation above mentioned, another is to be found among Donne's Poems, entitled *The Bait*, beginning thus,

> "Come live with me, and be my love,
> And we will some new pleasures prove
> Of golden sands," &c.

As for Chr. Marlow, who was in high repute for his dramatic writings, he lost his life by a stab received in a brothel, before the year 1593. See A. Wood, i. 138.

---

Come live with me, and be my love,
And we wil all the pleasures prove
That hils and vallies, dale and field,
And all the craggy mountains yield.

There will we sit upon the rocks,
And see the shepherds feed their flocks,
By shallow rivers, to whose falls
Melodious birds sing madrigals.

There will I make thee beds of roses
With a thousand fragrant posies,

[2] Since the above was written, Mr. Malone, with his usual discernment, hath rejected the stanzas in question from the other Sonnets, &c. of Shakspeare, in his correct edition of *The Passionate Pilgrim*, &c. See his Shakspeare, vol. x., p. 340.

A cap of flowers, and a kirtle
Imbrodered all with leaves of mirtle;

A gown made of the finest wool,
Which from our pretty lambs we pull;
Slippers lin'd choicely for the cold,
With buckles of the purest gold;

A belt of straw, and ivie buds,
With coral clasps, and amber studs:
And if these pleasures may thee move,
Then live with me, and be my love.

The shepherd swains shall dance and sing
For thy delight each May morning:
If these delights thy mind may move,
Then live with me, and be my love.

---

## THE NYMPH'S REPLY.

If that the World and Love were young,
And truth in every shepherd's toung,
These pretty pleasures might me move
To live with thee, and be thy love.

But time drives flocks from field to fold,
When rivers rage, and rocks grow cold,
And Philomel becometh dumb,
And all complain of cares to come.

The flowers do fade, and wanton fields
To wayward winter reckoning yield:
A honey tongue, a heart of gall,
Is fancies spring, but sorrows fall.

Thy gowns, thy shoes, thy beds of roses,
Thy cap, thy kirtle, and thy posies,
Soon break, soon wither, soon forgotten,
In folly ripe, in reason rotten.

Thy belt of straw, and ivie buds,
Thy coral clasps, and amber studs;
All these in me no means can move
To come to thee, and be thy love.

But could youth last, and love still breed,
Had joyes no date, nor age no need;
Then those delights my mind might move
To live with thee, and be thy love.

---

## XIII.

### Titus Andronicus's Complaint.

The reader has here an ancient ballad on the same subject as the play of *Titus Andronicus*, and it is probable that the one was borrowed from the other: but which of them was the original, it is not easy to decide. And yet, if the argument offered above in p. 182, for the priority of the ballad of the *Jew of Venice* may be admitted, somewhat of the same kind may be urged here; for this ballad differs from the play in several particulars, which a simple ballad-writer would be less likely to alter than an inventive tragedian. Thus in the ballad is no mention of the contest for the empire between the two brothers, the composing of which makes the ungrateful treatment of Titus afterwards the more flagrant: neither is there any notice taken of his sacrificing one of Tamora's sons, which the tragic poet has assigned as the original cause of all her cruelties. In the play, Titus loses twenty-one of his sons in war, and kills another for assisting Bassianus to carry off Lavinia: the reader will find it different in the ballad. In the latter she is betrothed to the Emperor's son: in the play to his brother. In the tragedy only two of his sons fall into the pit, and the third, being banished, returns to Rome with a victorious army, to avenge the wrongs of his house: in the ballad all three are entrapped, and suffer death. In the scene the

Emperor kills Titus, and is in return stabbed by Titus's surviving son. Here Titus kills the Emperor, and afterwards himself.

Let the reader weigh these circumstances, and some others wherein he will find them unlike, and then pronounce for himself. After all, there is reason to conclude, that this play was rather improved by Shakspeare with a few fine touches of his pen, than originally writ by him; for not to mention that the style is less figurative than his others generally are, this tragedy is mentioned with discredit in the Induction to Ben Jonson's *Bartholomew-fair*, in 1614, as one that had then been exhibited "five and twenty or thirty years:" which, if we take the lowest number, throws it back to the year 1589, at which time Shakspeare was but 25: an earlier date than can be found for any other of his pieces[1]: and if it does not clear him entirely of it, shows at least it was a first attempt[2].

The following is given from a copy in *The Golden Garland*, entitled as above; compared with three others, two of them in black letter, in the Pepys Collection, entitled *The Lamentable and Tragical History of Titus Andronicus, &c.* — To the tune of *Fortune.* Printed for E. Wright.—Unluckily none of these have any dates.

---

You noble minds, and famous martiall wights,
That in defence of native country fights,
Give eare to me, that ten yeeres fought for Rome,
Yet reapt disgrace at my returning home

1 Mr. Malone thinks 1591 to be the era when our author commenced a writer for the stage. See, in his *Shakspeare*, the ingenious "attempt to ascertain the order in which the Plays of Shakspeare were written."

2 Since the above was written, Shakspeare's memory has been fully vindicated from the charge of writing the above Play by the best critics. See what has been urged by Steevens and Malone, in their excellent editions of Shakspeare, &c.

In Rome I lived in fame fulle threescore yeeres,
My name beloved was of all my peeres;
Full five and twenty valiant sonnes I had,
Whose forwarde vertues made their father glad.

For when Rome's foes their warlike forces bent,
Against them stille my sonnes and I were sent;
Against the Goths full ten yeeres weary warre
We spent, receiving many a bloudy scarre.

Just two and twenty of my sonnes were slaine
Before we did returne to Rome againe:
Of five and twenty sonnes, I brought but three
Alive, the stately towers of Rome to see.

When wars were done, I conquest home did bring,
And did present my prisoners to the king,
The queene of Goths, her sons, and eke a moore,
Which did such murders, like was nere before.

The emperour did make this queene his wife,
Which bred in Rome debate and deadlie strife;
The moore, with her two sonnes did growe soe proud,
That none like them in Rome might bee allowd.

The moore soe pleas'd this new-made empress' eie,
That she consented to him secretlye
For to abuse her husbands marriage bed,
And soe in time a blackamore she bred.

Then she, whose thoughts to murder were inclinde,
Consented with the moore of bloody minde
Against myselfe, my kin, and all my friendes,
In cruell sort to bring them to their endes.

Soe when in age I thought to live in peace,
Both care and griefe began then to increase:
Amongst my sonnes I had one daughter bright,
Which joy'd, and pleased best my aged sight:

My deare Lavinia was betrothed than
To Cesars sonne, a young and noble man:
Who in a hunting by the emperours wife,
And her two sonnes, bereaved was of life.

He being slaine, was cast in cruel wise,
Into a darksome den from light of skies:
The cruell moore did come that way as then
With my three sonnes, who fell into the den.

The moore then fetcht the emperour with speed,
For to accuse them of that murderous deed;
And when my sonnes within the den were found,
In wrongfull prison they were cast and bound.

But nowe, behold! what wounded most my mind,
The empresses two sonnes of savage kind
My daughter ravished without remorse,
And took away her honour, quite perforce.

When they had tasted of soe sweete a flowre,
Fearing this sweete should shortly turn to sowre,
They cutt her tongue, whereby she could not tell
How that dishonoure unto her befell.

Then both her hands they basely cutt off quite,
Whereby their wickednesse she could not write;
Nor with her needle on her sampler sowe
The bloudye workers of her direfull woe.

My brother Marcus found her in the wood,
Staining the grassie ground with purple bloud,
That trickled from her stumpes, and bloudlesse armes:
Noe tongue at all she had to tell her harmes.

But when I sawe her in that woefull case,
With teares of bloud I wet mine aged face:
For my Lavinia I lamented more
Then for my two and twenty sonnes before.

When as I sawe she could not write nor speake,
With grief mine aged heart began to breake;
We spred an heape of sand upon the ground,
Whereby those bloudy tyrants out we found.

For with a staffe, without the helpe of hand,
She writt these wordes upon the plat of sand:
"The lustfull sonnes of the proud emperèsse
Are doers of this hateful wickednèsse."

I tore the milk-white hairs from off mine head,
I curst the houre wherein I first was bred,
I wisht this hand, that fought for countrie's fame,
In cradle rockt, had first been stroken lame.

The moore delighting still in villainy
Did say, to sett my sonnes from prison free
I should unto the king my right hand give,
And then my three imprisoned sonnes should live.

The moore I caus'd to strike it off with speede,
Whereat I grieved not to see it bleed,
But for my sonnes would willingly impart,
And for their ransome send my bleeding heart.

But as my life did linger thus in paine,
They sent to me my bootlesse hand againe,
And therewithal the heades of my three sonnes,
Which filld my dying heart with fresher moanes.

Then past reliefe I upp and downe did goe,
And with my teares writ in the dust my woe:
I shot my arrowes[3] towards heaven hie,
And for revenge to hell often did crye.

[3] If the ballad was written before the play, I should suppose this to be only a metaphorical expression, taken from that in the Psalms, "They shoot out their arrows, even bitter words." Ps. lxiv. 3.

The empresse then, thinking that I was mad,
Like Furies she and both her sonnes were clad,
(She nam'd Revenge, and Rape and Murder they)
To undermine and heare what I would say,

I fed their foolish veines[4] a certaine space,
Untill my friendes did find a secret place,
Where both her sonnes unto a post were bound,
And just revenge in cruell sort was found.

I cut their throates, my daughter held the pan
Betwixt her stumpes, wherein the bloud it ran:
And then I ground their bones to powder small,
And made a paste for pyes streight therewithall.

Then with their fleshe I made two mighty pyes,
And at a banquet served in stately wise:
Before the empresse set this loathsome meat;
So of her sonnes own flesh she well did eat.

Myselfe bereav'd my daughter then of life,
The empresse then I slewe with bloudy knife,
And stabb'd the emperour immediatelie,
And then myself: even soe did Titus die.

Then this revenge against the moore was found,
Alive they sett him halfe into the ground,
Whereas he stood untill such time he starv'd.
And soe God send all murderers may be serv'd.

[4] *i. e.* encouraged them in their foolish humours, or fancies.

---

## XIV.

### Take those Lips Away.

The first stanza of this little sonnet, which an eminent critic[1] justly admires for its extreme sweetness, is found in

[1] Dr. Warb. in his *Shakspeare.*

Shakspeare's *Measure for Measure*, act iv. sc. 1. Both the stanzas are preserved in Beaum. and Fletcher's *Bloody Brother*, act v. sc. 2. Sewel and Gildon have printed it among Shakspeare's smaller poems, but they have done the same by twenty other pieces that were never writ by him; their book being a wretched heap of inaccuracies and mistakes. It is not found in Jaggard's old edition of Shakspeare's *Passionate Pilgrime*[2], &c.

---

Take, oh take those lips away,
  That so sweetlye were forsworne;
And those eyes, the breake of day,
  Lights, that do misleade the morne:
But my kisses bring againe,
Seales of love, but seal'd in vaine.

Hide, oh hide those hills of snowe,
  Which thy frozen bosom beares,
On whose tops the pinkes that growe,
  Are of those that April wears:
But first set my poor heart free,
Bound in those icy chains by thee.

[2] Mr. Malone, in his improved edit. of Shakspeare's Sonnets, &c. hath substituted this instead of Marlow's Madrigal, printed above; for which he hath assigned reasons, which the reader may see in his vol. x. p. 340.

---

## XV.

## King Leir and his three Daughters.

The reader has here an ancient ballad on the subject of King Lear, which (as a sensible female critic has well observed[1]) bears so exact an analogy to the argument of Shakspeare's play, that his having copied it could not be doubted, if it were certain that it was written before the tragedy. Here is found the hint of Lear's madness, which the old

[1] Mrs. Lennox, *Shakspeare Illustrated*, vol. iii. p. 302.

chronicles[2] do not mention, as also the extravagant cruelty exercised on him by his daughters: in the death of Lear they likewise very exactly coincide. The misfortune is, that there is nothing to assist us in ascertaining the date of the ballad but what little evidence arises from within; this the reader must weigh, and judge for himself.

It may be proper to observe, that Shakspeare was not the first of our dramatic poets who fitted the story of LEIR to the stage. His first 4to. edition is dated 1608; but three years before that, had been printed a play entitled *The true Chronicle History of Leir and his three Daughters, Gonorill, Ragan, and Cordella, as it hath been divers and sundry times lately acted*, 1605, 4to. This is a very poor and dull performance, but happily excited Shakspeare to undertake the subject, which he has given with very different incidents. It is remarkable, that neither the circumstances of Leir's madness, nor his retinue of a select number of knights, nor the affecting deaths of Cordelia and Leir, are found in that first dramatic piece: in all which Shakspeare concurs with this ballad.

But to form a true judgment of Shakspeare's merit, the curious reader should cast his eye over that previous sketch: which he will find printed at the end of the Twenty Plays of Shakspeare, republished from the quarto impressions by George Steevens, with such elegance and exactness, as led us to expect that fine edition of all the works of our great dramatic poet, which he hath since published.

The following ballad is given from an ancient copy in the *Golden Garland*, bl. let. entitled, *A lamentable Song of the Death of King Leir and his three Daughters.* To the tune of *When flying Fame.*

[2] See Jeffery of Monmouth, Holingshed, &c., who relate Leir's history in many respects the same as the ballad.

King Leir once ruled in this land,
  With princely power and peace;
And had all things with hearts content,
  That might his joys increase.
Amongst those things that nature gave,
  Three daughters fair had he,
So princely seeming beautiful,
  As fairer could not be.

So on a time it pleas'd the king
  A question thus to move,
Which of his daughters to his grace
  Could shew the dearest love:
For to my age you bring content,
  Quoth he, then let me hear
Which of you three in plighted troth
  The kindest will appear.

To whom the eldest thus began;
  Dear father, mind, quoth she,
Before your face, to do you good,
  My blood shall render'd be:
And for your sake my bleeding heart
  Shall here be cut in twain,
Ere that I see your reverend age
  The smallest grief sustain.

And so will I, the second said;
  Dear father, for your sake,
The worst of all extremities
  I'll gently undertake:
And serve your highness night and day
  With diligence and love;
That sweet content and quietness
  Discomforts may remove.

In doing so, you glad my soul,
  The aged king reply'd;

But what sayst thou, my youngest girl,
  How is thy love ally'd?
My love (quoth young Cordelia then)
  Which to your grace I owe,
Shall be the duty of a child,
  And that is all I'll show.

And wilt thou shew no more, quoth he,
  Than doth thy duty bind?
I well perceive thy love is small,
  When as no more I find:
Henceforth I banish thee my court,
  Thou art no child of mine;
Nor any part of this my realm
  By favour shall be thine.

Thy elder sisters loves are more
  Than well I can demand,
To whom I equally bestow
  My kingdome and my land,
My pompal state and all my goods,
  That lovingly I may
With those thy sisters be maintain'd
  Until my dying day.

Thus flattering speeches won renown,
  By these two sisters here:
The third had causeless banishment,
  Yet was her love more dear:
For poor Cordelia patiently
  Went wandring up and down,
Unhelp'd, unpity'd, gentle maid,
  Through many an English town:

Untill at last in famous France
  She gentler fortunes found;
Though poor and bare, yet she was deem'd
  The fairest on the ground:

Where when the king her virtues heard,
And this fair lady seen,
With full consent of all his court
He made his wife and queen.

Her father king Leir this while
With his two daughters staid;
Forgetful of their promis'd loves,
Full soon the same decay'd;
And living in queen Ragan's court,
The eldest of the twain,
She took from him his chiefest means,
And most of all his train.

For whereas twenty men were wont
To wait with bended knee:
She gave allowance but to ten,
And after scarce to three:
Nay, one she thought too much for him,
So took she all away,
In hope that in her court, good king,
He would no longer stay.

Am I rewarded thus, quoth he,
In giving all I have
Unto my children, and to beg
For what I lately gave?
I'll go unto my Gonorell;
My second child, I know,
Will be more kind and pitiful,
And will relieve my woe.

Full fast he hies then to her court;
Where when she heard his moan
Return'd him answer, That she griev'd
That all his means were gone:
But no way could relieve his wants;
Yet if that he would stay

Within her kitchen, he should have
  What scullions gave away.

When he had heard, with bitter tears,
  He made his answer then;
In what I did let me be made
  Example to all men.
I will return again, quoth he,
  Unto my Ragan's court;
She will not use me thus, I hope,
  But in a kinder sort.

Where when he came, she gave command
  To drive him thence away:
When he was well within her court
  (She said) he would not stay.
Then back again to Gonorell
  The woeful king did hie,
That in her kitchen he might have
  What scullion boys set by.

But there of that he was deny'd,
  Which she had promis'd late:
For once refusing, he should not
  Come after to her gate.
Thus twixt his daughters, for relief
  He wandred up and down;
Being glad to feed on beggars food,
  That lately wore a crown.

And calling to remembrance then
  His youngest daughters words,
That said the duty of a child
  Was all that love affords:
But doubting to repair to her,
  Whom he had banish'd so,
Grew frantick mad; for in his mind
  He bore the wounds of woe:

Which made him rend his milk-white locks,
  And tresses from his head,
And all with blood bestain his cheeks,
  With age and honour spread.
To hills and woods and watry founts,
  He made his hourly moan,
Till hills and woods, and sensless things,
  Did seem to sigh and groan.

Even thus possest with discontents,
  He passed o're to France,
In hopes from fair Cordelia there,
  To find some gentler chance:
Most virtuous dame! which when she heard
  Of this her father's grief,
As duty bound, she quickly sent
  Him comfort and relief:

And by a train of noble peers,
  In brave and gallant sort,
She gave in charge he should be brought
  To Aganippus' court;
Whose royal king, with noble mind
  So freely gave consent,
To muster up his knights at arms,
  To fame and courage bent.

And so to England came with speed,
  To repossesse king Leir,
And drive his daughters from their thrones
  By his Cordelia dear:
Where she, true-hearted noble queen,
  Was in the battel slain:
Yet he good king, in his old days,
  Possest his crown again.

But when he heard Cordelia's death,
  Who died indeed for love

Of her dear father, in whose cause
  She did this battle move;
He swooning fell upon her breast,
  From whence he never parted:
But on her bosom left his life,
  That was so truly hearted.

The lords and nobles when they saw
  The end of these events,
The other sisters unto death
  They doomed by consents;
And being dead, their crowns they left
  Unto the next of kin:
Thus have you seen the fall of pride,
  And disobedient sin.

---

## XVI.

### Youth and Age,

Is found in the little collection of Shakspeare's Sonnets, entitled the *Passionate Pilgrime*[1], the greatest part of which seems to relate to the amours of Venus and Adonis, being little effusions of fancy, probably written while he was composing his larger Poem on that subject. The following seems intended for the mouth of Venus, weighing the comparative merits of youthful Adonis and aged Vulcan. In the *Garland of Good-will* it is reprinted, with the addition of four more such stanzas, but evidently written by a meaner pen.

---

Crabbed Age and Youth
  Cannot live together;
Youth is full of pleasance,
  Age is full of care:
Youth like summer morn,
  Age like winter weather,

[1] Mentioned above, Song xii. b. ii. (p. 190.)

Youth like summer brave,
  Age like winter bare:
Youth is full of sport,
Ages breath is short;
  Youth is nimble, Age is lame:
Youth is hot and bold,
Age is weak and cold;
  Youth is wild, and Age is tame.
Age, I do abhor thee,
Youth, I do adore thee;
  O, my love, my love is young:
Age, I do defie thee;
Oh sweet shepheard, hie thee,
  For methinks thou stayst too long.

---

*** See Malone's Shakspeare, vol. x. p. 325.

---

## XVII.

### The Frolicksome Duke, or the Tinker's Good Fortune.

The following ballad is upon the same subject as the Induction to Shakspeare's *Taming of the Shrew:* whether it may be thought to have suggested the hint to the dramatic poet, or is not rather of later date, the reader must determine.

The story is told of Philip the Good[1], Duke of Burgundy, and is thus related by an old English writer: "The said duke, at the marriage of Eleonora, sister to the king of Portugall, at Bruges in Flanders, which was solemnized in the deepe of winter; when as by reason of unseasonable weather he could neither hawke nor hunt, and was now tired with cards, dice, &c., and such other domestick sports, or to see ladies dance; with some of his courtiers he would in the evening walke disguised all about the towne. It so fortuned, as he was walking late one night, he found a countrey fellow

[1] By Ludov. Vives in *Epist.* and by Pont. Heuter, *Rerum Burgund.* b. iv.

dead drunke, snorting on a bulke; he caused his followers to bring him to his palace, and there stripping him of his old clothes, and attyring him after the court fashion, when he wakened, he and they were all ready to attend upon his excellency, and persuade him that he was some great duke. The poor fellow admiring how he came there, was served in state all day long; after supper he saw them dance, heard musicke, and all the rest of those court-like pleasures; but late at night, when he was well tipled, and again faste asleepe, they put on his old robes, and so conveyed him to the place where they first found him. Now the fellow had not made them so good sport the day before, as he did now, when he returned to himself; all the jest was to see how he looked upon it. In conclusion, after some little admiration, the poore man told his friends he had seen a vision, constantly believed it, and would not otherwise be persuaded, and so the jest ended."— Burton's *Anat. of Melancholy*, pt. ii. sec. 2, memb. 4. 2d ed. 1624, fol.

This ballad is given from a black letter copy in the Pepys Collection, which is entitled as above. "To the tune of *Fond boy.*"

---

Now as fame does report a young duke keeps a court,
One that pleases his fancy with frolicksome sport:
But amongst all the rest, here is one I protest,
Which will make you to smile when you hear the true jest:
A poor tinker he found, lying drunk on the ground,
As secure in a sleep as if laid in a swound.

The duke said to his men, William, Richard, and Ben,
Take him home to my palace, we'll sport with him then.
O'er a horse he was laid, and with care soon convey'd
To the palace, altho' he was poorly arrai'd:
Then they stript off his cloaths, both his shirt, shoes, and hose,
And they put him to bed for to take his repose.

Having pull'd off his shirt, which was all over durt,
They did give him clean holland, this was no great hurt:
On a bed of soft down, like a lord of renown,
They did lay him to sleep the drink out of his crown.
In the morning when day, then admiring he lay,
For to see the rich chamber both gaudy and gay.

Now he lay something late, in his rich bed of state,
Till at last knights and squires they on him did wait;
And the chamberling bare, then did likewise declare,
He desir'd to know what apparel he'd ware:
The poor tinker amaz'd, on the gentleman gaz'd,
And admired how he to this honour was rais'd.

Tho' he seem'd something mute, yet he chose a rich suit,
Which he straitways put on without longer dispute;
With a star on his side, which the tinker offt ey'd,
And it seem'd for to swell him 'no' little with pride;
For he said to himself, Where is Joan my sweet wife?
Sure she never did see me so fine in her life.

From a convenient place, the right duke his good grace
Did observe his behaviour in every case.
To a garden of state, on the tinker they wait,
Trumpets sounding before him: thought he, this is great:
Where an hour or two, pleasant walks he did view,
With commanders and squires in scarlet and blew.

A fine dinner was drest, both for him and his guests,
He was plac'd at the table above all the rest,
In a rich chair 'or bed,' lin'd with fine crimson red,
With a rich golden canopy over his head:
As he sat at his meat, the musick play'd sweet,
With the choicest of singing his joys to compleat.

While the tinker did dine, he had plenty of wine,
Rich canary with sherry and tent superfine.

Like a right honest soul, faith, he took off his bowl,
Till at last he began for to tumble and roul
From his chair to the floor, where he sleeping did snore,
Being seven times drunker than ever before.

Then the duke did ordain, they should strip him amain,
And restore him his old leather garments again:
'Twas a point next the worst, yet perform it they must,
And they carry'd him strait, where they found him at first;
Then he slept all the night, as indeed well he might;
But when he did waken, his joys took their flight.

For his glory 'to him' so pleasant did seem,
That he thought it to be but a meer golden dream;
Till at length he was brought to the duke, where he sought
For a pardon, as fearing he had set him at nought;
But his highness he said, Thou'rt a jolly bold blade,
Such a frolick before I think never was plaid.

Then his highness bespoke him a new suit and cloak,
Which he gave for the sake of this frolicksome joak;
Nay, and five hundred pound, with ten acres of ground,
Thou shalt never, said he, range the counteries round,
Crying old brass to mend, for I'll be thy good friend,
Nay, and Joan thy sweet wife shall my duchess attend.

Then the tinker reply'd, What! must Joan my sweet bride
Be a lady in chariots of pleasure to ride?
Must we have gold and land ev'ry day at command?
Then I shall be a squire I well understand:
Well I thank your good grace, and your love I embrace,
I was never before in so happy a case.

---

## XVIII.

### The Friar of Orders Gray.

Dispersed through Shakspeare's plays are innumerable little fragments of ancient ballads, the entire copies of which could not be recovered. Many of these being of the most beautiful and pathetic simplicity, the Editor was tempted to select some of them, and with a few supplemental stanzas to connect them together, and form them into a little Tale, which is here submitted to the reader's candour.

One small fragment was taken from Beaumont and Fletcher.

---

It was a friar of orders gray
  Walkt forth to tell his beades;
And he met with a lady faire
  Clad in a pilgrime's weedes.

Now Christ thee save, thou reverend friar,
  I pray thee tell to me,
If ever at yon holy shrine
  My true love thou didst see.

And how should I know your true love
  From many another one?
O by his cockle hat, and staff,
  And by his sandal shoone[1].

But chiefly by his face and mien,
  That were so fair to view;
His flaxen locks that sweetly curl'd,
  And eyne of lovely blue.

[1] These are the distinguishing marks of a Pilgrim. The chief places of devotion being beyond sea, the pilgrims were wont to put cockle-shells in their hats to denote the intention or performance of their devotion. Warb. *Shaksp.* vol. viii. p. 224.

O lady, he is dead and gone!
  Lady, he's dead and gone!
And at his head a green grass turfe,
  And at his heels a stone.

Within these holy cloysters long
  He languisht, and he dyed,
Lamenting of a ladyes love,
  And 'playning of her pride.

Here bore him barefac'd on his bier
  Six proper youths and tall,
And many a tear bedew'd his grave
  Within yon kirk-yard wall.

And art thou dead, thou gentle youth!
  And art thou dead and gone!
And didst thou dye for love of me!
  Break, cruel heart of stone!

O weep not, lady, weep not soe;
  Some ghostly comfort seek:
Let not vain sorrow rive thy heart,
  Ne teares bedew thy cheek.

O do not, do not, holy friar,
  My sorrow now reprove;
For I have lost the sweetest youth,
  That e'er wan ladyes love.

And nowe, alas! for thy sad losse,
  I'll evermore weep and sigh;
For thee I only wisht to live,
  For thee I wish to dye.

Weep no more, lady, weep no more,
  Thy sorrowe is in vaine:
For violets pluckt the sweetest showers
  Will ne'er make grow againe.

Our joyes as winged dreams doe flye,
  Why then should sorrow last?
Since grief but aggravates thy losse,
  Grieve not for what is past.

O say not soe, thou holy friar;
  I pray thee, say not soe:
For since my true-love dyed for mee,
  'Tis meet my tears should flow.

And will he ne'er come again?
  Will he ne'er come again?
Ah! no, he is dead and laid in his grave,
  For ever to remain.

His cheek was redder than the rose;
  The comliest youth was he! —
But he is dead and laid in his grave:
  Alas, and woe is me!

Sigh no more, lady, sigh no more,
  Men were deceivers ever:
One foot on sea and one on land,
  To one thing constant never.

Hadst thou been fond, he had been false,
  And left thee sad and heavy;
For young men ever were fickle found,
  Since summer trees were leafy.

Now say not so, thou holy friar,
  I pray thee say not soe;
My love he had the truest heart:
  O he was ever true!

And art thou dead, thou much-lov'd youth,
  And didst thou dye for me?
Then farewell home; for ever-more
  A pilgrim I will bee.

But first upon my true-love's grave
  My weary limbs I'll lay,
And thrice I'll kiss the green-grass turf,
  That wraps his breathless clay.

Yet stay, fair lady; rest awhile
  Beneath this cloyster wall:
See through the hawthorn blows the cold wind,
  And drizzly rain doth fall.

O stay me not, thou holy friar;
  O stay me not, I pray;
No drizzly rain that falls on me,
  Can wash my fault away.

Yet stay, fair lady, turn again,
  And dry those pearly tears;
For see beneath this gown of gray
  Thy owne true-love appears.

Here forc'd by grief, and hopeless love,
  These holy weeds I sought;
And here amid these lonely walls
  To end my days I thought.

But haply for my year of grace[2]
  Is not yet past away,
Might I still hope to win thy love,
  No longer would I stay.

Now farewell grief, and welcome joy
  Once more unto my heart;
For since I have found thee, lovely youth,
  We never more will part.

[2] The year of probation, or noviciate.

*** As the foregoing song has been thought to have suggested to our late excellent poet, Dr. Goldsmith, the plan of his beautiful ballad of *Edwin and Emma*, (first printed in his *Vicar of Wakefield*,) it is but justice to his memory to declare, that his poem was written first, and that if there is any imitation in the case, they will be found both to be indebted to the beautiful old ballad, *Gentle Herdsman*, &c., printed in the second volume of this work, which the Doctor had much admired in manuscript, and has finely improved. See vol. ii. book i. song xiv. ver. 37, &c.

END OF THE SECOND BOOK.

# RELIQUES
OF
# ANCIENT POETRY.
*&c.*

---

## SERIES THE FIRST.
## BOOK III.

---

### I.
### The more Modern Ballad of Chevy Chase.

At the beginning of this volume we gave the old original song of Chevy-Chase. The reader has here the more improved edition of that fine heroic ballad. It will afford an agreeable entertainment to the curious to compare them together, and to see how far the latter bard has excelled his predecessor, and where he has fallen short of him. For though he has every where improved the versification, and generally the sentiment and diction, yet some few passages retain more dignity in the ancient copy; at least the obsoleteness of the style serves as a veil to hide whatever might appear too familiar or vulgar in them. Thus, for instance, the catastrophe of the gallant Witherington is in the modern copy expressed in terms which never fail at present to excite ridicule, whereas in the original it is related with a plain and pathetic simplicity, that is liable to no such unlucky effect. See the stanza in page 12, which in modern orthography, &c. would run thus:

"For Witherington my heart is woe,
That ever he slain should be:
For when his legs were hewn in two,
He knelt and fought on his knee."

So again, the stanza which describes the fall of Montgomery is somewhat more elevated in the ancient copy:

"The dint it was both sad and sore,
He on Montgomery set:
The swan-feathers his arrow bore
With his heart's blood were wet." p. 11.

We might also add, that the circumstances of the battle are more clearly conceived, and the several incidents more distinctly marked in the old original, than in the improved copy. It is well known that the ancient English weapon was the long bow, and that this nation excelled all others in archery; while the Scottish warriors chiefly depended on the use of the spear: this characteristic difference never escapes our ancient bard, whose description of the first onset (p. 7, 8) is to the following effect:

"The proposal of the two gallant earls to determine the dispute by single combat being over-ruled, the English, says he, who stood with their bows ready bent, gave a general discharge of their arrows, which slew seven score spearmen of the enemy: but notwithstanding so severe a loss, Douglas, like a brave captain, kept his ground. He had divided his forces into three columns, who, as soon as the English had discharged the first volley, bore down upon them with their spears, and breaking through their ranks, reduced them to close fighting. The archers upon this dropt their bows and had recourse to their swords; and there followed so sharp a conflict, that multitudes on both sides lost their lives." In the midst of this general engagement, at length the two great earls meet, and after a spirited rencounter agree to breathe; upon which a parley ensues, that would do honour to Homer himself.

Nothing can be more pleasingly distinct and circumstantial than this: whereas the modern copy, though in general it has great merit, is here unluckily both confused and obscure. Indeed the original words seem here to have been totally misunderstood. "Yet bydys the yerl Douglas upon the *bent*," evidently signifies, "Yet the earl Douglas abides in the *field;*" whereas the more modern bard seems to have understood by *bent*, the inclination of his mind, and accordingly runs quite off from the subject[1];

"To drive the deer with hound and horn
Earl Douglas had the bent." v. 109.

One may also observe a generous impartiality in the old original bard, when in the conclusion of his tale he represents both nations as quitting the field without any reproachful reflection on either: though he gives to his own countrymen the credit of being the smaller number.

"Of fifteen hundred archers of England
Went away but fifty and three;
Of twenty hundred spearmen of Scotland,
But even five and fifty." p. 11.

He attributes *flight* to neither party, as hath been done in the modern copies of this ballad, as well Scotch as English. For, to be even with our latter bard, who makes the Scots to *flee*, some reviser of North Britain has turned his own arms against him, and printed an edition at Glasgow, in which the lines are thus transposed:

"Of fifteen hundred Scottish speirs,
Went hame but fifty-three:
Of twenty hundred Englishmen
Scarce fifty-five did flee:"

and to countenance this change, he has suppressed the two stanzas between ver. 240 and ver. 249. From that edition I have here reformed the Scottish names in p. 227, 228, which in the modern English ballad appeared to be corrupted.

When I call the present admired ballad modern, I only mean that it is comparatively so; for that it could not be writ much later than the time of Queen Elizabeth, I think may be made appear; nor yet does it seem to be older than

[1] In the present edition, instead of the unmeaning lines here censured, an insertion is made of four stanzas modernized from the ancient copy.

the beginning of the last century[2]. Sir Philip Sidney, when he complains of the antiquated phrase of *Chevy Chase*, could never have seen this improved copy, the language of which is not more ancient than that he himself used. It is probable that the encomiums of so admired a writer excited some bard to revise the ballad, and to free it from those faults he had objected to it. That it could not be much later than that time, appears from the phrase *doleful dumps;* which in that age carried no ill sound with it, but to the next generation became ridiculous. We have seen it pass uncensured in a sonnet that was at that time in request, and where it could not fail to have been taken notice of, had it been in the least exceptionable: see above, p. 162. Yet in about half a century after, it was become burlesque. See *Hudibras*, part i. c. iii. ver. 95.

This much premised, the reader that would see the general beauties of this ballad set in a just and striking light, may consult the excellent criticism of Mr. Addison[3]. With regard to its subject, it has already been considered in page 3. The conjectures there offered will receive confirmation from a passage in the *Memoirs of Carey*, *Earl of Monmouth*, 8vo. 1759, p. 165: whence we learn that it was an ancient custom with the borderers of the two kingdoms, when they were at peace, to send to the Lord Wardens of the opposite Marches for leave to hunt within their districts.

[2] A late writer has started a notion, that the more modern copy "was written to be sung by a party of English, headed by a Douglas in the year 1524; which is the true reason why, at the same time that it gives the advantage to the English soldiers above the Scotch, it gives yet so lovely and so manifestly superior a character to the Scotch commander above the English." See Say's *Essay on the Numbers of Paradise Lost,* 4to. 1745, p. 167.

This appears to me a groundless conjecture: the language seems too modern for the date above mentioned; and had it been printed even so early as Queen Elizabeth's reign, I think I should have met with some copy wherein the first line would have been,

God prosper long our noble queen,

as was the case with the *Blind Beggar of Bednal Green;* see vol. ii. book ii. no. 10.

[3] In the *Spectator,* Nos. 70, 74.

If leave was granted, then towards the end of summer, they would come and hunt for several days together, "with their *grey-hounds for deer;*" but if they took this liberty unpermitted, then the Lord Warden of the border so invaded, would not fail to interrupt their sport and chastise their boldness. He mentions a remarkable instance that happened while he was Warden, when some Scotch gentlemen coming to hunt in defiance of him, there must have ensued such an action as this of Chevy Chase, if the intruders had been proportionably numerous and well-armed; for upon their being attacked by his men at arms, he tells us, "some hurt was done, though he had given especiall order that they should shed as little blood as possible." They were in effect overpowered and taken prisoners, and only released on their promise to abstain from such licentious sporting for the future.

The following text is given from a copy in the Editor's folio MS. compared with two or three others printed in black letter. In the second volume of Dryden's *Miscellanies* may be found a translation of *Chevy-Chase* into Latin rhymes. The translator, Mr. Henry Bold of New College, undertook it at the command of Dr. Compton, bishop of London, who thought it no derogation to his episcopal character to avow a fondness for this excellent old ballad. See the preface to Bold's Latin Songs, 1685, 8vo.

---

God prosper long our noble king,
  Our lives and safetyes all;
A woefull hunting once there did
  In Chevy-Chace befall;

To drive the deere with hound and horne,
  Erle Percy took his way;
The child may rue that is unborne,
  The hunting of that day.

The stout Erle of Northumberland
  A vow to God did make,
His pleasure in the Scottish woods
  Three summers days to take;

The cheefest harts in Chevy-Chace
  To kill and beare away.
These tydings to Erle Douglas came,
  In Scotland where he lay:

Who sent Erle Percy present word,
  He wold prevent his sport.
The English erle, not fearing that,
  Did to the woods resort

With fifteen hundred bow-men bold;
  All chosen men of might,
Who knew full well in time of neede
  To ayme their shafts arright.

The gallant greyhounds swiftly ran,
  To chase the fallow deere:
On munday they began to hunt,
  Ere day-light did appeare;

And long before high noone they had
  An hundred fat buckes slaine;
Then having din'd, the drovyers went
  To rouze the deare againe.

The bow-men mustered on the hills,
  Well able to endure;
Theire backsides all, with speciall care,
  That day were guarded sure.

The hounds ran swiftly through the woods,
  The nimble deere to take[4],

Ver. 36, that they were. fol. MS.

[4] The Chiviot Hills and circumjacent Wastes are at present void both of

That with their cryes the hills and dales
An eccho shrill did make.

Lord Percy to the quarry went,
To view the slaughter'd deere;
Quoth he, Erle Douglas promised
This day to meet me heere:

But if I thought he wold not come,
Noe longer wold I stay.
With that, a brave younge gentleman
Thus to the erle did say:

Loe, yonder doth Erle Douglas come,
His men in armour bright;
Full twenty hundred Scottish speres
All marching in our sight;

All men of pleasant Tivydale,
Fast by the river Tweede:
O cease your sport, Erle Percy said,
And take your bowes with speede:

And now with me, my countrymen,
Your courage forth advance;
For never was there champion yett
In Scotland or in France,

That ever did on horsebacke come,
But if my hap it were,
I durst encounter man for man,
With him to break a spere.

deer and woods: but formerly they had enough of both to justify the description attempted here and in the Ancient Ballad of Chevy-Chase. Leland, in the reign of Hen. VIII., thus describes this county:—"In Northumberland, as I heare say, be no forests, except Chivet Hills: where is much Brushe-wood and some Okke; grownde ovargrowne with Linge, and some with Mosse. I have harde say that Chivet Hills stretchethe xx miles. There is greate plenté of Redde-dere, and Roo Bukkes."—*Itinerary*, vol. vii. p. 56. This passage, which did not occur when pp. 19, 20, were printed off, confirm the accounts there given of the Stagge and the Roe.

Erle Douglas on his milke-white steede,
  Most like a baron bold,
Rode formost of his company,
  Whose armour shone like gold.

Show me, sayd hee, whose men you bee,
  That hunt soe boldly heere,
That, without my consent, doe chase
  And kill my fallow-deere?

The man that first did answer make,
  Was noble Percy hee;
Who sayd, Wee list not to declare,
  Nor shew whose men wee bee:

Yet will wee spend our deerest blood,
  Thy cheefest harts to slay.
Then Douglas swore a solempne oathe,
  And thus in rage did say,

Ere thus I will out-braved bee,
  One of us two shall dye:
I know thee well, an erle thou art;
  Lord Percy, soe am I.

But trust me, Percy, pittye it were,
  And great offence to kill
Any of these our guiltlesse men,
  For they have done no ill.

Let thou and I the battell trye,
  And set our men aside.
Accurst bee he, Erle Percy sayd,
  By whome this is denyed.

Then stept a gallant squier forth,
  Witherington was his name,
Who said, I wold not have it told
  To Henry our king for shame,

That ere my captaine fought on foote,
  And I stood looking on.
You bee two erles, sayd Witherington,
  And I a squier alone:

Ile doe the best that doe I may,
  While I have power to stand:
While I have power to weeld my sword,
  Ile fight with hart and hand.

Our English archers bent their bowes,
  Their harts were good and trew;
Att the first flight of arrowes sent,
  Full four-score Scots they slew.

[5][Yet bides Earl Douglas on the bent,
  As Chieftain stout and good,
As valiant Captain, all unmov'd
  The shock he firmly stood.

His host he parted had in three,
  As Leader ware and try'd,
And soon his spearmen on their foes
  Bare down on every side.

Throughout the English archery
  They dealt full many a wound:
But still our valiant Englishmen
  All firmly kept their ground:

And throwing strait their bows away,
  They grasp'd their swords so bright:

[5] The four stanzas here inclosed in brackets, which are borrowed chiefly from the ancient copy, are offered to the reader instead of the following lines, which occur in the Editor's fol. MS.

To drive the deere with hound and horne,
  Douglas bade on the bent;
Two captaines moved with mickle might
  Their speres to shivers went.

And now sharp blows, a heavy shower,
  On shields and helmets light.]

They clos'd full fast on everye side,
  Noe slacknes there was found;
And many a gallant gentleman
  Lay gasping on the ground.

O Christ! it was a griefe to see,
  And likewise for to heare,
The cries of men lying in their gore,
  And scattered here and there.

At last these two stout erles did meet,
  Like captaines of great might:
Like lyons wood, they layd on lode,
  And made a cruell fight:

They fought untill they both did sweat,
  With swords of tempered steele;
Until the blood, like drops of rain,
  They trickling downe did feele.

Yeeld thee, Lord Percy, Douglas sayd;
  In faith I will thee bringe,
Where thou shalt high advanced bee
  By James our Scottish king:

Thy ransome I will freely give,
  And thus report of thee,
Thou art the most couragious knight,
  That ever I did see.

Noe, Douglas, quoth Erle Percy then,
  Thy proffer I doe scorne;
I will not yeelde to any Scott,
  That ever yett was borne.

With that, there came an arrow keene
  Out of an English bow,
Which strucke Erle Douglas to the heart,
  A deepe and deadlye blow:

Who never spake more words than these,
  Fight on, my merry men all;
For why, my life is at an end;
  Lord Percy sees my fall.

Then leaving liffe, Erle Percy tooke
  The dead man by the hand;
And said, Erle Douglas, for thy life
  Wold I had lost my land.

O Christ! my verry hart doth bleed
  With sorrow for thy sake;
For sure, a more renowned knight
  Mischance cold never take.

A knight amongst the Scotts there was,
  Which saw Erle Douglas dye,
Who streight in wrath did vow revenge
  Upon the Lord Percye:

Sir Hugh Mountgomerye was he call'd,
  Who, with a spere most bright,
Well-mounted on a gallant steed,
  Ran fiercely through the fight;

And past the English archers all,
  Without all dread or feare;
And thro' Earl Percyes body then
  He thrust his hatefull spere;

With such a vehement force and might
  He did his body gore,
The speare went through the other side
  A large cloth-yard, and more.

So thus did both these nobles dye,
  Whose courage none could staine;
An English archer then perceiv'd
  The noble erle was slaine;

He had a bow bent in his hand,
  Made of a trusty tree;
An arrow of a cloth-yard long
  Up to the head drew hee:

Against Sir Hugh Mountgomerye,
  So right the shaft he sett,
The grey goose-wing that was thereon,
  In his harts bloode was wett.

This fight did last from breake of day,
  Till setting of the sun;
For when they rung the evening bell[6],
  The battel scarce was done.

With brave Erle Percy, there was slaine,
  Sir John of Egerton[7],
Sir Robert Ratcliff, and Sir John,
  Sir James that bold Baròn:

And with Sir George and stout Sir James,
  Both knights of good account,
Good Sir Ralph Raby there was slaine,
  Whose prowesse did surmount.

For Witherington needs must I wayle,
  As one in doleful dumpes[8];

[6] Sc. the Curfew-bell, usually rung at eight o'clock; to which the moderniser apparently alludes, instead of the *Evensong-bell*, or bell for vespers of the original author, before the Reformation. Vide suprà, p. 11, v. 97.

[7] For the surnames, see the Notes at the end of the ballad.

[8] *i. e.* "I, as one in deep concern, must lament." The construction here has generally been misunderstood. The old MS. reads *wofull dumpes.*

For when his legs were smitten off,
He fought upon his stumpes.

And with Erle Douglas, there was slaine
Sir Hugh Mountgomerye,
Sir Charles Murray, that from the feeld
One foote wold never flee.

Sir Charles Murray, of Ratcliff, too,
His sisters sonne was hee;
Sir David Lamb, so well esteem'd,
Yet saved cold not bee.

And the Lord Maxwell in like case
Did with Erle Douglas dye:
Of twenty hundred Scottish speres,
Scarce fifty-five did flye.

Of fifteen hundred Englishmen,
Went home but fifty-three;
The rest were slaine in Chevy-Chace,
Under the greene wood tree.

Next day did many widowes come,
Their husbands to bewayle;
They washt their wounds in brinish teares,
But all wold not prevayle.

Theyr bodyes, bathed in purple gore,
They bare with them away:
They kist them dead a thousand times,
Ere they were cladd in clay.

This newes was brought to Eddenborrow,
Where Scottlands king did raigne,
That brave Erle Douglas suddenlye
Was with an arrow slaine:

O heavy newes, King James did say,
  Scottland can witnesse bee,
I have not any captaine more
  Of such account as hee.

Like tydings to King Henry came,
  Within as short a space,
That Percy of Northumberland
  Was slaine in Chevy-Chace:

Now God be with him, said our king,
  Sith it will noe better bee;
I trust I have, within my realme,
  Five hundred as good as hee:

Yett shall not Scotts nor Scotland say,
  But I will vengeance take:
I'll be revenged on them all,
  For brave Erle Percyes sake.

This vow full well the king perform'd
  After, at Humbledowne;
In one day, fifty knights were slayne,
  With lordes of great renowne:

And of the rest, of small account,
  Did many thousands dye:
Thus endeth the hunting of Chevy-Chace,
  Made by the Erle Percy.

God save our king, and bless this land
  In plentye, joy, and peace;
And grant henceforth, that foule debate
  'Twixt noblemen may cease.

---

*** Since the former impression of these volumes, hath been published a new edition of *Collins's Peerage*, 1779, &c. 9 vols. 8vo, which contains, in volume ii. p. 334, an historical passage that may be thought to throw considerable light on the subject of the preceding ballad: viz.

"In this .... year, 1436, according to Hector Boethius, was fought the battle of Pepperden, not far from the Cheviot Hills, between the Earl of Northumberland [second Earl, son of Hotspur] and Earl William Douglas, of Angus, with a small army of about 4000 men each, in which the latter had the advantage. As this seems to have been a private conflict between these two great chieftains of the Borders, rather than a national war, it has been thought to have given rise to the celebrated old ballad of *Chevy-Chase*, which, to render it more pathetic and interesting, has been heightened with tragical incidents wholly fictitious." — See Ridpath's *Border Hist.* 4to. p. 401.

The surnames in the foregoing ballad are altered, either by accident or design, from the old original copy, and in common editions extremely corrupted. They are here rectified, as much as they could be. Thus,

Page 227, ver. 202. *Egerton.*] This name is restored (instead of Ogerton, com. ed.) from the Editor's folio MS. The pieces in that MS. appear to have been collected, and many of them composed (among which might be this ballad) by an inhabitant of Cheshire; who was willing to pay a compliment here to one of his countrymen, of the eminent family *De* or *Of Egerton*, (so the name was first written,) ancestors of the present Duke of Bridgwater: and this he could do with the more propriety, as the Percies had formerly great interest in that county: at the fatal battle of Shrewsbury all the flower of the Cheshire gentlemen lost their lives fighting in the cause of Hotspur.

Ver. 203. *Ratcliff.*] This was a family much distinguished in Northumberland. Edw. Radcliffe, mil. was sheriff of that county in 17 of Hen. VII., and others of the same surname afterwards. (See Fuller, p. 313.) Sir George Ratcliff, knt.

was one of the commissioners of inclosure in 1552. (See Nicholson, p. 330.) Of this family was the late Earl of Derwentwater, who was beheaded in 1715. The Editor's folio MS. however, reads here "Sir Robert Harcliffe and Sir William."

The Harcleys were an eminent family in Cumberland. (See Fuller, p. 224.) Whether this may be thought to be the same name I do not determine.

Ver. 204. *Baron.*] This is apparently altered (not to say corrupted) from *Hearone*, in page 12, ver. 114.

Ver. 207. *Raby.*] This might be intended to celebrate one of the ancient possessors of Raby Castle, in the county of Durham. Yet it is written *Rebbye* in the fol. MS. and looks like a corruption of *Rugby* or *Rokeby*, an eminent family in Yorkshire. See pp. 12, 29. It will not be wondered that the Percies should be thought to bring followers out of that county, where they themselves were originally seated, and had always such extensive property and influence.

Page 228, ver. 215. *Murray.*] So the Scottish copy. In the common edition it is *Carrel* or *Currel;* and *Morrell* in the fol. MS.

Ver. 217. *Murray.*] So the Scot. edit. — The com. copies read *Murrel.* The fol. MS. gives the line in the following peculiar manner,

"Sir Roger Heuer of Harcliffe too."

Ver. 219. *Lamb.*] The folio MS. has

"Sir David Lamwell well esteemed."

This seems evidently corrupted from Lwdale or Liddell, in the old copy, pp. 12, 30.

---

## II.

## Death's Final Conquest.

These fine moral stanzas were originally intended for a solemn funeral song in a play of James Shirley's, entitled *The Contention of Ajax and Ulysses:* no date, 8vo. — Shirley flourished as a dramatic writer early in the reign of

Charles I.; but he outlived the Restoration. His death happened Oct. 29, 1666, æt. 72.

This little poem was written long after many of those that follow, but is inserted here as a kind of dirge to the foregoing piece. It is said to have been a favourite song with King Charles II.

---

The glories of our birth and state
  Are shadows, not substantial things;
There is no armour against fate:
  Death lays his icy hands on kings:
    Scepter and crown
    Must tumble down,
And in the dust be equal made
With the poor crooked scythe and spade.

Some men with swords may reap the field,
  And plant fresh laurels where they kill;
But their strong nerves at last must yield,
  They tame but one another still.
    Early or late
    They stoop to fate,
And must give up their murmuring breath,
When they pale captives creep to death.

The garlands wither on your brow,
  Then boast no more your mighty deeds;
Upon death's purple altar now
  See where the victor victim bleeds:
    All heads must come
    To the cold tomb,
Only the actions of the just
Smell sweet, and blossom in the dust.

---

III.

## The Rising in the North.

The subject of this ballad is the great Northern insurrection in the twelfth year of Elizabeth, 1569, which proved so fatal to Thomas Percy, the seventh Earl of Northumberland.

There had not long before been a secret negotiation entered into between some of the Scottish and English nobility, to bring about a marriage between Mary Queen of Scots, at that time a prisoner in England, and the Duke of Norfolk, a nobleman of excellent character, and firmly attached to the Protestant religion. This match was proposed to all the most considerable of the English nobility, and among the rest to the Earls of Northumberland and Westmoreland, two noblemen very powerful in the north. As it seemed to promise a speedy and safe conclusion of the troubles in Scotland, with many advantages to the crown of England, they all consented to it, provided it should prove agreeable to Queen Elizabeth. The Earl of Leicester (Elizabeth's favourite) undertook to break the matter to her; but before he could find an opportunity, the affair had come to her ears by other hands, and she was thrown into a violent flame. The Duke of Norfolk, with several of his friends, was committed to the Tower, and summons were sent to the northern earls instantly to make their appearance at court. It is said that the Earl of Northumberland, who was a man of a mild and gentle nature, was deliberating with himself whether he should not obey the message, and rely upon the queen's candour and clemency, when he was forced into desperate measures by a sudden report at midnight, Nov. 14, that a party of his enemies were come to seize on his person[1]. The earl was then at his house at Topcliffe in Yorkshire: when rising hastily out of bed, he withdrew to the Earl of Westmoreland, at Brancepeth, where the country

[1] This circumstance is overlooked in the ballad.

came in to them, and pressed them to take arms in their own defence. They accordingly set up their standards, declaring their intent was to restore the ancient religion, to get the succession of the crown firmly settled, and to prevent the destruction of the ancient nobility, &c. Their common banner[2] (on which was displayed the Cross, together with the five wounds of Christ) was borne by an ancient gentleman, Richard Norton, Esq., of Norton-Conyers; who with his sons (among whom, Christopher, Marmaduke, and Thomas, are expressly named by Camden,) distinguished himself on this occasion. Having entered Durham, they tore the Bible, &c., and caused mass to be said there: they then marched on to Clifford-moor near Wetherbye, where they mustered their men. Their intention was to have proceeded on to York; but altering their minds, they fell upon Barnard's castle, which Sir George Bowes held out against them for eleven days. The two earls, who spent their large estates in hospitality, and were extremely beloved on that account, were masters of little ready money; the Earl of Northumberland bringing with him only 8000 crowns, and the Earl of Westmoreland nothing at all for the subsistence of their forces, they were not able to march to London, as they had at first intended. In these circumstances, Westmoreland began so visibly to despond, that many of his men slunk away; though Northumberland still kept up his resolution, and was master of the field till December 13, when the Earl of Sussex, accompanied with Lord Hunsden and others, having marched out of York at the head of a large body of forces, and being followed by a still larger army under the command of Ambrose Dudley, Earl of Warwick, the insurgents retreated northward towards the borders, and there dismissing their followers, made their escape into Scotland. Though this insurrection had been suppressed with so little bloodshed, the Earl of Sussex and Sir George Bowes, marshal of the army, put vast numbers to death by martial law, without any re-

[2] Besides this, the ballad mentions the separate banners of the two noblemen.

gular trial. The former of these caused at Durham sixty-three constables to be hanged at once. And the latter made his boast, that for sixty miles in length and forty in breadth, betwixt Newcastle and Wetherbye, there was hardly a town or village wherein he had not executed some of the inhabitants. This exceeds the cruelties practised in the West after Monmouth's rebellion: but that was not the age of tenderness and humanity.

Such is the account collected from Stow, Speed, Camden, Guthrie, Carte, and Rapin; it agrees in most particulars with the following ballad, which was apparently the production of some northern minstrel, who was well affected to the two noblemen. It is here printed from two MS. copies, one of them in the editor's folio collection. They contained considerable variations, out of which such readings were chosen as seemed most poetical and consonant to history.

---

Listen, lively lordings all,
  Lithe and listen unto mee,
And I will sing of a noble earle,
  The noblest earle in the north countrìe.

Earle Percy is into his garden gone,
  And after him walkes his faire ladie[3]:
I heare a bird sing in mine eare,
  That I must either fight, or flee.

Now heaven forefend, my dearest lord,
  That ever such harm should hap to thee:
But goe to London to the court,
  And faire fall truth and honestìe.

Now nay, now nay, my ladye gay,
  Alas! thy counsell suits not mee;
Mine enemies prevail so fast,
  That at the court I may not bee.

[3] This lady was Anne, daughter of Henry Somerset, Earl of Worcester.

O goe to the court yet, good my lord,
And take thy gallant men with thee:
If any dare to doe you wrong,
Then your warrant they may bee.

Now nay, now nay, thou lady faire,
The court is full of subtiltìe;
And if I goe to the court, lady,
Never more I may thee see.

Yet goe to the court, my lord, she sayes,
And I myselfe will ryde wi' thee:
At court then for my dearest lord,
His faithfull borrowe I will bee.

Now nay, now nay, my lady deare;
Far lever had I lose my life,
Than leave among my cruell foes
My love in jeopardy and strife.

But come thou hither, my little foot-pàge,
Come thou hither unto mee,
To maister Norton thou must goe
In all the haste that ever may bee.

Commend me to that gentlemàn,
And beare this letter here fro mee;
And say that earnestly I praye,
He will ryde in my companìe.

One while the little foot-page went,
And another while he ran;
Untill he came to his journeys end,
The little foot-page never blan.

When to that gentleman he came,
Down he kneeled on his knee;
And took the letter betwixt his hands,
And lett the gentleman it see.

And when the letter it was redd
  Affore that goodlye companye,
I wis, if you the truthe wold know,
  There was many a weeping eye.

He sayd, Come hither, Christopher Norton,
  A gallant youth thou seemst to bee;
What doest thou counsell me, my sonne,
  Now that good erle's in jeopardy?

Father, my counselle's fair and free;
  That erle he is a noble lord,
And whatsoever to him you hight,
  I wold not have you breake your word.

Gramercy, Christopher, my sonne,
  Thy counsell well it liketh mee,
And if we speed and scape with life,
  Well advanced thou shalt bee.

Come you hither, my nine good sonnes,
  Gallant men I trowe you bee:
How many of you, my children deare,
  Will stand by that good erle and mee?

Eight of them did answer make,
  Eight of them spake hastilie,
O father, till the daye we dye
  We'll stand by that good erle and thee.

Gramercy now, my children deare,
  You showe yourselves right bold and brave;
And whethersoe'er I live or dye,
  A fathers blessing you shal have.

But what sayst thou, O Francis Norton,
  Thou art mine eldest sonn and heire:
Somewhat lyes brooding in thy breast;
  Whatever it bee, to mee declare.

Father, you are an aged man,
  Your head is white, your bearde is gray;
It were a shame at these your yeares
  For you to ryse in such a fray.

Now fye upon thee, coward Francis,
  Thou never learnedst this of mee:
When thou wert yong and tender of age,
  Why did I make soe much of thee?

But, father, I will wend with you,
  Unarm'd and naked will I bee;
And he that strikes against the crowne,
  Ever an ill death may he dee.

Then rose that reverend gentleman,
  And with him came a goodlye band
To join with the brave Erle Percy,
  And all the flower o' Northumberland.

With them the noble Nevill came,
  The erle of Westmorland was hee:
At Wetherbye they mustred their host,
  Thirteen thousand faire to see.

Lord Westmorland his ancyent raisde,
  The Dun Bull he rays'd on hye,
And three Dogs with golden collars,
  Were there sett out most royallye[4].

[4] Ver. 102, *Dun Bull, &c.*] The supporters of the Nevilles, Earls of Westmoreland, were two bulls argent, ducally collar'd gold, armed or, &c. But I have not discovered the device mentioned in the ballad among the badges, &c., given by that house. This however is certain, that among those of the Nevilles, Lords Abergavenny (who were of the same family) is a dun cow with a golden collar: and the Nevilles of Chyte in Yorkshire (of the Westmoreland branch) gave for their crest in 1513, a dog's (greyhound's) head, erased. So that it is not improbable but Charles Neville, the unhappy Earl of Westmoreland here mentioned, might on this occasion give the above device on his banner. After all, our old minstrel's verses here may have undergone some corruption; for, in another ballad in the same folio MS.

Erle Percy there his ancyent spred,
  The Half-Moone shining all soe faire[5]:
The Nortons ancyent had the crosse,
  And the five wounds our Lord did beare.

Then Sir George Bowes he straitwaye rose,
  After them some spoyle to make:
Those noble erles turn'd backe againe,
  And aye they vowed that knight to take.

That baron he to his castle fled,
  To Barnard castle then fled hee.
The uttermost walles were eathe to win,
  The earles have won them presentlie.

The uttermost walles were lime and bricke;
  But thoughe they won them soon anone,
Long e'er they wan the innermost walles,
  For they were cut in rocke of stone.

and apparently written by the same hand, containing the Sequel of this Lord Westmoreland's history, his banner is thus described, more conformable to his known bearings:

"Sette me up my faire Dun Bull,
  Wi' th' Gilden Hornes, hee beares soe hye."

5 Ver. 106, *The Half-Moone, &c.*] The *silver crescent* is a well-known crest or badge of the Northumberland family. It was probably brought home from some of the Crusades against the Sarazens. In an ancient Pedigree in verse, finely illuminated on a roll of vellum, and written in the reign of Henry VII., (in possession of the family,) we have this fabulous account given of its original. The author begins with accounting for the name of *Gernon* or *Algernon,* often borne by the Percies: who, he says, were

. . . . Gernons fyrst named of Brutys bloude of Troy:
Which valliantly fyghtynge in the land of Persè *(Persia)*
At pointe terrible ayance the miscreants on nyght,
An hevynly mystery was schewyd him, old bookys reherse;
In hys scheld did schyne a Mone veryfying her lyght,
Which to all the ooste yave a perfytte syght,
To vaynquys his enmys, and to deth them persue;
And therefore the *Persès* (Percies) the Cressant doth renew.

In the dark ages, no family was deemed considerable that did not derive its descent from the Trojan Brutus; or that was not distinguished by prodigies and miracles.

Then newes unto leeve London came
In all the speede that ever might bee,
And word is brought to our royall queene
Of the rysing in the North countrìe.

Her grace she turned her round about,
And like a royall queene shee swore[6],
I will ordayne them such a breakfast,
As never was in the North before.

Shee caus'd thirty thousand men be rays'd
With horse and harneis faire to see;
She caused thirty thousand men be raised,
To take the earles i' th' North countrìe.

Wi' them the false Erle Warwick went,
Th' erle Sussex and the lord Hunsdèn;
Untill they to Yorke castle came
I wiss, they never stint ne blan.

Now spred thy ancyent, Westmorland,
Thy dun bull faine would we spye:
And thou, the Erle o' Northumberland,
Now rayse thy half moone up on hye.

But the dun bulle is fled and gone,
And the halfe moone vanished away:
The Erles, though they were brave and bold,
Against soe many could not stay.

Thee, Norton, wi' thine eight good sonnes,
They doom'd to dye, alas! for ruth!
Thy reverend lockes thee could not save,
Nor them their faire and blooming youthe.

6 This is quite in character: her majesty would sometimes swear at her nobles, as well as box their ears.

Wi' them full many a gallant wight
  They cruellye bereav'd of life:
And many a childe made fatherlesse,
  And widowed many a tender wife.

---

## IV.

## Northumberland betrayed by Douglas.

This ballad may be considered as the sequel of the preceding. After the unfortunate Earl of Northumberland had seen himself forsaken of his followers, he endeavoured to withdraw into Scotland, but falling into the hands of the thievish borderers, was stript and otherwise ill-treated by them. At length he reached the house of Hector of Harlow, an Armstrong, with whom he hoped to lie concealed; for Hector had engaged his honour to be true to him, and was under great obligations to this unhappy nobleman. But this faithless wretch betrayed his guest for a sum of money to Murray, the regent of Scotland, who sent him to the castle of Lough-leven, then belonging to William Douglas. All the writers of that time assure us that Hector, who was rich before, fell shortly afterwards into poverty, and became so infamous, that *to take Hector's cloak*, grew into a proverb, to express a man who betrays his friend. See Camden, Carleton, Holingshed, &c.

Lord Northumberland continued in the castle of Lough-leven, till the year 1572; when James Douglas, Earl of Morton, being elected regent, he was given up to the Lord Hunsden at Berwick, and being carried to York, suffered death. As Morton's party depended on Elizabeth for protection, an elegant historian thinks "it was scarce possible for them to refuse putting into her hands a person who had taken up arms against her. But as a sum of money was paid on that account, and shared between Morton and his kinsman Douglas, the former of whom during his exile in England had been much indebted to Northumberland's friendship, the abandoning this unhappy nobleman to inevitable destruction, was deemed an ungrateful and mercenary act."—Robertson's Hist.

So far history coincides with this ballad, which was apparently written by some northern bard, soon after the event. The interposal of the *witch-lady* (v. 53.) is probably his own invention: yet even this hath some countenance from history; for about 25 years before, the Lady Jane Douglas, Lady Glamis, sister of the Earl of Angus, and nearly related to Douglas of Lough-leven, had suffered death for the pretended crime of witchcraft; who, it is presumed, is the witch-lady alluded to in v. 133.

The following is selected (like the former) from two copies, which contained great variations: one of them in the Editor's folio MS. In the other copy, some of the stanzas at the beginning of this ballad are nearly the same with what in that MS. are made to begin another ballad on the escape of the Earl of Westmoreland, who got safe into Flanders, and is feigned in the ballad to have undergone a great variety of adventures.

---

How long shall fortune faile me nowe,
  And harrowe me with fear and dread?
How long shall I in bale abide,
  In misery my life to lead?

To fall from my bliss, alas the while!
  It was my sore and heavye lott:
And I must leave my native land,
  And I must live a man forgot.

One gentle Armstrong I doe ken,
  A Scot he is much bound to mee:
He dwelleth on the border side,
  To him I'll goe right privilie.

Thus did the noble Percy 'plaine,
  With a heavy heart and wel-away,

When he with all his gallant men,
On Bramham moor had lost the day.

But when he to the Armstrongs came,
They dealt with him all treacherouslye;
For they did strip that noble earle:
And ever an ill death may they dye.

False Hector to Earl Murray sent,
To shew him where his guest did hide:
Who sent him to the Lough-levèn,
With William Douglas to abide.

And when he to the Douglas came,
He halched him right curteouslie:
Say'd, Welcome, welcome, noble earle,
Here thou shalt safelye bide with mee.

When he had in Lough-leven been
Many a month and many a day;
To the regent[1] the lord warden[2] sent,
That bannisht earle for to betray.

He offered him great store of gold,
And wrote a letter fair to see:
Saying, Good my lord, grant me my boon,
And yield that banisht man to mee.

Earle Percy at the supper sate
With many a goodly gentleman:
The wylie Douglas then bespake,
And thus to flyte with him began:

What makes you be so sad, my lord,
And in your mind so sorrowfullyè?
To-morrow a shootinge will bee held
Among the lords of the North countryè.

[1] James Douglas, Earl of Morton, elected regent of Scotland Nov. 24, 1572.

[2] Of one of the English Marches. Lord Hunsden.

The butts are sett, the shooting's made,
  And there will be great royalty:
And I am sworne into my bille,
  Thither to bring my lord Percye.

I'll give thee my hand, thou gentle Douglas,
  And here by my true faith, quoth hee,
If thou wilt ride to the worldes end,
  I will ride in thy companye.

And then bespake a lady faire,
  Mary à Douglas was her name:
You shall bide here, good English lord,
  My brother is a traiterous man.

He is a traitor stout and stronge,
  As I tell you in privitìe:
For he hath tane liverance of the earle[3],
  Into England nowe to 'liver thee.

Now nay, now nay, thou goodly lady,
  The regent is a noble lord:
Ne for the gold in all Englànd,
  The Douglas wold not break his word.

When the regent was a banisht man,
  With me he did faire welcome find;
And whether weal or woe betide,
  I still shall find him true and kind.

Between England and Scotland it wold breake truce,
  And friends againe they wold never bee,
If they shold 'liver a banisht erle
  Was driven out of his own countrie.

Alas! alas! my lord, she sayes,
  Nowe mickle is their traitorìe;

[3] Of the Earl of Morton, the regent.

Then let my brother ryde his ways,
And tell those English lords from thee,

How that you cannot with him ryde,
Because you are in an ile of the sea[4],
Then ere my brother come againe
To Edenbrow castle[5] Ile carry thee.

To the Lord Hume I will thee bring,
He is well knowne a true Scots lord,
And he will lose both land and life,
Ere he with thee will break his word.

Much is my woe, Lord Percy sayd,
When I thinke on my own countrie,
When I thinke on the heavye happe
My friends have suffered there for mee.

Much is my woe, Lord Percy sayd,
And sore those wars my minde distresse;
Where many a widow lost her mate,
And many a child was fatherlesse.

And now that I a banisht man,
Shold bring such evil happe with mee,
To cause my faire and noble friends
To be suspect of treacherie:

This rives my heart with double woe;
And lever had I dye this day,
Than thinke a Douglas can be false,
Or ever he will his guest betray.

If you'll give me no trust, my lord,
Nor unto mee no credence yield;
Yet step one moment here aside,
Ile showe you all your foes in field.

[4] *i. e.* Lake of Leven, which hath communication with the sea.
[5] At that time in the hands of the opposite faction.

Lady, I never loved witchcraft,
  Never dealt in privy wyle;
But evermore held the high-waye
  Of truth and honours, free from guile.

If you'll not come yourselfe, my lorde,
  Yet send your chamberlaine with mee;
Let me but speak three words with him,
  And he shall come again to thee.

James Swynard with that lady went,
  She showed him through the weme of her ring
How many English lords there were
  Waiting for his master and him.

And who walkes yonder, my good lady,
  So royallyè on yonder greene?
O yonder is the lord Hunsdèn[6]:
  Alas! he'll doe you drie and teene.

And who beth yonder, thou gay ladye,
  That walkes so proudly him beside?
That is Sir William Drury[7], shee sayd,
  A keen captàine he is and tryde.

How many miles is itt, madàme,
  Betwixt yond English lords and mee?
Marry it is thrice fifty miles,
  To saile to them upon the sea.

I never was on English ground,
  Ne never sawe it with mine eye,
But as my book it sheweth mee,
  And through my ring I may descrye.

[6] The Lord Warden of the east Marches.
[7] Governor of Berwick.

My mother shee was a witch ladye,
  And of her skille she learned mee;
She wold let me see out of Lough-leven
  What they did in London citie.

But who is yond, thou lady faire,
  That looketh with sic an austerne face?
Yonder is Sir John Foster[8], quoth shee,
  Alas! he'll do ye sore disgrace.

He pulled his hatt down over his browe,
  He wept: in his heart he was full of woe;
And he is gone to his noble Lord,
  Those sorrowful tidings him to show.

Now nay, now nay, good James Swynàrd,
  I may not believe that witch ladìe:
The Douglasses were ever true,
  And they can ne'er prove false to mee.

I have now in Lough-leven been
  The most part of these years three,
Yett have I never had noe outrake,
  Ne no good games that I cold see.

Therefore I'll to yond shooting wend,
  As to the Douglas I have hight:
Betide me weale, betide me woe,
  He ne'er shall find my promise light.

He writhe a gold ring from his finger,
  And gave itt to that gay ladìe:
Sayes, It was all that I cold save,
  In Harley woods where I cold bee[9].

[8] Warden of the middle March.
[9] *i. e,* Where I was: an ancient idiom.

And wilt thou goe, thou noble lord,
  Then farewell truth and honestie;
And farewell heart and farewell hand;
  For never more I shall thee see.

The wind was faire, the boatmen call'd,
  And all the saylors were on borde;
Then William Douglas took to his boat,
  And with him went that noble lord.

Then he cast up a silver wand,
  Says, Gentle lady, fare thee well!
The lady fett a sigh soe deep,
  And in a dead swoone down shee fell.

Now let us goe back, Douglas, he sayd,
  A sickness hath taken yond faire ladie:
If ought befall yond lady but good,
  Then blamed for ever I shall bee.

Come on, come on, my lord, he sayes;
  Come on, come on, and let her bee:
There's ladyes enow in Lough-leven
  For to cheere that gay ladie.

If you'll not turne yourself, my lord,
  Let me goe with my chamberlaine;
We will but comfort that faire lady,
  And wee will return to you againe.

Come on, come on, my lord, he sayes,
  Come on, come on, and let her bee:
My sister is craftye, and wold beguile
  A thousand such as you and mee.

When they had sayled[10] fifty myle,
  Now fifty mile upon the sea;

10 There is no navigable stream between Lough-leven and the sea: but a ballad-maker is not obliged to understand geography.

Hee sent his man to ask the Douglas,
  When they shold that shooting see.

Faire words, quoth he, they make fooles faine,
  And that by thee and thy lord is seen:
You may hap to think itt soon enough,
  Ere you that shooting reach, I ween.

Jamye his hatt pulled over his browe,
  He thought his lord then was betray'd;
And he is to Erle Percy againe,
  To tell him what the Douglas sayd.

Hold upp thy head, man, quoth his lord;
  Nor therefore lett thy courage fayle;
He did it but to prove thy heart,
  To see if he cold make it quail.

When they had other fifty sayld,
  Other fifty mile upon the sea,
Lord Percy called to Douglas himselfe,
  Sayd, What wilt thou nowe doe with mee?

Looke that your brydle be wight, my lord,
  And your horse goe swift as shipp att sea:
Looke that your spurres be bright and sharpe,
  That you may pricke her while she'll away.

What needeth this, Douglas? he sayth;
  What needest thou to flyte with mee?
For I was counted a horseman good
  Before that ever I mett with thee.

A false Hector hath my horse,
  Who dealt with mee so treacherouslie:
A false Armstrong he hath my spurres,
  And all the geere belongs to mee.

When they had sayled other fifty mile,
  Other fifty mile upon the sea:
They landed low by Berwicke side,
  A deputed 'laird' landed Lord Percye.

Then he at Yorke was doomde to dye,
  It was, alas! a sorrowful sight:
Thus they betrayed that noble earle,
  Who ever was a gallant wight.

V. 224. fol. MS. reads *land,* and has not the following stanza.

---

## V.

## My Mind to me a Kingdom is.

This excellent philosophical song appears to have been famous in the sixteenth century. It is quoted by Ben Jonson in his play of *Every man out of his Humour*, first acted in 1599, act i. sc. 1, where an impatient person says,

> "I am no such pil'd cynique to believe
> That beggery is the onely happinesse,
> Or, with a number of these patient fooles,
> To sing, 'My minde to me a kingdome is,'
> When the lanke hungrie belly barkes for foode."

It is here chiefly printed from a thin quarto music-book, entitled "Psalmes, Sonets, and Songs of Sadnes and Pietie, made into Musicke of five parts, &c. By William Byrd, one of the Gent. of the Queenes Majesties Honorable Chappell. Printed by Thomas East," &c. 4to. no date: but Ames, in his *Typog.* has mentioned another edition of the same book, dated 1588, which I take to have been later than this.

Some improvements, and an additional stanza (sc. the 5th) were had from two other ancient copies; one of them in black letter, in the Pepys Collection, thus inscribed, "A sweet and pleasant Sonet, intitled *My Mind to me a Kingdom is.* To the tune of *In Crete*," &c.

Some of the stanzas in this poem were printed by Byrd

separate from the rest: they are here given in what seemed the most natural order.

---

My minde to me a kingdome is;
  Such perfect joy therein I finde
As farre exceeds all earthly blisse,
  That God or nature hath assignde:
Though much I want, that most would have,
Yet still my mind forbids to crave.

Content I live, this is my stay;
  I seek no more than may suffice:
I presse to beare no haughtie sway;
  Look what I lack my mind supplies.
Loe! thus I triumph like a king,
Content with that my mind doth bring.

I see how plentie surfets oft,
  And hastie clymbers soonest fall:
I see that such as sit aloft
  Mishap doth threaten most of all:
These get with toile, and keep with feare:
Such cares my mind could never beare.

No princely pompe, nor welthie store,
  No force to winne the victorie,
No wylie wit to salve a sore,
  No shape to winne a lovers eye;
To none of these I yeeld as thrall,
For why my mind dispiseth all.

Some have too much, yet still they crave,
  I little have, yet seek no more:
They are but poore, tho' much they have;
  And I am rich with little store:
They poor, I rich; they beg, I give;
They lacke, I lend; they pine, I live.

I laugh not at anothers losse,
  I grudge not at anothers gaine;
No worldly wave my mind can tosse,
  I brooke that is anothers bane:
I feare no foe, nor fawne on friend;
I loth not life, nor dread mine end.

I joy not in no earthly blisse:
  I weigh not Cresus' welth a straw;
For care, I care not what it is;
  I feare not fortunes fatall law:
My mind is such as may not move
For beautie bright or force of love.

I wish but what I have at will:
  I wander not to seeke for more;
I like the plaine, I clime no hill;
  In greatest stormes I sitte on shore,
And laugh at them that toile in vaine
To get what must be lost againe.

I kisse not where I wish to kill;
  I faine not love where most I hate;
I breake no sleep to winne my will;
  I wayte not at the mighties gate;
I scorne no poore, I feare no rich;
I feele no want, nor have too much.

The court, ne cart, I like, ne loath;
  Extreames are counted worst of all;
The golden meane betwixt them both,
  Doth surest sit, and fears no fall:
This is my choyce, for why I finde,
No wealth is like a quiet minde.

My welth is health, and perfect ease;
  My conscience clere my chiefe defence:

I never seeke by brybes to please,
  Nor by desert to give offence:
Thus do I live, thus will I die;
Would all did so as well as I!

---

## VI.

## The Patient Countess.

The subject of this tale is taken from that entertaining colloquy of Erasmus, entitled, *Uxor Μεμψιγαμος, sive Conjugium:* which has been agreeably modernised by the late Mr. Spence in his little miscellaneous publication entitled "Moralities, &c., by Sir Harry Beaumont," 1753, 8vo. p. 42.

The following stanzas are extracted from an ancient poem entitled *Albion's England*, written by W. Warner, a celebrated poet in the reign of Queen Elizabeth, though his name and works are now equally forgotten. The reader will find some account of him in vol. ii. book ii. song 24 (p. 195).

The following stanzas are printed from the author's improved edition of his work, printed in 1602, 4to; the third impression of which appeared so early as 1592, in bl. let. 4to. The edition in 1602 is in thirteen books, and so it is reprinted in 1612, 4to; yet in 1606, was published "A Continuance of Albion's England by the first Author, W. W. Lond. 4to:" this contains books xiv. xv. xvi. In Ames's *Typography*, is preserved the memory of another publication of this writer's, entitled *Warner's Poetry*, printed in 1580. 12mo, and reprinted in 1602. There is also extant under the name of Warner, "Syrix, or sevenfold Hist. pleasant, and profitable, comical, and tragical," 4to.

It is proper to premise, that the following lines were not written by the author in stanzas, but in long Alexandrines of fourteen syllables; which the narrowness of our page made it here necessary to subdivide.

---

IMPATIENCE chaungeth smoke to flame,
But jelousie is hell;
Some wives by patience have reduc'd
Ill husbands to live well:
As did the ladie of an earle,
Of whom I now shall tell.

An earle 'there was' had wedded, lov'd;
Was lov'd, and lived long
Full true to his fayre countesse; yet
At last he did her wrong.

Once hunted he untill the chace,
Long fasting, and the heat
Did house him in a peakish graunge
Within a forest great.

Where knowne and welcom'd (as the place
And persons might afforde)
Browne bread, whig, bacon, curds and milke
Were set him on the borde.

A cushion made of lists, a stoole
Halfe backed with a hoope
Were brought him, and he sitteth down
Besides a sorry coupe.

The poore old couple wisht their bread
Were wheat, their whig were perry,
Their bacon beefe, their milke and curds
Were creame, to make him merry.

Meane while (in russet neatly clad,
With linen white as swanne,
Herselfe more white, save rosie where
The ruddy colour ranne:

Whome naked nature, not the aydes
Of arte made to excell)

The good man's daughter sturres to see
  That all were feat and well;
The earle did marke her, and admire
  Such beautie there to dwell.

Yet fals he to their homely fare,
  And held him at a feast:
But as his hunger slaked, so
  An amorous heat increast.

When this repast was past, and thanks,
  And welcome too; he sayd
Unto his host and hostesse, in
  The hearing of the mayd:

Yee know, quoth he, that I am lord
  Of this, and many townes;
I also know that you be poore,
  And I can spare you pownes.

So will I, so yee will consent,
  That yonder lasse and I
May bargaine for her love; at least,
  Doe give me leave to trye.
Who needs to know it? nay who dares
  Into my doings pry?

First they mislike, yet at the length
  For lucre were misled;
And then the gamesome earle did wowe
  The damsell for his bed.

He took her in his armes, as yet
  So coyish to be kist,
As mayds that know themselves belov'd,
  And yieldingly resist.

In few, his offers were so large
  She lastly did consent;

With whom he lodged all that night,
And early home he went.

He tooke occasion oftentimes
In such a sort to hunt.
Whom when his lady often mist,
Contràry to his wont,

And lastly was informed of
His amorous haunt elsewhere;
It greev'd her not a little, though
She seem'd it well to beare.

And thus she reasons with herselfe,
Some fault perhaps in me;
Somewhat is done, that soe he doth:
Alas! what may it be?

How may I winne him to myself?
He is a man, and men
Have imperfections; it behooves
Me pardon nature then.

To checke him were to make him checke[1],
Although hee now were chaste:
A man controuled of his wife,
To her makes lesser haste.

If duty then, or daliance may
Prevayle to alter him;
I will be dutifull, and make
My selfe for daliance trim.

So was she, and so lovingly
Did entertaine her lord,
As fairer, or more faultles none
Could be for bed or bord.

[1] To *check* is a term in falconry, applied when a hawk stops and turns away from his proper pursuit. To *check* also signifies to reprove or chide. It is in this verse used in both senses.

Yet still he loves his leiman, and
  Did still pursue that game,
Suspecting nothing less, than that
  His lady knew the same:
Wherefore to make him know she knew,
  She this devise did frame:

When long she had been wrong'd, and sought
  The foresayd meanes in vaine,
She rideth to the simple graunge
  But with a slender traine.

She lighteth, entreth, greets them well,
  And then did looke about her:
The guiltie houshold knowing her:
  Did wish themselves without her;
Yet, for she looked merily,
  The lesse they did misdoubt her.

When she had seen the beauteous wench
  (Then blushing fairnes fairer)
Such beauty made the countesse hold
  Them both excus'd the rather.

Who would not bite at such a bait?
  Thought she: and who (though loth)
So poore a wench, but gold might tempt?
  Sweet errors lead them both.

Scarse one in twenty that had bragg'd
  Of proffer'd gold denied,
Or of such yeelding beautie baulkt,
  But, tenne to one, had lied.

Thus thought she: and she thus declares
  Her cause of coming thether;
My lord, of hunting in these partes,
  Through travel, night or wether,

Hath often lodged in your house;
  I thanke you for the same;
For why? it doth him jolly ease
  To lie so neare his game.

But, for you have not furniture
  Beseeming such a guest,
I bring his owne, and come myselfe
  To see his lodging drest.

With that two sumpters were discharg'd,
  In which were hangings brave,
Silke coverings, curtens, carpets, plate,
  And al such turn should have.

When all was handsomly dispos'd,
  She prayes them to have care
That nothing hap in their default,
  That might his health impair:

And, Damsell, quoth shee, for it seemes
  This houshold is but three
And for thy parents age, that this
  Shall chiefely rest on thee;

Do me that good, else would to God
  He hither come no more.
So tooke she horse, and ere she went
  Bestowed gould good store.

Full little thought the countie that
  His countesse had done so;
Who now return'd from far affaires
  Did to his sweet-heart go.

No sooner sat he foote within
  The late deformed cote,
But that the formall change of things
  His wondring eies did note.

But when he knew those goods to be
His proper goods; though late,
Scarce taking leave, he home returnes
The matter to debate.

The countesse was a-bed, and he
With her his lodging tooke;
Sir, welcome home (quoth shee); this night
For you I did not looke.

Then did he question her of such
His stuffe bestowed soe.
Forsooth, quoth she, because I did
Your love and lodging knowe:

Your love to be a proper wench,
Your lodging nothing lesse;
I held it for your health, the house
More decently to dresse.

Well wot I, notwithstanding her,
Your lordship loveth me;
And greater hope to hold you such
By quiet, then brawles, 'you' see.

Then for my duty, your delight,
And to retaine your favour,
All done I did, and patiently
Expect your wonted 'haviour.

Her patience, witte and answer wrought
His gentle teares to fall:
When (kissing her a score of times)
Amend, sweet wife, I shall:
He said, and did it; 'so each wife
Her husband may' recall.

---

## VII.

## Dowsabell.

The following stanzas were written by Michael Drayton, a poet of some eminence in the reigns of Queen Elizabeth, James I., and Charles I.[1] They are inserted in one of his Pastorals, the first edition of which bears this whimsical title. "Idea. The Shepheards Garland fashioned in nine Eglogs. Rowlands sacrifice to the nine muses. Lond. 1593, 4to." They are inscribed with the author's name at length, "To the noble and valerous gentleman master Robert Dudley," &c. It is very remarkable, that when Drayton reprinted them in the first folio edition of his works, 1619, he had given those Eclogues so thorough a revisal, that there is hardly a line to be found the same as in the old edition. This poem had received the fewest corrections, and therefore is chiefly given from the ancient copy, where it is thus introduced by one of his shepherds:

Listen to mee, my lovely shepheards joye,
  And thou shalt heare, with mirth and mickle glee,
A prettie tale, which when I was a boy,
  My toothles grandame oft hath tolde to me.

The author has professedly imitated the style and metre of some of the old metrical romances; particularly that of *Sir Isenbras*[2], (alluded to in v. 3,) as the reader may judge from the following specimen:

Lordynges, lysten, and you shal here, &c.
*  *  *  *
Ye shall well heare of a knight,
That was in warre full wyght,
    And doughtye of his dede:
  His name was Syr Isenbras,
  Man nobler then he was
    Lyved none with breade.

He was lyvely, large, and longe,
With shoulders broade, and armes stronge,
  That myghtie was to se:

[1] He was born in 1563, and died in 1631.—*Biog. Brit.*
[2] As also Chaucer's Rhyme of Sir Topas, v. 6.

He was a hardye man, and hye,
All men hym loved that hym se,
For a gentyll knight was he:
Harpers loved him in hall,
With other minstrells all,
For he gave them golde and fee, &c.

This ancient legend was printed in black letter, 4to, by Wyllyam Copland: no date. In the Cotton Library (Calig. A. 2,) is a MS. copy of the same romance containing the greatest variations. They are probably two different translations of some French original.

---

Farre in the countrey of Arden,
There won'd a knight, hight Cassemen,
As bolde as Isenbras:
Fell was he, and eger bent,
In battell and in tournament,
As was the good Sir Topas.

He had, as antique stories tell,
A daughter cleaped Dowsabel,
A mayden fayre and free:
And for she was her fathers heire,
Full well she was y-cond the leyre
Of mickle curtesie.

The silke well couth she twist and twine,
And make the fine march-pine,
And with the needle werke:
And she could helpe the priest to say
His mattins on a holy-day,
And sing a psalme in kirke.

She ware a frock of frolicke greene,
Might well beseeme a mayden queene,
Which seemly was to see;
A hood to that so neat and fine,
In colour like the colombine,
Y-wrought full featously.

Her features all as fresh above,
As is the grasse that growes by Dove;
And lyth as lasse of Kent.
Her skin as soft as Lemster wooll,
As white as snow on Peakish Hull,
Or swanne that swims in Trent.

This mayden in a morne betime
Went forth, when May was in her prime,
To get sweete cetywall,
The honey-suckle, the harlocke,
The lilly and the lady-smocke,
To deck her summer hall.

Thus, as she wandred here and there,
Y-picking of the bloomed breere,
She chanced to espie
A shepheard sitting on a bancke,
Like chanteclere he crowed crancke,
And pip'd full merrilie.

He lear'd his sheepe as he him list,
When he would whistle in his fist,
To feede about him round;
Whilst he full many a carroll sung,
Untill the fields and meadowes rung,
And all the woods did sound.

In favour this same shepheards swayne
Was like the bedlam Tamburlayne[3],
Which helde prowd kings in awe:
But meeke he was as lamb mought be:
And innocent of ill as he[4]
Whom his lewd brother slaw.

[3] Alluding to *Tamburlaine the Great, or the Scythian Shepheard*, 1590, 8vo. an old ranting play ascribed to Marlowe.
[4] Sc. Abel.

The shepheard ware a sheepe-gray cloke,
Which was of the finest loke,
That could be cut with sheere:
His mittens were of bauzens skinne,
His cockers were of cordiwin,
His hood of meniveere.

His aule and lingell in a thong,
His tar-boxe on his broad belt hong,
His breech of coyntrie blewe:
Full crispe and curled were his lockes,
His browes as white as Albion rocks:
So like a lover true,

And pyping still he spent the day,
So merry as the popingay;
Which liked Dowsabel:
That would she ought, or would she nought,
This lad would never from her thought;
She in love-longing fell.

At length she tucked up her frocke,
White as a lilly was her smocke,
She drew the shepheard nye;
But then the shepheard pyp'd a good,
That all his sheepe forsooke their foode,
To heare his melodye.

Thy sheepe, quoth she, cannot be leane,
That have a jolly shepheards swayne,
The which can pipe so well:
Yea but, sayth he, their shepheard may,
If pyping thus he pine away,
In love of Dowsabel.

Of love, fond boy, take thou no keepe,
Quoth she; looke thou unto thy sheepe,
Lest they should hap to stray.

Quoth he, So had I done full well,
Had I not seen fayre Dowsabell
  Come forth to gather maye.

With that she gan to vaile her head,
Her cheeks were like the roses red,
  But not a word she sayd:
With that the shepheard gan to frowne,
He threw his pretie pypes adowne,
  And on the ground him layd.

Sayth she, I may not stay till night,
And leave my summer-hall undight,
  And all for long of thee.
My coate, sayth he, nor yet my foulde
Shall neither sheepe nor shepheard hould,
  Except thou favour mee.

Sayth she, Yet lever were I dead,
Then I should lose my mayden-head,
  And all for love of men.
Sayth he, Yet are you too unkind,
If in your heart you cannot finde
  To love us now and then.

And I to thee will be as kinde
As Colin was to Rosalinde,
  Of curtesie the flower.
Then will I be as true, quoth she,
As ever mayden yet might be
  Unto her paramour.

With that she bent her snow-white knee,
Downe by the shepheard kneeled shee,
  And him she sweetely kist:
With that the shepheard whoop'd for joy,
Quoth he, Ther's never shepheards boy
  That ever was so blist.

## VIII.

## The Farewell to Love.

From Beaumont and Fletcher's play, entitled *The Lover's Progress*, act iii. sc. 1.

Adieu, fond love, farewell you wanton powers;
I am free again.
Thou dull disease of bloud and idle hours,
Bewitching pain,
Fly to fools, that sigh away their time:
My nobler love to heaven doth climb,
And there behold beauty still young,
That time can ne'er corrupt, nor death destroy,
Immortal sweetness by fair angels sung,
And honoured by eternity and joy:
There lies my love, thither my hopes aspire,
Fond love declines, this heavenly love grows higher.

---

## IX.

## Ulysses and the Syren,

Affords a pretty poetical contest between Pleasure and Honour. It is found at the end of "Hymen's Triumph: a pastoral tragi-comedie," written by Daniel, and printed among his works, 4to. 1623[1]. Daniel, who was a contemporary of Drayton's, and is said to have been poet-laureate to Queen Elizabeth, was born in 1562, and died in 1619. Anne, Countess of Dorset, Pembroke, and Montgomery, (to whom Daniel had been tutor,) has inserted a small portrait of him in a full length picture of herself, preserved at Appleby Castle, in Cumberland.

This little poem is the rather selected for a specimen of Daniel's poetic powers, as it is omitted in the later edition of his works, 2 vols. 12mo. 1718.

[1] In this edition it is collated with a copy printed at the end of his "Tragedie of Cleopatra. Lond. 1607," 12mo.

SYREN.

COME, worthy Greeke, Ulysses come,
  Possesse these shores with me,
The windes and seas are troublesome,
  And here we may be free.
Here may we sit and view their toyle,
  That travaile in the deepe,
Enjoy the day in mirth the while,
  And spend the night in sleepe.

ULYSSES.

Faire nymph, if fame or honour were
  To be attain'd with ease,
Then would I come and rest with thee,
  And leave such toiles as these:
But here it dwels, and here must I
  With danger seek it forth;
To spend the time luxuriously
  Becomes not men of worth.

SYREN.

Ulysses, O be not deceiv'd
  With that unreall name:
This honour is a thing conceiv'd,
  And rests on others' fame
Begotten only to molest
  Our peace, and to beguile
(The best thing of our life) our rest,
  And give us up to toyle!

ULYSSES.

Delicious nymph, suppose there were
  Nor honor, nor report,
Yet manlinesse would scorne to weare
  The time in idle sport:
For toyle doth give a better touch
  To make us feele our joy;

And ease findes tediousnes, as much
  As labour yeelds annoy.

SYREN.

Then pleasure likewise seemes the shore,
  Whereto tendes all your toyle;
Which you forego to make it more,
  And perish oft the while.
Who may disport them diversly,
  Find never tedious day;
And ease may have variety,
  As well as action may.

ULYSSES.

But natures of the noblest frame
  These toyles and dangers please;
And they take comfort in the same,
  As much as you in ease:
And with the thought of actions past
  Are recreated still:
When pleasure leaves a touch at last
  To shew that it was ill.

SYREN.

That doth opinion only cause,
  That 's out of custom bred;
Which makes us many other laws,
  Than ever nature did.
No widdowes wail for our delights,
  Our sports are without blood;
The world we see by warlike wights
  Receives more hurt than good.

ULYSSES.

But yet the state of things require
  These motions of unrest,
And these great spirits of high desire
  Seem borne to turne them best:

To purge the mischiefes, that increase
  And all good order mar:
For oft we see a wicked peace,
  To be well chang'd for war.

SYREN.

Well, well, Ulysses, then I see
  I shall not have thee here;
And therefore I will come to thee,
  And take my fortune there.
I must be wonne that cannot win,
  Yet lost were I not wonne:
For beauty hath created bin
  T' undoo or be undone.

---

## X.

## Cupid's Pastime.

THIS beautiful poem, which possesses a classical elegance hardly to be expected in the age of James I., is printed from the fourth edition of Davison's Poems[1], &c. 1621. It is also found in a later miscellany, entitled *Le Prince d' Amour*, 1660, 8vo. Francis Davison, editor of the poems above referred to, was son of that unfortunate secretary of state, who suffered so much from the affair of Mary Queen of Scots. These poems, he tells us in his preface, were written by himself, by his brother [Walter], who was a soldier in the wars of the Low Countries, and by some dear friends "anonymoi." Among them are found some pieces by Sir J. Davis, the Countess of Pembroke, Sir Philip Sidney, Spenser, and other wits of those times.

In the fourth volume of Dryden's *Miscellanies*, this poem is attributed to Sidney Godolphin, Esq., but erroneously, being probably written before he was born. One edition of Davison's book was published in 1608. Godolphin was born in 1610, and died in 1642-3.—*Ath. Ox.* ii. 23.

1 See the full title in vol. ii. book iii. no. iv (p. 251).

---

It chanc'd of late a shepherd swain,
  That went to seek his straying sheep,
Within a thicket on a plain
  Espied a dainty nymph asleep.

Her golden hair o'erspred her face;
  Her careless arms abroad were cast;
Her quiver had her pillows place;
  Her breast lay bare to every blast.

The shepherd stood and gaz'd his fill;
  Nought durst he do; nought durst he say;
Whilst chance, or else perhaps his will,
  Did guide the god of love that way.

The crafty boy thus sees her sleep,
  Whom if she wak'd he durst not see;
Behind her closely seeks to creep,
  Before her nap should ended bee.

There come, he steals her shafts away,
  And puts his own into their place;
Nor dares he any longer stay,
  But, ere she wakes, hies thence apace.

Scarce was he gone, but she awakes,
  And spies the shepherd standing by:
Her bended bow in haste she takes,
  And at the simple swain lets flye.

Forth flew the shaft, and pierc'd his heart,
  That to the ground he fell with pain:
Yet up again forthwith he start,
  And to the nymph he ran amain.

Amazed to see so strange a sight,
  She shot, and shot, but all in vain;
The more his wounds, the more his might,
  Love yielded strength amidst his pain.

Her angry eyes were great with tears,
  She blames her hand, she blames her skill;
The bluntness of her shafts she fears,
  And try them on herself she will.

Take heed, sweet nymph, trye not thy shaft,
  Each little touch will pierce thy heart:
Alas! thou know'st not Cupids craft;
  Revenge is joy: the end is smart.

Yet try she will, and pierce some bare;
  Her hands were glov'd, but next to hand
Was that fair breast, that breast so rare,
  That made the shepherd senseless stand.

That breast she pierc'd; and through that breast
  Love found an entry to her heart;
At feeling of this new-come guest,
  Lord! how this gentle nymph did start!

She runs not now; she shoots no more;
  Away she throws both shaft and bow:
She seeks for what she shunn'd before,
  She thinks the shepherds haste too slow.

Though mountains meet not, lovers may:
What other lovers do, did they:
  The god of love sate on a tree,
  And laught that pleasant sight to see.

---

## XI.

## The Character of a Happy Life.

This little moral poem was writ by Sir Henry Wotton, who died Provost of Eton, in 1639. Æt. 72. It is printed from a little collection of his pieces, entitled *Reliquiæ Wottonianæ*, 1651, 12mo., compared with one or two other copies.

---

How happy is he born or taught,
  That serveth not anothers will;
Whose armour is his honest thought,
  And simple truth his highest skill:

Whose passions not his masters are;
  Whose soul is still prepar'd for death;
Not ty'd unto the world with care
  Of princes ear, or vulgar breath:

Who hath his life from rumours freed;
  Whose conscience is his strong retreat;
Whose state can neither flatterers feed,
  Nor ruine make oppressors great:

Who envies none whom chance doth raise,
  Or vice: Who never understood
How deepest wounds are given with praise;
  Nor rules of state, but rules of good:

Who God doth late and early pray
  More of his grace than gifts to lend;
And entertaines the harmless day
  With a well-chosen book or friend.

This man is freed from servile bands
  Of hope to rise, or feare to fall;
Lord of himselfe, though not of lands;
  And having nothing, yet hath all.

---

## XII.

## Gilderoy,

Was a famous robber, who lived about the middle of the last century, if we may credit the histories and story-books of highwaymen, which relate many improbable feats of him, as his robbing Cardinal Richelieu, Oliver Cromwell, &c. But these stories have probably no other authority than the records of Grub-street; at least the Gilderoy, who is the hero of Scottish songsters, seems to have lived in an earlier age; for, in Thompson's *Orpheus Caledonius*, vol. ii. 1733, 8vo. is a copy of this ballad, which, though corrupt and interpolated, contains some lines that appear to be of genuine antiquity: in these he is represented as contemporary with Mary Queen of Scots: *ex. gr.*

> "The Queen of Scots possessed nought,
> That my love let me want:
> For cow and ew to me he brought
> And ein whan they were scant."

These lines, perhaps, might safely have been inserted among the following stanzas, which are given from a written copy, that seems to have received some modern corrections. Indeed the common popular ballad contained some indecent luxuriances that required the pruning-hook.

---

Gilderoy was a bonnie boy,
Had roses tull his shoone,
His stockings were of silken soy,
Wi' garters hanging doune:
It was, I weene, a comelie sight,
To see sae trim a boy;
He was my jo and hearts delight,
My handsome Gilderoy.

Oh! sike twa charming een he had,
A breath as sweet as rose,
He never ware a Highland plaid,
But costly silken clothes;
He gain'd the luve of ladies gay,
Nane eir tull him was coy,
Ah! wae is mee! I mourn the day,
For my dear Gilderoy.

My Gilderoy and I were born
Baith in one toun together,

We scant were seven years beforn
  We gan to luve each other;
Our dadies and our mammies thay
  Were fill'd wi' mickle joy,
To think upon the bridal day,
  Twixt me and Gilderoy.

For Gilderoy that luve of mine,
  Gude faith, I freely bought
A wedding sark of holland fine,
  Wi' silken flowers wrought:
And he gied me a wedding ring,
  Which I receiv'd wi' joy,
Nae lad nor lassie eir could sing,
  Like me and Gilderoy.

Wi' mickle joy we spent our prime,
  Till we were baith sixteen,
And aft we past the langsome time,
  Among the leaves sae green;
Aft on the banks we'd sit us thair,
  And sweetly kiss and toy,
Wi' garlands gay wad deck my hair
  My handsome Gilderoy.

Oh! that he still had been content,
  Wi' me to lead his life,
But, ah! his manfu' heart was bent,
  To stir in feates of strife:
And he in many a venturous deed,
  His courage bauld wad try;
And now this gars mine heart to bleed,
  For my dear Gilderoy.

And when of me his leave he tuik,
  The tears they wat mine ee,
I gave tull him a parting luik,
  "My benison gang wi' thee!

God speed thee weil, mine ain dear heart,
For gane is all my joy;
My heart is rent sith we maun part,
My handsome Gilderoy."

My Gilderoy baith far and near,
Was fear'd in every toun,
And bauldly bare away the gear,
Of many a lawland loun;
Nane eir durst meet him man to man,
He was sae brave a boy:
At length wi' numbers he was tane,
My winsome Gilderoy.

Wae worth the loun that made the laws,
To hang a man for gear,
To 'reave of life for ox or ass,
For sheep, or horse, or mare:
Had not their laws been made sae strick,
I neir had lost my joy,
Wi' sorrow neir had wat my cheek,
For my dear Gilderoy.

Giff Gilderoy had done amisse,
He mought hae banisht been,
Ah! what sair cruelty is this,
To hang sike handsome men:
To hang the flower o' Scottish land,
Sae sweet and fair a boy;
Nae lady had sae white a hand,
As thee, my Gilderoy.

Of Gilderoy sae fraid they were,
They bound him mickle strong,
Tull Edenburrow they led him thair,
And on a gallows hung:
They hung him high aboon the rest,
He was sae trim a boy;

Thair dyed the youth whom I lued best,
My handsome Gilderoy.

Thus having yielded up his breath,
I bare his corpse away,
Wi' tears, that trickled for his death,
I washt his comelye clay;
And siker in a grave sae deep,
I laid the dear-lued boy,
And now for evir maun I weep,
My winsome Gilderoy.

***

---

## XIII.

## Winifreda.

This beautiful address to conjugal love, a subject too much neglected by the libertine Muses, was, I believe, first printed in a volume of "Miscellaneous Poems, by several hands, published by D. [David] Lewis, 1726." 8vo.

It is there said, how truly I know not, to be a translation "from the ancient British language."

---

Away; let nought to love displeasing,
My Winifreda, move your care;
Let nought delay the heavenly blessing,
Nor squeamish pride, nor gloomy fear.

What tho' no grants of royal donors
With pompous titles grace our blood:
We'll shine in more substantial honors,
And to be noble we'll be good.

Our name, while virtue thus we tender,
Will sweetly sound where-e'er 'tis spoke:
And all the great ones, they shall wonder
How they respect such little folk.

What though from fortune's lavish bounty
No mighty treasures we possess;
We'll find within our pittance plenty,
And be content without excess.

Still shall each returning season
Sufficient for our wishes give;
For we will live a life of reason,
And that's the only life to live.

Through youth and age in love excelling,
We'll hand in hand together tread;
Sweet-smiling peace shall crown our dwelling,
And babes, sweet-smiling babes, our bed.

How should I love the pretty creatures,
While round my knees they fondly clung:
To see them look their mothers features,
To hear them lisp their mothers tongue.

And when with envy time transported,
Shall think to rob us of our joys,
You'll in your girls again be courted,
And I'll go a wooing in my boys.

---

## XIV.

## The Witch of Wokey,

WAS published in a small collection of Poems, entitled *Euthemia, or the Power of Harmony*, &c., 1756, written in 1748, by the ingenious Dr. Harrington, of Bath, who never allowed them to be published, and withheld his name till it could no longer be concealed. The following contains some variations from the original copy, which it is hoped the author will pardon, when he is informed they came from the elegant pen of the late Mr. Shenstone.

Wokey-hole is a noted cavern in Somersetshire, which

has given birth to as many wild fanciful stories, as the Sybil's Cave in Italy. Through a very narrow entrance, it opens into a large vault, the roof whereof, either on account of its height, or the thickness of the gloom, cannot be discovered by the light of torches. It goes winding a great way under ground, is crost by a stream of very cold water, and is all horrid with broken pieces of rock: many of these are evident petrifactions, which, on account of their singular forms, have given rise to the fables alluded to in this poem.

---

In aunciente days, tradition showes,
A base and wicked elfe arose,
  The Witch of Wokey hight:
Oft have I heard the fearfull tale
From Sue, and Roger of the vale,
  On some long winter's night.

Deep in the dreary dismall cell,
Which seem'd and was ycleped hell,
  This blear-eyed hag did hide:
Nine wicked elves, as legends sayne,
She chose to form her guardian trayne,
  And kennel near her side.

Here screeching owls oft made their nest,
While wolves its craggy sides possest,
  Night-howling thro' the rock:
No wholesome herb could here be found;
She blasted every plant around,
  And blister'd every flock.

Her haggard face was foull to see;
Her mouth unmeet a mouth to bee;
  Her eyne of deadly leer;
She nought devis'd but neighbour's ill;
She wreak'd on all her wayward will,
  And marr'd all goodly chear.

All in her prime, have poets sung,
No gaudy youth, gallant and young,
  E'er blest her longing armes:
And hence arose her spight to vex,
And blast the youth of either sex,
  By dint of hellish charms.

From Glaston came a lerned wight,
Full bent to marr her fell despight,
  And well he did, I ween:
Sich mischief never had been known,
And, since his mickle lerninge shown,
  Sich mischief ne'er has been.

He chauntede out his godlie booke,
He crost the water, blest the brooke,
  Then—pater-noster done,
The ghastly hag he sprinkled o'er:
When lo! where stood a hag before,
  Now stood a ghastly stone.

Full well 'tis known adown the dale:
Tho' passing strange indeed the tale,
  And doubtfull may appear,
I'm bold to say, there's never a one,
That has not seen the witch in stone,
  With all her household gear.

But tho' this lernede clerke did well;
With grieved heart, alas! I tell,
  She left this curse behind:
That Wokey-nymphs forsaken quite,
Tho' sense and beauty both unite,
  Should find no leman kind.

For lo! even, as the fiend did say,
The sex have found it to this day,
  That men are wondrous scant:

Here's beauty, wit, and sense combin'd,
With all that's good and virtuous join'd,
Yet hardly one gallant.

Shall then sich maids unpitied moane?
They might as well, like her, be stone,
As thus forsaken dwell.
Since Glaston now can boast no clerks;
Come down from Oxenford, ye sparks,
And, oh! revoke the spell.

Yet stay—nor thus despond, ye fair;
Virtue's the gods' peculiar care;
I hear the gracious voice:
Your sex shall soon be blest agen,
We only wait to find sich men,
As best deserve your choice.

---

## XV.

## Bryan and Pereene,

A WEST-INDIAN BALLAD,

Is founded on a real fact, that happened in the Island of St. Christopher's, about 1760. The editor owes the following stanzas to the friendship of Dr. James Grainger[1], who was an eminent physician in that island when this tragical incident happened, and died there much honoured and lamented in 1767. To this ingenious gentleman the public is indebted for the fine *Ode on Solitude*, printed in the fourth volume of Dodsley's *Miscellanies*, p. 229, in which are assembled some of the sublimest images in nature. The reader will pardon the insertion of the first stanza here, for the sake of rectifying the two last lines, which were thus given by the author:

O Solitude, romantic maid,
Whether by nodding towers you tread,
Or haunt the desert's trackless gloom,
Or hover o'er the yawning tomb,

[1] Author of a poem on the Culture of the Sugar-Cane, &c.

Or climb the Andes' clifted side,
Or by the Nile's coy source abide,
Or starting from your half-year's sleep
From Hecla view the thawing deep,
Or at the purple dawn of day
Tadmor's marble wastes survey, &c.

alluding to the account of Palmyra published by some late ingenious travellers, and the manner in which they were struck at the first sight of those magnificent ruins by break of day.

---

The north-east wind did briskly blow,
The ship was safely moor'd;
Young Bryan thought the boat's-crew slow,
And so leapt over-board.

Pereene, the pride of Indian dames,
His heart long held in thrall,
And whoso his impatience blames,
I wot, ne'er lov'd at all.

A long long year, one month and day,
He dwelt on English land,
Nor once in thought or deed would stray,
Tho' ladies sought his hand.

For Bryan he was tall and strong,
Right blythsome roll'd his een,
Sweet was his voice whene'er he sung,
He scant had twenty seen.

But who the countless charms can draw,
That grac'd his mistress true;
Such charms the old world seldom saw,
Nor oft I ween the new.

Her raven hair plays round her neck,
Like tendrils of the vine;
Her cheeks red dewy rose buds deck,
Her eyes like diamonds shine,

Soon as his well-known ship she spied,
  She cast her weeds away,
And to the palmy shore she hied,
  All in her best array.

In sea-green silk so neatly clad,
  She there impatient stood;
The crew with wonder saw the lad
  Repel the foaming flood.

Her hands a handkerchief display'd,
  Which he at parting gave;
Well pleas'd the token he survey'd,
  And manlier beat the wave.

Her fair companions one and all,
  Rejoicing crowd the strand;
For now her lover swam in call,
  And almost touch'd the land.

Then through the white surf did she haste,
  To clasp her lovely swain;
When, ah! a shark bit through his waist:
  His heart's blood dy'd the main!

He shriek'd! his half sprang from the wave,
  Streaming with purple gore,
And soon it found a living grave,
  And ah! was seen no more.

Now haste, now haste, ye maids, I pray,
  Fetch water from the spring:
She falls, she swoons, she dies away,
  And soon her knell they ring.

Now each May morning round her tomb,
  Ye fair, fresh flowrets strew,
So may your lovers scape his doom,
  Her hapless fate scape you.

---

## XVI.

## Gentle River, Gentle River.

TRANSLATED FROM THE SPANISH.

Although the English are remarkable for the number and variety of their ancient ballads, and retain perhaps a greater fondness for these old simple rhapsodies of their ancestors than most other nations, they are not the only people who have distinguished themselves by compositions of this kind. The Spaniards have great multitudes of them, many of which are of the highest merit. They call them in their language *romances*, and have collected them into volumes under the titles of *El Romancero*, *El Cancionero*[1], &c. Most of them relate to their conflicts with the Moors, and display a spirit of gallantry peculiar to that romantic people. But, of all the Spanish ballads, none exceed in poetical merit those inserted in a little Spanish *History of the Civil Wars of Granada*, describing the dissensions which raged in that last seat of Moorish empire, before it was conquered in the reign of Ferdinand and Isabella, in 1491. In this History (or perhaps Romance) a great number of heroic songs are inserted, and appealed to as authentic vouchers for the truth of facts. In reality, the prose narrative seems to be drawn up for no other end, but to introduce and illustrate these beautiful pieces.

The Spanish editor pretends (how truly I know not) that they are translations from the Arabic or Morisco language. Indeed, from the plain, unadorned nature of the verse, and the native simplicity of the language and sentiment which runs through these poems, one would judge them to have been composed soon after the conquest of Granada above mentioned; as the prose narrative in which they are inserted, was published about a century after. It should seem, at least, that they were written before the Castilians had formed themselves so generally, as they have done since, on the model of the Tuscan poets, or had imported from Italy that fondness for conceit and refinement, which has for near two

[1] *i. e.* The ballad-singer.

centuries past so much infected the Spanish poetry, and rendered it so frequently affected and obscure.

As a specimen of the ancient Spanish manner, which very much resembles that of our old English bards and minstrels, the reader is desired candidly to accept the two following poems. They are given from a small collection of pieces of this kind, which the Editor some years ago translated for his amusement when he was studying the Spanish language. As the first is a pretty close translation, to gratify the curious it is accompanied with the original. The metre is the same in all these old Spanish ballads: it is of the most simple construction, and is still used by the common people in their extemporaneous songs, as we learn from Baretti's Travels. It runs in short stanzas of four lines, of which the second and fourth alone correspond in their terminations, and in these it is only required that the vowels should be alike; the consonants may be altogether different, as

| pone | casa | meten | arcos |
|---|---|---|---|
| noble | cañas | muere | gamo |

Yet has this kind of verse a sort of simple harmonious flow, which atones for the imperfect nature of the rhyme, and renders it not unpleasing to the ear. The same flow of numbers has been studied in the following versions. The first of them is given from two different originals, both of which are printed in the *Hist. de las Civiles Guerras de Granada.* Madrid, 1694. One of them hath the rhymes ending in *aa*, the other in *ia*. It is the former of these that is here reprinted They both of them begin with the same line,

Rio verde, rio verde[2],

which could not be translated faithfully:

Verdant river, verdant river,

would have given an affected stiffness to the verse, the great merit of which is its easy simplicity; and therefore a more simple epithet was adopted, though less poetical or expressive.

2 Literally, Green river, green river. Rio Verde is said to be the name of a river in Spain; which ought to have been attended to by the translator had he known it.

"Rio verde, rio verde,
Quanto cuerpo en ti se baña
De Christianos y de Moros
Muertos por la dura espada!

"Y tus ondas cristalinas
De roxa sangre se esmaltan:
Entre moros y Christianos
Muy gran batalla se trava.

"Murieron Duques y Condes,
Grandes señores de salva:
Murio gente de valia
De la nobleza de España.

"En ti murio don Alonso,
Que de Aguilar se llamaba;
El valeroso Urdiales,
Con don Alonso acababa.

"Por un ladera arriba
El buen Sayavedra marcha;
Naturel es de Sevilla,
De la gente mas granada.

"Tras el iba un Renegado,
Desta manera le habla;
Date, date, Sayavedra,
No huyas de la batalla.

"Yo te conozco muy bien,
Gran tiempo estuve en tu casa
Y en la Plaça de Sevilla
Bien te vide jugar cañas.

"Conozco a tu padre y madre
Y a tu muger doña Clara;
Siete años fui tu cautivo,
Malamente me tratabas.

Gentle river, gentle river,
  Lo, thy streams are stain'd with gore,
Many a brave and noble captain
  Floats along thy willow'd shore.

All beside thy limpid waters,
  All beside thy sands so bright,
Moorish chiefs and Christian warriors
  Join'd in fierce and mortal fight.

Lords, and dukes, and noble princes
  On thy fatal banks were slain:
Fatal banks that gave to slaughter
  All the pride and flower of Spain.

There the hero, brave Alonzo,
  Full of wounds and glory died:
There the fearless Urdiales
  Fell a victim by his side.

Lo! where yonder Don Saavedra
  Thro' their squadrons slow retires:
Proud Seville, his native city,
  Proud Seville his worth admires.

Close behind a renegado
  Loudly shouts with taunting cry;
Yield thee, yield thee, Don Saavedra,
  Dost thou from the battle fly?

Well I know thee, haughty Christian,
  Long I liv'd beneath thy roof;
Oft I've in the lists of glory
  Seen thee win the prize of proof.

Well I know thy aged parents,
  Well thy blooming bride I know;
Seven years I was thy captive,
  Seven years of pain and woe.

"Y aora lo seras mio,
  Si Mahoma me ayudara;
Y tambien te tratare,
  Como a mi me tratabas.

"Sayavedra que lo oyera,
  Al Moro bolvio la cara;
Tirole el Mora una flecha,
  Pero nunca le acertaba.

"Hiriole Sayavedra
  De una herida muy mala:
Muerto cayo el Renegado
  Sin poder hablar palabra.

"Sayavedra fue cercado
  De mucha Mora canalla,
Y al cabo cayo alli muerto
  De una muy mala lançada.

"Don Alonso en este tiempo
  Bravamente peleava,
Y el cavallo le avian muerto,
  Y le tiene por muralla.

"Mas cargaron tantos Moros
  Que mal le hieren y tratan:
De la sangre, que perdia
  Don Alonso se desmaya.

"Al fin, al fin cayo muerto
  Al pie de un pena alta. —
— Muerto queda don Alonso,
  Eterna fama ganara."

* * * * *

May our prophet grant my wishes,
Haughty chief, thou shalt be mine:
Thou shalt drink that cup of sorrow,
Which I drank when I was thine.

Like a lion turns the warrior,
Back he sends an angry glare;
Whizzing came the Moorish javelin,
Vainly whizzing thro' the air.

Back the hero full of fury
Sent a deep and mortal wound:
Instant sunk the renegado,
Mute and lifeless on the ground.

With a thousand Moors surrounded,
Brave Saavedra stands at bay:
Wearied out but never daunted,
Cold at length the warrior lay.

Near him fighting great Alonzo
Stout resists the Paynim bands;
From his slaughter'd steed dismounted
Firm intrench'd behind him stands.

Furious press the hostile squadron,
Furious he repels their rage:
Loss of blood at length enfeebles:
Who can war with thousands wage!

Where yon rock the plain o'ershadows,
Close beneath its foot retir'd,
Fainting sunk the bleeding hero,
And without a groan expir'd.

* * * * *

---

*** In the Spanish original of the foregoing ballad, follow a few more stanzas, but being of inferior merit were not translated.

*Renegado* properly signifies an apostate, but it is sometimes used to express an infidel in general; as it seems to do above in ver. 21, &c.

The image of the *lion*, &c. in ver. 37, is taken from the other Spanish copy, the rhymes of which end in *ia*, viz.

"Sayavedra, que lo oyera,
Como un leon rebolbia."

---

## XVII.

## Alcanzor and Zayda.

### A MOORISH TALE.

### IMITATED FROM THE SPANISH.

The foregoing version was rendered as literal as the nature of the two languages would admit. In the following, a wider compass hath been taken. The Spanish poem that was chiefly had in view, is preserved in the same history of the civil wars of Granada, f. 22, and begins with these lines,

"Por la calle de su dama
Passeando se anda," &c.

---

Softly blow the evening breezes,
Softly fall the dews of night;
Yonder walks the Moor Alcanzor,
Shunning every glare of light.

In yon palace lives fair Zaida,
Whom he loves with flame so pure:
Loveliest she of Moorish ladies;
He a young and noble Moor.

Waiting for the appointed minute,
Oft he paces to and fro;
Stopping now, now moving forwards,
Sometimes quick, and sometimes slow.

Hope and fear alternate teaze him,
Oft he sighs with heart-felt care. —

See, fond youth, to yonder window,
  Softly steps the timorous fair.

Lovely seems the moon's fair lustre
  To the lost benighted swain,
When all silvery bright she rises,
  Gilding mountain, grove, and plain,

Lovely seems the sun's full glory
  To the fainting seaman's eyes,
When some horrid storm dispersing,
  O'er the wave his radiance flies.

But a thousand times more lovely
  To her longing lover's sight,
Steals half-seen the beauteous maiden
  Thro' the glimmerings of the night.

Tip-toe stands the anxious lover,
  Whispering forth a gentle sigh:
Alla[1] keep thee, lovely lady;
  Tell me, am I doom'd to die?

Is it true the dreadful story,
  Which thy damsel tells my page,
That seduc'd by sordid riches
  Thou wilt sell thy bloom to age?

An old lord from Antiquera
  Thy stern father brings along;
But canst thou, inconstant Zaida,
  Thus consent my love to wrong?

If 'tis true, now plainly tell me,
  Nor thus trifle with my woes;
Hide not then from me the secret,
  Which the world so clearly knows.

[1] *Alla* is the Mahometan name of God.

Deeply sighed the conscious maiden,
  While the pearly tears descend:
Ah! my lord, too true the story;
  Here our tender loves must end.

Our fond friendship is discover'd,
  Well are known our mutual vows:
All my friends are full of fury;
  Storms of passion shake the house.

Threats, reproaches, fears surround me;
  My stern father breaks my heart:
Alla knows how dear it costs me,
  Generous youth, from thee to part.

Ancient wounds of hostile fury
  Long have rent our house and thine;
Why then did thy shining merit
  Win this tender heart of mine?

Well thou know'st how dear I lov'd thee
  Spite of all their hateful pride,
Tho' I fear'd my haughty father
  Ne'er would let me be thy bride.

Well thou know'st what cruel chidings
  Oft I've from my mother borne,
What I've suffer'd here to meet thee
  Still at eve and early morn.

I no longer may resist them;
  All, to force my hand combine;
And to-morrow to thy rival
  This weak frame I must resign.

Yet think not thy faithful Zaida
  Can survive so great a wrong;
Well my breaking heart assures me
  That my woes will not be long.

Farewell then, my dear Alcanzor!
  Farewell too my life with thee!
Take this scarf, a parting token;
  When thou wear'st it think on me.

Soon, lov'd youth, some worthier maiden
  Shall reward thy generous truth;
Sometimes tell her how thy Zaida
  Died for thee in prime of youth.

— To him all amaz'd, confounded,
  Thus she did her woes impart:
Deep he sigh'd, then cry'd, O Zaida!
  Do not, do not break my heart.

Canst thou think I thus will lose thee?
  Canst thou hold my love so small?
No, a thousand times I'll perish! —
  My curst rival too shall fall.

Canst thou, wilt thou yield thus to them?
  O break forth, and fly to me!
This fond heart shall bleed to save thee,
  These fond arms shall shelter thee.

'Tis in vain, in vain, Alcanzor,
  Spies surround me, bars secure!
Scarce I steal this last dear moment,
  While my damsel keeps the door.

Hark, I hear my father storming!
  Hark, I hear my mother chide!
I must go: farewell for ever!
  Gracious Alla be thy guide!

END OF THE THIRD BOOK.

# A GLOSSARY

OF

## THE OBSOLETE AND SCOTTISH WORDS IN THE FIRST VOLUME.

---

The Scottish words are denoted by s. French by f. Latin by l. Anglo-Saxon by A. S. Icelandic by Isl. &c. For the etymology of the words in this and the following volumes, the reader is referred to JUNII ETYMOLOGICUM ANGLICANUM. Edidit ED. LYE, Oxon. 1743, fol.

*For such words as may not be found here, the reader is desired to consult the Glossaries to the other volumes.*

A, au, s. *all.*
A Twyde, p. 6, *of Tweed.*
Abacke, *back.*
Abone, aboon, s. *above.*
Abowght, *about.*
Abraide, p. 143, *abroad.*
Acton, a kind of armour made of taffaty, or leather quilted, &c., worn under the habergeon, to save the body from bruises. f. *Hocqueton.*
Aft, s. *oft.*
Agayne, *against.*
Agoe, *gone.*
Ain, awin, s. *own.*
Al gife, *although.*
A-late, p. 89, *of late.*
An, p. 68, *and.*
Ancyent, *standard.*
Ane, s. *one, an.*
Aras, p. 5, arros, p. 8, *arrows.*
Arcir, p. 68, *archer.*
Assinde, *assigned.*
Assoyl'd, assoyled, *absolved.*
Astate, *estate;* also *a great person.*
Astound, astonyed, *stunned, astonished, confounded.*
Ath, p. 6, athe, p. 8, *o' th', of the.*
Aureat, *golden.*
Austerne, p. 247, *stern, austere.*
Avowe, p. 24, *vow.*
Avoyd, p. 178, *void, vacate.*
Axed, *asked.*
Ayance, p. 293, *against.*

B.

Ba, s. *ball.*
Bacheleere, p. 37, &c. *knight.*
Baile, bale, pp. 37, 72, *evil, hurt, mischief, misery.*
Bairne, s. *child.*
Baith, s. bathe, *both.*
Balys bete, p. 14, *better our bales,* i. e. *remedy our evils.*
Band, p. 43, *bond, covenant.*
Bane, *bone.*
Bar, *bore.*
Bar hed, *bare-head,* or perhaps *bared.*
Barne, p. 6, berne, p. 19, *man, person.*
Base court, *the lower court of a castle.*
Basnete, basnite, basnyte, bassonet, bassonette, *helmet.*
Bauzen's skinne, p. 263, perhaps, sheep's leather dressed and coloured red, f. bazane, *sheep's leather.* In Scotland, sheepskin mittens, with the wool on the inside, are called *Bauzon-mittens.* — *Bauson* also signifies a badger, in old English; it may therefore signify, perhaps, badger skin.
Be that, p. 6, *by that time.*

Bearyng arowe, p. 151, *an arrow that carries well.* — Or, perhaps *bearing*, or *birring, i. e.* whirring or whizzing arrow: from *Isl. Bir, ventus*, or A. S. Beþe, *fremitus.*
Bedight, *bedecked.*
Bedyls, *beadles.*
Beette, *did beat.*
Beforn, *before.*
Begylde, p. 82, *beguiled, deceived.*
Beheard, *heard.*
Behests, *commands, injunctions.*
Behove, p. 155, *behoof.*
Belyfe, p. 148, belive, *immediately, by and by, shortly.*
Ben, bene, *been.*
Bende-bow, *a bent-bow,* qu.
Benison, *blessing.*
Bent, p. 5, bents, p. 38, (where bents, long coarse grass, &c. grow,) *the field, fields.*
Benyngne, p. 85, benigne, *benign, kind.*
Beste, *beest, art.*
Bestis, *beasts.*
Be-strawghted, p. 162, *distracted.*
Beth, *be, are.*
Bickarte, p. 5, bicker'd, *skirmished.* (It is also used sometimes in the sense of *swiftly coursed*, which seems to be the sense, p. 5. Mr. Lambe[1].)
Bille, &c. p. 244, *I have delivered a promise in writing, confirmed by an oath.*
Blane, p. 10, blanne, did blin, i. e. *linger, stop.*
Blaw, s. *blow.*
Blaze, *to emblazon, display.*
Blee, *colour, complexion.*
Bleid, s. blede, *bleed.*
Blist, *blessed.*
Blive, belive, *immediately.*
Bloomed, p. 262, *beset with bloom.*
Blude, *blood,* bluid reid, s. *blood red.*
Bluid, bluidy. s. *blood, bloody.*
Blyve, belive, *instantly.*
Boare, *bare.*
Bode, p. 81, *abode, stayed.*
Boltes, *shafts, arrows.*
Bomen, p. 5, *bowmen.*
Bonnye, bonnie, s. *comely.*
Boone, *a favour, request, petition.*
Boot, boote, *advantage, help, assistance.*
Borowe, p. 137, *to redeem by a pledge.*
Borowed, p. 28, *warranted, pledged, was exchanged for.*
Borrowe, borowe, *pledge, surety.*
Bot and, s. p. 100, (it should probably be *both and,*) *and also.*
Bot, *but.*
Bote, *boot, advantage.*
Bougill, s. *bugle-horn, hunting-horn.*
Bounde, bowynd, bowned, *prepared, got ready.* The word is also used in the north in the sense of *went* or *was going.*
Bowndes, *bounds.*
Bowne ye, *prepare ye, get ready.*
Bowne, *ready;* bowned, *prepared.*
Bowne to dyne, p. 36, *going to dine.* *Bowne* is a common word in the north for *going; e. g.* Where are you bowne to? *Where are you going?*
Bowre, bower, *habitation: chamber, parlour, perhaps from* Isl. bouan, *to dwell.*
Bowre-window, *chamber window.*
Bowys, *bows.*
Braid, s. *broad, large.*
Brandes, *swords.*
Bred banner, p. 22, *broad banner.*
Breech, p. 263, *breeches.*
Breeden bale, *breed mischief.*
Breere, brere, *briar.*
Breng, bryng, *bring.*
Brether, *brethren.*
Broad arrow, *a broad forked-headed arrow,* s.
Brodinge, *pricking.*
Brook, p. 13, *enjoy.*
Brooke, p. 252, *bear, endure.*
Browd, *broad.*
Bryttlynge, p. 5, brytlyng, p. 6, *cutting up, quartering, carving.*
Bugle, *bugle horn, hunting horn.*
Bushment, p. 82, ambushment, *am-*

[1] Mr. Lambe also interprets "Bickering," by rattling, *e. g.*
"And on that slee Ulysses head
Sad curses down does bicker."
Translat. of Ovid.

*bush, a snare to bring them into trouble.*
Busk and boun, p. 102, *i, e. make yourselves ready and go.* Boun, *to go* (North country).
Buske ye, *dress ye.*
Busket, buskt, *dressed.*
Buskt them, p. 82, *prepared themselves, made themselves ready.*
But if, *unless,*
Buttes, *buts to shoot at.*
By thre, p. 131, *of three.*
Bydys, *bides, abides.*
Bye, p. 137, *buy, pay for;* also, abye, *suffer for.*
Byears, beeres, *biers.*
Byll, bill, *an ancient kind of halbert or battle-ax,* p. 5.
Byn, bine, bin, *been, be, are.*
Byrche, *birch-tree, birch-wood.*
Byste, beest, *art.*

C.

Calde, callyd, p. 7, *called.*
Camscho, s. *stern, grim.*
Can, p. 22, *began to cry.*
Cane, p. 25, *'gan to cry.*
Capull hyde, p. 76, *horse-hide.*
Care-bed, *bed of care.*
Carpe off care, p. 13, *complain thro' care.*
Cast, p. 6, *mean, intend.*
Cawte and kene, p. 22, *cautious and active,* l. cautus.
Caytiffe, caitif, *slave, despicable wretch,* p. 39.
Cetywall, p. 262, setiwall, *the herb valerian:* also, *mountain spikenard.* See Gerard's Herbal.
Chanteclere, *the cock.*
Chays, *chase.*
Check, *to rate at.*
Check, *to stop.*
Child, p. 90, *knight.* Children, p. 39, *knights.* See v. iii. p. 75.
Christentye, christiantè, *Christendom.*
Churl, *one of low birth, a villain, or vassal.*
Chyf, chyfe, *chief.*
Clawde, clawed, *tore, scratched;* p. 155, figuratively, *beat.*
Cleaped, cleped, *called, named.*
Clerke, *scholar.*
Clim, *the contraction of* Clement.
Clough, a north-country word for *a broken cliff.*
Clowch, *clutch, grasp.*
Coate, *cot, cottage.*
Cockers, p. 263, *a sort of buskins or short boots fastened with laces or buttons, and often worn by farmers or shepherds.* In Scotland they are called *cutikins,* from *cute,* the ankle. —*'Cokers: fishermen's boots.'* (Littleton's Diction.)
Cold bee, p. 247, *was.* Cowde dye, p. 27, *died* (a phrase).
Collayne, p. 25, *Cologne steel.*
Commen, commyn, *come.*
Confetered, *confederated, entered into a confederacy.*
Cordiwin, p. 263, cordwayne: properly Spanish or Cordovan leather; here it signifies a more vulgar sort.
Corsiare, p. 10, *courser, steed.*
Cote, *cot, cottage.* Item, *coat.*
Coulde, *cold.* Item, *could.*
Countie, p. 258, *count, earl.*
Coupe, *a pen for poultry.*
Couth, *could.*
Coyntrie, p. 263, *Coventry.*
Crancky, *merry, sprightly, exulting.*
Credence, *belief.*
Crevis, *crevice, chink.*
Cristes corse, p. 7, *Christ's curse.*
Crowch, *crutch.*
Cryance, *belief,* f. créance, [whence recreant]. But in p. 39, &c. it seems to signify *fear,* f. crainte.
Cum, s. *come,* p. 8, *came.*

D.

Dampned, p. 137, *condemned.*
De, dy, dey, pp. 6, 8, 12, *die.*
Deepe-fette, *deep-fetched.*
Deid, s. dede, *deed.* Item, *dead.*
Deip, s. depe, *deep.*
Deir, s. deere, dere, *dear.*
Dell, *deal, part;* p. 89, every dell, *every part.*
Denay, *deny* (rhythmi gratia).
Depured, *purified, run clear.*
Descreeve, *describe.*
Dight, *decked, put on.*
Dill, p. 36, *dole, grief, pain.* — Dill I drye, p. 37, *pain I suffer.* — Dill was dight, p. 36, *grief was upon him.*
Dint, *stroke, blow.*

Dis, p. 68, *this.*
Discust, *discussed.*
Dites, *ditties.*
Dochter, s. *daughter.*
Dois, s. doys, *does.*
Dole, *grief.*
Dolefulle dumps, pp. 162, 227, *sorrowful gloom; or heaviness of heart.*
Dolours, *dolorous, mournful.*
Doth, dothe, doeth, *do.*
Doughte, dougheti, doughetie, dowghtye, *doughty, formidable.*
Dounae, s. p. 34, *am not able;* properly, *cannot take the trouble.*
Doute, *doubt.* Item, *fear.*
Doutted, *doubted, feared.*
Drap, s. *drop.*
Dre, p. 11, drie, p. 100, *suffer.*
Dreid, s. dreede, drede, *dread.*
Dreips, s. *drips, drops.*
Drovyers, drovers, p. 221, *such as drive herds of cattle, deer, &c.*
Dryvars, p. 5, *idem.*
Drye, p. 26, *suffer.*
Dryghnes, *dryness.*
Duble dyse, *double* (false) *dice.*
Dughtie, *doughty.*
Dule, s. dole, *grief.*
Dyd, dyde, *did.*
Dyght, p. 10, dight, p. 46, *dressed, put on, put.*
Dynte, *dint, blow, stroke.*
Dysgysynge, *disguising, masking.*

E.

Eame, eme, p. 22, *uncle.*
Eathe, *easy.*
Ee, s. eie, *eye.* Een, eyne, *eyes.*
Ech, eche, eiche, elke, *each.*
Ein, s. *even.*
Eir, evir, s. *e'er, ever.*
Eke, *also.* Eike, elke, *each.*
Eldern, s. *elder.*
Ellumynynge, p. 84, *embellishing.* To *illumine* a book, was to ornament it with paintings in miniature.
Elridge[2], *Scoticè* Elriche, Elritch, Elrische; *wild, hideous, ghostly.* Item, *lonesome, uninhabited except by spectres, &c.* Gloss. to A. Ramsay. Elritcht-laugh, *Gen. Shep. a.* 5.
Ellyconys, *Helicon's.*
Endyed, *dyed.*
Enharpid, *&c.* p. 84, *hooked, or edged with mortal dread.*
Enkankered, *cankered.*
Envye, pp. 20, 22, *malice, ill-will, injury.*
Erst, s. *heretofore.*
Etermynable, p. 86, *interminable, unlimited.*
Everych-one, *every-one.*

F.

Fa, s. *fall.*
Fach, feche, *fetch.*
Fain, fayne, *glad, fond.*
Faine of fighte, *fond of fighting.*
Faine, fayne, *feign.*
Fals, *false.* Item, *falleth.*
Farden, p. 45, *fared, flashed.*
Fare, *pass.*
Farley, *wonder.*
Faulcone, *falcon.*
Faye, *faith.*
Fayre, p. 22, *fair.*

[2] In the ballad of SIR CAULINE, we have "Eldridge Hill." p. 37; "Eldridge Knight," p. 38, 45. "Eldridge Sworde," p. 40, 46.— So Gawin Douglas calls the Cyclops, the "ELRICHE BRETHIR," *i. e.* brethren (b. ii. p. 91, l. 16); and in his Prologue to b. vii. (p. 202, l. 3), he thus describes the night-owl:

"Laithely of forme, with crukit camscho beik,
Ugsome to here was his wyld ELRISCHE shriek."

In Bannatyne's MS. Poems, (fol. 135, in the Advocates' library at Edinburgh,) is a whimsical rhapsody of a deceased old woman travelling in the other world; in which

"Scho wanderit, and zeid by, to an ELRICH well."

In the Glossary to G. Douglas, ELRICHE, &c. is explained by "wild, hideous: Lat. *trux, immanis;*" but it seems to imply somewhat more, as in Allan Ramsay's Glossaries.

Faytors, *deceivers, dissemblers, cheats.*
Fe, *fee, reward:* also, *bribe.* But properly, Fee is applied to lands and tenements, which are held by perpetual right, and by acknowledgment of superiority to a higher Lord. Thus, p. 85, in fee, i. e. *in feudal service.* l. feudum, &c. (Blount.)
Feat, *nice, neat.*
Featously, *neatly, dexterously.*
Feere, fere, *mate, companion.*
Feir, s. fere, *fear.*
Fendys pray, &c. p. 86, *from being the prey of the fiends.*
Fersly, *fiercely.*
Fesante, *pheasant.*
Fette, *fetched.*
Fetteled, *prepared, addressed, made ready.*
Filde, *field.*
Finaunce, p. 86, *fine, forfeiture.*
Fit, p. 8, fyt, p. 137, fytte, p. 69. *Part or division of a song.* Hence in p. 61, *fitt* is a strain of music. See vol. ii. p. 143, and Glossary.
Flyte, *to contend with words, scold.*
Foo, p. 28, *foes.*
For, *on account of.*
Forbode, *commandment,* p. 153. Over God's forbode. [*Præter Dei præceptum sit,*] *q. d. God forbid.*
Forefend, *prevent, defend.*
Formare, *former.*
Forsede, p. 82, *regarded, heeded.*
Forst, *forced, compelled.*
Forthynketh, p. 149, *repenteth, vexeth, troubleth.*
Fosters of the fe, p. 150, *foresters of the king's demesnes.*
Fou, fow, s. *full;* also, *fuddled.*
Fowarde, vawarde, *the van.*
Freake, freke, freyke, *man, person, human creature.* Also, *a whim or maggot.*
Fre-bore, p. 69, *free-born.*
Freckys, p. 9, *persons.*
Freits, s. *ill omens, ill luck; any old superstitious saw, or impression* [3], p. 102.
Frie, s. fre, *free.*
Fruward, *forward.*
Fuyson, foyson, *plenty;* also, *substance.*
Fykkill, *fickle.*
Fyll, p. 81, *fell.*
Fyr, *fire.*

## G.

Gair, s. *geer, dress.*
Gane, gan, began.
Ganyde, p. 8, *gained.*
Garde, *garred, made.*
Gare, gar, s. *make, cause; force, compel.*
Gargeyld, p. 88, from Gargouille, f. *the spout of a gutter.* The tower was adorned with spouts cut in the figures of greyhounds, lions &c.
Garlande, p. 74, *the ring within which the prick or mark was set to be shot at.*
Gear, s. geer, *goods.*
Getinge, *what he had got, his plunder, booty.*
Geve, gevend, *give, given.*
Gi, gie, s. *give.*
Gife, giff, *if.*
Gin, s. *an, if.*
Give owre, s. *surrender.*
Glede, p. 6, *a red-hot coal.*
Glent, p. 5, *glanced.*
Glose, p. 81, *set a false gloss or colour.*
Goddes, p. 83, *goddess.*
Gode, *good.*
Goggling eyen, *goggle eyes.*
Gone, p. 44, *go.*
Gowd, s. gould, *gold.*
Graine, *scarlet.*
Gramercye, *i. e. I thank you,* f. Grand-mercie.
Graunge, p. 254, *granary;* also, *a lone country-house.*
Grea-hondes, *grey-hounds.*
Grece, *a step,* p. 88, *a flight of steps, grees.*
Greece, p. 145, *fat, (a fat hart,)* from f. graisse.
Gret, grat, *great.*
Greves, *groves, bushes.*
Groundwa, *groundwall.*

[3] An ingenious correspondent in the north thinks FREIT is not 'an unlucky omen,' but, 'that thing which terrifies:' viz. Terrors will pursue them that look after frightful things. FRIGHT is pronounced by the common people in the north, FREET, p. 102.

Growende, growynd, *ground.*
Grysely groned, p. 27, *dreadfully groaned.*
Gude, guid, geud, s. *good.*

## H.

Ha, hae, s. *have.* Item, *hall.*
Habergeon, f. *a lesser coat of mail.*
Hable, p. 82, *able.*
Halched, halsed, *saluted, embraced, fell on his neck; from* Halse, *the neck, throat.*
Halesome, *wholesome, healthy.*
Hand-bowe, p. 154, *the long-bow, or common-bow, as distinguished from the cross-bow.*
Haried, harried, haryed, harowed, p. 19, 139, *robbed, pillaged, plundered.* He *harried* a bird's nest. Scot.
Harlocke, p. 262, perhaps *charlocke,* or *wild rape,* which bears a yellow flower, and grows among corn, &c.
Hartly lust, p. 84, *hearty desire.*
Hastarddis, p. 80, perhaps *hasty rash fellows,* or *upstarts,* qu.
Haviour, *behaviour.*
Hauld, s. *to hold.* Item, *hold, strong, bold.*
Hawberk, *a coat of mail, consisting of iron rings, &c.*
Haylle, *advantage, profit* (p. 22, for the profit of all England). A. S. Hæl, *salus.*
He, p. 5, hee, p. 20, hye, *high.*
He, p. 146, hye, *to hye, or hasten.*
Heal, p. 9, *hail.*
Hear, p. 9, *here.*
Heare, heares, *hair, hairs.*
Hed, hede, *head.*
Heere, p. 77, *hear.*
Heir, s. here, p. 8, *hear.*
Hend, *kind, gentle.*
Hest, *hast.*
Hests, p. 40, *commands, injunctions.*
Hether, *hither.*
Hewyne in to, *hewn in two.*
Hewyng, hewinge, *hewing, hacking.*
Hi, hie, p. 68, *he.*
Hie, hye, he, hee, *high.*
Hight, p. 41, p. 9, *engage, engaged, promised* (page 131, *named, called*).
Hillys, *hills.*
Hinde, hend, *gentle.*
Hir, s. *her.*
Hirsel, s. *herself.*
Hit, p. 9, *it.*
Hode, *hood, cap.*
Hole, *whole;* holl, idem.
Holtes, *woods, groves,* p. 20. In Norfolk a plantation of cherry-trees is called a *cherry-holt.* Also sometimes *hills*[4].
Holy, *wholly.* Or perhaps hole p. 85, *whole.*
Hom, hem, *them.*
Hondrith, hondred, *hundred.*
Honge, *hang, hung.*
Hontyng, *hunting.*
Hoo, ho, p. 17, *an interjection of stopping or desisting: hence stoppage.*
Hoved, p. 88, *heaved; hung moving* (Gl. Chauc.). *Hoved* or *hoven* means in the north, *swelled:* but Mr. Lambe thinks it is the same as *houd,* still used in the north, and applied to any light substance heaving to and fro on an undulating surface. The vowel *u* is often used there for the conson. *v.*
Hount, *hunt.*
Hyght, p. 25, *on high, aloud.*

## I.

I' feth, *in faith.*
I ween, *(I think:) verily.*
I wot, *(I know:) verily.*
I wys, I wis, *(I know:) verily.*
Iclipped, *called.*

[4] HOLTES seems evidently to signify HILLS in the following passage from Tuberville's *Songs and Sonnets,* 12mo, 1567, fol. 56:

"Yee that frequent the hilles,
And highest HOLTES of all;
Assist me with your skilfull quilles,
And listen when I call."

As also in this other verse of an ancient poet:

"Underneath the HOLTES so hoar."

Iff, *if.*
Jimp. s. *slender.*
Ild. *I'd, I would.*
Ile, *I'll, I will.*
Ilka, s. *every.*
Im, p. 68, *him.*
In fere, I fere, *together.*
Into, s. *in.*
Intres, p. 88, *entrance, admittance.*
Jo, p. 272, *sweet-heart, friend.*
Jogelers, p. 114, *jugglers.*
Is, p. 68, *is, his.*
I-tuned, *tuned.*
Iye, *eye.*

K.

Kall, p. 86, *call.*
Kan, p. 83, can.
Karls, *carls, churls*, karlis of kynde, p. 81, *churls by nature.*
Kauld, p. 68, *called.*
Keepe, p. 263, *care, heed.* So in the old play of *Hick Scorner* (in the last leaf but one): "I keepe not to clymbe so hye." *i. e. I study not; care not, &c.*
Kempe, *a soldier.*
Kemperye man, p. 60, *soldier, warrior, fighting-man*[5].
Kems, s. *combs.*
Ken, kenst, *know, knowest.*
Kepers, &c. p. 156, Sc. those that watch by the corpse, shall tye up my winding sheet.
Kind, *nature.*
Kit, p. 84, *cut.*
Kithe or kin, *acquaintance nor kindred.*
Knave, p. 77, *servant.*
Knicht, s. *knight.*
Knightes fee, p. 77, *such a portion of land as required the possessor to serve with man and horse.*
Knowles, *knolls, little hills.*
Knyled, *knelt.*
Kowarde, *coward.*
Kuntrey, p. 84, *country.*
Kurteis, p. 85, *courteous.*
Kyrtill, kirtle, *petticoat, gown.*

L.

Laith, s. *loth.*
Laithly, s. *loathsome, hideous.*
Lang, s. *long.*
Langsome, s. p. 273, *long, tedious.*
Lauch, lauched, s. *laugh, laughed.*
Launde, p. 145, *lawn.*
Layden, *laid.*
Laye, p. 40, *law.*
Lay-land, p. 39, *land that is not ploughed: green sward.*
Lay-lands, p. 46, *lands in general.*
Layne, lain; *vid.* Leane.
Leane, *conceal, hide;* Item, *lye* (query).
Leanyde, *leaned.*
Learnd, *learned, taught.*
Lease, p. 145, *lying, falsehood.* Wythouten lease, *verily.*
Leasynge, *lying, falsehood.*
Lee, p. 102, lea, *the field.*
Leeche, *physician.*
Leechinge, *doctoring, medicinal care.*
Leer, p. 277, *look.*
Leeve London, p. 240, *dear London, an old phrase.*
Leeveth, *believeth.*
Lefe, p. 148; leeve, *dear.*
Lefe, *leave;* leves, *leaves.*
Leive, s. *leave.*
Leman, leaman, leiman, *lover, mistress*, A. S. leiꝼman.
Lenger, *longer.*
Lere, p. 44, *face, complexion*, A. S. hleaꞃe, *facies, vultus.*
Lerned, *learned, taught.*
Lesynge, leasing, *lying, falsehood.*
Let, p. 4, *hinder*, lett, p. 59, *hindred.*

[5] "Germanis *Camp* Exercitum, aut Locum ubi Exercitus castrametatur, significat: inde ipsis Vir Castrensis et Militaris *kemffer*, et *kempher*, et *kemper*, et *kimber*, et *kamper*, pro varietate dialectorum, vocatur; Vocabulum hoc nostro sermone nondum penitus exolevit; Norfolcienses enim plebeio et proletario sermone dicunt '*He is a kemper old man*, i. e. Senex vegetus est.' Hinc *Cimbris* suum nomen; '*kimber* enim homo bellicosus, pugil, robustus miles, &c. significat.' Sheringham de Anglor. gentis orig. pag. 57. Rectius autem Lazius (apud eundem, p. 49). *Cimbros* a bello quod *kamff*, et Saxonice *kamp* nuncupatos crediderim; unde bellatores viri *Die Kempffer, Die Kemper.*"

Lettest, *hinderest, detainest.*
Lettyng, *hindrance,* i. e. *without delay.*
Lever, *rather.*
Leyre, lere, p. 261, *learning, lore.*
Lig, s. *lie.*
Lightsome, *cheerful, sprightly.*
Linde, see Lynde.
Lingell, *a thread of hemp rubbed with rosin, &c.,* used by rustics for mending their shoes.
Lith, lithe, lythe, p. 131, *attend, hearken, listen.*
Lither, p. 59, *idle, worthless, naughty, froward.*
Liver, *deliver.*
Liverance, p. 244, *deliverance (money, or a pledge for delivering you up).*
Loke, p. 263, *lock of wool.*
Longes, *belongs.*
Looset, losed, *loosed.*
Lope, *leaped.*
Loveth, *love,* plur. number.
Lough, p. 143, *laugh.*
Louked, *looked.*
Loun, s. p. 274, lowne, p. 170, *loon, rascal, from the Irish* liun, *slothful, sluggish,*
Louted, lowtede, *bowed, did obeisance.*
Lowe, p. 76, *a little hill.*
Lurden, p. 139, lurdeyne, *sluggard, drone.*
Lynde, p. 143, 144, *the lime tree,* or collectively, *lime trees; or trees in general.* Lyne, p. 74.
Lyth, p. 262, lythe, *lithsome, pliant, flexible, easy, gentle.*

## M.

Mahound, Mahowne, *Mahomet.*
Majeste, maist, mayeste, *may'st.*
Mair, s. mare, *more.*
Makys, maks, *mates*[6].
Male, p. 8, *coat of mail.*
Mane, p. 6, *man.* Item, *moan.*
March perti, p. 13, *in the parts lying upon the Marches.*
March-pine, p. 261, march-pane, *a kind of biscuit.*
Mast, maste, *may'st.*
Masterye, p. 74, maystery, p. 151, *a trial of skill, high proof of skill.*
Mauger, maugre, *spite of.*
Maun, s. mun, *must.*
Mayd, mayde, *maid.*
Maye, p. 24, *maid* (rhythmi gratia).
Mayne, p. 47, *force, strength,* p. 72, *horse's mane.*
Meany, *retinue, train, company.*
Meed, meede, *reward.*
Men of armes, p. 25, *gens d' armes.*
Meniveere, *a species of fur.*
Merches, *marches.*
Met, meit, s. mete, *meet, fit, proper.*
Meynè, see Meany.
Mickle, much.
Mighttè, *mighty.*
Minged, p. 39, *mentioned.*
Miscreants, *unbelievers.*
Misdoubt, p. 257, *suspect, doubt.*
Misken, *mistake;* also in the Scottish idiom, *let a thing alone.* (Mr. Lambe.)
Mode, p. 143, *mood.*
Monnyn day, *Monday.*
Mores, p. 37, *hills, wild downs.*
Morne, s. p. 66, *on the morrow.*
Mort, *death of the deer.*
Most, *must.*
Mought, mot, mote, *might.*
Mun, maun, s. *must.*
Mure, mures, s. *wild downs, heaths, &c.*
Musis, *muses.*
Myllan, *Milan steel.*
Myne-ye-ple, page 8, *perhaps many plies, or folds.* Monyple is still used in this sense in the north. (Mr. Lambe.)
Myrry, *merry.*
Mysuryd, p. 83, *misused, applied to a bad purpose.*

## N.

Na, nae, s. *no, none.*
Nams, *names.*
Nar, p. 6, nare, *nor.* Item, *than.*
Nat, *not.*
Nee, ne, *nigh.*

[6] As the words MAKE and MATE were, in some cases, used promiscuously by ancient writers; so the words CAKE and CATE seem to have been applied with the same indifferency: this will illustrate that common English proverb, "To turn Cat (*i. e.* CATE) in pan." A PAN-CAKE is in Northamptonshire still called a PAN-CATE.

Neigh him neare, *approach him near.*
Neir, s. nere, *ne'er, never.*
Neir, s. nere, *near.*
Nicked him of naye, p. 54, *nicked him with a refusal.*
Nipt, *pinched.*
Nobles, p. 80, *nobless, nobleness.*
None, *noon.*
Nourice, s. *nurse.*
Nye, ny, *nigh.*

O.

O gin, s. *O if!* a phrase.
On, *one;* on man, p. 7, *one man.* One, p. 25, *on.*
Onfowghten, unfoughten, *unfought.*
Or, ere, p. 17, 20, *before.*
Or, eir, *before ever.*
Orisons, *prayers.*
Ost, oste, oost, *host.*
Out ower, s. *quite over: over.*
Out-horn, *the summoning to arms by the sound of a horn.*
Outrake, p. 247, *an out ride, or expedition. To* raik, s. *is to go fast. Outrake* is a common term among shepherds. When their sheep have a free passage from inclosed pastures into open and airy grounds, they call it a good *outrake.* (Mr. Lambe.)
Oware off none, p. 5, *hour of noon.*
Owre, owr, s. *o'er.*
Owt, owte, *out.*

P.

Pa, s. *the river Po.*
Palle, *a robe of state,* purple and pall, *i. e. a purple robe or cloak,* a phrase.
Paramour, *lover.* Item, *a mistress.*
Paregall, *equal.*
Parti, party, p. 7, *a part.*
Paves, p. 81, a pavice, *a large shield that covered the whole body,* f. pavois.
Pavilliane, *pavilion, tent.*
Pay, *liking, satisfaction;* hence, well apaid, *i. e. pleased, highly satisfied.*
Peakish, p. 254.
Peere, pere, *peer, equal.*
Penon, *a banner, or streamer borne at the top of a lance.*
Perelous, parlous, *perilous; dangerous.*
Perfight, *perfect.*
Perlese, p. 86, *peerless.*
Perte, *part.*
Pertyd, *parted.*
Plaining, *complaining.*
Play-feres, *play-fellows.*
Pleasance, *pleasure.*
Pight, Pyght, *pitched.*
Pil'd, p. 250, *peeled, bald.*
Pine, *famish, starve.*
Pious chanson, p. 157, *a godly song or ballad*[7].
Pitte, Pittye, Petye, pyte, *pity.*
Pompal, p. 202, *pompous.*
Popingay, *a parrot.*
Portres, p. 88, *porteress.*
Pow, pou: pow'd, s. *pull, pulled.*
Pownes, p. 255, *pounds* (rhythmi gratia).
Prece, prese, *press.*
Preced, p. 146, presed, *pressed.*
Prest, *ready.*
Prestly, p. 146, prestlye, p. 44, *readily, quickly.*
Pricked, *spurred on, hasted.*
Prickes, p. 74, *the mark to shoot at.*
Pricke-wande, p. 74, *a wand set up for a mark.*
Prowès, p. 83, *prowess.*
Prycke, p. 150, *the mark:* commonly a hazel wand.
Pryme, *day-break.*
Pulde, *pulled.*

Q.

Quadrant, p. 88, *four-square.*
Quail, *shrink.*
Quarry, p. 222, in hunting or hawking, is *the slaughtered game, &c.* See page 5.
Quere, quire, *choir.*
Quest, p. 140, *inquest.*
Quha, s. *who.*
Quhan, s. *when.*
Quhar, s. *where.*
Quhat, s. *what.*

[7] Mr. Rowe's edit. has, "The first Row of the Rubrick;" which has been supposed by Dr. Warburton to refer to the red-lettered titles of old ballads. In the large collection made by Mr. Pepys, I do not remember to have seen one single ballad with its title printed in red letters.

Quhatten, s. *what.*
Quhen, s. *when.*
Quhy, s. *why.*
Quyrry, p. 5. *See* Quarry *above.*
Quyte, p. 13, *requited.*

R.

Raine, *reign.*
Rashing, seems to be the old hunting term for the stroke made by a wild boar with his fangs. See p. 179.
Rayne, reane, *rain.*
Raysse, *race.*
Reachless, *careless.*
Reade, p. 19, rede, *advise, hit off.* Read, *advice.*
Reas, p. 5, *raise.*
Reave, *bereave.*
Reckt, *regarded.*
Reek, s. *smoke.*
Reid, s. rede, reed, *red.*
Reid-roan, s. *red-roan*, p. 49.
Rekeles, recklesse, *regardless, void of care, rash.*
Renisht, p. 54, 58, perhaps a derivation from reniteo, *to shine.*
Renn, *run*, p. 169.
Renyed, p. 82, *refused.*
Rewth, *ruth;* rewe, *pity.*
Riall, ryall, *royal*
Richt, s. *right.*
Ride, *make an inroad.*
Roche, *rock.*
Ronne, *ran*, p. 21; roone, *run.*
Roode, *cross, crucifix.*
Roufe, *roof.*
Routhe, ruth, *pity.*
Row, rowd, s. *roll, rolled.*
Rowght, *rout.*
Rowned, rownyd, *whispered.*
Rowyned, *round.*
Rues, ruethe, *pitieth.*
Ryde, p. 236, *i. e. make an inroad.* Ryde, in p. 57, (v. 136,) should probably be *rise.*
Rydere, p. 153, *ranger.*
Rynde, p. 24, *rent.*

S.

Sa, sae, s. *so.*
Saif, s. *safe.*
Sall, s. *shall.*
Sar, sair, s. *sore.*
Sark, *shirt, shift.*
Sat, sete, *set.*
Savyde, *saved.*
Saw, say, *speech, discourse.*
Say, p. 11, *saw.* Vol. ii. p. 229.
Say us no harme, *say no ill of us.*
Sayne, *say.*
Scathe, *hurt, injury.*
Schapped, p. 25, *perhaps* swapped. *Vide loc.*
Schip, s. *ship.*
Scho, p. 33, sche, p. 20, s. *she.*
Schone, *shone.*
Schoote, *shot, let go.*
Schowte, schowtte, *shout.*
Schrill, s. *shrill.*
Se, s. p. 83, *sea.*
Seik, s. seke, *seek.*
Sene, *seen.*
Sertayne, sertenlye, *certain, certainly.*
Setywall. *See* Cetywall.
Shaws, *little woods.*
Shear, p. 4, *entirely* (penitus).
Sheele, *she'll, she will.*
Sheene, shene, *shining.*
Sheits, s. shetes, *sheets.*
Shent, *disgraced.*
Shimmering, *shining by glances.*
Shoen, s. shoone, p. 211, *shoes.*
Shoke, p. 83, *shookest.*
Shold, sholde, *should.*
Shote, *shot.*
Shradds, p. 70, vid. locum.
Shrift, *confession.*
Shroggs, *shrubs, thorns, briars, G.Doug.* scroggis.
Shulde, *should.*
Shyars, *shires.*
Sib, *kin; akin, related.*
Sic, sich, sick, s. *such.*
Side, *long.*
Sied, s. *saw.*
Sigh-clout, p. 169, (sythe-clout) *a clout to strain milk through: a straining clout.*
Sik, sike, *such.*
Siker, *surely, certainly.*
Sithe, p. 6, *since.*
Slade, *a breadth of greensward between plow-lands or woods, &c.*
Slaw, *slew*, p. 262. (*Sc.* Abel.)
Sle, slee, *slay;* sleest, *slayest.*
Slean, slone, *slain.*
Sleip, s. slepe, *sleep.*
Slo, p. 81, sloe, *slay.*
Slode, p. 39, *slit, split.*
Slone, p. 40, *slain.*

Sloughe, p. 8, *slew.*
Smithers, s. *smothers.*
Soldain, soldan, sowdan, *sultan.*
Soll, soulle, sowle, *soul.*
Sort, *company.*
Soth, sothe, south, southe, *sooth, truth.*
Soth-Ynglonde, *South England.*
Sould, s. *should.*
Sowdan, soldain, *sultan.*
Sowden, sowdain, *sultan.*
Sowre, soare, *sour, sore.*
Sowter, p. 64, *a shoemaker.*
Soy, f. *silk.*
Spak, spaik, s. *spake.*
Sped, *speeded.*
Speik, s. *speak.*
Spendyd, p. 10, probably the same as Spanned, *grasped.*
Spere, speere, *spear.*
Spill, p. 168, spille, p. 48, *spoil, come to harm.*
Sprente, 9, *spurted, sprung out.*
Spurn, spurne, *a kick,* p. 14. *See* Tear.
Spyde, *spied.*
Spylt, *spoiled, destroyed.*
Spyt, p. 6, spyte, *spite.*
Stabille, p. 85, perhaps, *stablish.*
Stalwurthlye, *stoutly.*
Stane, s. stean, p. 68, *stone.*
Starke, p. 44, *stiff,* 83, *entirely.*
Steedye, *steady.*
Steid, s. stede, *steed.*
Stele, *steel.*
Sterne, *stern:* or, perhaps, *stars.*
Sterris, *stars.*
Stert, start, p. 269, *started.*
Sterte, sterted, *start, started.*
Steven, p. 74, *time,* p. 77, *voice.*
Still, *quiet, silent.*
Stint, *stop, stopped.*
Stonderes, *standers-by.*
Stound, stownde, *time, while.*
Stour, p. 11, 62, stower, p. 39, stowre, p. 26, 46, *fight, disturbance, &c.* This word is applied in the north to signify dust agitated and put into motion: as by the sweeping of a room.
Streight, *straight.*
Strekene, *stricken, struck.*
Stret, *street.*
Strick, *strict.*
Stroke, p. 8, *struck.*
Stude, s. *stood.*
Styntyde, stinted, *stayed, stopped.*
Styrande stagge, p. 19. A friend interpreted this, *many a stirring, travelling journey.*
Suar, *sure.*
Sum, s. *some.*
Sumpters, p. 258, *horses that carry clothes, furniture, &c.*
Swapte, p. 9, swapped, p. 26, swopede, *struck violently. Scot.* sweap, *to scourge* (vide Gloss. Gaw. Douglas). Or perhaps *exchanged, sc. blows:* so *swap* or *swopp* signifies.
Swat, swatte, swotte, *did sweat.*
Swear, p. 5, *sware.*
Sweard, *sword.*
Sweaven, *a dream.*
Sweit, s. swete, *sweet.*
Swith, *quickly, instantly.*
Syd, *side.*
Syde shear, p. 5, sydis shear, p. 5, *on all sides.*
Syne, *then, afterwards.*
Syth, *since.*

T.

Taine, s. tane, *taken.*
Take, *taken.*
Talents, p. 55, perhaps golden ornaments hung from her head, to the value of talents of gold.
Tear, p. 14, seems to be a proverb, "That tearing or pulling occasioned his spurn or kick."
Teenefu', s. *full of indignation, wrathful, furious.*
Teir, s. tere, *tear.*
Teene, tene, *sorrow, indignation, wrath;* properly, *injury, affront.*
Termagaunte, *the god of the Sarazens.* See a memoir on this subject in page 62 [8].
Thair, *their.* Thair, thare, *there.*
Thame, s. *them.* Than, *then.*

[8] The old French Romancers, who had corrupted TERMAGANT into TERVAGANT, couple it with the name of MAHOMET as constantly as ours; thus in the old *Roman de Blanchardin,*

> " *Cy guerpison tuit Apolin,*
> *Et Mahomet et* TERVAGANT."

The, *thee.*
The, *they.* The wear, p. 4, *they were.*
Thear, p. 5, *there.*
Thee, *thrive;* mote he thee, *may he thrive.*
Thend, *the end.*
Ther, p. 5, *their.*
Ther-for, p. 6, *therefore.*
Therto, *thereto.* Thes, *these.*
Theyther-ward, *thither-ward, towards that place.*
Thie, *thy.* Thowe, *thou.*
Thorowe, throw, s. *through.*
Thouse, s. *thou art.*
Thrall, p. 251, *captive,* p. 96, *thraldom, captivity.*
Thrang, s. *throng.*
Thre, thrie, s. *three.*
Threape, *to argue, to assert in a positive overbearing manner.*
Thrittè, *thirty.*
Thronge, p. 138, *hastened.*
Till, p. 13, *unto,* p. 60, *entice.*
Tine, p. 37, *lose;* tint, *lost.*
To, *too.* Item, *two.*
Ton, p. 6, tone, *the one.*
Tow, s. p. 101, *to let down with a rope, &c.*
Tow, towe, *two.* Twa, s. *two.*
Towyn, p. 19, *town.*
Treytory, traitory, *treachery.*
Tride, *tryed.*
Trim, *exact.*
Trow, *think, conceive, know.*
Trowthe, *troth.*
Tru, *true.*
Tuik, s. *took.* Tul, s. *till, to.*
Turn, p. 258, *an occasion.*
Twin'd, s. p. 33, *parted, separated,* vide G. Douglas.

## U. V.

Ugsome, s. *shocking, horrible.*
Vices, (probably contracted for *devices,*) p. 88, *screws;* or perhaps *turning pins, swivels.* An ingenious friend thinks *a vice* is rather "a spindle of a press" that goeth by a *vice,* that seemeth to move of itself.
Vilane, p. 80, *rascally.*
Undight, *undecked, undressed.*
Unmacklye, *misshapen.*
Unsett steven, p. 74, *unappointed time, unexpectedly.*
Untyll, *unto,* p. 137, *against.*
Voyded, p. 141, *quitted, left*

## W.

Wad, s. wold, wolde, *would.*
Wae worth, s. *woe betide.*
Waltering, *weltering.*
Wane, p. 9, *the same as* ane, *one:* so wone, p. 11, *is one*[9].
War, p. 5, *aware.*
Warldis, p. 50, s. *worlds.*
Waryson, p. 24, *reward.*
Wat, p. 7, wot, *know, am aware.*
Wat, s. *wet.* Wayde, *waved.*
Wayward, *froward, peevish.*
Weal, p. 13, *wail.*
Weale, p. 91, *happiness, prosperity.*
Wedous, p. 12, *widows.*
Weedes, *clothes.*
Weel, *we'll, we will.*
Weene, ween'd, *think, thought.*
Weet, s. *wet.*
Weil, s. wepe, *weep.*
Wel-away, *an interjection of grief.*
Wel of pitè, *source of pity.*
Weme, *womb, belly, hollow.*
Wend, wends, *go, goes.*

Hence Fontaine, with great humour, in his Tale, intituled *La Fiancée du Roy de Garbe,* says.

> "*Et reniant Mahom, Jupin, et* TERVAGANT,
> *Avec maint autre Dieu non moins extravagant.*"

Mém. de l'Acad. des Inscript. tom. xx. 4to p. 352.

As TERMAGANT is evidently of Anglo-Saxon derivation, and can only be explained from the elements of that language, its being corrupted by the old French Romancers proves that they borrowed some things from ours.

[9] In fol. 355 of Bannatyne's MS. is a short fragment, in which 'wane' is used for 'ane' or 'one,' viz. —

> "Amongst the Monsters that we find,
> There's WANE belovved of woman-keind
> Renowned for antiquity,
> From Adame drivs his pedigree."

Wende, p. 144, *weened, thought.*
Werke, *work.*
Westlings, *western,* or *whistling.*
While, p. 249, *until.*
Whoard, *hoard.*
Whos, p. 82, *whose.*
Whyllys, *whilst.*
Wight, p. 164, *person,* p. 249, *strong, lusty.*
Wightlye, p. 37, *vigorously.*
Wighty, p. 70, *strong, lusty, active, nimble.*
Wilfulle, 73, *wandering, erring.*
Will, s. p. 65, *shall.*
Windling, s. *winding.*
Winnae, p. 33, *will not.*
Winsome, p. 274, s. *agreeable, engaging.*
Wiss, p. 240, *know,* wist, *knew.*
Withouten, withoughten, *without.*
Wo, woo, *woe.*
Wode, wood, *mad, wild.*
Woe-begone, p. 44, *lost in woe, overwhelmed with grief.*
Won'd, p. 261, wonn'd, *dwelt.*
Wondersly, wonderly, p. 89, *wonderously.*
Wone, p. 11, *one.*
Wonne, *dwell.*
Woodweele, p. 70, *or* wodewale, *the golden ouzle, a bird of the thrush-kind.* Gloss. Chauc. The orig. MS. has *woodweete.*
Worthè, *worthy.*
Wot, *know,* wotes, *knows.*
Wouche, p. 8, *mischief, evil,* AS. ƿohȝ, *i. e.* Wohg, *malum.*
Wrang, s. *wrong.*
Wreke, wreak, *revenge.*
Wright, p. 84, *write.*
Wringe, p. 82, *contended with violence.*
Writhe, p. 247, *writhed, twisted.*
Wroken, *revenged.*
Wronge, *wrong.* Wull, s. *will.*
Wyght, p. 260, *strong, lusty.*
Wyghtye, p. 150, *the same.*
Wyld, p. 5, *wild deer.*
Wynde, wende, *go.*
Wynne, *joy.* Wyste, *knew.*

## Y.

Y-cleped, *named, called.*
Y-con'd, *taught, instructed.*
Y-fere, *together.*
Y-founde, *found.*
Y-picking, *picking, culling.*
Y-slaw, *slain.* Y-were, *were.*
Y-wis, p. 90, *(I wis,) verily.*
Y-wrought, *wrought.*
Yate, *gate.*
Yave, p. 239, *gave.*
Ych, yche, *each.*
Ychone, p. 26, *each one.*
Ychyseled, *cut with the chisel.*
Ydle, *idle.*
Ye bent, y-bent, *bent.*
Ye feth, y-feth, *in faith.*
Yee, p. 24, *eye.*
Yeldyde, *yielded.*
Yenoughe, ynoughe, *enough.*
Yerarrchy, *hierarchy.*
Yere, yeere, *year, years.*
Yerle, p. 7, yerlle, *earl.*
Yerly, p. 5, *early.*
Yestreen, s. *yester-evening.*
Yf, *if.*
Ygnoraunce, *ignorance.*
Yngglishe, Yngglyshe, *English.*
Ynglonde, *England.*
Yode, *went.*
Youe, *you.*
Yt, *it.*
Yth, p. 6, *in the.*

## Z.

Ze, zea, s. *ye.*
Zeir, s. *year.*
Zellow, s. *yellow.*
Zonder, s. *yonder.*
Zong, s. *young.*
Zour, s. *your.*

*** The printers have usually substituted the letter z to express the character ȝ which occurs in old MSS: but we are not to suppose that this ȝ was ever pronounced as our modern z; it had rather the force of y (and perhaps of gh), being no other than the Saxon letter ȝ which both the Scots and English have in many instances changed into y, as ȝeaꞃꝺ *yard,* ȝeaꞃ *year,* ȝeonȝ *young,* &c.

END OF VOL. I.

---

PRINTING OFFICE OF THE PUBLISHER.

Printed in Great Britain
by Amazon

45537482R00237